Fit for Life

Written by Anne D. Ager, Judith
Ferguson, Wendy Rose Neil, Ann
Carpenter, Miriam Polunin and
Cecilia Norman.
Photographed by Peter Barry and
Peter Pugh-Cook.
Designed by Philip Clucas.
Produced by Ted Smart and
David Gibbon.

CLB 1834
© 1986 Colour Library Books Ltd, Guildford, Surrey, England.
Text filmsetting by Acesetters Ltd, Richmond, Surrey, England.
Printed and bound in Barcelona, Spain by Cronion, S.A.
All rights reserved.
ISBN 0 86283 509 7
Dep. Leg. B-37.051-86

Fit for Life

A·GUIDE·TO·A·HEALTHIER·YOU

COLOUR LIBRARY BOOKS

Contents

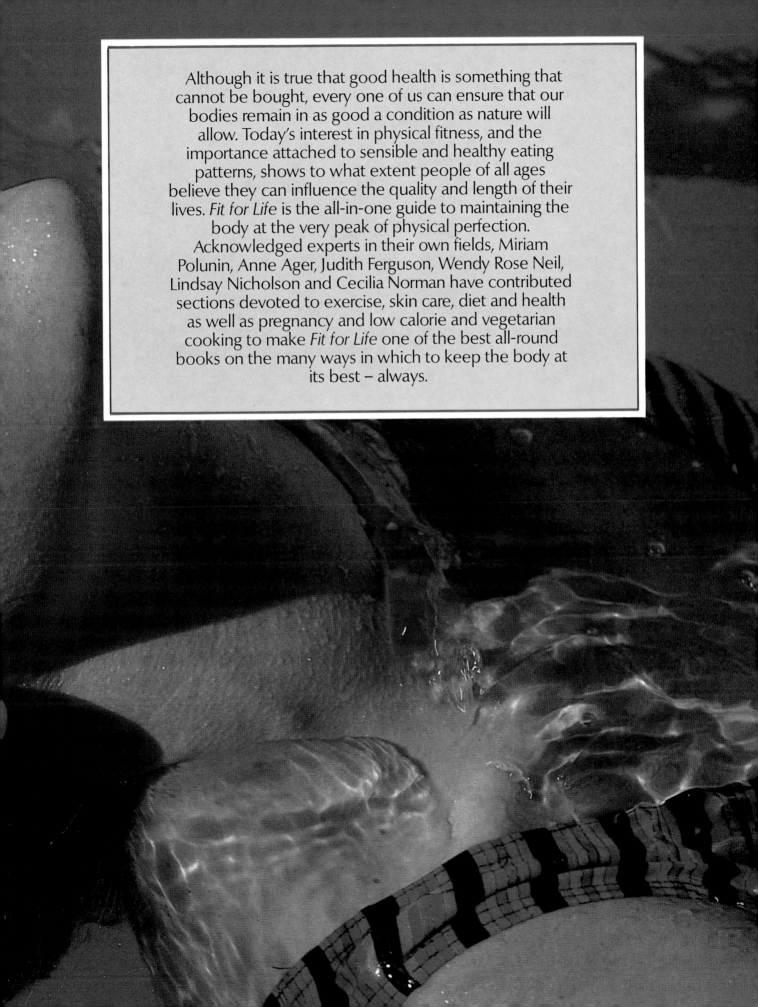

Although it is true that good health is something that cannot be bought, every one of us can ensure that our bodies remain in as good a condition as nature will allow. Today's interest in physical fitness, and the importance attached to sensible and healthy eating patterns, shows to what extent people of all ages believe they can influence the quality and length of their lives. *Fit for Life* is the all-in-one guide to maintaining the body at the very peak of physical perfection. Acknowledged experts in their own fields, Miriam Polunin, Anne Ager, Judith Ferguson, Wendy Rose Neil, Lindsay Nicholson and Cecilia Norman have contributed sections devoted to exercise, skin care, diet and health as well as pregnancy and low calorie and vegetarian cooking to make *Fit for Life* one of the best all-round books on the many ways in which to keep the body at its best – always.

Fit for Life
Body Watch

Your skin is the largest organ of your body. If it were laid flat it would cover 3,000 square inches and weigh around seven pounds. As well as protecting your inner body from damage or invasion by bacteria, it also works as an extremely effective thermostat, ensuring your body temperature remains constant whatever climate you are in.

Beautiful skin doesn't just happen. It's the result of good skin care habits practised day in, day out. Anyone can do it and it needn't be expensive.

There's so much hype surrounding skin care that you could be forgiven for thinking that best equals expensive. Not so. Cheap soaps, cleansers, toners and the rest –

provided they are reputable brand names – work just as well, sometimes better than the pricey stuff. Check out the chain stores for the best value.

It pays to choose unperfumed products wherever possible – most bad reactions to cosmetics are caused by the perfume rather than other ingredients –

Whether you use soap or cleanser, the secret of good skin care is to rinse, rinse and rinse again.

and don't bother with baby oils and lotions. What's right for a baby's bottom is not necessarily right for your face.

A good skin care routine needn't be time-consuming but it will pay dividends. Here's what to do...

skin cells, sweat and natural oils. And if you try to apply make-up on top of that lot without cleansing first you will end up with a sticky mess that will streak and smear and take the first possible opportunity to slide down your face.

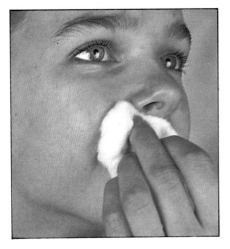
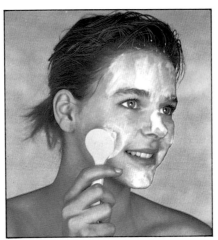
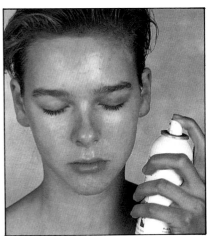

Come Clean

It might sound like stating the obvious, but to look good skin has to be clean – really clean. Otherwise its natural glow is obscured by a grimy film of dust, dirt, dead

The trouble is there's so much nonsense talked about cleansing, it's almost impossible to know what to do. Should you or shouldn't you use soap? Is water bad for the skin? Will going to bed without first removing your make-up give you spots? And so on.

The fact is that most of the anti-soap-and-water propaganda comes from the cosmetic houses who have a vested interest in persuading us to use expensive creams rather than cheap old soap. Yet soap and water does a superb job of shifting grease and grime. Older women with very dry skins may find it too harsh, but in your teens and twenties, especially if your skin is a little on the oily side, there is nothing to beat it.

So, morning and evening, wet your face with warm – not hot – water then work up a good lather with a mild, non-perfumed soap. Don't use a flannel unless you are prepared to use a clean one each day – damp, dirty flannels are a breeding ground for bacteria – simply use your fingers. Splash off as much soap as you can, then run a clean bowl of warm water and rinse again. Leaving traces of soap after washing can lead to irritation and sore patches. Pat your skin dry with a soft towel.

Soap and water will get rid of almost anything – except oil-based cosmetics. So on the days you wear make-up you need to use a special cleanser. And no, going to bed with your make-up on will not give you spots – just dirty pillowcases.

Choose a light cleansing milk rather than a rich cream which will feel sticky on your face. If you can get one that washes off with water, so much the better. To remove make-up smoothe the cleanser over your face with cotton wool then wipe it off with

chemistry lessons from school, alkalines neutralise acids. Left to its own devices you skin will return to its acid state – necessary to keep out bacteria – within 30 minutes or so of you washing your face. But you can balance it instantly by using a toner.

Unless you are made of money – and

Even apparently unpolluted country or seaside air deposits dust and grime on your skin which must be removed, along with the natural sweat and oil secretions, by thorough, twice-daily cleansings. Just because you haven't been wearing make-up, you can't skip this essential step in your skin care routine.

tissues or splash it off with warm water. *Then* wash your face with soap and water to ensure you have removed every trace of cleanser.

When people complain that a certain cleanser or soap has irritated their skin, it is often because they haven't been removing it properly. Cleansers are designed to combine chemically with the dirt or make-up so that the whole lot can be washed off together. Left on the skin the mixture of cleanser, dirt and make-up is disastrous. So feel free to rinse as much as you like.

Soap is an alkaline substance, but your skin is slightly acid. If you remember your

who is? – apply your toner with cotton wool dampened with cold water and wrung out. Wipe it quickly over your face, avoiding the sensitive skin around the eyes and lips, and allow it to dry naturally. Keep the lid of your bottle of toner tightly shut when you are not using it, as toners contain volatile substances that evaporate if the lid is left off.

Moisture Plus

The idea that water is somehow bad for your skin is laughable. Seventy-five per cent of your skin *is* water. Drop a sliver of dead skin into a test-tube of oil and it will stay

BodyWatch

There's no way to force water into the skin from the outside, but regular use of a moisturiser will slow down the loss of moisture through evaporation and keep your skin looking soft and fresh.

shrivelled and dead. Drop a sliver of dead skin into a test-tube of water and it will rehydrate to look fresh and new. Water gives skin its freshness and life and the idea of moisturisers is to seal that water in.

Young skin, as it happens, is very good at retaining water. You may curse the oiliness of your skin now, but the oil is acting like a natural moisturiser and preventing too much water being lost to the surrounding air through evaporation. As you get older your skin will become less oily, and centrally-heated rooms, hot atmospheres or windy weather will dry your skin out, making it feel and look uncomfortable.

Moisturising doesn't seal water into the skin for any length of time – a few hours at

the most. And it won't stop you getting wrinkles later on. Wrinkles are the result of damage deep in the skin and whether or not you moisturise makes no difference whatsoever. If you have dry patches, most likely on your cheeks, as the forehead, nose and chin are more oily, pat a little moisturiser there in the morning after cleansing and toning.

Forget products with fancy-sounding ingredients that promise the earth. They can't keep their promises. Simply choose one, unperfumed if possible, that you like the feel of. After all, a product is not going to do you any good sitting on the bathroom shelf.

If your skin feels oily rather than dry, don't moisturise. You won't be doing any

good, but simply wasting money and making the oil problem worse. Use your common sense. If your skin feels dry playing sports on windy days or sitting in overheated classrooms, then moisturise. Otherwise, don't bother.

Special Treats

The skin you have now is not the skin you had three weeks ago. Nor will it be the skin you have in three weeks' time. Surprised? You shouldn't be. Your skin is constantly renewing itself. New cells are formed in the deeper levels known as the dermis and then make their way up to the surface where the old cells are shed to make way for them. The whole process takes about 21 days when you are in your teens, longer as you get older. Most household dust is, in fact, made up of old skin cells, and during the course of your lifetime you will get rid of something like 40 lbs of skin in this way.

So what? Well, the furious speed at which young skin regenerates itself, can lead to problems. If new cells are coming up fast and the old cells haven't been shed quickly enough they can cause a blockage, in other words a blackhead or a pimple. Regularly sweeping the surface of your skin clean of these old skin cells that are on the point of flaking off makes your skin look better and helps prevent spots.

There are all sorts of ways of doing this sweeping or exfoliation, but the simplest is to use one of the many facial scrub creams on the market. They contain gritty particles in a creamy base and as you rub them over your skin they loosen and free any skin cells that were on the point of flaking off. When you rinse your face, grit, skin cells and cream are all washed away.

Use an exfoliating scrub once a week – no more often or you could make your face sore – after washing, but before toning.

Face packs work in a similar way. As they dry they pick up dirt and loose skin cells, and then the whole lot can be washed away. Face packs that contain fruit or flower extracts like strawberry, lemon or rose, have a double action because the natural juices dry out the loose skin flakes so that the edges curl and they are picked up more easily by the mask.

Generally speaking, packs that set hard are more effective than those that stay creamy, but they can be harsh. If your skin is not too sensitive you can get the best results by using a pack that dries and then,

instead of washing it off, rub it off with your fingers using small circular movements. Hold the area you are working on taut with the other hand.

Once a week you can give yourself a facial that is as good as anything you would get in an upmarket beauty salon – or invite a friend round and get to work on each other. First, remove your make-up and wash your face then use an exfoliating scrub, being careful not to use it on the delicate skin around the eyes and mouth. Rinse thoroughly, pat skin dry with a towel then apply a mask. Relax with pads of cotton wool soaked in cold water over your eyes.

When the mask has set, rub it off as described, and rinse away any last traces with warm water. Pat on skin toner with dampened cotton wool then, when that has dried, smoothe on a little moisturiser with gentle upward strokes.

Flawless Finish

Spots are the bane of teenage life. They appear in the worst possible places – like on the end of your nose – at the worst possible times – like before a very special date. So what do you do?

Spots are caused by a combination of the excess oil the skin produces in the teenage years and the fast rate of skin cell turnover happening at the same time. There are other factors, too, such as hormones – you are more likely to get a spot before your period – but these are less well understood.

Facing page: using a facial scrub once a week should lessen the likelihood of spots and pimples, but never rub so hard that your skin feels sore or irritated. Right: a face pack has a similar effect and can make you feel incredibly pampered. After giving yourself a facial, try to go without make-up for 24 hours to give your skin a chance to breathe.

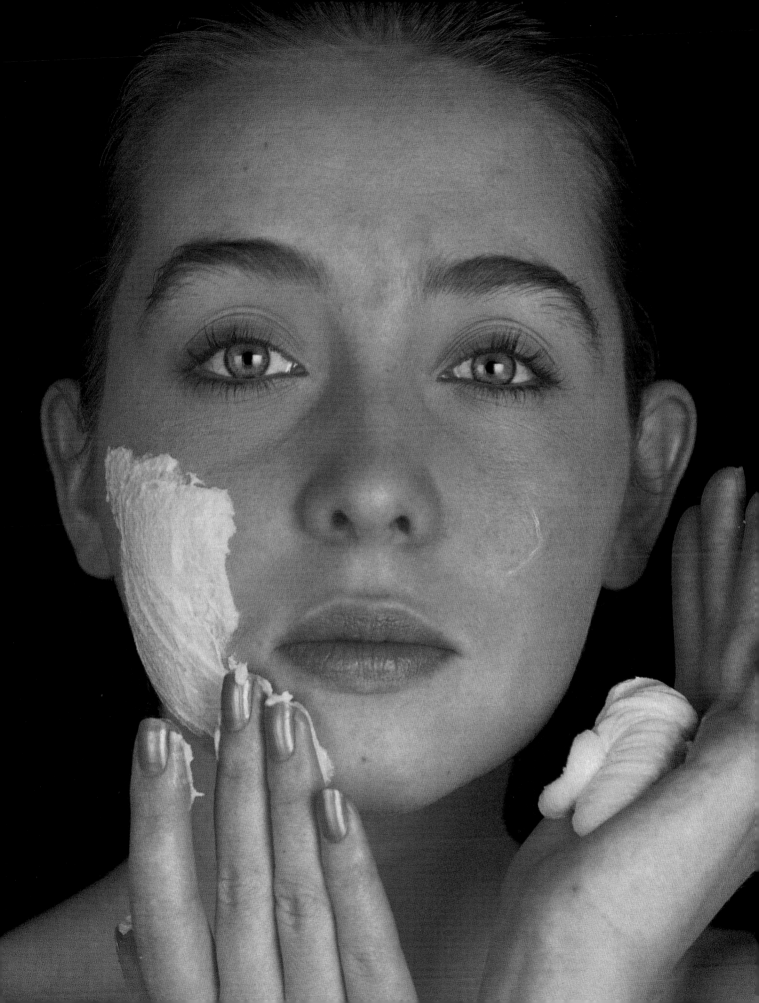

Right: eight out of every 10 teenagers suffer from acne, so if you have flawless skin count yourself very lucky indeed. Facing page: ensure you get plenty of sleep; frequent late nights can have a terrible effect on your skin. Most people need eight hours a night, but teenagers sometimes need more – 10 or even 11 hours.

What seems to happen is that the dead skin cells plug the opening of a pore and the oil builds up behind it. If that's all that happens the plug at the opening of the pore will turn black (because of the presence of melanin, the natural pigment that causes tanning) and you will have a blackhead. If so much oil builds up that it bursts through the walls of the pore into the neighbouring tissues, a small infection can set in causing swelling and pus – in other words a spot.

Once a week exfoliation, as described in the previous section, is the best way to stop spots and blackheads forming. But *be gentle*. Spot-prone skin is sick skin and needs special care.

Wash twice a day with unperfumed soap, and don't bother with the medicated variety. Spots happen inside the skin – all a medicated soap will do is aggravate the outside.

Once a blackhead has formed it can be gently squeezed out. Do this after a bath when the steam has softened the surrounding skin. Make sure your hands and nails are scrupulously clean, then wrap clean tissues around your fingertips and gently press on either side of the blackhead. It should pop out quite easily, but if it doesn't – leave it alone. Digging at it with your nails may lead to scarring and infection. Leave it a day or two then try again.

Once spots have come to a head, they too can be squeezed. Again make sure your hands and nails are very clean and wrap clean tissues around your fingers.

Sunbathing may make you feel good and appear to clear up your spots temporarily, but it may make them worse in the long run and too much sun can lead to wrinkles in later life. Only ever sunbathe in moderation and, when you've had enough sun for one day, cover up.

Very, very gently press the sides of the spot so the pus runs out. If the spot doesn't burst immediately, leave it. Pressing too hard can force the infection further under the skin and then you'll have real problems. Never, ever attempt to squeeze a spot that hasn't come to a head.

After you have successfully squeezed a spot, wash the area with soap and warm water then dab on antiseptic cream.

The best way to get rid of spots is to tackle them as soon as they appear, with one of the special spot preparations on the market. These contain chemicals such as

resorcinol or salicylic acid which dissolve the plug of dead cells. Ask your local pharmacist to recommend a good one for you to try, and follow the instructions on the packet carefully.

If you also have spots on your back they can be treated in the same way.

There are dozens of old wives' tales about spots – most of them untrue. Eating chocolate, for instance, won't give you spots, although if you follow a persistently unhealthy diet, neither your skin nor your figure will look very good. Wearing make-up won't cause spots – the pores get

clogged from the inside not the outside – in fact, make-up can be very useful for covering up spotty skin if you are going out.

Sunbathing doesn't get rid of spots. It may seem to dry them up for a while, but then the sunlight stimulates a thickening of the skin which blocks the pores again.

Having a fringe, or hair brushed forward onto your face, won't give you spots, although if hair is greasy it could irritate existing spots. The list goes on, but the truth is it's not what you do but your age that's responsible. Eight out of every 10 teenagers will be plagued with spots at some time or another.

If your spots are particularly bad or you have acne, those angry red lumps that rarely come to a head, ask your doctor for advice. New acne treatments are being developed all the time and 9 out of every 10 people who seek medical advice for acne are greatly helped by them. Even if you turn out to be the 1 in 10 who isn't, take heart from the fact that people who have bad acne in their teens turn out to get fewer wrinkles in later life. Well, it's something to look forward to.

Playing with Fire

It's not always easy to be disciplined about things now when you won't reap the rewards for 20 or 30 years to come. But if you care about your skin and don't want to look like a prune at 40, then you must limit your exposure to the sun.

Sunbathing in moderation is fine. Sunlight lifts your spirits and boosts the body's supplies of vitamin D, which is essential for health. But over the years too much sun will damage and age your skin.

A tan is the body's natural defence against ultra-violet light from the sun. It stimulates the production of the pigment melanin which stains the skin brown. Ultra-violet or UV light also thickens the outer layer of skin to give additional protection.

If you sunbathe for too long before you have built up a tan the ultra-violet rays will attack the skin's tissues making them swollen and inflamed in what is usually referred to as sunburn. Severe sunburn damages the skin so much that the burnt layers are shed in large flakes as the skin peels.

Apart from the pain of sunburn, which is bad enough, repeated burns year after year can increase the likelihood of serious skin problems later on.

The single most important thing you can do to keep your skin young-looking as long as possible is to limit your exposure to the sun. Using a good sunscreen whenever you sunbathe will pay dividends later on.

A sunscreen cream will stop you from burning. The Sun Protection Factor or SPF printed on the bottle will tell you how much protection it gives. Assume that you would start to burn after 15 minutes in the sun without any protection at all. An SPF4 would allow to spend 4x15 minutes or an hour in the sun without burning. An SPF6 would allow you to spend 6x15 minutes or an hour and a half in the sun without burning. An SPF8 would allow you to spend two hours sunbathing without risking a burn. Once you have established a tan you should use an SPF4 at least, all the time when sunbathing for added protection, unless you are very dark.

The colour you will go in the sun is dictated by your natural colouring. If you have blonde hair and blue eyes you will never go the colour of your brown-eyed, brown-haired friend – however hard you try. Redheads usually have trouble getting any sort of a tan at all. Freckles are a sign that the melanin pigment is poorly distributed throughout the skin. If you always burn in the sun and never tan, use a minimum SPF8 whenever your skin is exposed and don't even try to get a tan.

Ordinary sunscreens need reapplying every two hours and every time you go in the water, which can be a nuisance. Water-resistant sunscreens are better. Simply apply before you go down to the beach, then reapply just once halfway through the day.

You are much more likely to burn near water because the sea breezes fool you into thinking the day is cooler than it really is. So always use a high SPF water-resistant sunscreen when you are taking part in water sports.

Ultra-violet rays can pass through water so you need protection while you are swimming as well.

Never wear perfume when you sunbathe. It can react with the ultra-violet light to give you a very nasty burn that may make your skin permanently blotchy.

When you've had enough sun for one day, cover up or move into the shade. It can't be said too often that you should do everything in your power to avoid sunburn. If you are careless about exposing your skin to the sun you could be literally playing with fire.

Teeth 'n Smiles

No-one exactly enjoys a trip to the dentist,

but it helps if you regard it as a beauty investment. Bad, discoloured, crooked teeth can ruin your looks, and who wants to spend their life scowling because a smile would reveal a row of damaged enamel?

If you look after your teeth properly there is no reason why you should ever need a filling. Regular brushing and eliminating sugar from your diet are the two most important factors.

Visit your dentist every six months. If you look after your teeth properly between visits you won't have to have anything painful done. Cavities are caused when the bacteria, which exists in your mouth all the time, get to work on the sugar left on your teeth by sweets and sticky foods. They produce acid which rots away at your teeth enabling decay to set in causing holes. Unless these holes are filled they will get bigger and bigger until the tooth crumbles – a painful process.

If you have to have a front tooth filled ask about the new white fillings which look much more attractive than the old metal variety. White fillings are not usually strong enough for back teeth, which do most of the crunching and grinding.

You can avoid fillings altogether by looking after your teeth carefully. That means brushing twice a day – ask your dentist to show you the best way – with a good toothbrush and fluoride toothpaste. Toothbrushes wear out after three months or so, so change yours regularly. Brush for three minutes morning and evening. Time yourself for a few days to check you are brushing for long enough – most people don't.

To check whether you are getting your teeth completely clean you can buy disclosing tablets from the chemist which stain the unbrushed areas red.

Toothbrushes don't reach in between the teeth, so once a day use dental floss to clean these hard-to-reach places. Dental floss is like fine string and once you've been shown how to use it, it doesn't take long. Many dentists now employ hygienists to show patients the correct way to brush and floss teeth.

Avoiding sweets altogether is the best way to avoid fillings, but if you must have them, save them to eat after your meals then brush your teeth straight away. Remember biscuits, cakes, puddings and sugary drinks all contain lots of sugar, and so are bad for your teeth, too. If you are hungry between meals a piece of fruit, a stick of raw carrot or celery, some nuts or sunflower seeds make a healthier snack.

Your dentist may suggest you wear a brace for a few months to straighten your teeth. It's a nuisance but, on balance, you have to agree that it's preferable to a lifetime of crooked teeth.

By your teens you should have got all your permanent teeth with the exception of the four at the very back – your wisdom teeth. These usually emerge in your late teens or early twenties, but sometimes they come through crooked or not at all. If you have strange pains at the back of your jaw tell your dentist about it and he will X-ray your teeth to make sure the wisdom teeth are developing correctly.

Improving on Nature
Few of us are ever completely satisfied with the way we look. Most people, if asked, would like larger eyes, a smaller mouth or a general re-design. But for some people the shape or size of a particular feature causes real distress. An over-large nose or sticking-out ears can blight their life, making them shy, unhappy and reluctant to meet people. Luckily for people who suffer in this way cosmetic surgery is now so advanced that their problems can be very easily corrected.

Rhinoplasty is the correct term for a 'nose job'. It is usually carried out under general anaesthetic, although some surgeons now use a local anaesthetic and sedate the patient with a hefty dose of tranquillisers. The surgeon works inside the nose removing cartilage to give it a new shape. After the operation a plaster cast is operation can be carried out at any age, the sooner the better.

Cosmetic surgery is expensive; the total cost for each of these operations can be many hundreds of pounds. But you may be able to get treatment on the National Health if, in the opinion of the surgeon, your life is greatly affected by the size or shape

If you are shy or find it hard to get on with people, it's easy to blame it on the size of your nose, ears, chin or whatever. Before investigating the pros and cons of cosmetic surgery ask a friend whom you trust for an honsest opinion. You could, literally, be getting things out of proportion.

put on the nose for seven days. There is a great deal of swelling and bruising after a nose operation and this takes about three weeks to subside. Most surgeons prefer to wait until the patient is at least 16 before performing such surgery.

Prominent ears are corrected by folding the cartilage so that the ear lies close to the head and doesn't stick out. The operation is carried out using a local anaesthetic while the patient is sedated, and afterwards a turban bandage is worn for seven days. The stitches can be taken out on the seventh day, then the patient must wear a bandage in bed for the following month to avoid stretching out the ear. This of your nose or ears. If you feel you need cosmetic surgery, and your parents agree, your first step is to consult your GP and ask him to refer you to a reputable surgeon.

Advances are being made in cosmetic surgery all the time. Scars from acne or accidents can be made less obvious, a weak jaw given more shape, and many more. Cosmetic surgery should not be undertaken lightly. It can be painful, expensive and it won't make you wittier, more interesting or a nicer human being. But if you are embarrassed or upset by a particular feature of your face or body then it's good to know that you may not have to be stuck with it for ever.

Fit for Life
Body Work

The human body is a miracle of engineering. No man-made machine can compare with it. Every day, as the old cells are burnt out and used up by the bodily processes, new ones are generated to take their place – around five hundred thousand million of them. No machine or computer can constantly repair and regenerate itself in this way.

Yet, when it comes down to it, the human body is like a machine, a very sophisticated one, of course. And like all machines, how well it operates depends on the quality of fuel – or food – it receives and how well it is maintained through exercise.

It you eat properly and exercise regularly your personal machinery will operate at its best. This is the way to do it...

Get into the habit of eating well and taking plenty of exercise early on in life and you'll never have to worry about your figure. The best exercise for *you* is the kind you enjoy most. Try out different sports until you find out what suits you.

Food for Thought

What is a healthy diet? These days you can't open a newspaper or magazine without reading some new and crazy piece of information about how some perfectly innocent piece of food has turned out to be bad for you. Sometimes it makes you wonder how the human race has survived as long as it has, living as we do on *food*!

But from this barrage of largely useless information, it is possible to sift out some basic principles of healthy eating. Follow them conscientiously and you will reap the rewards of a slim figure, good skin, hair, teeth and nails, bright eyes and boundless vitality.

Don't wail that you can't bear the thought of life without burgers or cream cakes. No food is going to do you any harm if you only eat it occasionally. It's what you eat 99 per cent of the time that counts, not the odd treats that make up the other one per cent.

If you are living at home and are expected to eat the same meals as the rest of the family, show this section of the book to your parents and discuss with them how you can eat more healthily, if necessary. But, in all probability, the basic meals you have are fine – it's the extras like cakes, crisps, sweets and biscuits that turn a good diet into a bad one. And the solution to that is in your own hands, literally.

Eat more Fibre Fibre gives bulk to food so you feel fuller quicker and also smoothes the passage of food through the digestive system. Refined and processed foods usually contain very little fibre. Choose wholemeal bread not white bread; a wholegrain cereal like muesli; brown pasta and rice instead of white, and use wholemeal flour when making pastry, in order to get enough fibre in your diet. Don't think you are getting the same benefits by continuing to eat white bread and flour but sprinkling bran on cereals and drinks. For a start, it tastes disgusting, and secondly, you'll be missing out on the many other nutrients that wholemeal bread provides.

Eat more Raw Food This sounds alarming, but it doesn't mean raw meat and potatoes, simply that you should eat more fresh fruit and raw salads. Many of the vitamins and minerals our bodies need to function properly can be stored by the body so, if we go a day or two without eating them, we can use up the reserve supplies instead. But vitamin C and the B vitamins cannot be stored and must form part of our everyday diets. The best sources are fruit and vegetables and, since cooking often destroys these vitamins, it's a good idea to eat them raw.

Fruit and vegetables are also extremely low in calories and high in fibre, so you'll be getting other benefits, too. Try to eat a salad every day. If you take a packed lunch to college or work you could pack a selection of salad foods like lettuce, tomato, cucumber, beetroot, watercress, grated carrot, celery, bean sprouts, mushrooms, grated white cabbage and so on (not everything every day, of course) in an airtight plastic container. Take some dressing separately in a small bottle (the ones they serve spirits in on trains are good) and add it at the last minute or the salad will go soggy.

Always choose fresh fruit, fruit salad, or fruit with yoghurt to round off a meal, rather than pudding or ice cream.

Eat less Sugar Sugar is bad for your teeth and extremely fattening, so stop taking it in tea and coffee and sprinkling it on cereals. Sweets, chocolates, biscuits, cakes, puddings, soft drinks and ice-cream are also loaded with sugar so cut them out. If you must snack between meals, choose sunflower seeds, fresh fruit, raw carrot or celery or bread.

Eat less Fat Most dietary experts agree that it's healthy to limit the amount of animal fat you eat. That means choosing fish or poultry rather than red meat, which has a high percentage of hidden fat; opting for skimmed milk rather than creamier varieties; choosing low-fat cheeses like cottage cheese instead of cream cheese, and Edam instead of Cheddar and spreading your bread with a margarine that's high in polyunsaturates rather than butter.

Never fry food when you can grill it instead, and watch out for rich, creamy sauces that turn an otherwise healthy meal into an unhealthy one. Potatoes are, contrary to popular belief, very nourishing and good for you. But when they are fried as chips or covered with fat and roasted, the amount of fat they soak up outweighs the health benefits. Eat them boiled, baked or mashed instead.

As well as providing long-term health benefits, a low-fat diet is also less likely to make you put on weight. And that can't be bad.

Vegetarian diets are not only quite safe, but often healthier than conventional diets because the beans and pulses used in preparing vegetarian savoury dishes are naturally low in fat. Vegan diets (where no animal products, not even milk, butter, eggs or cheese, are eaten) can also be healthy, vitamins and minerals, but they are also high in natural sugars. Always dilute fruit juices half and half with water before drinking.

Tea and coffee contain stimulants which may make you anxious and keep you awake at night. A couple of cups a day

Above: pasta need not be fattening. Choose the wholemeal variety and eat it with light vegetable sauces rather than rich, creamy ones. Above right: sparkling mineral water is the most refreshing drink going.

but require a great deal of planning to ensure you are getting all the necessary nutrients, and should not be undertaken lightly.

Eat less Salt Too much salt encourages high blood pressure and water retention, which can give you a bloated feeling just before your period. Don't add salt to your food at the table, and steer clear of over-salted snacks like nuts and crisps.

Drink more Water Water has no calories at all and comes out of your taps free, so make the most of it. It's the healthiest drink you'll find. For parties and special occasions sparkling mineral waters are fun, especially if you liven them up with ice-cubes and a slice of lemon or lime. Try to drink between six and eight glasses of water every day.

Fruit juices are often thought of as healthy because they contain plenty of

is OK but don't drink any more than that, and don't drink them just before going to bed. A milky drink before bed may help you sleep, but make it with skimmed milk or you'll be getting too much fat.

Soft drinks tend to be packed with sugar, artificial sweeteners and colourants, and provide no goodness whatsoever. They also tend to be expensive. Only drink them occasionally.

Alcohol is, in fact, a dangerous drug, so be wary of it. If your parents allow you to try it at home before you are 18, drink it very sparingly. Wine can be diluted with water, as the French do, to make a longer drink, and beer can be mixed with lemonade for shandy. Avoid spirits. It's unfair but true that a female body is less able to cope with alcohol than a male's. It's also the case that a young liver is less able to cope with

Healthy food doesn't have to be boring. Cram a wholemeal bap full of saladstuff for your lunch and finish off with a juicy apple. If you snack between meals choose fruit or a stick of raw celery rather than biscuits or a sticky bun.

alcohol than an older person's. If you drink too much alcohol you will, in the short term, make a fool of yourself because even in very small quantities alcohol affects the decision-making part of the brain. In the longer-term, you could be storing up very real health problems for yourself.

Don't Smoke You would have had to be living in a cave for the past 10 years not to know of the dangers of smoking. The trouble is that it is extremely addictive and very hard to stop once you've started. The solution is simple: don't start. The same goes for other, illegal, drugs – if you don't take them you won't have the problem of giving up.

Eat Right and Look Good
Try to follow this eating plan as far as possible.

Breakfast
Muesli (with no added sugar) or wholegrain breakfast cereal with skimmed milk or low-fat yoghurt and topped with fresh fruit. Small glass of fruit juice...
or Lightly boiled, poached or scrambled free-range eggs with wholemeal toast spread with polyunsaturated margarine. Half a grapefruit or a small glass of fruit juice...
or Stewed fresh or dried fruit topped with low-fat yoghurt, seeds and nuts,

Crash diets don't work. You may lose weight on a starvation regime, but the chances are you'll put it all back on again... and more besides. It's better by far to follow a healthy, nutritious eating plan than to overindulge and then try to put the damage right with a gimmicky diet.

Wholemeal toast spread with poly-unsaturated margarine. Small glass of fruit juice...
or Porridge made with skimmed milk or water topped with fresh or dried fruit and nuts. Half a grapefruit or a small glass of fruit juice.

Lunch (or light evening meal)
Large salad made from a selection of lettuce, tomato, cucumber, endive, white cabbage, carrots, celery, beetroot, watercress, onion, green pepper, mustard and cress, bean sprouts, raw broccoli, raw mushrooms, raw cauliflower or any other salad stuff, dressed with a mixture of olive oil and vinegar or lemon juice...
with A handful of (unsalted) nuts, or a hard-boiled egg (eat no more than four eggs a week), or a tub of cottage cheese, or grated Edam or other low-fat cheese, or a small tin of tuna or pilchards, or a few slices of chicken or ham...
with A wholemeal roll, or a couple of slices of wholemeal bread spread with polyunsa-turated margarine, or a potato baked in its jacket...
with A piece of fresh fruit.

Dinner (or main meal of the day)
Grilled fish, or chicken, or lean meat, or vegetarian savoury dish...
with A selection of lightly cooked or steamed vegetables...
with A potato baked in its jacket, or boiled potatoes, or mashed potatoes, or brown rice, or wholemeal pasta...
with Fresh fruit, or fruit salad, or fruit fool, or stewed dried or fresh fruit, or fruit served with yoghurt.

Slim Chances
Diets are horrible things. They make you feel bad-tempered, irritable and hungry, stop you enjoying your food, and, worst of all, 95 out of every 100 women who go on diets put all the weight back on and more.

This is because, when you go on a diet your body thinks you've been stranded on a desert island, or somewhere, without enough food, so it slows down your body's metabolism to conserve supplies. When you start eating normally again – and who can stay on a diet all their lives? – your metabolism is still slowed down so you need less food than you did before you went on the diet. Even if you eat normally you will start to pile the weight back on,

possibly ending up fatter than before.

There's worse. If you go on a crash diet of around 1000 calories a day, or less, your body burns the most easily available form of fuel simply to keep you alive. This is a substance known as glycogen, which is you could end up suffering from malnutrition. Diets of between 1000 and 1500 calories a day simply can't supply all the vitamins and minerals you need to stay healthy, unless they are extremely well planned.

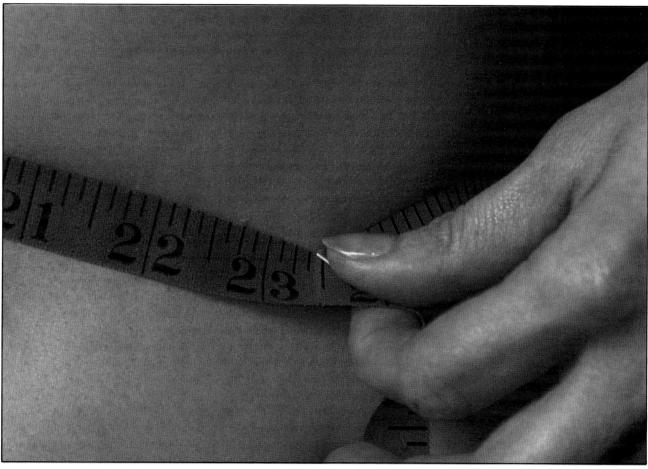

It's useful to know what size you are and how much you weigh, but don't make an obsession of it. If you are trying to lose weight, take regular exercise and follow a healthy eating plan, but don't weigh yourself more often than once every two weeks.

stored in the muscles. Glycogen is bound up with a great deal of water and when the glycogen is used up the water is eliminated. This is how crash diets can produce astonishing weight losses like 10lbs in 10 days. The trouble is that of that 10lbs at least 5lbs will be water which will go back on the minute you stop dieting. Of the remaining 5lbs half of that could be muscle tissue which may be used up as fuel on very low calorie diets, meaning that you've lost only 2½lbs in fat. Unless you exercise as well, as the weight goes back on it will all go on as fat, not muscle and fat. So if you go on a crash diet and then regain the weight you will end up with more body fat than when you started.

Plus, as if all that wasn't bad enough, follow a starvation diet for long enough and

Anorexia nervosa is another fear. No-one knows exactly what sparks this off, but the result is excessive dieting, sometimes to the point of death. *Bulimia nervosa* is similar, except that sufferers appear to eat normally but secretly vomit up everything they eat. Quite apart from the other dangers of bulimia, the stomach acids rot away sufferers' teeth. In fact, bulimics are often first diagnosed by their dentists.

So what do you do if you suffer from puppy fat? There's no denying that society demands girls and women to look slim rather than chubby. Excess fat is not usually very healthy anyway. Well, the good news is that reasonably active teenage girls need a great deal of food – around 2800 calories worth every day – just to fuel their bodies. Now 2800 calories worth of cream cakes,

chocolate, burgers and chips is not that much, but 2800 calories worth of the healthy food described in the previous section is as much food as anyone can eat in a day.

So, forget about counting calories and simply aim to eat a healthy, balanced diet. Unless you are cheating on it, you won't gain weight and you may lose some very gradually. If you need to lose weight faster, take more exercise as described in the next section. Forty minutes vigorous activity three or four times a week should burn up the calories and speed your metabolism, making puppy fat a thing of the past.

The combination of healthy diet and plenty of exercise won't have the weight rolling off as it would if you went on a crash diet. On the other hand, it won't roll back on again in the same way. It's a slow but sure method. Try it for at least three months, preferably six. If at the end of that time you are still overweight, see your doctor. It could be that you have a naturally slow metabolism, or a great deal of weight to lose, and need specialist advice.

Figure it Out

A beautiful body is the result of good food and regular exercise. As a child you probably rushed about playing games, climbing trees and getting plenty of exercise without even thinking about it. As you get older you expend less energy in this way and unless you take part in sports or exercise classes your body can become flabby and your joints stiff and unsupple.

Schools, sadly, do little to prepare teenagers for life in this way. You may have loved hockey or netball at school, but once you leave, it's not always easy to find others to make up a team – and other teams to play against. If you hated organised sports at school, you are probably quite relieved when they are no longer compulsory.

Yet the human body was made to be active. Until the last century, the majority of men did physically punishing work every day. Although they suffered from dirt and infectious diseases, the heart and circulatory diseases, which are major killers in the Western world now, were extremely rare. No-one wants to go back to the bad old days, but everyone feels better and looks better for incorporating a little more physical activity into their lives.

The most important aspect of whatever form of sport or exercise you

More and more women are taking up weight training these days. It's an extremely fast and effective way of shaping up your body. And no, it won't give you massive muscles, women simply don't have the right hormones for that.

decide on is that you should enjoy it. If you regard it as a chore, you won't keep it up. And the thing about exercise is that little and often has much better results than an out-and-out blitz followed by a month of inactivity.

There's a lot of talk now about aerobic exercise as if this were something special. But aerobic simply means 'with air', and any activity which makes you puff and pant can be described as aerobic. Certainly aerobic exercise is the sort of exercise which does most for your heart, lungs and weight problems, but if you prefer the tranquillity of yoga to the freneticism of a dance class, then stick with yoga. All exercise is good, and the more you do the better it is. At least forty minutes, three or four times a week is what you should aim for.

Apart from organised sports and exercise classes, make your daily life more active, too. Walk or cycle short distances rather than hopping on a bus, or asking your parents to drive you. Run upstairs in preference to taking lifts or escalators. Take the dog (if you have one) for regular walks – he'll love you for it. Meet friends to go swimming or for a game of tennis rather than going to a coffee bar. Don't be a lounge lizard.

Sports to Try

Cycling On your bike. If you have a bicycle, or the use of one, you have a great way of exercising, plus free transport. Cycling is aerobic and a good way of improving leg muscles. Simply cycling to and from college or work will save you money on bus fares and give you a good workout every day. At weekends you can cycle out into the country for picnics with friends. If the sport really grips you, you can join a local cycle club and get to know fellow enthusiasts.

Dancing There's a form of dance to suit just about everyone. Choose from ballet, jazz, modern dance, rock and roll, ballroom, folk, aerobic dance, even belly dancing. The thing about dancing is that you get carried away by the music and forget about being too lazy, tired or bored to exercise. Most forms of dance are aerobic and give all the muscles, especially the legs, a good workout, as well as improving flexibility and coordination.

Fencing is extremely aerobic and does wonders for your leg muscles. If you are the competitive sort, you will love fighting to win. There are a surprisingly large number

Riding is very expensive if you live in a city. Out in the country it's usually cheaper and, if you can ride already, you may get to know someone who will let you exercise their horse in return for help with the stable duties. Riding itself is not very aerobic, nor does it give your muscles much of a workout, but all that mucking out, grooming, tack cleaning and sweeping down the stable yard that goes with it works every muscle in your body.

Swimming is one of the best all-round forms of exercise there is. If you can't swim already, you should be able to learn at your local baths. Swimming is highly aerobic and gives your body a complete workout. If you're the solitary sort, settle for swimming lengths, but if you prefer company and competition join a swimming club. Whatever you do, get in the swim.

Tennis improves your coordination and upper body strength. Singles is fairly aerobic, doubles less so. Unless you have access to indoor courts you won't be able to play all year round, so give badminton or squash a try. It's usually possible to book courts at your local sports centre. Don't worry if you are not very good at racquet sports – the more time you spend running after the shuttlecock or ball, the more exercise you get.

Walking is a vastly under-rated form of exercise. So long as you stride out briskly, you are getting virtually the same aerobic benefits as if you were jogging. It's also the best way of getting from A to B. If the distance is under three miles, put on your trainers and put your best foot forward.

Weight training is not just for the boys. It's the quickest way of improving your figure, but you need to be properly taught. Weight training involves using small weights and frequent repetitions of exercises and should not be confused with weight lifting, where the objective is to lift heavier and heavier weights, or body building. Find out if your local gym or sports centre runs courses for women.

Yoga is a superb form of relaxation and a good way of improving flexibility. Most local education authorities run yoga evening classes and you should be able to find one near you. If you find you get very wound up about exams or work, then yoga may be a great help to you.

These are just 10 sports; there are literally hundreds more. Check out what's available in your area. If you live near water

If a sport isn't fun, you won't be bothered to do it however good it is for you. If you love horse-riding, for instance, don't force yourself to go to an aerobics class instead – you'll get bored and find excuses not to go. Jogging is more fun if you can find a friend to run with you.

of fencing clubs run at sports centres and at local education authority evening classes around the country.

Jogging If you can't bear team sports or being organised in any way then jogging is for you. All you need are a good pair of training shoes (bought from a specialist sport shop) and loose, comfortable clothes and you're off. The point about jogging is that it's the time you spend doing it that counts, not the distance or the speed at which you run. Start by brisk walking interspersed with jogs of a minute or less. If you can't catch your breath, walk until you are breathing evenly again. Gradually build up the amount of jogging you do until you can jog for 20 minutes without stopping. Always warm up and cool down by brisk walking for 10 minutes. Jogging is very aerobic.

you may be able to try sailing, or you could have fun on a dry ski slope or ice rink if they are situated nearby. Whatever activity you choose, make sure you learn the basics from a properly qualified instructor or you will hurt yourself. And if special clothes or equipment – like shoes for aerobics or running, or a crash hat for riding – are needed, don't think you can get by without. Sports injuries can be painful and may cause permanent damage.

Whatever sport you choose, you should warm up by running on the spot and doing stretching exercises for 10 minutes beforehand. Cool down the same way afterwards. If any exercise or activity hurts, stop at once. If you are unused to exercising you may feel stiff the next day, but if you are sore or in pain, something is wrong. Think about it: is the teacher pushing you too hard, or not checking you are performing the exercises correctly?

Whether or not you normally wear a bra, you should always wear a sports bra for any sort of physical activity. Choose one that binds your breasts firmly to your chest and doesn't rub or chafe.

Bathing Belles

Not only do the hormones unleashed by puberty send your skin's oil-producing glands into overdrive, they also 'switch on' a new set of sweat-producing glands known as the apocrine glands, which are found in the armpits, groin and around the nipples.

Unlike the sweat glands you have on the rest of your body, these apocrine glands don't only produce sweat to cool your body in the heat or during physical exertion, they respond to any sort of stress, emotion or nervous tension. All of a sudden you find it harder to keep your cool.

Sweat is 99 per cent water mixed with natural salts, and when it is fresh it doesn't smell. It's only after it has been in contact with the bacteria on the skin for a few hours that it becomes unpleasant. A daily bath or shower is the best way to stop sweat building up. If the hot water supplies in your household don't run to that, ensure you wash your underarms, groin and feet daily with warm water and mild, unscented soap.

Bubble baths are fun to use once in a while, but if you bathe in them frequently you could find they dry your skin out and even lead to irritation in the sensitive genital area. Bath oils won't dry your skin out, but they do leave a slippery film which can be dangerous for the next user, so be sure to clean the bath out after you've finished.

Anti-perspirants give extra protection against wetness and body odour, but you should only use them under your arms, never on any other part of the body. They contain metallic salts which prevent the production of sweat. If possible, don't apply an anti-perspirant directly after bathing as it won't work so well. Deodorants simply kill the bacteria which cause the unpleasant odour but do not prevent wetness. They are useful for people who are allergic to anti-perspirants. If you sweat so much that anti-perspirants are ineffective, see your GP who may suggest several ways of tackling the problem.

Supporting Features

Treat your feet well and they'll happily take you wherever you want to go. Treat them badly and you'll suffer for it. Most important, choose shoes that fit you. That's not as daft as it sounds. How many times have you squashed your feet into shoes half a size too small because you liked the look of them? Shoes should fit snugly around your heels, but give you plenty of freedom to wriggle your toes at the front.

For everyday wear choose low-heeled – maximum 1½ inches – shoes that come up high over your instep or have a bar or strap to keep the shoe in place, otherwise you'll have to claw your toes to keep them on. Save high-heeled, fancy shoes for parties and special occasions. Whenever you have to do a lot of walking wear well-fitting trainers. Go barefoot around the house as much as possible.

Once a week, while you have a bath, tackle rough skin on your soles and heels with a pumice stone. Work up a good lather with soap first, then gently rub the roughened head skin away. Never try to tackle corns, callouses, veruccae or any other foot problems yourself – visit a state registered chiropodist who will get rid of them quickly and painlessly.

Toenails should be cut straight across and level with the tops of the toes to avoid ingrowing toenails. Smoothe the edges with an emery board to stop them snagging on your tights. For summer, toenails look pretty painted with nail polish. But remove the polish or touch it up

Go barefoot as often as possible to exercise the muscles in your feet. Some fashion shoes act like splints, preventing the feet from moving properly and leading to aching legs and poor posture. If you have to walk any distance wear well-fitting trainers or walking shoes and save high heels for when you arrive at your destination.

as soon as it starts to chip – nothing looks worse with open-toed shoes.

Barely There

Whether or not you remove what is known as superfluous body hair is entirely your own decision. These are the options available to you, should you decide to do it. *Shaving* is suitable for removing hair on the legs, underarms and around the bikini line.

Buy your own razor – borrowing someone else's can lead to infections – and make sure the blade is sharp. It's easiest to shave in the bath. Simply work up a good lather with soap then shave in the direction of hair growth. Shaving does not make hair grow any thicker or faster, but stubble will appear within a few days to a week. The main advantages of shaving are that it is cheap and quick.

Waxing is suitable for removing hair on the legs and around the bikini line. It is best done in a salon as home waxing kits are messy and expensive. Hair must be at least a quarter of an inch long before waxing. The wax is painted on warm in strips then quickly ripped off, taking the hairs with it. For a few days afterwards the skin will be red and blotchy, but regrowth takes a month to six weeks to appear. Whether or not you can bear to have your legs waxed depends on your threshold of pain. It also works out fairly expensive.

Depilatory creams can be used to remove hair on the underarms. Special mild formulations can be used on the face and around the bikini line. Although creams can be used to remove hair from the legs, it is an expensive way of doing it. Depilatory creams contain the same active ingredient as perming lotions, but you leave them on long enough for the hair to break just below the skin surface and then be wiped away.

well, but works out very expensive. Use a reputable make of cosmetic bleach – don't mix your own concoction – and follow the instructions to the letter. Eyebrow bleaching must be carried out by a qualified beautician because of the risk of bleach getting in the eyes.

Electrolysis is the only permanent form of hair removal. A fine needle is inserted into the follicle and a small electric current kills the hair at the root. Electrolysis should only be carried out by a member of the Institute of Electrolysis. It is very expensive, and treatment for even a small patch of hair on the face can take a year or more because only a few hairs can be treated at each session, and not all the follicles are destroyed the first time they are treated. Some people find electrolysis painful and it should not be carried out on anyone who has keloid scar formation.

Plucking is the best way to thin dense eyebrows, but never pluck above the arch of the brow or you will destroy the line.

Take some tips from the men when you shave. Work up a good lather and use a sharp blade. Rinse the blade frequently in hot water while shaving to prevent it from becoming clogged with hairs. After shaving, rinse away any excess soap, pat dry then smoothe on a little body lotion.

It is important to follow the instructions carefully when applying depilatory creams, and to patch test for sensitivity or allergic reactions before use. Most depilatory creams smell awful, by the way, and you can't apply anti-perspirant for a day or two after treating underarms.

Bleach can be used to lighten hair on the face. It can be used on the arms and legs as

Hairs growing out of moles and around the nipple should never be plucked.

Cutting off hairs close to the skin is the best way to deal with growth around the nipples and navel area. Use a small, sharp pair of scissors. Never try to remove pubic hair or eyelashes as the skin is extremely sensitive in these parts and soreness and infections could set in.

Fit for Life
Try a Gym Workout!

On the following pages, fitness expert Dave Prowse takes you through one of his specially worked out routines. Before you attempt each exercise, make sure your feet are firmly positioned for good support. If you have any back trouble, take medical advice before attempting the exercises.

★ Easy
★★ Medium
★★★ Advanced

Exercise 1. ★

This warm-up exercise is for the muscles of the waist and lower back. Stand erect, hands on hips, and move down to one side as low as possible, back to the upright position and then down to the other side as low as possible. Repeat the movement 50 times (25 times each side).

Exercise 2. ★

This warm-up movement series is for the lower back and the hamstrings. Start from an upright position with hands on hips. Bend forward as far as possible. Come up and arch backwards. Repeat 20 times.

Exercise 3. The Dumbbell Press ★

An arm and shoulder movement.
This is where the dumbbells are pushed from the shoulders overhead alternately. Do three sets of 10-15 repetitions.

Exercise 4. The Dumbbell Curl ★

Our next exercise is specifically for the fronts of the upper arms.
Stand erect, palms to the front, weights resting at the thigh and, by simply bending at the elbow, bring the dumbbells up until they touch your shoulders. Do three sets of 10-15 repetitions.

Exercise 5. The Bench Press ★★★

On to the next exercise which is the first of the bust movements.
Lie on a comfortable bench. It will need to be about ten inches wide and somebody will have to hand you the barbell at arms length as performed in picture. Take a hand spacing slightly wider than shoulder width and, taking a deep breath, lower the barbell down to the throat area, i.e. to the top of the bust or chest. Immediately start to push the barbell up to starting position, exhaling at the finish, and repeat the exercise 10 times. This is specifically for the big chest muscles and an improvement in your pectoralis region will result in an improved bust.

Exercise 6. The Two-Hands Clean ★★★

This is designed for the whole body as well as being an excellent fitness movement.
A barbell is lifted from the floor to shoulder level in one movement and most of the work is done with the legs, arms and shoulders. If you get sufficient leg drive, you will automatically come up on your toes as in the picture *right*. You will end up with the bar resting across your breastbone as shown *far right*. A great all-round exercise, it should be performed 10 times, then rest for 2-3 minutes, repeat a further 10 times, rest another 2-3 minutes, and repeat for a third and last set of 10 times.

Exercise 7. The Grip Press-up ★★★

For the backs of the arms we use a table or, a low bench.
Lean up against the bench with hands fairly close together, thumbs touching. Keeping the body stiff, lower it until the bust or chest touches the bench, then return to the starting position. Most women are not very strong in this exercise, so do as many repetitions as you can, working up to 15 times.

Exercise 8. The Flyer ★★

Our next exercise is also a bust exercise.
This time we use dumbbells and we also utilise
the bench again. Hold the dumbbells at arms
length, lying on a bench. Take a deep breath
and, keeping the arms fairly straight, let the
dumbbells go downward and out to the side.
Get as big a stretch across your chest muscles
as possible. This should be done 15-20 times,
making sure you inhale on the way down and
exhale on the way up. Three sets once again.

Exercise 9. The Two Hands Dead Lift ★★★

From the lower back we do an exercise called
the Two Hands Dead Lift which although with
men has become a competition lift with
weights up nearly 1,000 pounds being lifted,
we are going to do with dumbbells. Basically
all the exercise consists of is lifting two
dumbbells off the floor, standing up straight
and returning to starting position. This is for
the lower back and provided you have nothing
wrong in that area – e.g. disc problems – some
heavy weights can be lifted. Three sets of 15
repetitions will suffice.

Exercise 10. The Squat ★★★

Finally we come to a marvellous fitness, thigh and hip exercise.

Once again you will see we have utilised dumbbells plus a small block to put your heels on. This is to help you maintain your balance. It consists of holding the dumbbells at the shoulders and doing deep knee bends. Squat as deeply as you can. Each exercise necessitates a big deep breath on the way down and an exhalation on the way up. At the end of 20 repetitions, you should be puffing and blowing quite well. Three lots of 20 will round off this brief weight training routine.

The Nautilus

1. Double Shoulder Machine/Overhead Press.

Muscles used: deltoids and triceps.
Grasp handles above shoulders and press them overhead. Slowly lower the resistance making sure to keep elbows wide.

Repeat.

2. Abdominal Machine.

Muscles used: abdominal.
Place ankles behind lower pads and sit erect. Grasp handles over shoulders and pull down, contracting abdominal muscles only. Pause in contracted position and return slowly to starting position.

Repeat.

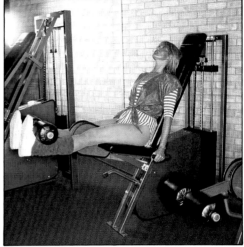

3. Leg Extension Machine.

Muscles used: fronts of thighs.
Place feet behind roller pads with knees against seat. Make sure head and shoulders are firm against back of seat. Straighten both legs to fully extend. Pause. Slowly bend knees to lower the resistance and repeat.

4. Double Chest Machine.

Muscles used: chest, deltoid muscles in shoulders.
Place forearms firmly against pads. Keeping head against seat back, grasp handles. Push forearms to try and touch elbows together in front of chest. Pause and slowly move arms out again with control.

5. Double Shoulder Machine/Lateral Raise.

Muscles used: deltoid muscles of shoulders.
Pull handles back until knuckles rest against pads. Raise both arms from the elbows until parallel with the floor. Pause, then slowly lower the resistance and repeat.

Fit for Life
Looking Good...Feeling Great

Back to Basics

More mistakes are made choosing foundation than any other item of cosmetics. Choose a light fluid formulation rather than a cream or solid base which will be too rich for your skin. Match it exactly to the colour of the skin on your neck. Many women opt for too dark a colour thinking it will make them look healthier; in fact, it just means that your make-up will look like a mask.

Another common mistake is to go for a pinky shade. Skin isn't pink at all, but shades of beige through to brown. Look for a flat, putty colour if you are pale, a dull brown if you are darker skinned.

Only ever apply make-up to scrupulously clean skin. Moisturise any dry patches or the make-up will sink in too quickly and look patchy. Apply a camouflage stick to any spots first, then put foundation over the top.

For a really professional finish you need to use a flat, soft cosmetic sponge which can be bought cheaply at any chemist's. Dampen it with cool water and wring out well. Pour a little foundation into the palm of your hand then use the sponge to sweep it lightly and smoothly across your face.

Cover your eyelids and lips with foundation and make sure you have even coverage on the nose and cheeks where skin tone is often blotchy. Don't take foundation right up to the hairline or beyond the jaw. If you have chosen the colour well, you should be able to gradually fade it out leaving no harsh lines.

If you wear foundation, you must set it with powder or your face will look moist and sweaty. Choose a light, translucent powder and apply it with a puff or a ball of cotton wool. Pat it generously all over your face where you have put foundation and don't worry at this stage if it looks too floury. Next, take a large, soft make-up brush – as large as you can find – and gently brush away all the excess powder. Brush

Get together with a friend and spend an evening experimenting with new make-up techniques. Try unusual colours and aim at creating different effects: casual, sophisticated, romantic and so on. Never try a new look for the first time when you are going somewhere special, always practise first.

All it takes is practice. Build up a good selection of inexpensive cosmetics in a variety of colours so you can experiment with different looks. If you have any cash to spare spend it on a good set of make-up brushes. Look after them and keep them clean by washing in warm, soapy water, rinsing then propping upright to dry. They will last you all your life.

Applying a lot of make-up is easy, but it looks false and unnatural. The secret is to apply very little at first and gradually build up the colour. Develop a light hand with a make-up brush and you are half way there.

Spots always seem to appear when it is most important that you look your best. Concealer cream followed by foundation and powder does a very good job of covering blemishes, but remember to blend in well to ensure the concealer matches the surrounding skin tone. Keep a tube of concealer cream in your handbag for emergency cover-ups.

downwards because this is the direction in which the tiny facial hairs lie. When you have finished your face should look beautifully matt, smooth and even – the perfect canvas for the eye and lip colours that are to come.

For a more natural look, or when you simply don't have time to apply foundation *and* powder, use a tinted moisturiser just to give your skin a little extra glow. Again, match it to the actual colour of your skin rather than choosing a colour you would like your skin to be, or it will look like a mask. After washing and toning, carefully smoothe tinted moisturiser over your face, blending it in with your natural skin tone as you approach the hair or jaw line. Don't let the colour end abruptly in a dark line or it will look unnatural. Once you get the hang of this you will find it takes no longer than applying your usual moisturiser.

Shaping Up

Few teenage girls have high, elegant cheekbones. Usually they are obscured by a layer of puppy fat, giving the face a young, round look. But don't despair. By the time you reach your mid-twenties your hormones will have been working to redistribute any excess fat, concentrating it around your hips. You will probably by then have the cheekbones you always craved, although, of course, you may also have a pear-shaped figure problem, too, but that's another story.

For photography, make-up artists use darker make-up to shade away chubby cheeks when necessary. And that looks fine under strong photographic lights and when the model holds her face in just one position. It doesn't work so well on a 'real' person. In fact, face-shaping can simply look as if you have a dirty smudge on your cheeks.

Rather than trying to achieve the impossible, it's better to emphasise your good points like your lips and eyes and ignore the fact that your cheeks are rounder than you would like them to be, the chances are most people won't realise either.

Blusher is fast going out of fashion, but if you think you need a little extra colour to lift your face, use it sparingly. If you are one of those people who blushes naturally at the slightest provocation, don't use cosmetic blusher – your face will have enough colour anyway.

Apricot or a pinky brown are undoubtedly the most flattering colours for blusher. If you are wearing powder, choose a powder blusher. If you have simply opted for tinted moisturiser, use a cream blusher. Remember the rule: wear powder colours with powder, and cream colours or gels with tinted moisturisers.

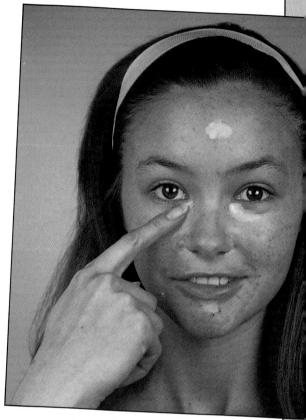

To find out where to put blusher, hold a pencil up to your face. Find the vertical line down from the mid-point of your eye and at the point where this line crosses your cheekbone – you can feel it under your skin with your fingers – is where you should start your blusher. You can then blend it out along your cheekbone towards the hairline, but fading away well before it. Never apply blusher any closer to your nose than below the mid-points of your eyes.

To apply powder blusher, wait a few moments after you have powdered over your foundation for your base make-up to set. Then load blusher colour onto a fairly thick brush. Tap the brush on the back of your hand to get rid of any excess then brush it along your cheekbones, as described. Cream blusher can be blended in with your fingers.

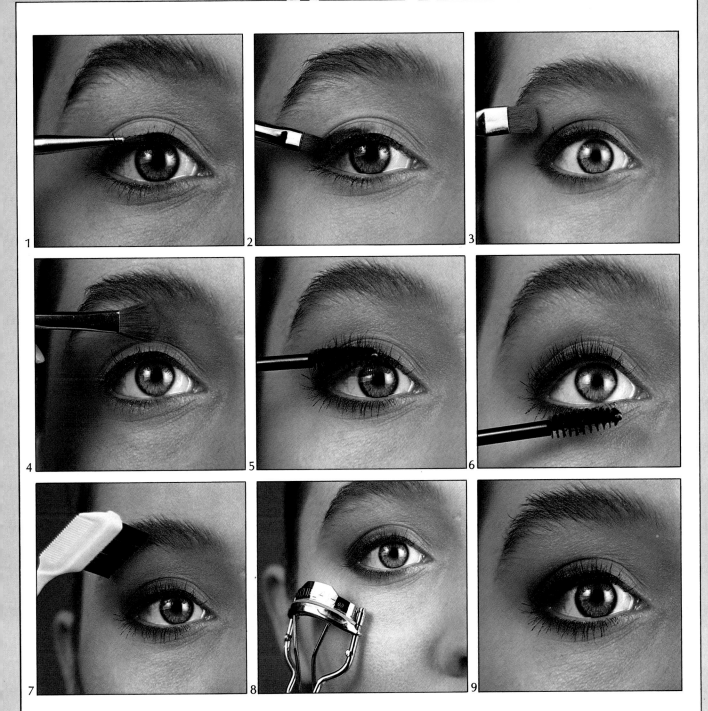

1 2 3
4 5 6
7 8 9

1 Add definition by outlining your eyes with eyeliner or eye pencil. **2** Use a basic shade, like brown or grey, on your upper lids. **3** A touch of gold shadow emphasises the brow bone. **4** Pink, cream or even white shadow on the inner eye prevents eyes looking too close together. **5** Apply

Eyes Right

Eye make-up is tricky but looks really impressive when properly applied. Powder eyeshadow lasts longest, especially if you remembered to put foundation and powder on your lids first to give the colour something to cling to. When you are just wearing tinted moisturiser, choose a creamy eye colour in a plain shade, or, for a more natural look, don't wear any eye make-up at all.

To give your eyes depth and definition, start by outlining their shape. Liquid eyeliner is best, but you need a steady hand. Eye pencil is easier for beginners – dark colours like grey, brown, navy, burgundy or emerald green look good. Run a line along the upper lids close to the lashes and dot the same colour between the lashes on the outer edges of the lower lids. Smudge the colour with a cotton wool bud to make it softer.

mascara to the upper lashes first and allow to dry. **6** Then apply mascara to the lower lashes. **7** Brush the brows into shape. **8** If you have eyelash curlers, use them *before* you apply your mascara.

The basic eyeshadow colours are grey and brown. You should aim to have both of these in your make-up collection. But you can also use literally any colour you like – matched to your eyes or your outfit – to create any effect you want. There are no rules. Experiment and see what looks good.

For the simplest eye make-up use one colour and brush it over your upper lids, following the shape of your eyes. Blend it in well with the eye pencil or line close to your lashes, but don't take it beyond the eye socket. With a clean eyeshadow brush, blend the colour to get rid of any hard lines.

difficult to remove you end up rubbing and pulling at the delicate skin around your eyes.

The best colour for mascara is black – it suits almost everyone, although if you are very fair you may prefer brown. Navy mascara looks good if you have blue eyes, and emerald green perks up green or hazel eyes. You can even get purple or burgundy mascaras now, which are great fun.

Mascara is easiest to apply if you look down into a magnifying mirror. Brush gently from the roots of the lashes towards the tips and be very careful not to jab your eye

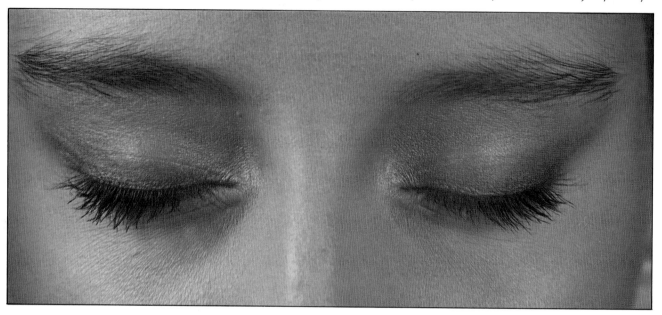

Above: strong eyeshadow colours look best lightly winged out from the corners of the eyes. Facing page: for those special occasions, however, you can let your imagination run away with you.

To ring the changes, simply brush eyeshadow in a line along the edge of the upper lashes and wing it out when you reach the corners of the eyes. Blend well with a clean brush.

These are the two basic eyeshadow techniques, but for special occasions you can add more colours to build a new look. Try adding a darker shade on the inner half of the eyelid, or a lighter, even silver or gold, shadow on the outer half – and blend it up towards the browbone. Use a contrasting colour underneath as well. Or go completely mad, the only limit is your imagination. Eye make-up looks unfinished without mascara. This is how to apply it. Start by curling your upper lashes with eyelash curlers to give your eyes a wide-awake look. Cream mascara in a tube is easier to use and longer-lasting than block mascara. Look for a smudge-proof variety but avoid waterproof mascara – it's so

with the mascara wand – it can be excruciatingly painful.

Apply one light coat of mascara, allow it to dry then apply a second. If it clogs or blobs, gently brush an old, clean mascara wand over your lashes to tidy them up. You can stop mascara splashes landing on your freshly-made up cheeks by holding a tissue under the eye you are working on.

Your eyebrows frame your face and add character. Don't pluck them into a hard, mean line, simply remove any straggling hairs with a pair of slant-tipped tweezers, then brush them in shape and remove any stray traces of powder with an old, clean mascara brush. A tiny dab of hair gel will hold them in place.

If you swim a great deal or simply can't be bothered with fiddling around with mascara, consider having your eyelashes dyed. Most good beauty salons do this very cheaply and the effects last four to six

Looking Good...Feeling Great

1 Outline your lips with lip pencil for a more precise shape – this also gives you the chance to even up crooked lips. **2** Use a lipbrush to fill in with colour; it makes the lipstick stay on longer and is more economical. **3** A dash of lip gloss in the middle of the lower lip adds the finishing touch.

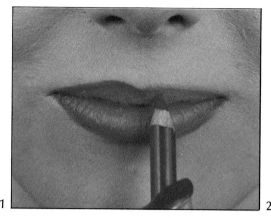

1

3

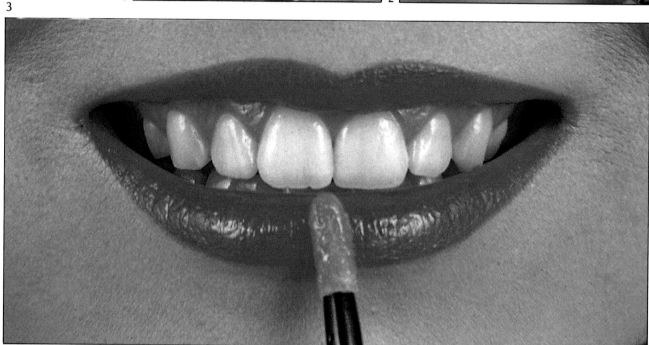

Facing page: match your lipstick to your outfit, your glasses, or whatever you fancy. Strong-coloured lipstick draws attention to your teeth, so if yours are less than perfect consider paler pinks or peach colours.

weeks. Don't try to do it yourself, you could get the dye in your eyes, which is painful and can be dangerous.

Contact lens wearers should avoid mascara with lash-building filaments, as these can irritate the eyes. Put your lenses in *before* applying eye make-up, so you can see what you are doing – but *remove* them before you take it off otherwise they will become smeared and possibly damaged.

If you wear glasses, you can have just as much fun with eye make-up as those with 20-20 vision. Use a magnifying glass to help you see where to apply it. Just remember not to choose eyeshadow colours that clash with your frames.

The best way to remove eye make-up is with a good, non-oily eye make-up remover. Soak a pad of cotton wool in eye make-up remover, then hold it to an eye for

a second or two. Gently wipe make-up away, always working from the inside towards the outside. Repeat with the other eye, then wash your face in the usual way.

A Lot of Lip

For beautiful lips, outline first with a lip pencil. Correct any minor imperfections this way, but don't take the pencil more than a hair's breadth outside the natural lip line or you will look like a clown. Fill in with colour. Red, pink, peach and coral always look good, simply make sure they tone with what you are wearing. Brown is an unusual choice, but can look stunning. Burgundy and plum colours are good in winter but look too heavy in summer.

Applying your lipstick with a lipbrush gives a better finish and is more economical. Blot your lips with tissue and

apply a dash of lip gloss in the middle of your lower lip as a finishing touch.

Lip gloss – either colourless or tinted – is a good bet on the days when you don't want to be bothered with too much make-up as it will moisturise your lips and prevent them becoming chapped.

Nailed

Over-long nails look vicious. Keep yours all at a reasonable length by filing them – in one direction only, sides to middle – with an emery board. If you break a nail, cut it off and smoothe the edges with an emery board then trim the other nails down to match.

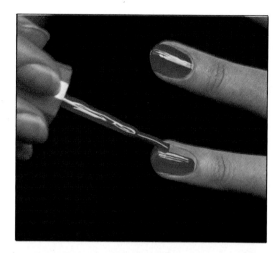

If you have slim fingers and well-shaped nails, make the most of them with nail polish in vivid colours. But touch it up or remove it the moment it starts to flake, as nothing looks worse than neglected nails. If you are trying to grow your nails a coat or two of clear or pale pink polish may help to strengthen them.

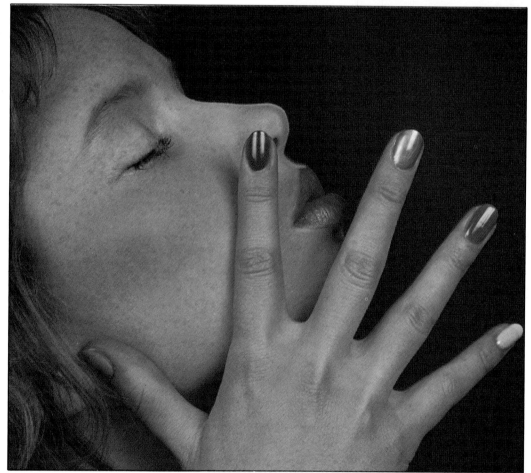

Some people have naturally weak nails, and if yours break easily, settle for having them short and well-shaped rather than trying to battle against nature and grow them. If you bite your nails, you can buy a preparation from the chemist to paint on them. It tastes disgusting and should cure you of the habit quite quickly.

Once a week, after you have softened the skin in a bath, push your cuticles back with a cotton wool bud. If they are still stubborn, soften them further with a cuticle cream. Never, ever cut or tear at cuticles.

Well-shaped nails look pretty painted with clear or pale pink nail polish. If you choose a stronger colour you must be sure

it tones with your lipstick and your outfit. Either touch it up or remove it as soon as it starts to chip. Cracked and flaking nail polish looks awful.

Remove old polish by soaking pads of cotton wool in nail polish remover. Hold the pads against your nails for a few seconds then wipe the polish away. Wash your hands to get rid of the last traces of polish remover. Dry.

If you want to wear a bright colour use a base coat first to stop the polish staining your nails. Apply polish to each nail using no more than three strokes of the brush. Paint a broad stripe from the cuticle to the tip then fill in with a brush-stroke on each side. If you fiddle about it will look messy. Allow the first coat to dry, then apply a second. A top coat of clear polish adds gloss and lessens the likelihood of chipping.

Naturally Pretty

A woman who wears make-up all the time is a woman who has something to hide. Or at least that's what it looks like. Playing sports, on the beach or walking in the countryside, make-up looks unnatural and unnecessary. A dab of moisturiser or sunscreen is all you need to protect your face from the elements, with perhaps a slick of lip gloss to stop your lips from becoming chapped.

For weekend outings with friends or as a fast make-up for busy mornings you could try wearing tinted moisturiser with a pale-coloured lipgloss and one coat of mascara – unless you have had your lashes dyed.

The lightest touch of gel blusher or cream eyeshadow makes this a look that's right any time, anywhere.

If your school, college, place of work or parents don't approve of make-up, don't push your luck by wearing any. As an adult you will be able to wear as much as you like. Until then, bide your time.

Carrie didn't want to look overly made-up, so we just used tinted moisturiser and a dusting of translucent powder to even out her skin tones. One coat of brownish-black mascara added emphasis to her eyes and a coral-tinted lip gloss completed this fresh, natural look.

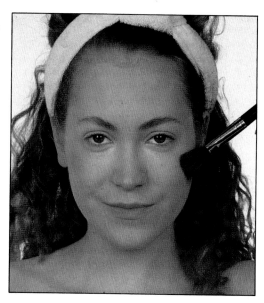

Jenna is a very attractive girl, but her usual style wasn't suitable for her new job in a bank. Foundation and powder gave her skin a matt, sophisticated look and a touch of brown eyeshadow and coral lipstick emphasised her strong features. With her hair slicked back off her face and held in place with a hairspray she presented a much more business-like image.

Look Smart

For interviews or starting you first job, make you make-up very low-key and unobtrusive. Use foundation and powder as a base, or if you feel that is not right for you, tinted moisturiser. Keep eye make-up to a minimum. Stick to grey or brown eyeshadow or even none at all and one coat of mascara. Avoid brightly-coloured lipstick. Choose, pink, coral or peach, or a pale lip gloss. Don't wear coloured nail polish, it doesn't look very businesslike, or perfume, other than a dash of cologne. Keep your hair sleek and under control. Whatever you do, don't go for an interview or start your first job without practising your make-up and hairstyle beforehand. If you know you look good you'll have more confidence.

The Look of Love

When romance is a possibility make sure it will be you, not your make-up he'll be looking at. A foundation and powder base lasts longer than tinted moisturiser. Avoid blusher unless you are deathly pale to begin with. Excitement and nervous tension bring a flush to most people's cheeks.

For a romantic look emphasise your eyes. Carefully applied eye liner and dark eyeshadow look smoky and mysterious. Use two, even three coats of mascara. Don't make your lips compete for attention with your eyes by choosing a fiery red lipstick. A soft pink or brown is more subtle. A dash of cologue adds the finishing touch.

Party Party

Have fun with colour. Anything goes. For parties, think about combining your outfit, your hairstyle and your make-up to create a complete look. Go for a one-colour theme. Pile your hair into a 60s style and wear false lashes and white lipstick like the Mods. Or simply sizzle up your usual make-up with dashes of silver or gold or glitter.

Zoe wanted a romantic look for a very special date. We suggested she emphasise her eyes with brown eye pencil, eyeshadows in smoky colours and lashings of black mascara. Her soft pink lipstick toned with her dress and she twisted some matching pink fabric into a bow for her long hair.

Debi didn't think she could do much with her short hair, but we showed her it's ideal for the '60s look. Eyeliner and false lashes are the hallmark of this era, with pale, pale pink or white lipstick. She brushed her hair forward, too, for a '60s fringe. We suggested that while Debi was getting ready she had a drink of milk or a sandwich, in case there was no food available at the party.

The Last Detail

You've done your make-up, styled your hair, your outfit looks good and you are ready to go out. But wait. There's one final touch that makes all the difference: your fragrance. Choosing a fragrance is a very individual thing. You may love a perfume on your friend but hate it on yourself. If a teacher you loathed at school always wore a certain fragrance, you may think of her every time you smell it for years to come.

All perfumes have three different notes. The top note is the one that emerges a few minutes after you apply it and is usually light and fresh. The middle note or heart of the perfume emerges about 20 minutes later. After several hours only the musky base note will be left.

Rehearse your make-up beforehand so you can be sure it will look all right on the night. A foundation and powder base will last longer and provide a better background for the colours you plan to use. Lipsticks and eyeshadows come in all shades now so don't double up and use lip colours on your eyes or eye colours on your lips. They won't look as good as the ones that are designed for the job, and could irritate your skin.

The only way to discover which perfumes you like is to try as many as possible. Spray yourself from the tester bottle every time you pass the perfumery counter in your local department store, but just try one fragrance at a time or your nose will become confused. When you've found a fragrance you like all three notes of, only then consider buying.

Perfume is expensive, and the more concentrated it is, the more costly it will be.

Light, floral fragrances are very popular now, especially for daytime. Heavy, oriental perfumes are usually more suitable for the evenings, but experiment and work out what suits you best. No-one can decide for you.

Unfortunately, once opened it doesn't keep for longer than 18 months to two years so it's no good being frugal with it. The best way to get value for money is to buy – or be given – a small spray of the more dilute eau de parfum or eau de cologne. That way you can use it lavishly – perfume concentrate, or extrait, is overpowering in any more than tiny quantities – and use it up before it goes off.

Spray perfume on your wrists, neck, behind your ears, shoulders, back and the backs of your knees, if you like. Only ever apply it to clean skin or it will mingle with perspiration and smell foul. Now look in the mirror again. Your hair, make-up and clothes look as good as they did before, but your fragrance has added that indefinable something. You look more confident, and true beauty comes from confidence. It's the last detail.

Fit for Life
Go Get Ahead!

Glossy, well-cared-for hair is your most important accessory. Whether it's straight or curly, fine or thick, blonde, brown, red or black, a few minutes attention every day will bring rewards.

You have somewhere between 120,000 and 150,000 hairs on your head, each growing at the rate of about one centimetre a month. After growing for about six years each hair will rest for a few months then fall out to be replaced by a new one. This accounts for the 100 to 200 hairs that you find in your brush or comb every day.

The hair you can see is dead. The growth happens in what are known as follicles buried in your scalp. But just because hair is dead it doesn't mean you can treat it any old how. Just as cleaning and polishing a pair of leather shoes makes them last longer and look better, so the way you care for your hair has a lot to do with how shiny and manageable it is.

There is hardly a woman on this earth who wouldn't swap her hair type for something different if she could. Girls with curly hair long for locks as straight as tap

water. Blondes would prefer to be dark, mysterious brunettes. Anyone who has had to battle with thick, wiry hair wishes it were soft and fine. Those with limp, flyaway locks long for a mass of curls. But all hair can look beautiful and the secret of success is to work *with*, not *against*, nature.

The new, frequent-wash shampoos have made hair care simpler than ever before. Now you can wash your hair whenever it needs it and you don't have to worry about stripping away the natural oils as with the old-style detergents. If you need to wash your hair daily, a short or medium-length, simple haircut will speed things up.

Bubbling Over

Along with spots, greasy hair is the hallmark of adolescence. But unlike spots there's no need to put up with greasy hair. Since the introduction of the new, mild, frequent-wash shampoos a couple of years back, it has been possible to wash your hair as often as you like without damaging it. Now you can certainly wash your hair every day if need be, and twice a day if you like. And no, frequent washing won't make your hair more greasy in the long run.

Before you wash your hair, bend forward from the waist and give it a good brushing with a natural bristle brush. This will remove some of the dust and dirt and any loose hairs that would otherwise block

up the sink. Next, thoroughly wet your hair with warm water making sure that the underneath and the parts behind your ears aren't missed out.

The purpose of a shampoo is to combine with the dirt and grease on your hair and scalp, and then rinse out. So don't waste your money buying a fancy brand that contains herbs, eggs, flowers or anything else that is supposed to do amazing things to your hair – it won't be there long enough to make any difference. Simply look for an inexpensive product by a well-known manufacturer and marked 'frequent wash'.

Some people think that by diluting shampoo with water in the bottle it will last longer and be kinder to hair. The opposite is true. The manufacturers put in just enough preservative to keep the product in good condition. If you dilute it, it could well go 'off'. At best you would be wasting your money – at worst you could damage your scalp or hair.

You don't need to use a lot of shampoo – just enough to cover a 10 pence piece. Pour it onto your hands then smear it across your palms before massaging it into your scalp and hair. Rub gently, you don't want to tear hair out by the roots, but thoroughly, making sure you cover your whole head. Then rinse. One shampoo is sufficient; two simply add to the manufacturer's profits. Many cases of dull, matted hair, dandruff and even scalp infections are caused by inadequate rinsing. If you have a shower attachment, use that to rinse hair until it is squeaky clean. If not, run bowl after bowl of warm water until you are sure you have removed every trace of shampoo.

If you don't have a shower you may be tempted to wash your hair in the bath. This is fine so long as you don't use any soap in the water before you wash your hair as it leaves a scum, and provided you get out of the bath and rinse your hair in fresh, clean water in the basin.

When you are sure your hair is clean, wrap it in a soft towel to blot the excess moisture. Don't try and comb it straight away and don't rub vigorously with a rough towel. Hair is extremely vulnerable when it is wet and rough handling will stretch and break it.

Greasy hair often goes hand in hand with dandruff. If you are a sufferer it could be that you are simply not washing your hair often enough – at least every three

Condition's the Thing

If you were to examine a hair under a microscope – in fact, if you have access to a microscope do try it – you would see that the surface is not smooth, but is made up of tiny overlapping scales. The job of these scales is to protect the inner parts of the hair which give it its curl and bounce.

If the scales, which make up what is known as the cuticle, lie flat they do a good job of protection and also reflect light well, making hair look shiny. But if they are ruffled or rubbed away in parts then the hair looks dull and will be in poor condition.

Unfairly, some people are born with naturally good cuticles to their hair. These are the people who can use heated rollers day in day out, have perms and never use a conditioner and still have a glossy, healthy-looking head of hair. Others naturally have cuticles that do a very poor job of protection and, unless it is very well looked after, their hair looks dull and flyaway.

Because the hair you can see is dead, once it is damaged it cannot be mended. Heated rollers, over-hot hairdryers, too vigorous brushing, perms and colouring treatments all wear away the scales of the cuticle, and once lost they cannot be replaced. The ends of the hair are the oldest part and the most vulnerable. If you have long hair the ends have had to endure five or so years of rough treatment.

If the cuticle becomes worn away the inner parts will dry out and split – a split end. And once hair has split it cannot be stuck together again, it must be trimmed to prevent the split from travelling further up the hair.

Top: using conditioner once or twice a week after shampooing will make your hair easier to manage. Above: switch your hairdryer to 'cool' to finish drying your hair to prevent split ends caused by excess heat.

days – or rinsing out all of the shampoo when you do so. Try washing your hair using the method described above for a few weeks and see whether that brings any improvement.

If your dandruff doesn't clear up straightaway try using a special shampoo containing zinc pyrithione (ask your pharmacist to help you choose). Follow the instructions on the label to the letter. Medicated shampoos should be avoided as they may make dandruff worse.

Occasionally, dandruff doesn't respond to any of these measures and you will need to consult your GP, who may refer you to a dermatologist.

Regular haircuts are the basis of good hair condition, along with gentle washing as described in the previous section and going easy on the heated rollers and perms. Conditioners have their place, too, but must be used with care on hair that has a tendency to become greasy or you will end up with limp, lank locks.

Rollers may have a frumpy image, but you can use them to create styles that are anything but! Try not to use heated rollers every day, and step up your conditioning programme to prevent the ends of your hair drying out after use.

Only use a conditioner if your hair is hard to comb through while wet. This indicates that the scales of the cuticle are ruffled, leading to snarls and tangles. Shampoo and rinse your hair thoroughly and blot dry. Pour enough conditioner to cover a five pence piece onto the palms of your hands then work it through the ends of your hair *only*. Conditioner doesn't need to go anywhere near the scalp. Using a wide-toothed comb – preferably one marked 'saw-cut' as these are kindest to hair – comb the conditioner through your hair.

If there are any tangles, start at the ends and gently unravel them, working up towards the roots. Some conditioners must then be left on the hair for a few minutes, others can be rinsed out immediately – read the label. Either way, when you come to rinse your hair use lots of clean, warm water and make sure you get rid of every trace of conditioner.

Style Counsel

Blow drying is easy – when you know how to do it. Before you start remove as much moisture as you can from your hair with towels then, using a wide-toothed comb, make your parting and comb hair into shape. With your hairdryer set to medium – never hot, as too much heat dries out and damages hair – hold the dryer at least six inches away from your head and play the jet of warm air all over your hair, never resting on the same spot for more than a second or two, until hair is just damp.

If you have a good cut and all you want is more volume, you can then simply bend forward from the waist and continue to dry your hair in this way, brushing it forward all the time to encourage plenty of lift in the under layers of hair.

To encourage curl, dispense with the hair brush and simply scrunch up hair with the fingers as you dry it. This is called scrunch-drying and works best on hair with a natural wave to it.

If your hair is very long, thick or cut in a complicated style you will need to work a bit harder at it. Section off the upper layers of hair and hold them in place with clips. Use a circular or semi-circular brush, preferably one with vents to allow the air to circulate through it, and brush the underneath strands of hair down and under, playing with warm air over the hair as you do it. When the underneath sections are completely dry, unclip the upper layers and do the same with them. Never, ever direct the hot air at one piece of hair for longer than a second or two, and try switching your dryer to 'cold' when hair is almost dry as this is when it is most vulnerable to heat damage.

Curling tongs are useful styling aids provided you don't use them too often – once or twice a week at most. If you have a style that needs tonging more often that that you will dry out the ends of your hair. Choose a reputable make of curling tongs that have a thermostat fitted so they can't overheat. Only ever use tongs on completely dry hair. Grip the very ends of the hair between the tongs and quickly roll

It's incredible what you can do with a pair of curling tongs and plenty of patience. Less dramatically, you can use them simply to flick up a fringe or turn under the ends of your hair. As with all heated appliances, take care not to damage your hair with overuse.

up a strand. Don't hold the hair in the tongs for more than a second or two before releasing the curl. Allow the hair to cool before fingering or combing into shape. If you have a straight bob that just needs more bounce, it's possible to buy styling wands that are covered in wire hoops and simply give lift not curl.

Heated rollers, like tongs, are fine for special occasions but shouldn't be used on a daily basis. Again, they must only be used on dry hair. Choose a reputable make and heat them up to the required temperature.

Section hair off into strands and roll hair, in a downwards direction, over the roller. Secure with the grips provided. Use large rollers on the top layers of hair, smaller ones underneath. When the rollers have cooled, gently unwind the strands of hair with your fingers then lightly comb into shape.

A Cut Above
Good haircuts don't come cheap, but the right style will make your hair easy to manage and you will have the confidence of knowing it looks good. If you can't afford

1 Assessing the hair type and condition. **2** The hair is sectioned off and the cutting begins. **3, 4, 5** Small sections of hair are cut and then the length is checked; avoid hairdressers who try to cut too much in one go. **6** The front hair is pinned up and the back blow-dried into shape. **7** The front hair is combed into shape ready for blow-drying. **8** The finished effect.

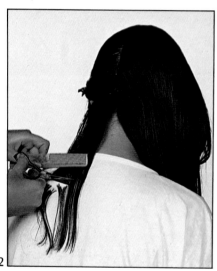

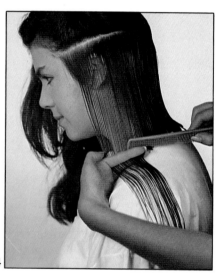

It helps if you have some idea of the style you want – or don't want – but it's no good asking a stylist to reproduce the one you liked in a magazine. No two people have exactly the same facial structure or hair style, and so no two haircuts will ever be exactly the same.

To ask how long a good cut should take is like asking how long is a piece of string. It varies. Thick hair, for instance, takes longer to cut than thin simply because there is more of it. Some of the best stylists work very fast, but if you are in and out of the salon in under half an hour then you have probably not had the best possible service.

If you don't have much time to spend on your hair in the mornings, or if you have to have your hair tied back for school or work, explain this to the hairdresser before she begins work. Don't daydream or lose

to visit a top-class salon find out whether any of the ones near you need models for trainee stylists to practise on. It sounds alarming, but it needn't be. The trainee will be closely supervised by an experienced cutter and will be concentrating extremely hard on getting everything right. Salons usually only charge a nominal fee to cover shampoo, heat and lighting for this service, and the only snag is that you'll get the cut that the trainee needs to learn, not necessarily the one you want.

A good hairdresser will always examine your hair dry first to assess the curl, thickness and condition, and discuss with you how you would like it cut, and then wash it in order to cut it wet. Dry hair is too springy to be cut properly.

yourself in a magazine while your hair is being cut. Watch what is going on then, if you think the fringe is going to be too short, you can say so while there is still time to do something about it.

Hard-and-fast rules about who suits what styles are a waste of time. You may think you don't suit a fringe, but do you mean a short fringe, a long fringe, a shaped fringe, a graduated fringe a wispy fringe or a side-swept fringe? A good hairdresser sees dozens of people day in, day out, and can usually tell at once what will suit your unique looks.

Take particular note of how the stylist dries your hair so you can copy it yourself at home. If you can't see what he's doing at the back of your head – ask.

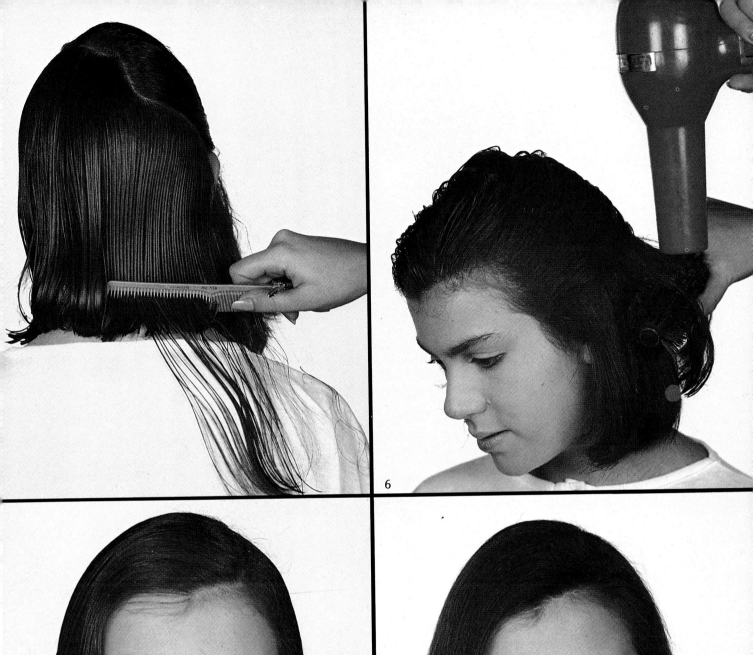

6

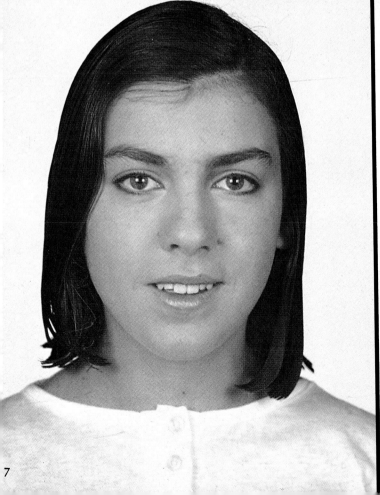

7

8

Right: hair gel is ideal for creating spiky styles like the one shown facing page. Below: work the gel through your hair with your fingertips, shaping it into spikes. Below right: blow-dry holding the strands vertically as you do so. Use your fingers rather than a brush or comb.

Attempting to take legal action over a bad haircut is usually fruitless unless the salon put some treatment on your hair which has made it turn green or fall out. Trying to explain to a judge the finer points of a graduated bob is not usually worth the effort, and can work out to be costly.

Should you cut your own hair? The answer must be No. If haircutting was that easy hairdressers wouldn't need to spend years training to do it. Even trimming a fringe can be dodgy, and there's no way you can cut around the back of your head. It's not like making you own clothes when if you don't like the result you can stuff it in the back of a drawer. If you have a bad haircut you have to wear it day in, day out, until it grows out.

Depending on how fast your hair grows, it will need cutting every two to three months. If you are really strapped for cash you could have it styled at a good

If you don't like your style, say so there and then. It may be embarrassing, but the hairdresser would rather have the opportunity to put it right himself than have you go home in tears and tell all your friends that so-and-so's salon is awful. If you don't realise how bad it is until you get home, ring up straight away and tell the stylist or the manager. They should arrange for you to come in and have it put right at no extra charge, but the longer you leave it the less helpful they are likely to be. They may think you are just trying to get a free haircut out of them.

(expensive!) salon then simply have the ends trimmed more cheaply by a local hairdresser. But don't be mean about having your hair cut. A good style is going to do a lot more for your looks than expensive cosmetics or fancy clothes. And on a cost-per-day basis will probably work out cheaper, too.

Go Set... Go
Most people's hair has a tendency to flop downwards. However good your cut and skillful your blow-drying, you cannot expect your hair to defy gravity – well not

For soft cùrls use mousse and scrunch dry. Right: work mousse through your hair. Far right: gently blow-dry hair, using your fingers to scrunch it into natural-looking curls. The longer you spend doing this, the curlier the final result will be.

If you have naturally curly hair, a squirt of hair spray will give lift and hold. Gently backcomb hair with fingers or a wide-toothed comb, then aim the spray at the roots of your hair. Leave a few minutes for the spray to dry, or speed the process up with a hairdryer on its coolest setting.

for very long, at least. If you want to lift or even spike your hair you have to give it some help in the form of one of the many gels, mousses and hairsprays on the market today.

Gels usually give the strongest hold. They coat each strand of hair with a light and harmless chemical that sets hard, holding the hair in shape. They should only be used on wet hair and, because gels don't distribute very easily, they are best for spikes, individual curls and flipped-up fringes.

To use a gel, dampen your hair then dip your fingers in gel and work it into a strand. Hold the strand upright if you want a spike or bend it around your fingers for a curl and blow-dry until it has set in position. It should then stay in place until you next wash your hair.

If you don't like the way you have styled your hair or you need a more conventional style for school or work the next day, simply dampen your hair slightly – use a fine spray of water from a plant mister – and re-style. The gel will hold the new style as well as the old. Gels simply coat the outside of the hair and do not harm it. They wash out with warm-to-hot water and shampoo.

Hair Flair

Even if your hair is really quite short you can still have fun experimenting with different styles. The first thing to do is make a collection of as many scarves, scraps of lace and pretty fabrics, ribbons, ties, shells, beads, broken pieces of jewellery, slides and combs as you can find. Then let your imagination run riot.

Simplest of all – and something you can

do whatever the length of your hair – is to wrap a length of fabric around your hair bandeau-style and twist the ends into a bow. Stretchy fabric is the easiest to do this with. You can even cut the bottom off an old T-shirt and use that. Pull strands of hair out from under the fabric and gel into curls.

Backcombing instantly gives hair more body and forms the basis for wonderful 60s bouffant styles. Section off a strand of hair and comb it straight up from your head. With your finger or a comb, very gently push some of the hairs back down towards the roots. If you do this too enthusiastically you won't be able to comb it out. Clip into any style you like and hold in place with a squirt of hairspray.

Anyone with hair longer than chin-length should know how to plait. If you are

Right: twist your hair into a topknot and secure with grips and a fun hair slide. Below: (left) long hair can be pulled back into a plait and the fringe gelled into strands at the front, or backcombed for height and fixed in a French pleat at the back (right). Facing page: Ring the changes with short hair by using a scarf or fabric scraps as a bandeau.

not very good at it, practise with wool or string until you are. Hair looks prettiest in what is known as an American plait. Start to plait at the crown of the head then gradually draw in strands from each side to give a woven effect.

By the time you reach the nape of the neck you should have drawn in all the hair

towards the head to form a knot. Tuck the end in and secure in place with grips.

French pleats are fun for a 50s look. You need good thick hair that's at least shoulder-length. Brush all the hair at the back of the head over to one side and secure with grips. Fold the loose hair over to make a pleat and clip in place.

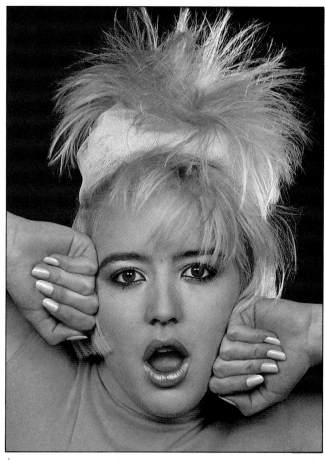

Above: make a collection of all the scraps of fabric, lace, net and ribbon you can lay your hands on. There's no end to the dozens of different ways you can fix them in your hair. Facing page: a thick plait not only looks stunning but keeps your hair in place, off your face, all day long. Control any short hairs that can't be woven into the plait with gel or hairspray.

and can finish off the plait in the conventional way. Once you've mastered a single American plait, try doing two, one on each side to form pigtails, or just one down the side. The cornrow plaits that look so good on Black hair are simply variations on this theme.

Tie plaits and pigtails with pretty ribbons or lace, or weave them in and out of the plait. Threading beads, shells or pieces of jewellery onto the ribbons first makes them look really special.

For a cute top-knot fix hair on top of the head in a ponytail. Brush up the pony tail holding it vertically above your head and divide it into two sections. Keeping the hair pulled upwards, twist the two strands tightly around each other then push down

Dyeing for a Change

There has been a revolution in hair colour – and it's fun. Tints used to be just for elderly ladies who wanted to cover up the grey. Now there's a whole range of marvellous shades to try. It's not *yet* quite as simple as changing your outfit, but it's fast moving that way.

Temporary colours can be sprayed on, painted on or used like a shampoo. The important thing is that they wash out the next day. They don't penetrate the hair so they don't damage it, but if your hair is very dark they won't show up at all.

Outrageous temporary shades like pink, green and blue show up best on blonde or light brown hair. Red tints that wash in one day and out the next can give a

If you are a blonde, or have very light brown hair, you can have fun with spray-on, temporary tints in crazy colours. Don't try to colour all your hair, just work on the fringe or the tips of your hair and choose a shade that matches your outfit. To remove, simply shampoo your hair.

lift to darker hair. They can be used at home with complete safety. The only disadvantage is that they may rub off on pillowcases and can 'run' in the rain.

Semi-permanent colours last through four to six washes. They are usually applied to wet hair and lathered up like shampoo then left in place for 10 or 20 minutes before being rinsed out. They can be safely used at home and don't damage the hair. Nor do they alter the colour a great deal unless your hair is very light to start with.

Choose a colour that is recommended for your hair type. If you put red on blonde hair you can end up looking like a carrot. *Permanent hair colours* incorporate a bleach that penetrates the inner layers of the hair, removing the old colour and replacing it with a new. They can be used to change hair colour dramatically from blonde to black and all shades in between. The trouble is that they give a heavy, solid colour whereas natural hair is made up of a variety of colours, so they can look ageing and dull. Some people are sensitive to the ingredients in permanent colours so a patch test should always be carried out before treating the whole head. If hair is in bad condition to start with, permanent colours can make it worse. Because the results of permanent hair colouring are, well, permanent, it's best to place your head in the hands of an experienced hairdresser rather than attempting to do it yourself.

Right: brown hair gets a soft auburn glow with a semi-permanent tint. Simply shampoo in, leave for a few minutes (read the instructions on the packet carefully) then rinse out. The colour should last through six to eight washes. Below: home highlighting kits are fairly cheap but don't always give very good results. For natural-looking highlights like those facing page it may be better to put your hair in the hands of a professional.

Bleaches simply lighten the hair by stripping colour. The effects are permanent – until the hair grows out – and unless hair is in good condition to start with bleach will ruin it. Again the problem is that dying or bleaching hair all one colour looks very unnatural, especially when the regrowth starts to show. Some hairdressers simply refuse to do it. A much better way of lightening hair is by highlighting.

Highlighting involves bleaching up to 25 per cent of the hair. Strands are sectioned off and coated with bleach then wrapped in foil so that the bleach doesn't run off onto the rest of the hair. It looks much more natural than all-over bleaching and re-growth doesn't become obvious for much longer. On very dark hair the highlighted strands can be tinted red for a lovely auburn glow.

The major drawback with highlighting is that it is usually very expensive because it is fiddly to do and takes a great deal of the hairdresser's time. You can buy kits to use at home but these usually involve pulling hair through a plastic hat and don't give very good results. And, of course, anything involving bleach is permanent and can damage your hair. The only way to cut the

cost of having you hair highlighted is to find out whether you can have it done more cheaply by trainees under supervision.

Henna is a great way of colouring dark brown or black hair. The effects fade gradually over several months. Henna does not harm hair, it may even improve the condition, but doing it at home can be messy. It's easier if you have a friend to help you.

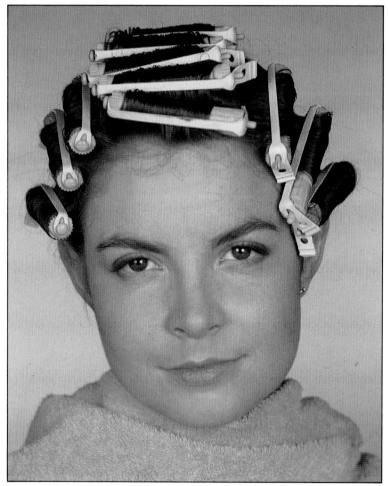

Above: leave perming to the experts. If hair is wound too tightly around the rollers it may break off – too loose and the curls won't take. Facing page: skilfully-permed hair is very easy to handle. Simply wash and leave to dry naturally. Take special care over conditioning though, as chemical treatments rob the hair of its natural oils.

Henna can be bought from health food stores. It looks like a fine green powder. Mix it up with boiling water to form a thick paste. When it has cooled enough not to burn you, plaster it over your hair, making sure you cover every bit. This part is very messy, so cover your clothes with old towels and the floor with newspaper. If you spill any, clean it up straight away.

When all of your hair is covered with the paste, wrap your head in tin foil and towels to keep the heat in and leave in place for anything up to two hours. Rinse out thoroughly – it takes ages – then

shampoo your hair. When it is dry your hair should be soft, shiny and a beautiful, deep red. Don't use henna on blonde or light brown hair as the effects could be disastrous.

New Waves

Perming is a fairly sophisticated chemical process. First a solution is applied to the hair to loosen the molecular bonds. Then strands of hair are wound around rods to curl them. A neutralising lotion is applied to harden the molecular bonds again so the hair keeps its curly shape. The effect is permanent – at least until the hair grows out.

Not surprisingly, such a complex procedure is fraught with hazards. If the hair is in poor condition it will split and break. If the strands are wound around the rods unevenly the curls will be of different sizes. The timing is crucial. Apply the neutralising lotion too soon and the perm won't have taken. Apply it too late and you'll be left with a frizzy mess that you can't even get a comb through. You can buy home perming kits, but can you really be sure you won't make any of these mistakes?

A hairdresser will probably insist on cutting your hair before he perms it to make absolutely sure there are no split ends. He will also match the strength of the perm to your hair type. Anything from loose waves to tight corkscrew curls are possible. If your hair is naturally dead straight it's not a good idea to have tight curls as the regrowth looks strange.

Increasingly, hairdressers are just perming part of the hair to give a little extra lift to a style. These are called weave perms when a few strands only are sectioned off to be permed, or root perms when only the hair nearest the scalp is treated.

Perming is a good way of giving body to limp, greasy hair as it dries up some of the oil and gives hair more body. If you want your hair coloured and permed have the perm carried out first and the colouring a week or two later. Permed hair needs careful conditioning every time you wash it.

Hair that is very curly to start with can be straightened by a process that is very similar to perming. However, the ingredients used can be very dangerous if any of them get into your eyes, and so you should always have this done at a reputable salon.

Fit for Life
The Goal of Good Health

Good health is one of the most precious possessions you can have, but if you think it's just a matter of luck, think again.

It's true that you inherit from your parents characteristics which will influence your health, but many illnesses – or plain lack of 'bounce' – have nothing to do with luck. They are the direct result of our own style of living. That means the food we eat, the amount and type of exercise we take, and our attitudes towards life. They all work together and they are all our choice. That's encouraging, because it means we can change them, once we become aware of how they affect our health. Whatever your health when born, you can make the most of it. Good health really does make a difference, and the health you build for yourself can help give your children a better start in life.

This book is about how to choose a life style – particularly a style of eating – that will do most to improve and maintain your health. In the process you'll also be helping your looks, and before you give up any idea of dazzling the world, take a look at some famous good-lookers. You'll find that their features are often no better than those of people around you. What often makes the difference is an inner sparkle that makes them appear outstandingly attractive, even if they have far smaller eyes, bigger ears, or a weaker chin than the accepted ideal.

Inner sparkle is partly tied to personality,

Far right and right: life isn't fair in what looks and physique we inherit. But your own attitude to life – positive or negative – and the health habits you choose, are just as important to your health and appearance.

Opposite: we know now that a child's health can be affected by the mother's health habits even before she becomes pregnant! There's no greater gift to pass on to children than the habit of eating well, taking exercise, good posture, deep breathing and knowing how to relax.

Right: feeling 'good in your skin' isn't a pleasure reserved for the young and perfectly shaped. You can revel in feeling well and in shape at any age: it's never too early – or too late – to start.

but it's also hugely influenced by health. You know for yourself how your own looks suffer when you're feeling unwell. Building up your health builds up your potential for looking great. Without good health, it doesn't matter how wonderful your features are: your eyes won't shine, your skin won't bloom, your hair won't gleam, and you're not likely to have a lovely smile, either.

Today's style of beauty is more closely tied to a healthy vitality than ever before. Once upon a time, models may have wanted to look pale and interesting; now they'd just look anaemic. Heavy make-up is out and, anyway, the one effect it can't produce is that of glowing health.

Feeling really chock full of health is good for your mood, too. It's not surprising that you are more cheerful when you're full of energy and in shape. That 'glow' is essential to today's kind of good looks, as well as making life much more fun.

Deciding to live in a healthier way is like stepping on to an upwards spiral staircase. Choosing food that does more for you and taking exercise don't just improve your level of health by staving off illness, they also give you a good mental feeling that you're looking after yourself and that you are someone worth looking after.

As your body improves – healthy food happens to be the kind that does most for your figure, skin and hair – your confidence goes up. That helps you in social and professional life, and you therefore feel even better.

When you have a good level of self-confidence, which is a mile away from being bigheaded, you find that life's ups and downs are easier to 'ride'. They still happen, but you don't react with large swings in mood nearly so much. You're able to be philosophical, maintain your sense of wellbeing and come out smiling.

So here's the carrot! Good health habits are worth a little effort because they bring quick, as well as long-term rewards:

✳ You feel good for more of the time.
✳ You have a better level of energy to put into work and leisure.
✳ Life looks rosier, thanks to your added stamina and confidence in your looks.
✳ Robust health may mean better earning potential.
✳ Your looks improve in a way that make-up and clothes can't achieve.
✳ You don't need to worry about losing your looks or health early in life.
✳ Your children may inherit a better constitution.
✳ You can cope more easily with life's problems.

Right: the glow that make-up can't give. The way you choose to eat is a vital part of how confident you feel about yourself, and how serenely you cope with life.

Fit for Life
How's Your Balance Sheet?

A good way to start improving the parts of your life style that affect health is to take a look at what you do now. Here's a check list of factors known to affect your health. It's like playing snakes and ladders; you'll find that some of your regular habits are helping your health without you realising it. Some of the 'snakes' your health can slither down may come as surprises, too. Take a look and be honest with yourself!

Opposite: taking 20 minutes to take stock of your living habits, and what they are doing to you, is your best investment.

effects on health. Women who smoke, for instance, suffer more stillbirths and their babies are more likely to be underweight or die. People who smoke 20 cigarettes a day are twice as likely to die from a heart attack

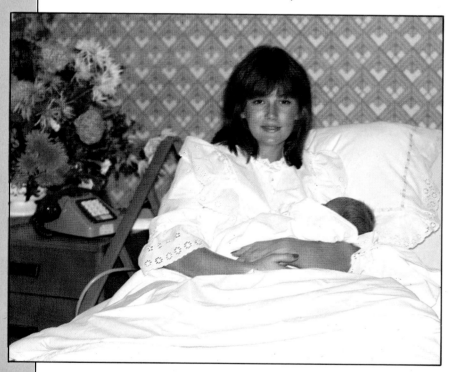

Above: smoking is now seen as taboo for the woman who wants to do the best for her baby – and herself. Much of a baby's health is decided before a woman even knows she is pregnant – so give up before you plan to conceive.

Smoking is your biggest health 'snake'. It isn't just that one in eight of those who smoke over 20 a day will get lung cancer. It's also that smoking is linked with an estimated one in three of all cases of cancer, associated with cancer of the lips, tongue, palate, throat and larynx. In men, there's a link between smoking and cancer of the bladder and, perhaps, cancer of the prostate gland, too.

Most smokers won't get cancer, but there's little chance of escaping its other

as non-smokers. Then there's bronchitis and emphysema, both serious lung complaints which can kill you. Bronchitis that is bad enough to need hospital admission is five times more likely for a heavy smoker.

However, forget the long-term hazards for a minute. You may think 'I'll stop before I get old enough for those problems', but any cigarette you smoke is hurting your health in other ways:

＊It's affecting your stomach. Smokers

who suffer from heartburn, nausea, flatulence or tummy discomfort often find that stopping solves the problem.

* It's affecting your face: smokers tend to screw up their faces as they puff – watch people doing it – and hence get wrinkles more quickly.

* It's using up extra vitamin C, reducing your protection against infections.

* It's making you smell like an old ashtray. However often you bathe, the smell of tobacco hangs around your breath, your clothes, your home and even your pets and children.

* It's putting off other people. Look at how many advertisements for jobs, flat-sharers and mates now specify 'non-smoker'. There are now considerably more non-smokers than smokers and, even if they say nothing, non-smokers may avoid you if you smoke.

* It's taking your breath away. Exercise is good for you, but you can't be very good at it while your lungs are struggling with the effects of a drug like nicotine.

* It's costing you a small fortune. Even 10 cigarettes a day now costs you the equivalent of a Mediterranean holiday each year.

Smoking and Your Figure With all these reasons to stop, why do almost four out of every ten of us still smoke? Apart from the fact that nicotine is an addictive drug – although that hasn't stopped thousands of people from giving it up – some people may go on smoking because they are frightened to stop; they're worried about putting on weight.

It's true that most people do put on some weight when they stop smoking, but they don't have to stay at that weight. In any case, with care, many avoid gaining even a pound. Although stopping smoking means that your appetite and digestive system get back to normal, so you may feel hungrier and absorb food better, you can counter gaining weight as follows:

* Put a temporary 'stop' on alcohol at the same time. Smokers tend to drink more and alcohol has lots of calories. If you stop drinking those calories for a month or two after smoking, you'll reduce your chances of gaining weight, without losing any vitamins or minerals for which alcohol is pretty useless.

* Take up an extra form of exercise at the same time. The cash you save on tobacco can pay for an exercise class, for instance. So you'll be using up the extra calories, as well as keeping your mind off the urge to

Exercise can help you stop smoking – by giving you something else to do, by providing the relaxation that you may try to get by smoking, and by strengthening your will-power as you find how much not smoking helps your breathing and muscles.

Facing page: if you've always found the idea of giving up smoking daunting, then perhaps pregnancy, or the birth of your first baby, will give you just the push you need.

Exercise does not have to hurt, in fact it shouldn't. Push, don't jerk – and don't be put off by your limitations. You'll still feel good – and look better – for each session.

smoke. You'll find you have more 'breath', once you stop smoking, for dancing or just running for a bus.

✳ Change to healthier food at the same time. As you'll find later in the book, it tends to give you more to eat without more calories, so you always have something to chew instead of smoking that cigarette.

Exercise is a good 'ladder' which you may already be using. Whether you have an energetic job, such as teaching swimming, or a regular active sport, if you are taking vigorous exercise three or more times a week, you've got a head start for health.

For many people, exercise is mainly a way of improving the figure. It certainly does that by toning up muscles and using up calories, so you end up in better shape. However, exercise does even more. It improves circulation, bringing more oxygen to every cell and so promoting alertness and good body function. It strengthens the internal 'slings' which hold your organs in place, so they are able to work well, and it improves your heart and lung efficiency. It is also one of the best ways of relaxing, partly because it takes your mind off anxieties – you can't think of anything but what you are physically concentrating on and, when you come back to your usual 'grind', you get a fresher view – and partly because energetic exercise stimulates the production of mood-raising chemicals in the body.

A 'sitting-still' job is a small 'snake' we can offset by exercise. However, make sure you aren't increasing its chance of affecting your health by one of the following habits:

The wonderful world of fruit and vegetables. Make a resolution to make the most of their colours, flavours and variety, instead of spending just as much money on fatty, sugary foods.

sitting in a way that constricts your circulation – slumping, having a chair that digs into the back of your legs, constantly crossing one knee over the other or twisting your back because your chair doesn't fit your needs – or downing cup after cup of tea or coffee and perhaps lots of 'nibbles', too. Even if you don't take sugar or have a packet of peppermints handy, the amount of caffeine in several cups of either tea or coffee can leave you feeling nervy and your system overstimulated.

Eating plenty of fruit and vegetables is a good ladder to health because they provide the least processed form of

vitamins and minerals, and are full of useful fibre in a low-calorie form.

Fruit is useful for minerals and yellow fruit, like apricots, yellow melons, peaches or bananas, provide sources of vitamin A. However, the main advantage of fruit is that its sweetness keeps us away from unhealthy sticky buns and sweets, and it's also a way of getting vitamin C. We all know that citrus fruit, like an orange, is high in vitamin C. However, remember that the level in strawberries is even higher and other soft fruits – particularly the famous blackcurrants, which are one of the highest sources of all – combine vitamin C with a particularly high amount of fibre.

Of course, you'll only be getting all this good value if you eat fruit fresh or freshly cooked with the juice. Fruit that's been chopped into a fruit salad hours ago and is browning at the edges, or that's tinned in heavy sugar syrup, has already lost a large amount of its nutritional value and gained unwanted sugar, which doesn't have vitamins or minerals.

Some people never eat fruit but stay healthy because they eat vegetables, which are really more important. As well as providing vitamin C and A – again, mainly in yellow or red items like carrots and tomatoes, but also in leafy greens – vegetables provide the main source of other vitamins: the B vitamin folic acid, vitamin E and vitamin K. They also contain

Above and right: vegetables – fresh, leafy, crunchy and colourful – can be your daily health 'insurance'. The more you eat raw, the better – try thinly sliced courgettes, mushrooms, green beans and peas, as well as familiar celery and carrots, for your meals and the snacks that help keep you away from chocolate bars.

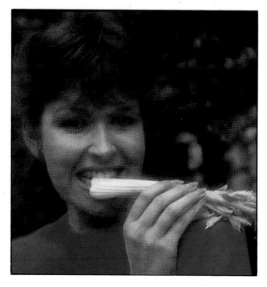

calcium, iron, magnesium and other useful minerals. Green, leafy vegetables are the best for promoting health. So anyone who regularly buys watercress, mustard and cress, spring greens or Chinese leaves, for instance, has a health habit worth cherishing.

Overeating is a 'snake' most of us know well, because it shows, but it doesn't just mean eating too much. It also refers to the kind of food that you eat. Basically, fat and sugar provide a lot of calories in even a small amount of food. Weigh out for yourself an ounce of butter or margarine, and it's astonishing to realise that this little lump contains 10 per cent of all the calories an average woman would eat in a day. Weigh out an ounce of sugar, about 4 teaspoonfuls, and it's the same story.

Because most of us have to eat a certain amount of food to feel full, any dish that includes a lot of these high-calorie-for-their-bulk foods is likely to end up consuming a very large amount of calories. Calories aren't 'bad' – they're the energy input we need to keep us alive and kicking – but if we eat more than we use up in energy, we store those calories as fat.

Above: sugar *isn't* needed for exercise – or romance. But soft drinks and alcohol, such as sweeter wines, can hide a lot. Try 'drier' drinks – like fruit juice or dry wine, mixed half-and-half with sparkling mineral water.

We all know someone who seems to be able to eat any amount of rich, sugary foods without gaining weight. These people react to extra food, it seems, by turning up their body 'thermostat', so that the surplus is burnt off. However, few people can do that permanently if they keep swallowing too many calories. By the time they are thirty years old, the extra starts to show on many a previously slender frame. Also, those who stay permanently hungry and thin are likely to be nervous, highly strung individuals; so we shouldn't envy them too much.

The fact remains that meals with lots of sugar or fat are deceptively high in calories, and we can overeat even if we don't seem to eat large platefuls. In contrast, if you choose food that's low in fat and sugar, you can eat much more and feel fuller, and still end up with fewer calories. Here's where healthy eating shows its double benefit. Reducing the amount of fat and sugar you eat tends to help you control your weight without having to think about it all the time, and it also helps your general health.

Sugar is the only food we eat that contains none of the 40-plus vitamins and minerals we need for good health. It's often described as 'empty calories'. So cutting out sugar, and you don't *need* crystal sugar for energy or for any other purpose, saves a lot of calories – 110 per ounce – which you can 'spend' on more nourishing foods. Anything else you eat instead, apart from fat, will provide some of the nourishment you need. With the average person consuming one in five of all their calories through sugar, in food, drinks and alcohol, that's a lot of extra goodness you can get by eating other foods instead. Usually this means fewer calories too, as other foods are more filling.

Fat isn't 'empty calories' and you shouldn't try a 'fat-free diet' because you need some fat to stay healthy. On the other hand, most people eat around four out of every ten calories in the form of fat. That's around twice as much fat as we need for good health. The surplus half merely provides a whopping amount of calories: 205 per ounce for butter or margarine, 255 for oil. So reducing fat saves you more calories than reducing any other food, but you lose less volume off your plate, because fat is so compact.

Eating too much fat or sugar hurts your health prospects in other ways; you'll read later in this book how. For the moment, however, just keep in mind that if you eat 1oz less sugar and 1oz less fat each day – most of us down about 3-4oz of each – that's at least 315 calories you can either spend on more nutritious foods, or save in a diet. A pound of unwanted flesh comprises some 3,500 surplus calories, and 315 saved calories daily adds up to around 321lb a year less you! You'll probably use some of those calories on other foods but, even so, it's the easiest way to keep your weight under control without thinking about it.

Overeating may be a 'snake' for you because you eat too much fat and sugar, therefore too many calories, or because you go on eating and eating even when you know you aren't hungry. Compulsive eating is so common, it's nothing to be ashamed of or to hide. Lots of people around you do

Opposite and below: you don't need a leotard to benefit from exercise and active hobbies. Here are two that make life fun. Gardening and riding can be energetic, or just absorbing. Either way, they'll relax you by giving your mind a refreshing break from tension and worries, in the fresh air.

it, but some do it more than others. If you find yourself turning to food – especially chocolate, cakes and other sweet and gooey foods – when you're upset, angry, bored, worried or fed up with your life, cutting down fat and sugar isn't the answer for you. You won't to able to, unless you tackle the troubled state of mind behind the urge to 'binge'.

Relaxation can help as you will see later in this book. As one of the most difficult things is admitting the seething emotions underneath those cream cakes, you may need to find someone you can 'let it all out' to, such as a professional counsellor or a self-help group of other overeaters who understand and can offer their success stories to give you hope of getting out of the cream pit!

Hobbies that keep you interested and on the move are another 'ladder'. Energetic ones, such as running a playgroup or gardening, are the most useful but anything that you're really keen on has a health value. That's because it puts you in a good mood, enhances your confidence in yourself as a capable and useful person, and absorbs the energy you might otherwise spend on worrying, feeling bored, frustrated, or depressed at the apparent emptiness of your life.

There's little doubt that feeling miserable is bad for you. We take for granted such sayings as 'bored to tears', 'painfully lonely' or, when angry, 'it makes me sick', but they reflect the way that our emotions can make us feel ill and even reduce our resistance to infection. Studies of American students

Above and opposite: when you are absorbed in a hobby where you acquire knowledge and skill, your confidence, together with your ability to cope with stress, will benefit.

have shown, for example, that at the times of year when they were most worried about examinations, their body's defence system against infection worked far less efficiently.

A sense of self-value is important to all of us in day-to-day self-confidence and also in making us feel less depressed when life goes wrong. One of the best ways of gaining a permanent improvement in how you see yourself is to develop a skill. It doesn't really matter what it is: stamp-collecting, flower-arranging, card tricks, folk songs or growing azaleas. What's important is to know that you are unusually knowledgeable and skilled in at least one area of life; something of which you can

remind yourself when you doubt your abilities in other fields. With shorter hours spent in work inside or outside the home, there's more opportunity than ever to develop such a skill and more people eager to teach it in evening classes or clubs.

Too much alcohol is a 'snake' that can easily get out of hand. While the odd glass of wine or beer doesn't seem to harm people, the number of those whose lives are dominated by their addiction to alcohol is rising, particularly among women. The increase may be due to a mixture of influences and it's interesting to look hard at one's own drinking pattern to see how and why one drinks. It's more acceptable for women to drink than it used to be and young people still see getting drunk as part of growing up and being sophisticated. Many people have more spare time – some by choice, some not – and drinking can grow to dangerous amounts almost without realising it, through having more hours to socialise.

It's now medically established that women are more at risk from heavy drinking than men, suffering from liver damage more easily. Also, drinking in pregnancy affects babies badly and, unfortunately, by the time a woman knows she's pregnant, the baby has usually been developing for several weeks. The alcohol drunk during that period can already have given it a setback, for the very early weeks of pregnancy are the time of fastest brain development for the foetus. Today, the advice to women is that if you plan to have a baby, or even know you're liable to accidents, don't drink, or limit it to a maximum of a glass a day.

Alcohol is bad for your figure in two ways. Firstly, it's got a surprising number of calories. Secondly, it's spoiled many a diet by relaxing the willpower of the dieter, so that after a glass of wine the person concerned tucks into the gateaux or peanuts.

Like sugar, alcohol is 'empty calories', so omitting it can only help. If you eat more of other things with the saved calories, you're bound to get more goodness out of them than you would out of the alcohol, without the bleary eyes, headache and bags under your eyes!

Alcohol isn't good for mental health, either. Beyond a modest amount, people become aware that they aren't fully in control – an uncomfortable feeling – and they also feel weak-willed, losing self-respect. The idea that hard drinking is somehow 'strong' is losing ground and, while a small amount of alcohol is a stimulant, what goes up comes down with a thump: it's really a depressant in any quantity.

Not being a rusher is a help up the ladder of health. People who are not always trying to fit too much into their time make far less tension for themselves; they aren't constantly struggling to keep up with their tight schedule, worrying about the clock or cutting short their personal relationships because they're rushing off elsewhere.

Tension doesn't just take the enjoyment out of life. It also affects your health. Mental tension produces physical tightening of muscles; feel how tight the back of your neck gets when you are worried, for instance. Prolonged tension, if you don't take time to relax, can produce all kinds of backache, headache and other ills. Your chest muscles will tighten too, restricting how deeply you breathe. One of the first reactions in a tense situation is to start breathing shallowly. It doesn't matter for a short while, but the habit can set in, precipitating asthma attacks and headaches, as well as limiting the supply of oxygen to your body.

Do you remember how it feels when you're stuck in a traffic jam or a delayed train and you know you're going to be late for an important appointment or plane? If your memory is accurate, it will recall that churning of the stomach and possibly even the feeling that you couldn't breathe properly or felt sick. Day-to-day tension may not be so extreme, but it can certainly divert your body from digesting food properly. The result that's best known is ulcers but feeling bloated, and attacks of heartburn and indigestion, are bad enough.

Being in a rush is almost certain to mean that you eat less good food. You'll be more inclined to grab a take-away or open a bar of chocolate, just because it's quick. Unfortunately, both are full of excess fat, sugar and additives; well, not quite all, as you'll see later. It is possible to eat 'fast food' that's good for you, but you have to make a little more effort. If you don't, you may gradually run your system down by not supplying it with the vitamins and minerals you need, especially since stress results in more B group vitamins and vitamin C being used up.

Drinking too much tea, coffee, cola drinks or chocolate is a habit that often goes hand in hand with the person who is always rushing and under stress; it isn't an accident. Unconsciously, most of us are attracted to all four because they contain chemicals which are stimulants; mild stimulants, but strong enough for the person who drinks cup after cup, or eats bar after bar of chocolate, to find it hard to stop. They all contain caffeine and related stimulants which, in excess, make you feel jumpy, 'hepped up' and incapable of sleeping or even slowing down. They affect your digestive as well as nervous systems and, if you give your body a chance to see what it feels like without them, you'll usually find that after a few weeks in which you really miss coffee, suffer from headaches and, perhaps, constipation,

Opposite: don't let life turn into a race against the clock. It will create unnecessary tension, which can lead to headaches, stomach problems, backache and more. You *don't* have to rush: learn to say 'no' charmingly!

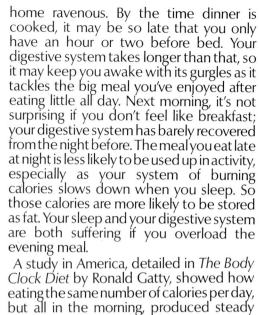

you'll feel far calmer and more in control of your life.

Late night eating is yet another 'snake' which modern life encourages by its rush through each day. It's almost standard to skip breakfast, except for a quick cuppa; pick up a sandwich and cake for lunch to fit round shopping or socialising, and come home ravenous. By the time dinner is cooked, it may be so late that you only have an hour or two before bed. Your digestive system takes longer than that, so it may keep you awake with its gurgles as it tackles the big meal you've enjoyed after eating little all day. Next morning, it's not surprising if you don't feel like breakfast; your digestive system has barely recovered from the night before. The meal you eat late at night is less likely to be used up in activity, especially as your system of burning calories slows down when you sleep. So those calories are more likely to be stored as fat. Your sleep and your digestive system are both suffering if you overload the evening meal.

A study in America, detailed in *The Body Clock Diet* by Ronald Gatty, showed how eating the same number of calories per day, but all in the morning, produced steady weight loss in a group of volunteers, even though they ate just as much. You wouldn't want to go to such extremes, but the principle is worth remembering.

Skipping breakfast isn't a help in slimming; it's much more effective to move some calories from later in the day to breakfast time. If you do so, your evening meal will be lighter and you'll feel hungrier at breakfast, especially if you also try to eat earlier at night.

A settled home life with regular meals is a 'ladder' because it favours healthier eating habits. The more cooking you do at home, the more likely you are to eat plenty of fruit and vegetables, which don't figure highly on restaurant menus and, when they do, have often been overcooked so they've lost a lot of their vitamin C. You're less likely to rely regularly on café fry-ups and take-aways, too.

An old toothbrush is a give-away 'snake' in your bathroom. The main benefit of brushing your teeth well and often is not to brush off sugar and so avoid holes in your teeth; the evidence is that the damage starts very quickly after eating the sugar and that only avoiding its consumption will really make much difference to tooth decay. Tooth brushing's value is in preventing the other 'mouth disease' from which adults lose more teeth than from tooth decay, such as *gingivitis*, or inflammation of the gums from bacterial infection, in which the teeth may become loose in their sockets. The tooth sockets themselves can also become filled with pus, following infection, in the condition *pyorrhoea alveolaris*.

Being good at relaxing is a 'ladder'. Some people are just naturally relaxed; others can learn to be more so by taking up exercise, yoga, meditation or other techniques which show you how to slow down and unwind. Not only does this undo the tension we all experience, which is part of life, so it can't affect our health; it also avoids some of that tension occurring. That's the part that comes not because a train is late, or someone is rude to us, but because we overreact to that upset. You may think that your reactions aren't under your control, but you can almost certainly recall something you got very upset about in the past, which now makes you wonder why. People can learn to take life more philosophically. The first step towards doing so is to become aware of how you react to events and often just watching yourself provides a restraining influence on your emotions!

Other Snakes and Ladders

✱ *Long hours of car driving*, especially if you use your wheels when you could walk, reduce your exercise and can leave you with a stiff back and tension from negotiating heavy traffic.

✱ *Eating in staff restaurants* or canteens can unbalance your diet through lack of fresh fruit and vegetables, unless you choose carefully.

✱ *Walking to work*, or at least to the station or bus stop, can give you a surprising amount of exercise, just because you do it so often. A simple way of upping your exercise is to extend this walk by 10 minutes by taking a longer route or walking a few more stops.

✱ *Having a good laugh now and then* helps your health! When you laugh you relax tense muscles, breathe deeper and put your worries in perspective.

✱ *Love of cream buns* is more of a psychological hang-up than a real, physical love affair; otherwise, we'd all have the craving! Willpower on its own is a less effective 'cure' than watching yourself to see what emotions spark off the urge. Then transfer them to some non-food, harmless outlet, such as doing a crossword puzzle, buffing your nails, or taking a walk round the block. If you can stave off the urge for 15 to 20 minutes, you'll probably find it's gone; another clue that it's a reaction to emotion, not hunger.

✱ *Lack of knowledge about healthy eating* is still a major reason why people don't eat better than they do. So now you've had a look at some of the ways you help or hurt your health, here's a closer look at how food can be your ally or your enemy in feeling and looking great.

Lifestyle Quiz

1 *Do you smoke?* A. Never. B. Under 5 a day. C. Over 5 a day.
2 *How often do you eat fresh vegetables or fruit?* A. Daily. B. Weekly. C. An orange at Christmas.
3 *Do you know what your blood pressure is?* A. Yes. B. No idea.
4 *Do you sometimes use sleeping tablets?* A. Yes. B. Never.
5 *Are you happy about your shape, more or less, when you see yourself naked?* A. Ugh! B. Love it! C. Reasonably content.
6 *How many alcoholic drinks do you have a week?* A. Around 1 per day. B. None at all. C. Under 3 a day. D. More, but can't count!
7 *Have you had a health check-up in the last 2 years?* A. Yes. B. No.
8 *Do you consider yourself in general:* A. Relaxed? B. Tense?

Answers

1 Score 0 for A, 2 for B or 6 for C.
2 Score 0 for A, 2 for B or 4 for C.
3 Score 0 for A, 2 for B. It's sensible to have your blood pressure measured from time to time as it's a measure of how hard your heart is having to work to push blood round the body. High blood pressure indicates that your heart is having to work too hard and is a sign of greater risk of heart disease, stroke or kidney problems.
4 Score 3 for A, 0 for B.
5 Score 4 for A, 0 for B, and 0 for C. Liking or being realistically content with your shape – if you're telling the truth – is healthy, suggesting that you've got a reasonably good self-image and confidence, and are in reasonably good shape; not model girl shape but not flabby.
6 Score 0 for A or B, 3 for C and 5 for D. Over 24 drinks a week means you have a drinking problem. Tolerance varies, but many women could be suffering health damage on less. Almost anyone on more than 2 drinks per day would be better off cutting down, both to avoid the excess calories and the heavy workload that alcohol imposes on the liver.
7 Score 0 for A, 2 for B. Check-ups can catch problems while they are still trivial, or show you where your health habits are slipping; for instance, if you find your blood pressure is inching upwards.
8 Score 0 for A and 3 for B. Being a tense person doesn't always bode ill for health – you may just be highly strung like a racehorse – but many people can't cope and develop stress-induced complaints, like stomach problems or skin rashes.

If you've scored:

Over 20: you're fighting your own health! Take action now, before your body rebels.
Over 10: not bad, provided you don't smoke, but wouldn't you like to get even more spring in your step?
0-10: you're heading in the right direction; keep going!

Fit for Life
Eating for Vitality and Vigour

Some people think that eating healthily will turn them into a rabbit: all carrots, lettuce and timidity! Well, it won't. What you eat is one of the most important elements in your health programme, but you don't have to be a fanatic about it, or spend more time, trouble or money. Healthy food can taste good, too.

Some people say that they won't bother about healthy eating because experts disagree so much on what you should eat. Although there's a lot we still don't know about how food affects health, there's enough general agreement, however, to have produced government reports in both the United Kingdom and the United States of America. The advice they've advocated doesn't have to spoil your meals, or make you a social outcast, and it applies just as much to slim people as to fatter ones.

Start eating well before you are pregnant and you will be giving your child a better chance than if you start once you know you are: development starts very early. From then on, mother and child are getting the best chance to bloom – and for babies to learn healthy eating habits as natural.

Dad's eating habits matter too: children learn by example. Slim people shouldn't assume they eat healthily: quality is as important as the right quantity.

Many people think that if you're slim, you must be healthy, but look around you and you'll see that it isn't true. Some slim people don't eat much and may be undersupplied with nourishment; no wonder they don't sparkle with vitality. Others eat, but for one reason or another – physical or that stomach-churning tension – don't absorb food very efficiently or burn it off. It's just as important to look after your health by eating well if you're fashionably slender, as if you are struggling with your weight.

Most important of all is the way that mothers eat, both before and during pregnancy. Because the major development of a baby occurs very early in pregnancy, a woman changing to a healthy diet only when she discovers she's pregnant, some six or more weeks after conception, is far from ideal. It would be better if every woman planning a baby were to eat healthily for at least three months before conceiving.

Mothers and fathers of young children have another reason for healthy eating: children start copying what their parents do at a very early age. Why should a child avoid sweets if he sees Dad taking a bar of chocolate for his lunchbox, or Mum piling sugar into her tea?

The following five chapters offer guidelines that nutrition experts recommend.

Fit for Life

Fats and Your Fitness

At the moment, the average Westerner gets around 4 out of every 10 calories he eats in the form of fat. That doesn't mean that 40% of what we eat is fat. Fat has twice as many calories as most other foods, so you only need to eat 20% of your food as fat to get that 40%. If someone eats around 2,000 calories a day, the 40% of calories can be produced by just over 88 grams, or 3 ounces, of fat a day. One gram of fat produces about 9 calories, so 88 grams is about 800 calories.

Provided we aren't overweight, why does the proportion of fat consumed matter? Because it's about twice as much fat as we need for good health and the extra can harm us. Too much fat doesn't only encourage overeating and overweight. Populations with a high fat diet have much higher rates of heart disease; and other health problems – such as the West's high incidence of gallstones – may be linked with excess fat.

There's suspicion that other 'epidemics of the 20th century' are at least partly linked with too much fat in our diet. They include the rising rate of diabetes, cancer of the breast and cancer of the colon or large intestine. Women used to be concerned about heart disease mainly on behalf of their men, and men are still much more prone to heart problems, but the rate is rising among younger women. Although eating too much fat is certainly not the sole cause – another may be more heavy smokers among women – it certainly doesn't help.

Why we are eating more fat? A major reason seems to be that we're better off. In the past, the main foods in the meals of almost everyone, except the wealthy few, were bread, potatoes, vegetables and beans. They're all very low in fat, but between them they provide enough protein for good health. With the advent of higher incomes and more food products, people were able to choose more of what used to be 'luxury' foods, like meat, dairy foods and eggs. By switching more of our food to these, we still get plenty of protein – more than we need in fact – but we unintentionally get a lot of fat, too. Even the leanest rump steak, for instance, has more than twice as much fat as bread; while beans and vegetables have hardly any.

At the same time, the kind of fat we eat has changed. Fats that are hard at room temperature – like most, but not all, animal fats – are known as saturated, because the bonds in their chemical structure are filled by hydrogen atoms and are hence incapable of undergoing additional reactions. It seems that these fats are more likely to raise the level of fat in the bloodstream. It's fats collecting in the bloodstream, gradually leaving deposits on the inside of artery walls, that eventually leads to the arteries becoming blocked or to clot formation, both being causes of heart attacks. If a clot lodges in the brain's arterial blood supply, restricting oxygenated flow, the result is a stroke. The story isn't a simple one, and fats certainly aren't the only cause – smoking, lack of exercise and reactions to stress are others – but hard fats are one factor we can change.

Fats which are liquid, but still thick, at room temperature, make up most of those which are called unsaturated; they could take a few more hydrogen atoms. From a health point of view, they seem to be neutral. Countries where such fats are the main ones used, such as olive oil in Greece, don't have particularly high rates of heart disease; in fact, much lower rates than the hard fat using communities.

Fats which are thoroughly runny at room temperature are called polyunsaturated, because their chemical structure has room for many more hydrogen atoms. These are the vegetable oils, such as sunflower, safflower, soya and corn. Others hover between polyunsaturated and unsaturated. These fats are not associated with a build-up of fats in arteries. On the other

Exercise won't undo bad eating habits, although it will help you eat plenty of food (increasing your chance of getting plenty of vitamins and minerals) – without getting fat. But you have to run a long, long way to work off calories if you don't change your diet as well.

hand, they have just as many calories and overweight is, in itself, a contributor to many illnesses as far apart as aching joints and heart disease.

Above: high fat foods to be wary of, because you may not realise just how fatty they are – such as mayonnaise on salad (79% oil) or chocolate (30% fat). Don't say 'never', say 'hardly ever' – and tuck into the spread (opposite) of tasty, low fat foods, from trout to pasta. The bowls contain (from left): low fat soft cheese, ideal for making dips, dressings for salad, cheesecakes with less fat or instead of cream; low fat yoghurt; cultured buttermilk and smetana – like sour cream, but with less fat.

Fat is Important for Health Never aim for a fat-free diet. Fats are important for a whole range of body functions. Animal fats are the main sources of one form of vitamin A, retinol, and of vitamin D, which is necessary for the body to absorb calcium. We can get both vitamins from other sources. Another, but just as useful form of vitamin A, is the provitamin called carotene, which is rich in orange and yellow vegetables and fruit, and in leafy greens. The action of sunlight – it doesn't have to be shining – on the skin results in the formation of vitamin D. However, northern winters don't allow for much sunbathing and most people don't eat many vegetables.

The polyunsaturated fats provide important substances, which we don't get anywhere else, called 'essential fatty acids'. The body relies on food to provide them, instead of being able to make them, as it can some nutrients, from other ingredients in food.

The main item you need is called linoleic acid. It's rich in oils like safflower, sunflower (and in sunflower seeds), soya and corn. Linoleic acid is necessary for several body functions to work properly.

A popular way of getting linoleic acid is in soft margarine, but unless the packet is labelled 'high in polyunsaturates', don't bother; it may not be a good source. Some soft margarines now give the linoleic acid content on the label. It's usually got the words 'cis-cis' next to it. This mystifying term means that the linoleic acid hasn't been artificially hardened, which would spoil it. Have you ever wondered how margarine can be made from liquid oils? The answer is that some are hardened by a process called hydrogenation. As the name suggests, this involves making the polyunsaturated fat fill up its multiple bonds with hydrogen, which turns it into something hard like the saturated fats. Unfortunately, the artificially hardened fats end up different in structure from natural hard fats and they may be worse for our health, so avoid hard margarines. In the soft margarines labelled 'high in polyun- saturates', they've hardened just the minimum of oil to produce a solid-enough consistency, while keeping the high level of polyunsaturates or PUFAs. But while we all need some polyunsaturates, we only need an estimated 15 grams or ½ ounce a day at the most.

The aim is still to eat less fat of all kinds, although you are better off cutting the hard animal fats. Just to confuse things, not all hard fats are animal in origin. Palm and coconut 'oil', for example, are both solid and naturally saturated. Palm oil is often used in margarines. Animal fats which are soft, like fish oil, contain a high proportion of unsaturated and PUFAs, while semi-hard ones like chicken fat contain a mixture of saturated and unsaturated.

The aim is to eat only 2 spoonfuls of fat for every 3 you eat now.

Eating Less Fat You may think that you already eat little fat. Perhaps you're right, but most people are surprised to learn how much fat is 'hidden' in food. To eat less fat, go warily with all high fat foods, as well as the obvious steps of avoiding fried foods and spreading less margarine or butter on bread. It doesn't mean you must never eat them. Keep them for occasional, not everyday, use though even then the use of a little fat is fine.

Don't damn all high fat content foods as 'rubbish'. Some are full of food value, as well

Opposite: fats worth keeping because these foods contain other useful nutrients: eggs, nuts, oily fish like herring, a little safflower, sunflower or soya oil, and wheat germ – delicious added to cereals and puddings.
Oily fish like sardines and mackerel have a different kind of fat from most animal hard fats: their soft oil is more useful to the body, along with the vitamins A and D they're so rich in.

as the fat which means you shouldn't eat too much of them. The 'goodies' to keep in mind for occasional enjoyment are: peanuts and peanut butter, which are packed with protein, B vitamins and other goodness; avocado pears, containing vitamins A and E; herrings, a rich food for vitamins A and D, with mainly PUFA-type fats; and hard cheese for its high protein, vitamin B and calcium content.

On the other hand, some of the following foods have few redeeming features; keep them for a blue moon! They include fried bread, crisps, mayonnaise, chocolate, cream cheese, savoury and sweet pastries (pastry is always high in fat, especially when it is the puff or flaky type), pork chops and other fatty meats and pies, suet and most commercial biscuits.

There's still plenty left to eat; just look at our appetising low fat foods which can become the 'regulars' on your shopping list. Of course, without all that fat they are also very much lower in calories. So you either save calories and lose weight, or eat more of them and stay the same weight; you choose. You can also discover that eating less fatty foods won't make your meals more expensive.

How can you turn foods like pasta and beans into delicious meals without adding fat to them? Here are some secrets of low fat cooking:

1 When you're browning an onion or greasing a pan, use a new bristle paintbrush dipped in cooking oil, instead of pouring oil or adding a dollop of fat. You'll use far less fat and the recipe will work as well. Don't use a nylon bristled brush, or it will melt if it meets a hot pan.

2 Use fish and the least fatty meats. Even apparently lean meat has a surprising amount af fat hidden in it. The meat with the least hidden fat is turkey, followed by rabbit, chicken and then game, which also has more PUFAs and less saturated fats. White fish is leanest of all, followed by trout, salmon and then the oilier fish. But even oily fish, apart from eel and mackerel, is leaner than most meat.

3 Use more non-meat recipes. You may think that bread, rice and pasta are 'just stodge' but, in fact, they provide enough protein for main meals and contain almost no fat, as is the case with beans and lentils. Dishes like risotto, pizza, sandwiches and baked beans are all low in fat, provided you don't add too much. Be mean with oil when cooking, spreading bread or when adding cheese. Pick low fat sandwich fillings, such as chicken, low fat cheese, salad, yeast extract, mashed bananas or apple slices. Sprinkle these last two with orange or lemon juice so they don't go brown.

4 Remember that most of us eat much more protein than we need. So use more light salad meals and plain bread or potatoes to replace the fancier, rich foods.

Useful Fats Here are some foods which have a high level of fat, but which also contain so much goodness that it's a good idea to keep them on your shopping list; just use them a little less often than normal. Because their fats are still in the food and unprocessed, they are fresher and more natural.

✳ Use 3-4 eggs a week – the national average – if you like them.

✳ Herrings provide the richest source of vitamins A and D, plus useful minerals, B vitamins and vitamin E. In winter, when vitamin D from the action of sunlight on skin is in short supply, it's a good idea to eat oily fish once a week.

✳ Nuts provide protein, B vitamins and vitamin E, plus useful minerals. They also contain plenty of fibre. Use small helpings to add flavour and protein to vegetable and rice dishes, but not more than 40 to 55 grams (1½-2oz) per person for a main dish. Hazelnuts are much less fatty than the others; walnuts highest in PUFA, although they all contain some; almonds and sunflower seeds are good for protein, along with peanuts.

✳ Wheat germ is so packed with protein (25% – more than meat), B group vitamins and vitamin E, it's as good as a vitamin pill! Sprinkle a tablespoonful here and there on cereals, stewed fruit or savouries, but after cooking so the goodness won't get cooked out of it. Wheat germ goes stale quickly, so keep it in the refrigerator and use it within a few weeks while it's still sweet in flavour. Throw it away if it goes bitter.

✳ Oils are the most natural way, apart from nuts and seeds, to get the vital PUFAs. Keep sunflower, safflower and soya oil for use on salads. They burn too easily to be heated to high temperatures, but are fine in baking. For frying, olive and corn oil are the most stable. In health food stores, you'll see 'cold-pressed oils' for sale. These are thicker and have more flavour. They are extracted from the plant by pressure, rather than by heat or chemical treatment. They're expensive, but they are more natural. As you are aiming for a low fat diet, you won't use much, so why not buy the best?

Fit for Life
Sugar: a Balance for Health

Sugar is so more-ish, it's the main feature of 'bingeing'. It's often done for comfort, but leads to the opposite – self-hate. The urge can be transferred to harmless, more filling foods like bananas. Because they are very low in fat, you'll find it hard to tuck away too many calories – you'll get too full.

Everyone knows that sugar is bad for your teeth, but what other reasons are there for saying we should eat less of it? The main argument is that sugar contains no vitamins, minerals or other substances useful and necessary for health. So eating sugar, while it supplies calories or energy, is pushing out of our meals other foods which would provide important nutrients.

Because sugar is so concentrated, it's easy to eat too much of it, and anyone who has ever 'eaten for comfort' will recognise that eating sugar is sometimes almost irresistible. When people go on a food 'binge', it's almost always sugary foods – from chocolate to doughnuts – that they crave. You'd be surprised how many people have eaten their way through half a dozen or more such items, one after the other, when upset about something.

The old phrase 'You are what you eat' has never seemed truer than when you're looking at a cream bun fan, who often looks as though the cream is just about to squidge out of her rounded frame! Why say 'her'? Although some men also crave sweet foods, the unconscious use of sweet and sticky foods as an outlet for emotion when upset seems mainly to affect women. Men seem more likely to turn to alcohol or other outlets.

It's important not to get the idea that cream cakes are somehow 'wicked'. That may just make them seem more desirable, or make you feel horribly guilty when you eat one. Eating the occasional cake, bar of chocolate, gateau or pastry never hurt anyone. It shouldn't be a reason for feeling a failure, even if you're trying to lose weight. Just enjoy it and then go back to eating healthily. Don't go the other way and feel so bad – 'I've ruined my diet' – that you promptly eat a plateful more of sweet stodge.

If you know you are one of those people who can't open a bar or box of chocolates without wolfing the lot, it's safest to keep

away from sugar almost all the time. However, if you can cope, a little sugar – say up to 25g (1oz) per day – is unlikely to harm you. It won't do you any good either, but it's a lot less than most people eat. The national average is a colossal 110g (3⅞oz) approximately each day from food and drink, including alcohol. That means that some women are eating their weight in sugar each year, and many more of us are almost achieving this dubious feat. No wonder official reports would like us to eat less sugar and replace it with other foods

which provide something more useful to the body.

Don't we need sugar for energy? Sugar does provide energy, which is just another word for calories, but so do many other foods. Sugar doesn't have any magical, special energy. Your body can turn almost anything you eat into energy.

sugar. While we all know that buns and cakes contain sugar, some contain very much more than others. With some foods, reading the label is a guide to how much sugar has been added. Ingredients are listed in descending order of weight. So a food product with an ingredients list showing sugar at, or near the top, means

that it has a higher proportion of sugar than a similar product with sugar near the bottom of the list. This is a useful point to remember when deciding which kind of breakfast cereal, pickle or biscuit to buy.

Here are eight pairs of foods, all sweet. However, one of each pair has considerably more sugar than the other.

Currant bun, average 14% sugar.
Blackcurrant cream tartlet; fancy cakes average 54% sugar.

Digestive biscuits, average 16% sugar.
Milk chocolate – ½ a 100-gram bar – average 56% sugar.

Dry wine, average 0.6% sugar.
Sweet wine, average 6% sugar.

Tomato ketchup, average 23% sugar.
Marmalade, average 70% sugar.

Black cherry yogurt, average 14% sugar, or 20g (¾oz) per 5oz pot.
Plain yogurt with grapes, average 13%

The invisible difference: three examples of why it pays to get to know where invisible sugar in food is – so you can dodge it and enjoy the less-sweet alternative.

Eating Less Sugar As your body doesn't need crystal sugar at all, you can trim as much as you want from your meals without any fear of ill-effects. It's easiest to trim the sugar you can see: any you add to drinks, cereal or puddings, and also any sweets you eat, or sweet drinks.

These are the most obvious sugars to reduce, but one reason why we eat so much sugar is that sugar is an invisible ingredient in many common foods. Do you think of jam as mainly fruit or mainly sugar, for instance? By law, it can be two-thirds

More 'hidden' sugars: there's always something nice to eat that has less sugar. Your tastebuds will quickly adapt too, so that you find high sugar foods too sweet.

natural sugars, but to eat 20g (¾oz), you can eat 10½oz fruit and yogurt.

Strawberry jam, average 69% sugar.
Apple purée with the minimum of honey or sugar, average 10% sugar.

Cornflakes with 2 tsp sugar, average 7% and 100% sugar respectively, giving about ½oz sugar per helping of 1oz cornflakes with sugar.

Porridge with 2 tsp bran, average sugar negligible.

Apricot chutney, average 50% sugar.
Piccalilli pickle, average 2.6% sugar.

So, you can often choose a replacement for a very sweet food that does the job, or satisfies your sweet tooth, but has only a fraction of the sugar. The sugar in fruit and milk, by the way, can almost be discounted

because it's well diluted, so you don't get such a large amount, and it's treated differently by your digestive system.

Is there anything you can sweeten food with that's better for you than sugar is?

Here's a guide to alternative sweeteners. Some are much better than sugar, but it has to be said that the healthiest move is to eat less sweet things in general. Your taste buds will adapt and you'll find you aren't tempted by sweets and cakes nearly so much. If you do ever slip back to sweet foods, you may find that they taste revoltingly sickly!

Below: starting with the dark honey at the top, go anti-clockwise for molasses sugar, Demerara sugar, fruit sugar, aspartame (artificial sweetener), saccharin, and muscovado sugar

Opposite: anti-clockwise from top: molasses, black treacle, sultanas, maple syrup, concentrated apple juice, dates and dried apricots – the natural sweeteners with advantages over sugar in more refined, crystal form.

Molasses: thick, almost black syrup left when sugar cane is boiled and the sugar extracted. Contains only about half as much sugar and has such a strong flavour, you'd find it impossible to eat a lot. However, useful for adding a taste-plus-sweetness to gingerbread, milk drinks, stewed fruit or porridge. It also has roughly only half the calories of sugar, plus useful minerals, especially iron, calcium and magnesium. Fine if you only use say 2 tablespoons a day, otherwise its laxative properties will begin to take effect.

Black treacle: taken from another stage in the refining process, it has a little more sugar and calories, rather less but still useful amounts of minerals, and makes a less dramatic impact with its flavour. Fine in small amounts, it has a laxative effect, like molasses, if you take more than a spoonful or two.

Sultanas: together with raisins, these are one of the best sweeteners. At around 71 calories per 28 grams (1oz), they are still very sweet, but 'pay' for their calories with fibre, minerals and a small amount of B vitamins. Use them in small amounts instead of sweets (but remember that you should still clean your teeth afterwards), and in cooking. The way to get most sweetness from them is to liquidise washed sultanas or raisins with the liquid in a recipe before cooking. If you like sweet cereal, for instance, liquidise the fruit in the milk you are going to pour over it. You can use the same technique to sweeten stewed fruit, doing the blending before adding the sweetened water to the raw fruit and cooking.

Maple syrup: is more like honey in composition than sugar, so see the reference to honey for ideas on its use. Make sure that what you buy is genuine maple syrup and not maple flavour syrup, which will be just flavoured sugar syrup. The real thing is expensive but has a delicious·flavour, which should help you enjoy even small amounts.

Concentrated apple juice: is mainly used as an economical way of making apple drinks; you just add hot or cold water. It's certainly better for you than soft drinks high in sugar, colourings and often caffeine. It's still sweet, without the addition of sugar. You can also use it to sweeten dishes, too, provided you keep to small amounts because it is quite acidic under the sweetness. Good uses include in fruit cakes, or when you want a touch of sweetness in a curry or casserole; a tablespoon goes quite a long way. To make an apple drink, just use like a concentrated fruit drink.

Dates: are the most useful natural sweetener for making fruit cakes and puddings. They're very sweet indeed. A good way to use them is to prepare a purée by cooking dates in enough water to cover, until you have a soft consistency. Make sure the mixture contains no stones, then purée

Right: unsweetened fruit juice is sweet enough for most of us, so why add ounces of sugar to other foods and drinks?
Opposite: no, you don't need to eat sugar 'for energy'. You can swim, run or play sports just as energetically on any other food. The body can turn all your meals into energy, and any food will give you more vitamins, minerals or fibre than sugar will.

in a blender or by mashing thoroughly with a fork. Use this purée, weight for weight, in place of the sugar required by the recipe, remembering to reduce the amount of liquid to allow for the extra water you've added. The easiest way to do this is to add liquid to the recipe cautiously until you've achieved the consistency the recipe suggests, which is much easier than measuring. This mixture contains about 70 calories per ounce.

Dried apricots: a versatile alternative to sugar as a source of sweetness, dried apricots can be munched as they are instead of sweets; stewed with sour fruit or porridge, which the apricots will sweeten; made into a thick purée, which can be used instead of jam to spread on bread, or to fill cake; or served stewed, hot or cold, as a sweet but nourishing pudding. They contain approximately 52 calories per ounce, under half the level in sugar, because their sweetness is diluted with a high level of fibre, as well as having one of the highest levels of vitamin A (in carotene form), iron and other useful nutrients. Before cooking or eating apricots it's useful,

if possible, to boil them in some water, simmer for a minute or two, then drain, throwing the water away. This is an effective way of cleaning them and also helps to remove some of the preservative sulphur dioxide which keeps them pale. It is sometimes possible to buy darker 'unsulphured' apricots.

Honey: is sometimes treated by nutritionists as no better than sugar, but it does have advantages. These are, first, that it contains fewer calories: roughly 82 per ounce, versus sugar's 110. Second, it is somewhat sweeter, especially when added to cold foods, so you may use less. Third, a major part of its sweetness is in a form which is more slowly released to the body as energy, a useful property for diabetics or those with diabetic tendencies who need to avoid sudden surges in the level of energy supplied to the body. On the other hand, don't replace a high level of sugar with a high intake of honey and expect to gain greatly. Honey contains small amounts of many minerals and vitamins, but such small amounts that it contributes only tiny quantities compared

Opposite: snacks to remember next time you get that craving for something sweet. From an apple sandwich to a health food shop no-added-sugar fruit bar to a bowl of porridge with a little honey, you get more goodness for your calories, and usually fewer calories, this way.

to our needs. So it's wisest to treat it as a not particularly nutritious food, to be used to avoid the problems of sugar, but not in large quantities; one ounce a day, which is about one tablespoonful, would be sensible.

Molasses sugar: the most nourishing kind of sugar, molasses sugar has a strong, treacly taste but doesn't have a lot of vitamins and minerals. Use it sparingly; it's less worthwhile than molasses or black treacle and can overpower other ingredients with its strong flavour, if you use more than a spoonful or two. Like other sugars, it contains about 110 calories per ounce.

Demerara sugar: a few traces of minerals are all that make this sugar better than white. However, it is still that bit better, provided you don't use more than about one ounce per day. Another reason is that it has a flavour, unlike white sugar which is just sweet. This can make it a more effective flavouring agent in small amounts. Of brown sugars, this is the most versatile in cooking and for serving to guests to put in drinks; even though it's also the palest and one of the lowest in minerals. Contains 110 calories per ounce.

Fruit sugar: looks just like a fine-crystal white sugar, but once you taste it, it behaves differently. Firstly, it's considerably sweeter to most people's taste buds than sugar, especially when used in cold foods and drinks. This means that less need be used. Secondly, it provides a kind of sugar which is absorbed more slowly by the body as energy, which is good for diabetics – who should ask their medical advisor before using it – but also for those who react to sugar with a brief burst of energy, followed by a slump! Fruit sugar, also known as fructose or levulose, is extracted from plants and attracts water, so it needs to be stored in a tightly sealed jar. You can use it to replace sugar in many dishes, but use less both for the nutritional advantage and also

because it will produce more sweetness. You can't simply swop fruit sugar for ordinary sugar in baking sponges or jam-making; write to the manufacturer for special recipes. Fruit sugar is not particularly slimming, unless you use less than ordinary sugar; both contain 110 calories per ounce.

Aspartame: is the newest artificial sweetener. It's made from two proteins, so although it isn't natural, its 'parents' are. It contains almost no calories, so can be used just like saccharin, i.e. where sweetness is wanted, without the recipe requiring bulk. It contains phenylalanine, a natural amino acid which some people cannot tolerate, but this is labelled on the product and most people with this problem are well aware of it. Products based on aspartame are claimed not to have the bitter aftertaste associated with other artificial sweeteners.

Saccharin: is the longest-established and most widely used artificial sweetener. Doubts have been raised about its safety, but it is not proven that it has any ill-effects. You may prefer to avoid it for another reason: it certainly isn't natural and does not help you retrain your taste buds to want less sweetness. It contains no calories.

Muscovado sugar: available in dark and light versions, is the 'halfway house' between molasses sugar and demerara sugar, in both strength of flavour and in mineral content. Again, use it if you like it, but in small amounts, say around one ounce per day. It contains 110 calories per ounce.

What to eat when you get that craving for something sweet.
Here is a list of foods that give you sweetness and food value:

bowl of porridge with one tsp honey
oatcake, scone, banana
fruit bar, dried apricots, apple
wholemeal apple sandwich
wholemeal biscuit

Lifestyle Quiz

Quiz – Are You a Sugar Addict? Find out if you're an unconscious sugar 'addict' by answering these questions – truthfully!

1 *Is a day without something sweet unthinkable?* A. Yes. B. No.
2 *Do you find it hard to eat only part of a bar*

of chocolate or packet of chocolate biscuits? A. Yes. B. No.
3 *Do you find you want sweet foods more when you're upset or bored?* A. Yes. B. No.
4 *Are you almost afraid to buy sweet foods, because you think you may wolf the lot?* A. Yes. B. No.

If you score more than two 'Yesses', you're fairly hooked, but don't give up hope. Once you realise how much you depend on sugar, it's easier to divert that attention to another harmless, or even healthy activity, such as eating apples, gardening or cleaning your shoes when you get that sugary urge.

Fit for Life
Fibre in Your Diet

As incomes have risen, Westerners have eaten less bread, rice, pasta, potatoes and all the other basic grains and carbohydrate foods. People have generally thought of this as 'progress'. The animal and dairy foods they eat instead contain more protein, they point out. For a long time, people also had the idea that these animal foods were less fattening, while thinking of bread and potatoes as 'just stodge'. Now expert opinion agrees that the change has not been a healthy one. It's had two main results: the foods we eat more of do have more protein, but they also have much more fat, and the foods we eat less of provided us with something very important that is now deficient in our diet – fibre.

Fibre is a 'family' word used to describe several substances found in the walls of plant cells. They all share the property that little of them is digested, so they pass through the body in roughly the same bulk in which they're eaten. This bulk 'pads out' the waste products of other foods eaten, so that the result is a neat and fairly large parcel that the muscles of the wall of the intestine can get a good grip on and move faster down the tube!

Comparisons between Westerners and natives of communities which still eat a lot of fibre, show that the latter are freer from several of the intestinal ailments which are virtual epidemics here. That doesn't prove the connection but this evidence, coupled with tests on the result of fibre in food here, are fairly convincing.

Eating more fibre is the easiest and most efficient way of avoiding or curing constipation, and also of making food travel more quickly through the body. This may have an advantage, some experts say, by shortening the time for which harmful waste products in food are in contact with the vulnerable, absorbent wall of the bowel. Other intestinal problems have been relieved by taking extra fibre – from haemorrhoids to a common problem in older people, diverticulitis.

The message now is: eat more fibre foods. They are not so high in protein, but still high enough, since most of us eat very much more protein than we need. They are certainly no more fattening than most protein foods, since most meat, cheese and milk/cream products gain many extra calories from their high fat content. The exceptions are the lean meats, especially poultry, game, rabbit and turkey, and white fish, low fat cottage cheese and low fat yogurt. If you combine foods from this last list with fibre foods like bread, breakfast cereals and potatoes – but go easy on other, fattier animal foods – you can enjoy a surprising amount of the breads and pasta most of us enjoy and gain no weight, but have a better-balanced style of eating.

However, at the same time as the move from bread to beef was beginning, refining of flour changed to remove almost all the fibre from bread. It also removed most of the B vitamins and minerals, and some of the protein. White bread contains very little fibre; wholemeal or wholewheat bread (the same thing), about 3 times as much. It's the same story with pasta, rice and breakfast cereals. To get the fibre, and more vitamins and minerals, you need to choose the 'whole' version. These are once more widely available, as more and more people want to put the fibre back into what they eat. Also having a revival are the beans and lentils, which provide protein and fibre with very little fat. Fruit and vegetables, and nuts, are the third source of fibre. So eating more fruit and vegetables helps your health in more ways than one.

Because the fibres from different kinds of food behave differently inside us, it's wise to include all kinds of fibre in what we eat. Since it makes food bulkier, it can often mean that people feel fuller quickly and eat less. This is why changing to a high fibre style of eating can help people lose weight.

Eating More Fibre You'll eat more fibre automatically if you choose natural foods, rather than packaged, processed ones; and if you replace some of the animal foods you eat, such as cheese, eggs or meat, with vegetable protein foods, like grains or cereals, beans or lentils, fruit, nuts and vegetables. If you do this, and choose the wholemeal versions of rice, bread and so on, you won't need to add bran to food. It'll be built in to the foods you are eating.

Don't suddenly start stuffing yourself with high-fibre foods. If your digestive system isn't used to them, you're likely to react to large amounts by feeling 'blown out' and uncomfortable, because of the unaccustomed bulk. It's better to change over to more fibre foods over several weeks, or even a few months.

Aim regularly to include in your meals some from each of the following groups:

1 Wholemeal bread, pasta, or cereals, or wholemeal crispbread. Brown rice.

2 Oatmeal, porridge oats or oatcakes. Beans or lentils, in soups, stews, salads, dhal etc. Peas or broad beans.

3 Fruit and vegetables, especially soft fruit such as blackcurrants and leafy vegetables such as spinach; or runner beans; or sweet corn.

Right: fibre isn't all bran. All these foods are especially rich in fibre – so put them on your shopping list. Clockwise from coconut: blackberries, sweetcorn, puffed cereals, prunes, runner beans, dried apricots, blackcurrants (and other soft fruit like raspberries), lentils, soya beans, brown rice, nuts of all kinds, passionfruit.

More carbohydrate can mean less calories. Right: grilled hamburger and coleslaw loses to less fatty, higher fibre baked beans on toast with tomatoes. Opposite: 'slimmer's' meal of steak and salad has more fat, and more calories than the egg salad sandwiches.

Here are examples of how meals with plenty of carbohydrate are healthier than the conventional equivalents:

1 *A 5oz beef hamburger with shop-bought coleslaw, versus 7oz baked beans on a slice of wholemeal toast, with 3 tomatoes.*
When you want a take-away meal, both these will generally be available. Choose the hamburger and you're clocking up about 16% fat, according to a Consumers' Association survey of minced beef; roughly 350 calories are likely to be involved, while the coleslaw will provide some 100-plus more, depending on the weight of mayonnaise or French dressing.
The baked beans provide plenty of protein, with a little more from the toast, but both also give a wealth of fibre; something the hamburger has none of and the coleslaw only a little. The meal contains about 300 calories and also provides plenty of vitamins A and C.

2 *Two rounds of wholemeal sandwiches, filled with egg and salad, versus 8oz steak with mustard and radiccio (red lettuce).*
Both meals provide protein, but while the wholemeal version provides fibre from the bread too, lettuce isn't particularly fibrous. The sandwiches meal, provided you are mean with butter or margarine and don't add mayonnaise to the egg, contains about 460 calories, using 1 large egg. The steak, even if it's lean, contains about the same, but you may find it difficult to avoid adding chips! So the advantage of the sandwiches is fibre.

Above: potatoes aren't fattening – when compared to the meal with lamb chops; that plateful has less than half the calories.
Opposite: two pub lunches – and the shepherd's pie has less calories as well as less fat and more fibre, and more to eat.

3 *A large, 9oz baked potato filled with 2oz cottage cheese, and a generous plate of mixed salad, versus 7oz lamb chops with 4oz chips and 2oz peas.*

Because of the amount of fat on chops, this 'meat and two vegetables' meal carries around 500 calories for the meat, 30 for the peas and 280 for the chips! That makes about 810. The chips contain only a small amount of fibre, so the peas are the only good source. The potato – which many of us like to eat, but some imagine is too fattening – contains around 300 calories including cottage cheese and salad. It isn't as high in protein as lamb chops, but when you add in the cottage cheese and salad protein, you end up with a meal that provides about a quarter of an adult's total daily protein need, plus fibre from potato and salad. If you wanted extra protein, you could add more cottage cheese for a 'lean' protein meal.

4 *A ploughman's lunch of 112g (4oz) Cheddar cheese, 40g (1½oz) French roll, 20g (¾oz) butter and 1tbsp chutney, versus 200g (7oz) shepherd's pie with cauliflower, carrots and green beans.*

You may think of the first meal as 'light', but with this amount of cheese, you'll be getting about 2oz pure fat if you count the butter and, if the bread is white, virtually no fibre. The shepherd's pie meal has a potato topping, which is usually low fat and includes some fibre, plus all the fibre from the vegetables. It's considerably lower in calories, depending on vegetable portions and the proportion of fat in the meat; 400 calories versus about 640.

Right: quiche has a 'healthy' image, but is high in fat and calories. You're better off with the whole-meal pizza.
Opposite: "I just had a sandwich for lunch" can mean more calories, if you choose cheese (30% fat) on buttered bread, than a good plate of chicken, rice and vegetables. Brown rice, with its extra fibre, vitamins and minerals, scores over white bread, too.

5 *Two small rounds of toasted cheese sandwiches, with tomato and watercress, versus 4oz roast chicken with carrots, 3oz (cooked weight) brown rice and browned mushrooms.*

You might think the first meal is lighter, but because the bread is white, even the admirable tomato and watercress mean it's low fibre, with considerable fat from the cheese. The calorie count: about 500, allowing for 1½oz grated cheese and about ½oz butter. It's easy to spread butter liberally on hot toast and bought toasted sandwiches are often buttered on the outside, too.

The chicken meal has about 400 calories, allowing for 1 tsp oil to brown the mushrooms in – they contain so few calories, you can have as many as you want – and a generous helping of carrots. It will contain about 60 calories fewer if you don't eat the chicken skin, which carries most of the fat, which this meal has little of. The chicken meal provides two kinds of fibre, from the brown rice and the vegetables.

6 *Wholemeal pizza with mixed salad, versus quiche with tomato and mayonnaise coleslaw.*

The wholemeal pizza has more fibre than the quiche, because it's made with wholemeal flour, and it contains more vitamins and minerals, too. It also has less fat, because the bread dough used in pizza is low fat, while shortcrust pastry is about 30% fat. Quiche fillings are high in fat from milk, cheese, eggs and often bacon, too. The salad with the pizza isn't deluged in greasy mayonnaise (79% fat) like the coleslaw, and you actually eat more salad, so get more fibre from it. The pizza still provides enough protein, but mainly from the low fat wheat, plus cheese in topping. For the same calories as a 5oz piece of quiche (approximately 550 calories), you can eat an 8oz piece of pizza, or you could save some calories by eating the same amount. Every tablespoon of mayonnaise or a bought coleslaw adds about 100 calories, 80 of them from fat, to your meal.

Bread – the Staff of Life

If you go into a supermarket or bakery, the choice of bread can be both delightful and confusing! Which is the healthiest?

All brown bread will contain more fibre than white, with Granary tm the next highest in fibre after wholewheat. All the same, brown bread may contain only about a third as much fibre as wholewheat, so the '100%' label indicating that the loaf is wholemeal or wholewheat is worth looking for. You're getting more B vitamins

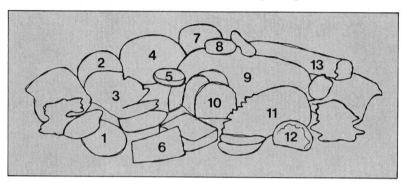

Key to bread photo, previous page: 1. wholemeal pitta bread; 2. brown soda bread; 3. wholemeal raisin-and-sesame cob; 4. round French country bread (made with little yeast and long rising time to give special tangy flavour); 5. black rye loaf; 6. pumpernickel slices with linseed; 7. Granary™ cob; 8. wheatmeal muffin; 9. long French brown bread; 10. rye and wheat pumpernickel; 11. Dr. Vogel mixed grain loaf; 12. Granary™ roll; 13. wholemeal French stick.

and more minerals too. Wholemeal bread also has slightly fewer calories, and if you are planning to increase your fibre intake by getting more of your protein from bread, this can add up to quite a substantial saving. If you usually eat 5 slices a day, changing to wholemeal will save about 30 calories, which over a year represents 3lb from your waistline. Even among wholemeal breads, you'll find a fascinating choice which is widening yearly: pumpernickel, sourdough and more.

Wheatmeal is another name used for brown but not wholemeal bread, and the term covers a wide range of breads which vary from almost white to almost wholemeal. Apart from the high fibre Granary loaf, you'll find mixed grain loaves, which may be as good as wholemeal in food value, but can't call themselves wholemeal because their ingredients include some not included in the legal definition of wholemeal, such as linseed or sunflower seed.

Wheat germ breads are made by adding back to white flour a larger amount of wheat germ than would naturally be there. This provides more B vitamins and vitamin E, some fibre – but less than Granary – and makes the bread slightly sweet. Wheatmeal 'soda' breads are raised with soda rather than yeast, from Irish traditions.

Pick the wholemeal loaf most often, but even the brown ones are better than white, and better than alternatives such as high fat quiches or pies.

What to Spread Bread may be low in fat, 'but what about the butter?', you may ask. It's certainly possible to unbalance your healthy bread by a high fat spread. Here's a choice of spreads to keep your bread healthy and unfattening:

Butter: you don't need to give it up, but use it sparingly, most easily done if you don't keep it too cold. Try keeping butter for the day in the week when you have most time to enjoy breakfast, but using other fats for other days and for cooking. It contains 205 calories per ounce. Unsalted or slightly salted types are preferable.

Soft margarine high in polyunsaturates: is the only margarine worth giving up butter for! It has the same 205 calories per ounce, but provides more of the fats the body really needs and has less tendency to raise the level of fat in the blood. However, you should still use this sparingly, choosing lower-fat spreads most of the time. You can bake well with this kind of margarine.

Low fat spreads: contain only half as much fat as either butter or margarine, approximately 105 calories per ounce. This makes them worth trying for taste; some contain more PUFAs than others but all are useful.

Sunshine spread: is a way of getting a more natural spread than margarine, which is always processed, and getting some taste of butter too! You just beat into some softened butter about half its weight of an oil very high in polyunsaturates, say sunflower or safflower. It will look odd at first, but when chilled again forms into an easy-to-spread consistency. You will probably need an electric beater to save on the hard work. It contains around 220 calories per ounce, so you don't save any calories but just produce a spread, mixing butter taste and PUFAs, without additives.

Smoothie: an unprocessed lower fat spread, made by mixing equal amounts of slightly softened butter or high PUFA margarine (no need to soften this), with low fat curd or cottage cheese (sieve the latter). It contains around 120 calories per ounce.

Curd and cottage cheese: both make good spreads for bread on their own, at around 36 or 30 calories per ounce respectively. In this case, make sure you get your polyunsaturates by using oils high in them for salads or cooking.

Other spreads: keep in mind that sandwiches don't have to have a spread before filling, providing the filling is moist.

You are what you spread: Clockwise from top: butter, soft margarine high in polyunsaturates, low-fat spreads sold in tubs, sunshine (butter-and-oil) spread, smoothie (butter-and-soft-cheese) spread, curd cheese and cottage cheese.

Try yeast extract, mashed bananas, mashed sardines and dried apricot purée, for instance, and skip the butter or margarine.

Other high fibre foods: as well as wholemeal bread include coconut, blackberry, sweetcorn, puffed wheat, prunes, dried apricots, blackcurrants, green beans, lentils, brown rice, beans, nuts, passion fruit, and variations on the same foods i.e. unrefined cereals, dried fruit, berry fruit, dried beans and lentils, nuts.

How Much Fibre Do You Need? The ideal amount of fibre for good health is unknown, but for practical purposes, the target is at least 30 grams a day. This is about twice the fibre eaten in a typical Western

Fibre doesn't mean stringy! Above: high fibre baked apple versus no fibre caramel cream. Opposite: chili con carne (bean fibre) and high fibre peas and brown rice, versus low fibre white rice, no fibre chicken. Both delicious – so why not pick the fibre foods more often?

diet with white bread and little vegetables. However, it's not difficult to add fibre without adding bran from a packet.

Aim to have about 5 'fibre foods' a day at least, mixing the types. Here are some of the choices:

Wholemeal bread, fresh fruit, bean salads, baked beans, chilli con carne, unrefined breakfast cereals, porridge, crispbread, brown rice, beansprouts, banana, carrots, humus, dhal (Indian spiced lentils), dried fruit, vegetables, especially green beans, peas, sweet corn, broad beans, nuts, soft fruit, wholemeal pasta, potato, large helping.

Here's an example of how keeping fibre in mind can produce a high fibre style of eating without you even noticing, compared to a low fibre meal.

High	Low
Chilli con carne	Chicken casserole
Brown rice	White rice
Celery	Cauliflower
Peas	

The low fibre menu contains virtually no fibre, except for the cauliflower. The high fibre menu includes all three types of fibre: from beans, in chilli, from brown rice and from vegetables, especially the peas. You certainly don't need to add bran to this style of eating.

Fibre in Pudding	*No Fibre*
Baked apple stuffed with minced dried fruit	Caramel dessert from shop

Fit for Life
The Salt Factor

We all need some sodium, the main ingredient of table salt, but thanks to the amount added to foods in processing, and added by us in cooking or at table, the average person eats some 2 or 3 times as much as the level considered desirable. Excess salt can encourage high blood pressure in people who are vulnerable to this condition; which comes to some 1 in 4 or 5 of us at some time in our lives. High blood pressure isn't a disease in itself, but a warning signal that the heart is having to overwork and that we are more vulnerable to a heart attack, stroke or kidney illness. We are more likely to retain excess fluid, too.

Reducing salt can help bring blood pressure down, in a more natural way than taking drugs and without any side-effects. This is most easily done by reducing the number of processed foods that you use; if you read the ingredients labels of food packets, you'll find that almost all of them have added salt. Take-away foods also tend to be very salty.

Salt isn't the only influence on blood pressure; the amount of fibre, especially the kind of fibre in oats and beans, can have an effect, if you step it up. Eating less fat can also reduce blood pressure. Other factors: being too heavy encourages blood pressure to rise too high; smoking is linked with high blood pressure; lack of exercise is a bad influence and being under stress can push up blood pressure, at least temporarily.

If you say that it's easier to take drugs than to counter high blood pressure by natural means, remember that most people have to continue taking the drugs for the rest of their lives, and many experience unpleasant side-effects. It's healthier to get into the habit of eating less salt early in life; you won't miss the surplus provided you have some salt.

Eating Less Salt You can reduce the amount of salt you eat very quickly just by using a salt pourer with a smaller hole, and not salting a plateful of food before you even taste it!

It's easy to dodge some of the most obvious salty foods, too: crisps, salted nuts, highly salted coated chicken or fish and other snack and take-away foods whose saltiness is outstanding.

Opposite: it's much easier to remove a little of the unnecessary heap of salt we eat than to face years of taking drugs to control the high blood pressure extra salt can encourage in many older people. Old age may seem a long way away, but the habit of taking too much salt can start trouble building up early. And it's a habit that most people can easily change, using only half as much.

However much salt you may think you 'sweat off', you don't need as much as you eat. Clockwise from top right, opposite: yeast extract, Biosalt, mustard, salt substitutes, stock cubes, seaweed (sea vegetables), olives, Cheddar cheese, soya sauce, sesame salt, sea or rock salt crystals, herb salt, lemon juice.

Get out of the habit of automatically salting vegetables, rice or pasta cooking water; it's often unnecessary. If you cook vegetables only until they are just tender, not mushy, they'll have more of their own flavour and not need added salt. Let people add their own at table.

Choose unsalted or slightly salted butter instead of the saltiest, and flavour your cooking with other tastes instead of plain salt.

Here are some of the flavourings you can use to salt foods or give them flavour in other ways, so you don't need to use so much plain salt:

Yeast extract: is very salty, but it has a lot of other flavours too. So use it sparingly to flavour cooking or as a spread, and omit other salt from the recipe.

Biosalt: contains less sodium, because it is a mixture of minerals, all of which have some flavouring power. Still, use it sparingly.

Mustard: is a good salt substitute; if you make it up from powder it won't contain more than a trace of sodium. Made-up jars have added salt, but you can still end up with a lower-salt dish if you omit other salt from the recipe when using mustard.

Salt substitutes: contain other natural minerals, based on potassium, and virtually no sodium. They don't taste much like salt,

Right: added salt in food can be dangerous for babies, whose systems find it hard to cope with. To make baby food at home, remove child's portion from family meal before adding seasoning. But why add salt to the adults' food either? Apart from damage to health, excess salt can encourage fluid retention, blurring the clean lines of jaw and cheek with puffiness.

but try them to see whether you find they help you use less sodium. Anyone with a heart condition or on a low-potassium diet must check with their doctor before using these products.

Stock cubes: are usually very salty and are to be avoided, in favour of using your own cooking water from vegetables and meat as stock. You can buy low-salt stock cubes from health food stores. If you use stock cubes, omit other salt from recipe.

Nori: sheets of crisp, paper-thin seaweed from Japan with a naturally high salt content give flavour from other minerals. Use chopped nori or other cooked seaweed instead of salt to flavour meals.

Olives: are preserved in salty brine. So if you use them in pizza or other dishes, leave out any other salt.

Cheddar cheese: like almost all cheese, has a lot of salt added when it's made, as well as some natural sodium in milk. As it's high in fat too, use sparingly to replace salt in savouries, choosing the strongest-flavour type so you get more flavour with less cheese.

Soya sauce: is a salty Chinese and Japanese flavouring. Use sparingly; it will give you more taste than salt alone, so you need not use much.

Sesame salt: has only about half the sodium of ordinary salt, because it's mixed with toasted, crushed sesame seeds which contribute their own special flavour.

Sea salt: contains other useful minerals, especially iodine, which table salt doesn't have unless it's labelled 'iodized'. But it's still mainly sodium, so use as reluctantly as ordinary salt. You may find it easier to use less if you grind it each time in a salt mill.

Herb salt: has less sodium because it's mixed with powdered, dried herbs and vegetables. So if you use it like salt, you'll be getting extra flavour with less sodium. Use sparingly, unless you pick the type with no salt, only the vegetables.

Lemon juice: is the ideal salt substitute: it adds flavour, vitamin C and almost no sodium to food. Use freely, especially from fresh lemons.

Fit for Life

Fresh Food for Fitness

Fruit and vegetables are our sole source, apart from milk and liver, of vitamin C (ascorbic acid). It's essential for many reasons, which can be summed up as protecting the body from vulnerability to infection and helping it recover if it does succumb.

Vitamin C is barely stored by the body, so it's important to eat some virtually every day. Vegetables are just as good sources as fruit, provided you pick at least some of them as leafy greens and eat a good proportion in salads, as even careful cooking causes some vitamin C loss.

When cooking either fruit or vegetables, the rules for keeping the best flavour *and* vitamin and mineral value are:

1 Only expose the cut or peeled surfaces to air for as short a time as possible. So don't cut or shred produce hours before it's going to be cooked or eaten.

2 Don't soak prepared produce, as vitamins and minerals will dissolve into the liquid. For the same reason, prefer methods

Eating plenty of fruit and vegetables – at least 2 or 3 helpings every day – gives the body plenty of the materials it needs to keep skin, hair, eyes and nails in good condition. And you can eat plenty of it while staying slim. But careless cooking can remove many of the vitamins and minerals from the food – so make the small effort to keep the goodness in.

of cooking using no water, or the minimum: steaming, pressure cooking (a version of steaming), microwave cooking, or 'conservative' cooking, where you put only half a cup of water in a pan, boil it, add the vegetables, cover tightly and cook over a low-to-medium heat for several minutes. This is a 'half-steaming' method, where most of the vegetable barely touches water and little liquid is left at the end.

Any liquid left after cooking vegetables is worth keeping for the stock jug. It not only adds flavour to soups, casseroles or sauces, but also means you 'regain' some minerals and vitamins which may have dissolved in it.

Below: vegetables are even more valuable than fruit, but use both. Yellow, red and orange types like carrot and pepper tend to be richest in vitamin A; leafy greens and citrus fruit, peppers and strawberries are top for vitamin C, but they are all good – and so delicious to eat, too.

3 Cook produce for the minimum of time. This reduces vitamin loss and keeps texture and flavour good, minimising the need for added butter or salt to make the produce enjoyable.

4 Avoid keeping vegetables hot, which causes substantial vitamin loss. Only start cooking them when everyone's at table.

5 If you want to use ready-prepared vegetables or fruit, frozen produce has a higher food value than tinned. If using tinned, use the liquid in cooking to regain minerals dissolved in it.

Aim to have fresh food with every meal, from fruit at breakfast time, to a salad as a daily habit, to snacks of raw carrots or bananas. Fruit and vegetables can be good 'convenience foods', because salads are easy to make and fruit can be eaten wherever you are.

Apart from their vitamin C, fresh produce is a major source of vitamin A in carotene form. This is richest in yellow and orange vegetables and fruit, together with leafy green vegetables. Leafy green vegetables also provide the best sources of folic acid (a

Think of yourself as someone special, worth feeding with the fresh and natural foods that will nourish you best. Don't see food as unimportant fuel, and eat the first food that comes to hand. You'll enjoy food – and life – more if you like yourself too much to fill up on 'junk'.

constituent of the vitamin B complex), vitamin E, vitamin K and a variety of minerals, including iron and calcium. This makes them particularly important, more so than fruit, and most useful of all if you don't want to eat much meat or milk products, which are the alternative and richest sources of iron and calcium respectively.

Leafy greens that are eaten raw, such as mustard and cress, celery leaves, shredded green cabbage (white is not so nutritious), watercress or alfalfa sprouts, are especially valuable because no food value is lost in cooking. Aim to eat leafy greenstuff at least once daily.

On top of all this, fruit and vegetables supply fibre, giving a satisfying bulk to meals without too many calories. Their rich variety of colours and flavours is vital to good cooking and means that you don't have to rely on high-fat butter, cream or oil to make food look and taste good. Make them a major part of your shopping list and keep them for as short a time as possible. Store vegetables in the refrigerator for crisp freshness: heat, light and exposure to air on cut surfaces are the major enemies of their freshness and food value.

Fit for Life
The Four-Week Health Diet

Why carry suitcases around with you – in the shape of excess poundage? It's nice to travel light, without wanting to be skinny. Keeping active while you lose weight makes the job much easier.

Follow this four-week eating plan for a sleeker, livelier you.

Being skinny isn't fashionable any more. Now the aim is to be in good shape; firm rather than frail. Beauty is the gleam of hair, skin and smile that comes from health. Give yourself the glossy good looks that come from the inside. The diet provides around 1,400 calories a day; more than the typical weight loss diet, less than the average woman's daily intake. If you know you find it hard to maintain a neat shape, trim the diet as suggested later.

Team the meal plan with 30 minutes of exercise each day. It'll not only firm up your shape, but also act as a mood-booster. If you feel lethargic, exercise can improve your energy level, which is another essential for good looks and success. If you feel tense or restless, exercise can help you relax. It can also help you stick to your eating plan. How? When you become more aware of your body, through sport or movement, you'll find you're keener to keep it in peak form by eating well. Also, when you keep active, you have less time

to be tempted towards the wrong foods.

This eating plan is different from other diets because its first aim is vitality; foods that give you best value-for-calorie are packed into it. Feeling good stops you eating for comfort when depressed, too. The foods that don't earn their keep with the meal plan through not having the right food to hand. To protect vitamins, keep all your vegetables cool and dark in the 'fridge'. Invest in the vitality foods; you'll save overall because you won't be spending money on soft drinks, sweets or take-away snacks.

food value are booted out. If you find you've eaten the wrong thing one meal, don't worry, or give up. Just go back to the plan and notice how well you feel when you stick to it. You don't need to check this diet with your doctor unless you are under treatment for an illness.

Choose one breakfast, one light meal and one main meal every day. You don't have to try all the meals, but don't eat the same thing every day. Variety improves your chances of getting every vitamin or mineral you need.

If you don't usually eat breakfast, a style of eating like this may make you feel hungrier in the morning. If you don't eat breakfast, keep fruit and a made-up tub of one of the cereal or stewed fruit breakfasts handy for mid-morning, when you may otherwise be drawn to chocolate or bun!

Shop in advance, so that you don't give up

Measure out your daily allowance of spread and milk, so you know how much you are eating. It's useful to weigh out portions of other foods until you can judge by looking how large a 4oz potato is, for instance.

Your 28-Day Plan
Repeat the cycle 4 times.

Daily allowances
* 15g (½oz) butter, margarine high in polyunsaturates or other spread (105 calories). You can also use low fat spread, saving half these calories, but choose a type with a reasonable level of vegetable oils for PUFAs, e.g. mix soft margarine high in PUFA half and half with cottage cheese.
* 285ml (½ pint) skim milk (about 110 calories)
* Vegetables from 'free' list
* Drinks from 'free' list

Beautiful bodies, above and opposite, should inspire you, and not make you give up because yours is so much fatter! We're all individuals, and there are many different body shapes which are beautiful, as great painters have proved. Find a model you are content with that's close to your figure type – then work gradually towards your target. It's better to change slowly and keep the weight off than to crash diet, then crash gain!

Breakfast Choices

1 *Total Calories 288*	*Approx. Cals.*	*Main food value*
1oz breakfast cereal, wholegrain such as muesli, unsugared brand	105	protein, fibre, B vitamins, E, minerals
1 apple (4oz approximately)	50	fibre, minerals
¼ pint unsweetened fruit juice <u>or</u> extra skim milk (not allowance)	50	vitamin C, minerals especially potassium <u>or</u> protein, B vitamins, calcium
2 tsp wheat germ (½oz)	40	protein, vitamins B and E, minerals, high-PUFA oil
1 tsp chopped nuts (¼oz)	43	high-PUFA oil, protein, B vitamins, minerals
drink from allowance, e.g. coffee	–	

N.B. Soak muesli in liquid overnight. In the morning, grate in apple and nuts, stir in wheat germ.

Below: breakfast 1: plenty to eat, thanks to soaking muesli overnight. Decaffeinated coffee.

Right: breakfast 2: beautiful food is more satisfying, and no one can complain that this breakfast takes too long to make. Peppermint tea – or try limeflower for a morning boost.

2 *Total Calories 225*	*Approx. Cals.*	*Main food value*
10oz any fruit but banana	120	vitamins, minerals, fibre
5oz unsweetened low fat yogurt	75	protein, calcium, B vitamins
1 tsp clear honey	30	trace minerals
drink from allowance, e.g. peppermint tea	–	

N.B. Chop fruit or slice. Mix yogurt with honey.

3 Total Calories 262	Approx. Cals.	Main food value
1 large boiled egg	90	protein, vitamins, iron, 13% fat
2 slices wholemeal 'soldiers'	122	protein, fibre, vitamins, minerals
spread from allowance	–	
1 piece of fruit (e.g. 4 oz apple)	50	fibre, minerals
drink from allowance, e.g. weak China tea	–	

N.B. Use as little salt as possible on egg.

Below: breakfast 3. Choose 'real' 100% wholemeal bread, not halfway-house 'brown' or 'wheatmeal', for the full benefit of fibre, vitamins and minerals. China tea.

Opposite: breakfast 4 – a perfect starter to a summer's day. Vary the fruit as much as you like to suit what's in season and good value. Home-made lemon barley water is a wonderfully refreshing drink. (Boil 1oz barley and rind of 1 lemon, simmer for a few minutes, pour into jug, cool. Add juice of lemon and honey to taste. Strain and chill.)

4 Total Calories 287	Approx. Cals.	Main food value
Fresh and dried fruit salad: 2oz stewed dried fruit, mixed	106	fibre, iron, other minerals
8oz fresh fruit, chopped	96	vitamins, especially C, and minerals, fibre
juice from stewing fruit	–	
2 tsp coarse bran	neg.	fibre
2 tsp wheat germ	40	protein, B and E vitamins, minerals, high-PUFA oil
3 tbsp (3oz) low fat yogurt	45	protein, B vitamins, calcium
drink from allowance, e.g. lemon barley water	–	

Below: breakfast 5. For a change, use grilled mushrooms instead of tomatoes, and other kinds of fresh fruit. You can add tea – herb or regular – without sweetening, if you like.

5 *Total Calories 207*	*Approx. Cals.*	*Main food value*
4 halves grilled tomato	20	vitamins A and C, fibre, minerals
spread from allowance	–	
1 slice wholemeal toast (1¼oz)	77	protein, fibre, B and E vitamins, minerals
5oz pear	60	fibre, minerals
5oz glass buttermilk	50	protein, calcium, B vitamins

Opposite: breakfast 6. Ideal for a frosty morning, porridge really warms you up, with a hot glass of tea. The dried fruit can be mashed into the porridge to give extra sweetness.

6 *Total Calories 365*	*Approx. Cals.*	*Main food value*
Porridge using 1½oz oats	165	protein, fibre, B vitamins, minerals
¼ pint extra skim milk	50	protein, calcium, B vitamins
2oz dry weight prunes and apricots, stewed	100	fibre, minerals
1 piece fresh fruit, not banana	50	vitamin C (not particularly high in apples), minerals, fibre
drink from allowance, e.g. rosehip tea	–	

Above: breakfast 7: the bread isn't burnt, it's spread with yeast extract, a perfect flavour to go with cottage cheese. Swap the apricot nectar for your favourite juice, if liked, and sip slowly, you can add tea, herb or regular, without sweetening, if you like, or decaffeinated coffee.

1 *Total Calories 340*	*Approx. Cals.*	*Main food value*
2 good slices (2½oz total) wholemeal bread	155	protein, fibre, B vitamins, E, minerals
spread from allowance	–	fats, vitamins A and D
yeast extract topped with 2oz cottage cheese	70	protein, calcium, B vitamins, salt
1 large piece fruit or small banana	65	vitamin C, minerals (banana: vitamin A rather than C), fibre
small glass apricot nectar	50	vitamin A, minerals, fibre
drink from allowance if wanted	–	

Light meals

Can be eaten midday or evening, as convenient. The exact quantities of vegetables are not given as calorie values are low enough to let you eat according to appetite without making much difference.

Below: the maxi-sandwich that's mini in calories. Opposite: the burger platter – including a glass of wine. It's worth arranging meals prettily, even if they're just for you. You'll find you eat with more enjoyment and tend to feel satisfied with less.

2 Burger platter:
calories around 410 including 90 for wine

Double decker Vegeburger on 2oz sesame wholemeal bun, sliced tomato, cucumber, spring onion
5oz glass of dry white wine

Vegetable burger mixes take only a few minutes to prepare to packet instructions. Grill or sauté in pan lightly brushed with oil.

4 Maxi-sandwich:
calories around 400

3 slices wholemeal bread
spread from allowance
filled with:
shredded carrot
yeast extract
3oz cottage cheese
sliced cucumber
side salad:
cauliflower chunks
carrot sticks
3oz unsweetened orange juice

Make bread into 3 super-filled sandwiches, using generous amounts of carrot and cucumber (plus watercress or mustard and cress if wanted).

Above: the bean salad platter, good and crunchy with satisfying chick peas. Easy to take to work as these vegetables don't go soggy quickly. You can drink as many mugs of bouillon or yeast extract as you like: the calorie count is very low.

Opposite: the rice salad platter, much more filling made with brown rice. You can add more vegetables if you like. In cold weather, tomato juice is delicious hot.

1 Bean salad platter:
calories around 390

2oz chick peas or any dried bean
chopped fresh vegetables
2 tsp safflower or sunflower oil
good squeeze of lemon juice
2 tsp cider vinegar
1½oz wholemeal roll
Yeast extract hot drink

Soak beans in water overnight or during day. Change water, boil and simmer covered for about 40-60 minutes until tender. (Boil beans vigorously for 10 minutes before simmering.) Mix with all other ingredients while warm.

7 Rice salad platter:
calories around 340

2oz (raw weight) brown rice, cooked
½oz peanuts, toasted but not salted
½ bunch watercress, mustard and cress
or parsley
1 tbsp yogurt
squeeze of lemon juice
strips of green or red pepper
tomato juice with celery stick garnish

Cook rice as under Autumn salad. Mix with other ingredients, using vegetables generously.
Use yogurt as dressing.

Above: Lentil soup with pate bap. Lentil soup is high in protein and fibre, as well as B vitamins, minerals and flavour! It can be kept hot in a vacuum flask without losing any goodness or taste.
Opposite: baked potato platter allows you to enjoy a really big potato. You can keep it hot in a wide-mouthed vacuum flask, if wished, then add cottage cheese when you are ready to eat it.

5 Soup and pâté bap:
calories around 430

Lentil soup:
1 tsp vegetable oil
1 onion, finely sliced
1 carrot, washed and sliced
1oz split red lentils
1 bay leaf
¼ pint stock
sea salt and pepper to taste
yeast extract to taste

2oz wholemeal roll filled with ½oz Tartex^tm
vegetable pâté
sliced cucumber
apple juice drink from concentrate

Heat oil in saucepan, soften onion with lid on for 5 minutes over lowest heat. Add carrot, lentils, bay leaf and stock. Simmer, covered, for 20 minutes.

Season, adding yeast extract if liked and more water if too thick. Remove bay leaf, liquidise. Transfer to vacuum flask if eating away from home.

6 Baked potato platter:
calories around 460

10oz baked potato
Coleslaw:
shred carrots, cabbage, add ½oz raisins
¼oz hazel nuts or sunflower seeds
3oz cottage cheese
½ bunch watercress or mustard and cress
Mineral water

Split potato, stuff with half the cottage cheeses (<u>no</u> butter!). Use rest of cheese to dress salad, with a squeeze of lemon juice if liked. Mix all salad ingredients together.

Above: autumn salad – a really generous plateful, with a delicate and relaxing cup of chamomile tea. Don't dismiss beans as too much trouble: cook a triple batch when you have time, then refrigerate or freeze until you want them for soups, casseroles or salad.

Opposite: younger women don't have all the cards. Mature good looks often go with greater self-confidence, serenity and the ability to enjoy life.

Autumn salad:
calories around 410

2oz (dry weight) beans or brown rice, cooked
generous selection of shredded vegetables, such as carrot, celery, leeks, cauliflower etc.
½oz hazel nuts, toasted but not salted
3oz cottage cheese or 1oz cheddar cheese
lemon juice or vinegar to flavour if liked
chamomile tea (or favourite herb tea)

Cook beans as for Bean salad; rice by simmering with 2½ times its volume of water, covered, for 40-50 minutes, when water will have been absorbed.
Mix with other ingredients, shredding cheddar cheese if used.

N.B. Hazel nuts have about 108 calories per ounce, compared to 150-170 for other nuts; this is due to their lower oil content.

Main Meals

Choose one of these:
✱ Medium portion of white fish, occasionally herring or kipper, and shellfish.
✱ Joint of chicken, turkey or rabbit; liver or kidneys at least once a week.
✱ Repeat any 'light meal'.
✱ Vegetables with skim milk white sauce and a little grated cheese.

Cook by baking, grilling or casseroling, i.e. don't add fat.
Add:
✱ 2 generous helpings of lightly cooked vegetables, 1 green (no potatoes)
✱ dessert of fresh fruit, or baked apple stuffed with dried fruit, or grilled grapefruit (pint type for preference) brushed with honey, or unsweetened yogurt with chopped fresh fruit.

Above: an old trick, but it works. Keep a good stock of prepared (washed or peeled) vegetables chilled and handy for hungry moments when you might be tempted to dive into biscuits or ice cream. Opposite: a wide choice of drinks for flavour without calories or nerve-twitching caffeine. From top: chamomile tea – traditionally relaxing; top right: refreshing rosehip tea; next row, left: dandelion coffee, and opera singer's special (1 teaspoon each of honey, lemon juice and cider vinegar, with very hot water); bottom row, left: decaffeinated black coffee, lime flavoured tea, bouillon made with yeast extract.

✱ Drink from allowance.
Calories will average around 400.

'Free' Drinks
Too much caffeine and tannin from coffee, tea, cola drinks or chocolate can over-stimulate you and make you nervy. Therefore, try to use the following instead:
 Decaffeinated coffee
 Weak tea
 Dandelion and grain 'coffee'
 Lemon juice with hot water and 1 tsp honey, plus a dash of cider vinegar
 Tomato juice
 Lemon barley water (pour boiling water over lemon rind and barley in a jug, strain when cold, add minimum of honey to taste)
 Fruit juices, unsweetened – up to ½ pint a day.
 Fruit nectars, which are slightly sweetened, in small amounts.

Mineral water.
 Vegetable cocktail juices.
 Herb teas, e.g. rosehip, chamomile, peppermint, fennel, mixed fruit.
 Apple juice, including drinks made from juice concentrate with hot or cold water.
 Glass of dry wine not more than 3 times a week. Try making it go further by mixing with sparkling mineral water.

'Free' Vegetables
All vegetables provide good food value per calorie, but to control weight use freely all but the following: sweet corn, sweet potatoes, peas, baked beans, broad beans. Use small amounts of these, but avoid avocado pears completely if calorie-counting; they are very high indeed, thanks to their oil content.

Eating Well... Anywhere

Fit for Life

Right and opposite: many of us make an effort to eat healthily and get in shape at home, then give up when we go away. But the food that makes us feel confident in our swimwear can taste just as delicious as the stuff that brings out the spots and bulges.

Business lunches, holidays and having to eat out are all used as reasons for not being able to eat healthily. It's true that they do present you with many dishes which are richer in fat, sugar and salt than you might eat at home, but you'd be surprised how many healthy foods are there for the choosing.

Holidays: apply the same yardsticks as at home. You want to avoid excess fat and sugar, but increase fibre, fruit and vegetables. So choose salads (easy when it's hot), fish, poultry and fruit rather than fried or sugary dishes. That could mean, for instance, picking a *tjatziki* (cucumber and yogurt) dish if you're in Greece, rather than the high fat *tyropitta* pastries as your first course, and going for the many bean and vegetable dishes on offer, rather than fried food. Fish is good at most seaside holiday places, but opt for it grilled, barbecued or casseroled rather than fried in batter; or leave the batter aside.

Avoiding meat and rich puddings will also reduce your chances of getting food

Below: dessert trolley temptation! There's always fresh fruit salad or fresh pineapple, or a simple 'no', which may be hard to say but you'll soon be pleased you did.
A moment in the mouth, an hour in the stomach, a lifetime on the hips...
If you seldom eat puddings,

poisoning, which is more liable to affect animal foods like cream, custard, ice cream and meat.

Look out for local specialities such as corn on the cob (avoid the butter or most of it), melons, or barbecued food, which reduces fat. You'll often find it hard to find wholemeal bread or cereal, so it can be worth taking with you packets of pumpernickel,

Business lunches: it's never been so easy to avoid the business paunch! Restaurants are increasingly catering for the health-minded. However, you may have to make a few requests; don't be nervous, they'll accept it as normal. Ask for salad dressings to be served separately, so you can control the amount you add. Ask for sauces to be left off dishes like seafood cocktail or

or confectionery say once a month, then of course you can say 'yes' cheerfully. But once you are used to healthy eating, you may not want to.

which keeps well until opened, and muesli (sugar-free brand). If you are going self-catering, you can take you own brown rice and pasta, for instance.

To stay well on holiday, don't eat fruit unless you've peeled it yourself. Don't drink unboiled water or have ice in drinks, and be wary of seafood around the polluted Mediterranean. Alcohol and sun are a potent mixture which can lead to tummy upsets all on their own, especially if you drink an unfamiliar local brew.

puddings, and again served separately so you can reduce the amount you eat. Ask for sauces on main courses, like fish, to be reduced or omitted; they usually consist of butter and cream.

Easy-to-find first courses include: melon, grapefruit cocktail, seafood cocktail without dressing, thin soups, mixed salads, oysters, asparagus (with only a drop of dressing), artichoke (ditto), moules marinière (mussels), crudites (raw vegetable sticks with a dip – ask for cottage cheese instead, or use dip cautiously), and smoked fish.

Main courses: pick a plain poultry, fish, game or rabbit dish, with vegetables (ask for them not to be buttered). More restaurants now offer vegetarian main dishes, but avoid fried croquettes, rich in nut oil. Choose jacket-baked or boiled potatoes, rather than creamed or chipped, and in preference to white rice or white noodles.

Puddings: try eating fresh fruit salad, fresh fruit such as raspberries, strawberries, orange sliced in liqueur or stewed figs, crème caramelle or crumble, leaving most of the topping. Don't pick cheese and biscuits unless you've had a very light meal, such as a salad.

persuade you, resist; why should you drink more than you want? Alcohol provides 'empty calories' and can't help your health or your looks.

Take-Aways Most of us want a take-away meal at some time. Here's the choice you'll usually have; which is best for your health?

Baked potato (9oz) with baked beans (2½oz). If you ask for the pat of butter to be omitted, totals about 265 calories. Excellent for health with vitamin C from potato, plus fibre, minerals and protein with B vitamins, fibre and minerals for beans.

Fried chicken pieces (9½oz) with chips (4½oz). Poor health choice, with too much fat and little fibre. A little vitamin C is found in the chips. Contains around 800 calories.

Double cheeseburger (4oz meat) with

The take-away choice. Top row from left: baked potato with baked beans; fried chicken with chips; cheeseburger and milk-shake; pork pie and stout; coffee and Danish pastries. Bottom row from left: frankfurter with fried onions; chicken chop suey, pizza, doner kebab; vegetable curry with chapattis; tuna and cucumber sandwich; fish and chips.

Coffee: ask for decaffeinated. More restaurants now offer it and, if more of us ask for it, they all will. Otherwise, carry sachets of decaffeinated coffee or herb tea in your pocket, and ask them to make them up. You can always plead your doctor's advice!

Alcohol: stick to a glass or two of dry wine, remembering that more will blunt your business judgement (it is a working lunch, isn't it?) as well as your health. If they try to

1oz cheese, chips (2¼oz) and 2oz bun. Thin chips like these tend to be highest in fat in proportion to amount of potato. No vitamin C in this one, almost no fibre, with plenty of fat. Contains around 880 calories, including milk shake. Only advantage: plenty of protein, from hamburger, cheese, bun and shake's milk content.

Bottle of stout (275ml) and pork pie (5oz). One of the worst choices, providing some 628 calories, of which a high proportion come from fat. Virtually no fibre, no vitamin C at all, few vitamins and minerals compared to what the same number of calories would provide in the form of other foods.

Keep a note of what to look for in food value – low fat, freshness, wholemeal or bean-based dishes for fibre, and you'll be able to choose the healthiest of what's available wherever you travel. Remember basic rules too: avoid unboiled water, including ice in drinks, peel fruit and vegetables, refuse seafood unless you're very confident.

Cup of coffee and Danish pastries. With 14ml cream from the standard portion tub and 6oz for the pastries, this provides a colossal 1,000-odd calories, is mainly fat and has almost no fibre and no vitamin C. Bottom of the list, and the coffee may also make you feel nervy!

Hot dog. A 4oz frankfurter in a typical 2¾oz roll with 1½oz fried onion provides roughly 625 calories, complete with protein but little else apart from fat. Virtually no fibre or vitamin C.

Pizza. An 8oz slice of pizza or complete pizza made with wholemeal flour (easier to find now) provides about 520 calories, with around 11% fat. Cheese and flour provide the protein, and there's vitamin C in tomato topping (ask for peppers – they're very high in vitamin C), and the base also provides fibre. This is one of the best choices.

Chicken chop suey. This will vary from one restaurant to another but, basically, the Chinese stir-frying method results in a low fat result and chicken is one of the meats lowest in fat, especially as most restaurants remove the fattiest part, the skin. A 12oz portion might provide 4oz chicken, 8oz mixed vegetables – which should supply some vitamin C and fibre – and a typical 300 calories; a good choice.

Doner kebab, salad and pitta bread. With 3oz of each, this provides about 440 calories. The salad provides vitamin C and a little fibre and, if the pitta bread were wholemeal (now available), the meal would be well-balanced, because the fat content is low and the bread would then provide more fibre and vitamins.

Vegetable curry and 2 chapattis. A 9oz curry will vary considerably in food value according to the cook's use of fat and length of cooking time for the vegetables. It provides some fibre and a little vitamin C, for about 400 calories. Many Indian restaurants use wholemeal flour for chapattis, which would make this a good meal as it's relatively low in fat, if you supplied the vitamin C with an orange for afters.

Tuna and cucumber sandwich in wholemeal bread. With about 2½oz tuna and little butter or margarine, this clocks up about 330 calories, complete with protein, vitamin C from the cucumber and fibre from the bread. A very good choice, especially if you ask for extra salad to be included.

Fish and chips. A generous 7oz fish and 10oz chips gave this meal a solid 1,266 calories! This amount of chips would provide some fibre and a good helping of vitamin C, but an awful lot of fat with it. If you peeled the batter off the fish, you'd be peeling off a lot of the fat too. Keep this one for special occasions.

Summary of Best Buys:
✽ Baked potato with baked beans
✽ Tuna and cucumber wholemeal sandwich
✽ Chicken chop suey
✽ Vegetable curry with wholemeal chapattis

Runners-Up Pizza and doner kebab would be good if wholemeal, and pizza needs salad for vitamin C.

Fit for Life
Exercise and Relaxation

Food can't be discussed without taking into account the other side of the balance: the energy we use.

Exercise has benefits you may not have considered. As well as helping to control your weight, and keeping you in shape with trim muscles, exercise can:

✳ Increase your energy level, by making your body stronger.

✳ Improve your stamina.

✳ Help you resist stress by improving stamina and helping you relax.

✳ Mean you can eat more while staying in shape. The more you eat, provided you choose natural foods, the more vitamins and minerals you'll be eating too, to supply your body with materials for good health. Lots of people also find another benefit worth having from exercise; it puts them in a good mood!

You don't have to be a natural athlete or fanatical sports fan to benefit.

When people talk about aerobics, they simply mean exercise which increases the body's need for oxygen. A sure sign of that happening is getting hot – and that's a simple target to aim for when choosing how active to be!
To be safe from overstrain, don't be competitive; take breaks, treat it as fun, don't go on when you feel tired.

Exercise experts agree that the most valuable exercise for almost everyone, no matter what their age or fitness, is **swimming**, because it uses many muscles in a situation where you are unlikely to hurt yourself. Three sessions of 20-30 minutes a week can improve your stamina, especially if you swim with concentration and don't just splash around.

Next best comes **walking**, provided it is brisk. It has the advantage that you can do it anywhere and every day, so although it doesn't have such a high rating for energy use, the amount you do will build up to something useful. Include some hills or stairs for maximum benefit.

Cycling is another exercise which many people can fit into their daily routine, so increasing its beneficial effect on their fitness. Mainly benefits the lower half of your body and, as you don't want to be schizophrenic – with a fit bottom, but flabby top – ideally combine it with another kind of exercise.

Bouncing on a mini-trampoline is a bit like jogging on the spot, with less risk of foot and ankle jar or injury, because you land on a surface that 'gives'. Exercises your heart, lower half of your body and shakes out tension.

Dancing: this doesn't have to be dazzling stuff to keep you fit. Ballroom, disco, folk or

Relaxation

How relaxed you are will affect both your attitude to food and the use your body can make of it. Anxious people don't digest as well and are more inclined to eat poorly, or to binge on sweet foods; both of which should be avoided.

Exercise of all kinds can help you relax, both by shaking the tension out of your muscles as you move and by giving your mind a rest. It must be exercise, though,

ballet dancing will all tone up muscles and heart capacity if done to the extent where you get hot and breathless.

Housework: varies in its exercise value. Scrubbing the floor and polishing are excellent; dusting is not so hot. Just going up and down stairs is good exercise. Put your back into the household chores: stretch, bend, rub hard, and you'll be toning muscles without realising it.

Exercise classes: certainly tone muscles and help use up calories. However, choose them carefully, avoiding anything that's intended for people fitter than you. Injuries are common and can plague you for a long time. The most important element of a class is proper attention to warming up muscles, so you don't jerk or tear them when you exercise.

Swimming is accepted as the ideal form of exercise. Jacuzzi baths don't provide exercise – although they are ideal places in which to perform stretching exercises, as your muscles will be very relaxed.

that keeps your mind fully occupied, so you can't carry on worrying at the same time.

Have You Considered?

✳ **Breathing lessons**: shallow breathing encourages anxiety and rations the body's oxygen supply. Deep breathing is essential to relaxation and can be learned from classes or tapes.

✳ **Yoga**: is one of the most widely-available relaxation techniques, particularly useful for breathing and for learning how to put problems in perspective. By increasing your body awareness, it can also encourage you to eat more healthily.

✳ **Massage**: can help you relax. If you live with someone, why not both learn and treat each other?

✳ **Relaxation exercises**: can be learned at classes or from books. Again, they emphasize breathing, but can also point out to you personal habits that bring

tension, such as the way you sit or stand, which you may be unaware of but which can be changed for the better.

✳ **Water therapies**: from Turkish baths, saunas, jacuzzis and sitz baths to health farm-type underwater massage and herb baths, can help your muscles relax with warmth and rubbing. Sitz baths, which alternate hot and cold water showers or put one half of you in cold water, the other half in hot, then change round, improve circulation, as do saunas which also alternate hot and cold.

✳ **Hobbies**: like gardening are relaxing in three ways. They use up your attention, so you can't worry about daily life; they provide fresh air, and they give you something life-enhancing and beautiful to think about. Looking after animals outdoors, bird-watching, flower-photography and watercolour painting are among other pursuits with these benefits.

Fit for Life

Yoga: to Balance Body and Mind

Here is a selection of yoga exercises for you to try at home. If you have a history of back trouble, either seek medical advice before attempting them, or work under the guidance of a qualified teacher. If you are a complete beginner, don't expect to be able to do them all correctly. Although you should naturally be putting effort into the postures, if you feel any pain while doing them, then stop straight away.

Remember, it takes years to become adept at yoga and even the most experienced enthusiast is likely to have difficulty with one movement or another. The photographs illustrate the kind of posture to aim for, but read the captions carefully in order to see exactly how you should be positioned. The very stiff, out of condition among you will not be able to do the forward bends very well – so just go as far as you can. And please don't be disheartened if that's not very far! Proficiency will come with practice. The very supple will probably find they can execute the postures better than our model!

The yoga exercises are divided into two parts. The first comprises a series of 12 movements which should be done in sequence. This sequence is called Salute to the Sun or Surya Namaskara, as it is known in Sanskrit. An effective, all-around routine, it is designed to stretch all parts of the body. It is traditionally done first thing in the morning (in the open air facing the sun – according to the climate!) and will revitalise and tone the entire body and mind, ready for the day's events.

Because this is a sequence of postures, the movements should flow naturally from one to another but each posture can be held for a couple of seconds or for a count of ten, depending on comfort. The idea is to start off with the feet in one place and end up with them in the same position.

Salute to the Sun

Position 1. Stand with feet firm and together, toes spread forward and comfortably positioned. The back and neck should be in a straight line so check you aren't hollowing your back. Release all tension from the body. Place the palms of the hands together in front of your chest and inhale slowly and deeply. Hold breath for a couple of seconds and then slowly breathe out. This simple, positive stance prepares you for the work to come.

Position 2. *(Not Illustrated)* Keeping legs straight, breathe in and tip your body forward

4

from the hips, stretching your arms straight out in front. Making a wide curve, take them back behind your head, stretching your torso back as they go.

Position 3. Keeping arms straight in front of you and knees stiff, breathe out while bending forward and reach towards the floor. If you have a stiff back and can only comfortably touch your knees, then don't strain further. If it is easy to touch the floor, bring nose and forehead to the knees.

5

Position 4. In a single movement, bend your right knee and stretch left leg straight behind while placing your palms either side of your right foot. Arch your back and stretch your head back at the same time. Note the toes of the extended leg are inverted. Keep arms stiff. Feel the stretch in the front of the neck, the extended leg, the toes, feet and hands.

6

Position 5. Dropping the head to the front, move your bent leg back to meet the other one keeping arms, back and legs stiff and in a straight line. Press down hard on hands and toes for support. This strengthens arms and wrists and tones the leg muscles. For extra pull on the calf muscles, try to push heels towards the floor.

7

8.

9.

Position 6. With your hands and feet in the same position, bend your arms and knees and lower your chest to the floor with your head between your palms. Check your breathing is correct at this point. You should be breathing *in*! Now breathe out and then *in* again as you go into the next pose.

Position 7. Breathing in, straighten the legs and lift your head up and back. Your arms should automatically straighten and your pelvic area be resting on the floor.

Position 8. Breathing out, supporting yourself with your palms and with toes pointing in, drop the head to the floor and arch your back into the 'mountain' position. Keep the heels down on the floor and advanced students can try to touch the floor with their heads.

Position 9. Bending the left knee, bring the foot forward to rest squarely between your hands. Keeping arms and extended right leg straight, with toes inverted, arch the neck, head and back.

Position 10. In one sweeping movement, bring right leg to meet the left foot and straighten legs keeping the torso dropped forward.

Position 11. *(Not Illustrated)* Breathe in deeply, keep arms straight and sweep them forward, up and back in a curve. Stretch head and neck back at the same time.

Position 12. *(not illustrated)* Breathing out, return to the starting position and stand with palms together in front of your chest, legs straight and head, neck and back in a straight, tall but relaxed line.

10.

Yoga Postures

Here are some more traditional yoga postures to try at home – and some postures that are based on yoga. Needless to say, you don't have to do the whole lot in one go! If you *are* trying several postures, though, take rests in between every three of four, in the 'corpse' pose. The object is not to exhaust yourself but to stretch, work and revitalise your body and mind. Always begin a yoga routine and end it with the 'corpse'.

Remember, never attempt too much – and if it hurts, STOP! Try to relax in a pose and *feel* the stretch. Attempt each pose only once unless otherwise directed. And don't rush. Just take each posture slowly, making sure you are in the right position first.

It would be ideal if you could get a friend to help you by reading the postures out while you try them.

The instructions are very important, especially since some of them are not suitable for people with back problems unless they are carried out under qualified supervision.

Do not attempt these postures after a heavy meal, otherwise you will feel sick. It is best to do them three hours after a meal.

A

1. The Corpse Pose. ★

This is the basic relaxation pose of yoga.
Lie flat on the floor, chin in line with pubic bone, feet a few inches apart and falling naturally outwards. Thighs do not touch. Arms are straight but relaxed and down, slightly away from the sides. Palms face upwards. (This has a more relaxing effect than when palms and fingers are touching the floor.) To relax the neck, shoulders and spine further, lift the head, tilt the chin slightly forward and drop the head back to the floor again. Breathe deeply a couple of times, then breathe normally.

> **The Star Guides**
> ★
> Easy
> ★★
> Medium
> ★★★
> Advanced

B

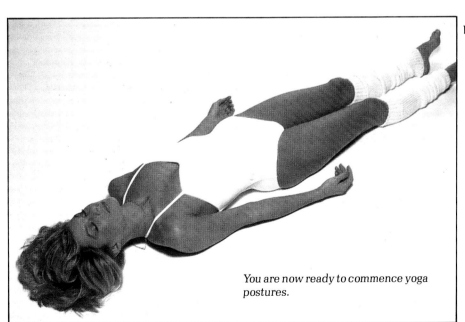

You are now ready to commence yoga postures.

2. The Revolving Triangle. ★★

Stand with feet two and a half feet apart. Knees are stiff. Bend forward from the lower back and, turning your head to the right, try to grasp the right knee (if your are a beginner) or the right ankle (if you are advanced). Advanced students can also try to bring the chest or head to the right knee. Twist torso and look up at the ceiling. With one movement, sweep round to grasp the left ankle (**B**). Great stretch for the whole body: shoulders, neck, back, waist, arms and legs!

3. The Spinal Twist. ★★

Sit with both legs straight out in front. Bend the left knee then, keeping the knee on the floor, draw the left foot round under the right buttock. Now bend the right knee and step over the left knee so foot rests on the other side of the left knee. Straighten the back and check you have all the directions correct so far. It is very easy to do this posture the wrong way. With your back straight, twist the trunk, neck and head round to the right, so the abdomen is pressed against the thigh. Put your right palm on the floor behind you so it is in line with your hips and legs. Bring your left elbow over your right knee and clasp your left ankle. Breathe in and out deeply three times. As well as massaging the abdominal muscles and intestines, this stretches the thighs, neck, waist and back. It also loosens the shoulder joints.

Remember to repeat the posture on the other side.

4. Knee Bend in Corpse Pose. ★

Lie in corpse pose and either ball hands or press palms down on floor for support. Exhale while pulling back and waist into floor. Bend your knees, join the soles of your feet and inhale as you pull your knees apart and towards the chest. This is excellent for limbering-up the pelvic area and lower spine while stretching insides of thighs. Exhale and release.

5. The Cat Stretch. ★

Kneel on the floor, arms straight, palms down, with arms and thighs at right angles to the body. Inhale deeply, stretch head up and back and arch the body. Exhale, drop head down and arch the back up into a hump. Repeat several times. Very relaxing for the back, neck and spine. A good limbering-up pose.

6. Leg Flex in Corpse Pose. ★

This is not suitable for people with back problems since it puts pressure on the lower spine.
Stretch arms out to sides so they are in line with shoulders. Place palms down on the floor for support. Pull waist and back into the floor. Bend knees to join soles of the feet and, keeping them stretched out as much as possible, inhale as you try to lift your legs. Exhale as you release and return them to the floor. Repeat a few times.

A   B

7. Modified Version of Headstand. ★★

Kneel on the floor with elbows bent, hands forward. Resting body weight on right leg, keep left knee tight and, dropping the forehead to the floor, sweep leg up at the back. Point toes. Try to get a straight line through the body and don't sway over to the right. Remain in this position, breathing normally, for a few moments.

B. Bend the left knee and take the foot towards your head. Try and raise your left hip for greater stretch. Breathe normally. Return to original position and repeat both postures on the other side. Tipping your body upside down like this gets the circulation going and has a rejuvenating effect. Bending the leg stretches thighs and tightens buttocks at the same time.

8. The Dancing Pose. ★

Stand in a straight position, feet firmly on the ground, toes spread. Raise arms above the head and place palms together. Keep elbows bent. Now gently move your head and shoulders over to the right. Press palms together and squeeze. Repeat on the left side.

This posture is excellent for poise and balance. The palm squeezing also helps improve the bust. To further improve your balance, stand on your toes before raising your arms and completing the pose.

A variation on this posture can be done to strengthen legs and back, too. With your arms above your head and your back straight, very slowly bend your knees and go into a squatting position. Squat as low as you can while keeping your back straight and stiff.

9. A Variation of the Plane Pose. ★★★

(Previously shown in Salute to the Sun.)
Lie down with face to the floor, legs straight behind. Relax. Place your palms flat under your shoulders and invert your toes. Keep your chin on the floor. Now inhale and push your hands so your body rises and rests in a straight position. Arms are now straight. Tuck your tummy in and tense your legs so your buttocks tighten. Breathe out and slowly return to the floor again. This firms the bust, arms, legs and buttocks. It also strengthens the wrists and exercises the toes.

10. The Mountain Pose. ★★

With feet 18 inches apart, palms down in front of head (also apart in line with feet) raise buttocks. Keep arms and legs straight, knees tight. Push heels down to the floor. Try to lower head between arms to the floor (our model can't do this). This strengthens wrists and ankles, stretches calves and backs of thighs.

11. The Tiger. ★★

Take up position as at start of **9**. Drop head and bring left knee up to the chin. Inhale and stretch head back while taking leg up and out behind. Keep knee tight. Exhale, drop head and bring knee back to the chin. Repeat once, relax and do the posture on the other side. Tightens buttocks, stretches neck, legs and abdomen, relaxes the back and spine.

12. Tensing Posture. ★★

Start in the corpse pose. Now make balls of your fists and tense all muscles: calves, thighs, buttocks, arms and abdomen. Point toes, breathe in and exhale as you raise your legs, head, shoulders and arms. Keep arms and legs straight. Hold for a couple of seconds and release to corpse pose again. Relax totally. This posture tones all the muscles and then, through the releasing action, relaxes the entire body.

B

13. Full Spinal Twist. ★★

This is for advanced students and is a harder version of pose **3**. If you have short arms you will find it more difficult. Get into position as pose **3**. Now bend right forward from the lower back, put your left arm under your right knee and try to clasp your hands behind (as in pose **B**). Straighten up and twist around to the right. Now breathe deeply three times and repeat on the other side. An easier version is not to cross your right foot over the left knee.

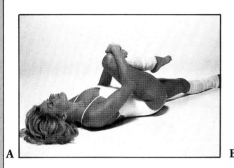

A

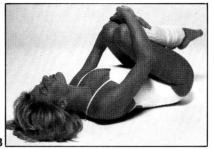

B

C

14. Preparation for the Plough and Shoulder Stand. ★

Lie flat on the floor in the corpse pose. Inhaling, raise one leg vertically and bend it to the chest, exhaling. Breathing normally, hold the bent knee and tug towards the chest. Hold pose. Repeat with other leg.

B. Now raise both legs vertically, inhaling, and bend them to the chest exhaling. Breathe normally. Grasp legs in both arms and hug to the chest.

C. Still grasping both knees to chest, inhale and exhale as you raise your forehead to touch your chest. These postures stretch and prepare the neck and spine for the Plough and the Shoulder Stand. They also massage the abdominal area and stretch thighs and buttocks.

B

15. The Plough. ★★★

If you have back trouble, do not attempt this pose without a qualified teacher present. This should be done to prepare the neck and spine for the Shoulder Stand. Beginners can try this pose with their hands supporting their backs.

Lie flat on the floor, palms facing down for support. Raise head, tilt chin forward then drop head back again. This will make the neck more comfortable. Slowly raise your legs to a vertical position, breathing in, then, very slowly take them over towards the floor behind you. Relax in a straight line, breathing out.

B. Breathing normally, take your feet to the floor behind you. Tighten knees and stretch the backs of the legs. Both these poses massage the neck, abdomen and chest area while stretching the whole spine at the same time.

To return to the original position, press palms down on the floor or in your back for support and gently lower the back and buttocks to the floor. Raise legs to the vertical position and slowly lower the spine and legs to the floor. This also massages the spine and tightens the abdomen.

16. Variation on The Plough. ★★★

Pressing palms down on the floor for support and breathing normally, stretch legs wide apart and hold. Scissor open and closed, keeping toes on the floor. Good for inner thighs and limbering-up the pelvic area.

A B C D

17. Variation of the Shoulder Stand. ★★★

For advanced students only. *If you have back trouble this should not be attempted without a qualified teacher present.* Lie on your back with arms down to sides, palms flat on floor. Raise head, tilt chin forward and drop head back again. Make sure your body is in a straight line. Pressing down on palms, breathe in and raise both legs vertically. Breathe out.

Now support your back firmly with your hands, breathe in and raise your body into the shoulder stand (**B**). Breathe out. You should now be supported by your shoulders, elbows, hands and neck. If you can't raise your legs into this pose from a straight position, then bend them first and straighten them up when you are on your shoulders. Breathe normally when holding pose.

To vary this posture, take your feet and legs slowly down behind your head, into the Plough. Move your hands out behind your back, for support, and 'scissor' your legs up and down, keeping the knees tight. (**C**).

Another variation (**D**) is to support your back with your hands and try to touch the floor behind your head with one toe. Stretch the raised leg back over your buttocks as far as it will go. Repeat with other side. Breathe normally while doing this pose.

The Shoulder Stand should only be attempted when the back is limbered up first. Benefits: revitalises the whole system, notably the head area. Especially benefitted is the pituitary gland which is the control centre of the endocrine system. By pressure in the neck area, the thyroid gland is also massaged. The whole system is refreshed and revitalised. **Not suitable before retiring.**

N.B. The Shoulder Stand should always be followed by **The Fish** *(not illustrated)*. The aim of The Fish is to stretch the neck in the opposite direction after it has been compressed. Slowly lower your back from the Shoulder Stand into the corpse pose. Relax for a few moments. Bend your elbows, place your hands under your back for support and raise your abdomen and chest while keeping the head on the floor. Now take your head backwards until the crown is resting on the floor and your neck is arched. Hold this pose for half the time you maintained the Shoulder Stand. Breathe normally.

18. Forward Bend with Side Stretch. ★★

In sitting position with legs wide apart, beginners hold left knee or ankle, inhale, and take right arm over head towards the left knee. Exhale. Look towards the ceiling trying to turn your chest and shoulders up at the same time. Advanced students put elbow on the floor inside the left knee, inhale and reach over to try and grasp the ankle. Relax in pose, breathing normally. Return to upright position and repeat on other side. Stretches waist and insides of thighs.

A B

19. The Leg Stretch. ★★★

Sit up tall with back straight, abdomen pulled in and legs wide apart. Bend right knee and tuck right foot in to touch the top of the inside left thigh. Rest right hand on right knee. Grasp the left ankle or the inside of the left foot. Keeping legs straight, inhale and try to raise your leg up (B) keeping knee tight, back straight. Hold. Exhale. Keeping hold of the left ankle or foot, inhale, raise left leg and take it across to the right . Excellent for inner thighs. Repeat on other side.

20. Variation on the Forward Bend. ★★

Remain sitting on the floor with legs apart, one leg bent. Face forward, back straight. Inhale, stretch arms to grasp knee or ankle and bend forward from the lower back. Beginners go as far as is comfortable. Advanced students can try to touch their knee with their forehead. Exhale. Relax in pose. Return to upright position and repeat on other side. Stretches lower back and pelvic area.

21. The Spider. ★★★

For advanced students only. *On no account to be attempted at home by those with back problems or neck trouble.* Lie flat on the floor, palms pressed down for support, or flat on the back. Raise head, tilt chin forward and lower head. This prepares the back of the neck for the pose. Slowly raise legs vertically and take them back to the floor behind, into the Plough. Now bend the knees either side of head, pressing them against ears.

A   B

22. The Sphinx. ★

This is a marvellous posture for flexing and strengthening the back and relieving tension in that area. *It is not dangerous for people with back trouble, providing they only go as far as they comfortably can and take things very slowly.*

Lie on your stomach with your face to one side, elbows bent, palms flat on the floor.

Stretching fingers out in front, move palms so they are either side of your forehead. Very slowly lift the head **(B)** and then raise the back as far as you can. You are now resting on your forearms. Move them for comfort, if necessary. Inhale deeply, expanding the stomach to the floor. Exhale and relax. Very slowly roll the chest back down taking the head to the floor last.

23. The Sleeping Thunderbolt. ★★

Advanced students can do this straight from The Fish. Return to the kneeling position, widen feet and sit between them. Some people will find this painful to do and they could put a cushion on the floor between their calves for

support. Supporting yourself with your hands on the floor, lie back between your calves. Fold your arms under your neck or head. Relax. This can be a beautifully relaxing posture to stretch the spine, shoulder blades, thighs, knees and ankles.

A   B   C

24. The Bow. ★★★

For advanced students only. *If you have back problems, consult a qualified teacher before you attempt this.*
Many people find this pose extremely difficult but when you master it, it's very invigorating. The trick is to be relaxed and to pull hard on the feet rather than trying to strain to lift the thighs. Do not tense the neck area. Lie on stomach, inhale and exhale. Grasp feet or ankles and, in inhalation, raise thighs, head

and chest **(B)**. Now try breathing deeply as you automatically rock backwards and forwards **(C)**. Relax to the floor and gently try to push feet to the floor either side
This posture is easier when the knees are apart.

This is a marvellous posture for toning and relaxing the arms, shoulders, back, buttocks, legs and ankles. It relaxes the pelvic area, strengthens the deeper muscles of the back. Now counteract this posture with The Swan.

25. The Swan. ★

This is a very relaxing posture and is often recommended for alleviating insomnia. Try it before retiring. It is a good, effective posture to counteract all backward bends. Kneel with your forehead on the floor and arms stretched in front. You could cross your wrists while keeping palms down.

A   B

26. Variations on the Swan. ★

Relax on knees and stretch arms out in front. Now take one leg straight back and hold. This limbers up the pelvic area, firms the thighs.

B. Now stiffen your elbows and raise your head and chest. This puts more pressure on the thighs and buttocks. Relax and repeat both postures on the other side.

27. The Pose of the Child.

Again this is a very relaxing posture which encourages sleep and counteracts backward bends. Unlike The Swan, hands are flat behind the buttocks or can be clasped at the wrists.

The yoga postures are now complete. Return to the corpse posture and relax!

Fit for Life
New Life... New Horizons

Every day all over the world thousands of babies are born. Yet for each couple, the birth of their own baby is a unique experience in their lives. Your baby is your own small miracle that grows during the space of nine months from the fusion of two minute cells into a fully-formed human being with his or her own special personality.

Embarking on parenthood is a great adventure for which few of us are fully prepared. In this book you'll find guidelines about preparing for a healthy pregnancy, about what to expect during the coming months and when you go into labour, and information about the first few weeks after the birth.

To all readers who are planning a family, I wish you great happiness and many years of satisfying and fulfilling parenthood.

To avoid confusion throughout the text, the pronoun "he" has been used when referring to the baby. This is not for any sexist reason, but simply to make it easier when talking about the mother and baby together.

Fit for Life
The Best Possible Start!

Before the arrival of effective contraception, most parents had little choice about when to have a baby or about how many children they wanted. But things are very different now and the majority of couples have the opportunity to prepare themselves in advance before their baby is conceived. There's no doubt that it's well worthwhile making sure that you are as healthy as possible before your pregnancy so that your baby has the best possible start in life, right from the moment of conception.

A strong, well-nourished mother and father are more likely to produce a healthy child than those who are badly fed or who suffer from frequent illnesses. For this reason, more and more attention is being paid nowadays to helping couples understand the simple rules of good health and to encouraging them to become as fit as possible before they embark on a pregnancy.

Your Emotions In ideal circumstances, every couple would be well-prepared for parenthood, both physically and psychologically. From an emotional point of view, this means that they have made a joint decision to have a child and are aware of the love and commitment which are involved, both to each other and the baby.

Having a baby involves a great deal of hard work as well as enormous pleasure, so it makes sense to read as much as you can about the changes which are likely to happen to you, both during pregnancy and afterwards. Talking to friends and relatives who are already parents can also help you to understand more about what to expect.

But it's probably not until you become pregnant that you begin to appreciate fully how much your decision will affect your lives. Bringing a baby into the world is a major landmark for most men and women, one that involves excitement, anticipation, responsibility and an awareness that their lives will be changed forever. Very soon there won't be just the two of you; before long you'll be a family of three – and more if you decide to have another child. So it's important not to underestimate the quite dramatic changes that parenthood brings, and to realise that things will never be the same again for you.

Being emotionally ready to have a baby involves other things, too. For many people it means having sufficient financial security to be able to afford the expense that's involved. After all, you'll need quite a lot of equipment in the form of clothing and nursery goods and perhaps extra space in your home to accommodate your child as he or she gets older. This could mean that you might have to move somewhere larger if you don't have room at the moment.

All of this can add up to quite a lot of money and, if you're unemployed or on a low income, it can be very stressful to look at the cost of everything you'll need. Many couples feel quite ready to make the financial sacrifices which having a baby brings and are happy to give up the mother's earnings, so that she can devote herself to looking after the baby when he or she is born. In a few cases, a couple decides that the father is in a better position to stay at home, especially if he is unemployed. This option of role-swapping is becoming more popular among people who feel that it's appropriate in their circumstances.

If you're single and planning to have a baby, as some women do nowadays, then you'll need to think particularly carefully about how you'll manage the dual responsibility of earning a living and being a parent on your own. Some women do cope successfully and those who manage best are able to call on a supportive network of friends and relatives to share the work, or else to make arrangements for good childcare if they plan to continue in their job. The same applies, of course, if you hope to carry on working after your baby is born, even if you do have a partner to help you at home.

All of these aspects need careful consideration and are an important part of reducing the amount of stress which you'll undergo when you become pregnant. Joy and excitement are in themselves a form of stress, even though they're pleasant ones, so if you can reduce the stress in other areas of your life before you conceive, then you'll find that you enjoy your pregnancy more – which can only be good for you and your baby.

The Right Kind of Food The kinds of food you eat before you become pregnant play a vital part in getting as healthy as possible, and this applies to your partner, too. This may mean changing the eating habits of a lifetime if you haven't thought much about your diet before. If so, you'll probably find it easier to make these changes gradually, rather than suddenly trying to switch over to a new way of eating.

The most important point to remember is to eat as much of your food as possible in its natural state, which means that it should be unrefined and unprocessed. In this way, you'll make sure that your body is getting the maximum amount of goodness with all the essential nutrients it needs. Here are some guidelines to follow:
* Eat plenty of fresh fruit and vegetables every day. One way of doing this is to include a raw salad with a variety of ingredients and a couple of pieces of fresh fruit in season. You can make fresh fruit and vegetable juices if you have an extractor or blender, but otherwise unsweetened natural juices are a good alternative.

Avoid removing the skins of vegetables such as potatoes; they simply need to be scrubbed well and cooked. Steaming and baking are good ways of preserving vitamins and minerals, but if you boil your vegetables, then keep the cooking time to a minimum and use as little water as possible. Keep the cooking liquid to make stock for soups and sauces.
* Make sure you eat enough protein every day. Good sources of protein include fresh meat and fish and dairy foods such as milk, eggs, cheese, yogurt and so on. If you are vegetarian, you can obtain good quality protein by mixing wholegrain cereals and pulses in your meals.

There are plenty of pulses to choose from. They include all kinds of kidney beans, soya beans, lentils, split peas, chickpeas, mung and aduki beans and so on. Other good sources of protein, plus vitamins and minerals, include nuts and sunflower, sesame and pumpkin seeds, which also make ideal snacks when you're feeling hungry.
* Try to make sure that all the cereal foods you eat are unrefined. This means using wholewheat bread, crispbread, rolls, muesli and wholegrain breakfast cereals, such as Weetabix, Shreddies and others. Use wholewheat spaghetti, macaroni and other pasta products instead of the white varieties, and wholewheat semolina and brown rice. Try to use wholewheat flour for your home baking, too.
* You may not want to use a lot of fat or oil in your diet for health reasons, but it's important to have some of the right kind every day. Try to use polyunsaturated oils such as sunflower, sesame, corn, safflower or soya for salad dressings and cooking, and unsaturated margarine if you prefer not to use butter. If you follow the guidelines given above, you'll obtain sufficient fat anyway from many of the foods already mentioned.

By making sure that you eat a wide variety of these groups of foods every day, you'll obtain all the nourishment you need. It's important to make your meals as attractive and interesting as possible, so it's worth trying foods and recipes that you may not have thought of using before.

If you eat these kinds of foods, you'll automatically be excluding many of the less desirable ones, from the health point of view. Here's a summary of the main ones to avoid as much as you can:
* Any food containing chemical additives, such as colours, preservatives and artificial flavourings. These are found in many tinned fruits and vegetables, in preserved meats

and fish and in some frozen foods. It's a good idea to read the labels before you buy anything, so that you know what you're eating and can avoid unnecessary synthetic chemicals in your diet.

* Any food which is made from white flour. Refined flour has had the wheatgerm and the fibre removed from it, together with many important vitamins and minerals. So watch out for white bread, cakes, pastries, pasta, rolls, puddings and biscuits, and choose the wholegrain varieties whenever possible.

* Foods which contain white sugar. It's important to keep sugar to a minimum in your diet for health reasons, as it contains empty calories which just help you to put on weight. If you have a sweet tooth, it may take a little while to become used to the natural sweetness of fruits, but you'll gradually notice that you become more sensitive to the taste of fresh foods. Use raw sugar, honey or molasses for cooking if necessary – and in moderation.

These guidelines form the basis for a healthy diet for everyone, not just for expectant parents. Try to follow them as much as you can during your pregnancy, too, and later on after the birth of your baby.

Risks to Avoid Apart from eating well, there are other things you can do to improve your health, and it's worth embarking on this kind of a programme for three to six months before you try to conceive. Again, the following guidelines apply to both partners, so that you produce healthy sperm and egg cells when the time comes.

It's now well-known that smoking and alcohol reduce your resistance to illness and lay the foundations for many preventable diseases. So, if you do smoke, now is the time for both of you to give up – after all, you'll never have a better reason to do so! The same applies to drinking alcohol. It's generally believed that the occasional glass of wine won't do any harm, but it's sensible to keep drinking to a minimum or to cut it out completely, if you can. If you have problems with either of these two aspects of your health, talk to your doctor, who will be able to give you more advice or suggest where you can go for help.

Try to avoid all drugs, wherever possible. This includes prescription drugs as well as over-the-counter pills and medicines. If you do need medication for any reason, tell your doctor that you are planning a pregnancy, so that he or she can take this into account. Your pharmacist will be able to advise about commercial preparations so that you can choose the safest that are available. Herbal and homeopathic remedies are often a safe substitute during this period for minor illnesses and aches and pains.

It's known that environmental pollution affects our health and unfortunately there's not much that most of us can do about this, especially if we live in or near a large city with lots of traffic or industry. However, a good diet will help to protect you from some of the effects of pollution, so it's even more important if you feel you're at risk in this way.

If you've had any recent illnesses, it's worth discussing with your GP about the way they might affect your pregnancy. The same applies to chronic conditions, such as diabetes, arthritis, asthma and so on, or to any inherited disorders in your family. Your doctor can refer both of you for genetic counselling so that you can assess any risks involved in your pregnancy.

Check that you're immune to rubella (German measles), which can cause defects in the baby if you develop the disease during the first three months of pregnancy. A simple blood test will tell if you are immune, and you can be inoculated in advance if you aren't.

If you've been taking the contraceptive pill, it's sensible to change to another method during this period of preparation. The best alternative is a barrier method, such as the sheath or diaphragm, so that your natural hormonal rhythms have a chance to become well-established before you become pregnant.

If you've had a recent miscarriage, your doctor will probably advise you to wait for up to three months before becoming pregnant, to give your body a chance to recover fully.

If you haven't been used to taking much exercise up to now, think about ways in which you can begin to get in trim. Walking, swimming, jogging, yoga and

dancing are all easy ways to tone up your muscles and improve your health generally before you conceive. The emphasis should be on regular exercise which you find enjoyable and easy to fit into your everyday life, rather than suddenly taking up strenuous activities which you aren't used to.

Problems in Conceiving Even with the most careful planning, some couples find that they don't conceive when they want to. The average length of time is around six months, although many are lucky and conceive much sooner than this. If you find that it's taking longer than you thought, then check that you're making love at the right time of your menstrual cycle. This means at about day 14, counting from the first day of your last period and assuming that you have a 28 day cycle. Some couples fail to conceive for very simple reasons, such as not making love at the right time of the month, or not frequently enough.

It's been estimated that about one in seven couples have difficulty in conceiving, and if you don't become pregnant after a year or so of trying, then you should consult your doctor for help. He or she can then refer you to a specialist for investigation, if necessary.

Many problems can be put right fairly quickly and only a very few women need to resort to the time-consuming and expensive last resort of in vitro fertilisation – the 'test tube' method. Remember that your partner may also need to undergo tests for infertility, as it's known that between 30 and 40 per cent of men may be affected when there is a problem in conceiving.

Fit for Life

Conception and the First 3 Months

Two weeks after your baby has been conceived, you will miss your period, and this is the classic sign of pregnancy. But many women are aware of other signs, especially if they have been pregnant before. One of the most common of these are feelings of nausea and sickness, which can begin even before you have missed your period.

About 70 per cent of all pregnant women experience some kind of nausea which usually stops by the end of the first three months, although in a few cases it can last throughout the whole of the pregnancy. It can be very distressing if it's severe, particularly if you are at work. Most doctors are reluctant to prescribe drugs to treat the problem because of the possibility of side effects and there are simple ways of coping which we'll look at later in this chapter.

Tiredness is a common symptom, too, and you may notice that you seem to need much more sleep than normal. The tiredness may occur at unusual times of the day, such as the morning or afternoon. If this happens to you, listen to the messages your body is giving you and try to rest whenever you have the chance. Just putting your feet up at lunchtime instead of rushing around to do the shopping, and going to bed early can combat the fatigue. Some women, on the other hand, become very energetic shortly after they conceive and feel they are ready to take on anything.

Going off certain foods or drinks is another well-known sign of early pregnancy. This might be something like tea, coffee or fried foods, as well as perhaps alcohol or cigarette smoke. Quite a few women experience cravings for particular foods and, if this happens to you, there's no harm in indulging them, unless they're among the kind it's better to avoid, as mentioned in the previous chapter.

You may notice that you want to pass water more frequently than usual. The reason for this is that as the womb begins to enlarge it presses on the bladder. By about the twelfth week of pregnancy this pressure stops, because the womb has risen up into the pelvis.

You may also notice changes in the sensitivity and appearance of your breasts very early on and these will continue as your pregnancy progresses. Your nipples may feel sore or tingling and your breasts might feel heavier and fuller. The veins often become more prominent and the nipples and surrounding areola become enlarged and darker in colour. Even at this early stage, your body is beginning to prepare for the vital task of breastfeeding your baby after the birth.

Pregnancy Tests Confirming that you're pregnant is a simple matter nowadays since the development of home testing kits. There are a number of these on the market and all of them are between 95 and 98 per cent accurate, as long as the instructions are followed exactly. Some of the tests are so sensitive that they can detect pregnancy as early as one day after you have missed your period.

The advantage of using a home kit is that you have the result very quickly in complete privacy. It's worth buying one which includes a second test, in case the first one is negative and you still think you're pregnant. If this happens, use the second test a few days later. A negative result doesn't necessarily mean you aren't pregnant; it could simply be that your body hasn't produced enough of the pregnancy hormone which is excreted in your urine to be detected by the test.

You can also have your pregnancy

confirmed by taking an early morning specimen of urine to your doctor. He or she will send it away to a laboratory for confirmation, which will probably take a few days.

Because of National Health Service cuts, however, some doctors are now refusing to carry out these free tests and may suggest that you return at about eight weeks, when the pregnancy can be confirmed by an internal examination. If this happens to you, and you can't afford the £5 or £6 necessary for a commercial test, you may be able to get a free one at your local family planning clinic if you are already a patient there.

Another less expensive alternative to a home test is to get one done by your chemist, which will normally cost in the region of £3 to £4.

Whichever method you choose, it's important to have your pregnancy confirmed as soon as possible so that you can begin your antenatal care straight away. By doing this, any problems which you may have or which are likely to develop can be spotted and treated early. If you haven't already seen your doctor for a free test, then now's the time to visit him to let him or her know you're pregnant.

Ask to make an appointment which allows you to have plenty of time for discussion about your pregnancy, to talk over any fears or worries you may have and to find out about the facilities for antenatal care and the delivery of your baby in your area. Your doctor will then arrange for you to make your first appointment at your antenatal clinic.

You and Your Partner You and your partner are probably feeling excited, overwhelmed and perhaps a little scared when you finally know for certain that a baby is on the way. It's common for many couples to experience a mixture of emotions, both positive and negative, and you need to remember that these are absolutely normal and that you shouldn't feel guilty about them.

This is a time when you should be feeling very close, but if you are worried about any aspect of the pregnancy or birth, these fears can often get in the way of your happiness. So do talk to each other, rather than keep these feelings to yourself. Worries can often be magnified when you try to bottle them up and they're always easier to cope with when you share them with another person.

You'll also need your partner's love and support during the coming months. After all, he's about to become a father and the more involved he is from the very start, the more likely you are to be able to work as a team when the baby is born.

Making Choices During these early weeks you'll have lots of questions about what's likely to happen during your pregnancy, labour and the birth of your baby, and you'll also have a lot of decisions to make. During the last few years, many women have come to realise that they have a certain amount of choice about the way their baby is born, and many doctors and midwives have become more flexible about meeting individual women's needs.

All of this means that you need to start thinking about where you want your baby to be born, whether you want to have drugs during your labour, what kind of antenatal classes you'd like to attend and whether you want your partner with you during the birth. The only way you can.

make these choices is by getting as much information as possible, and this means talking to the medical staff who are looking after you, by reading as much as you can and by contacting various organisations which exist to help expectant parents (listed at the end of this book).

Some women feel that they want to give birth without the use of lots of technology, drugs and medical intervention. Others believe that they will be safer with all of these and prefer to experience as little pain as possible during labour and birth. Deciding which group you belong to will help you to choose where you want your baby to be born. Basically, there are five options, although not all of them are universally available:

Home Only about two per cent of babies are born at home nowadays, but for healthy women who are expected to have a normal labour, it can be ideal. Research has shown that women who give birth at home usually feel happier and recover more quickly than those who go into hospital.

Not all areas have good facilities for home deliveries and you may need to be very persistent about getting what you want. By law, however, you are entitled to have a home birth and you only need a midwife to be present. For the birth of your first baby however, your doctor may recommend that you go into hospital.

Domino Scheme This is an arrangement where the midwife who looks after you during your pregnancy takes you into hospital when you go into labour and delivers your baby there. You can usually return home within six to 48 hours, as long as all is going well with you and the baby.

General Practitioner Unit Not all areas have GP units but many women prefer them to large hospitals. Your own GP or midwife delivers your baby in a smaller and more friendly environment and you have the advantage of personal contact with them throughout your antenatal care.

Maternity Homes With the current trend towards larger hospitals, there aren't many

of these left. Normally, your antenatal care is shared between your doctor and the clinic at the maternity home and you go in when your labour starts. Because of their small size, the atmosphere is usually less rushed and more personal than in large hospitals.

Consultant Maternity Unit These are in the charge of a consultant obstetrician and are always needed for women who are likely to have complications during their delivery. They have the full array of medical equipment at hand to deal with any emergencies which may arise. If you choose this or it is recommended for you, you will attend the hospital antenatal clinic where you will probably see a number of different doctors or midwives during your pregnancy.

Unfortunately, this system offers little continuity of care and you're unlikely to have the personal contact offered by the other options. Many women do, however, have satisfying deliveries and more and more hospitals are trying to offer a variety of styles of delivery, rather than a standard 'high tech' approach for all mothers, regardless of their individual needs. So it's quite possible to have a drug-free delivery in many of these units nowadays. Do ask how flexible the unit is before you make your final choice about this.

Your First Visit to the Clinic Your first visit to the antenatal clinic will probably take place when you're about 12 weeks pregnant.

Most clinics are attached to the hospital or unit where your baby will be born, although some group medical practices hold clinics in their own health centres. You may be able to choose shared care, which means that you see your own doctor or midwife for most of your appointments and only attend the hospital clinic occasionally for special tests. This can eliminate a lot of travelling and also offers more continuity of care.

At your booking-in visit, you'll be asked a lot of questions about your health, medical history, your family's health, your age, race, date of birth, your work and your partner's work, and so on. These are all important questions and help the staff determine whether you are likely to have any problems during your pregnancy and delivery, so don't feel that they are just being nosey. If you are planning a home confinement, they will want to make sure that you have the facilities which will be needed, such as adequate heating, hot water and so on.

You'll also be asked to undergo a few tests at this visit. For example, your urine and blood will be tested to screen for possible infections, for diabetes and protein, for rubella immunity and anaemia, and to classify your blood group. Your weight and height will also be measured and you'll be given an internal examination to check the size of your baby. You'll also have a cervical smear to rule out any abnormalities, and your blood pressure will be taken to make sure that it is within the normal range.

This visit gives you the opportunity to ask questions and to bring up any worries which you may have. It's a good idea to make a note of these before you attend, so that you don't forget them in the general activity of the clinic. If you have any strong preferences about your pregnancy and delivery, this is the time to discuss them and ask for them to be included in your notes. After the first visit, you will probably attend the clinic every four weeks until the 28th week, and then every two weeks until the 36th week, and after that weekly until you go into labour.

Pregnancy normally lasts for 40 weeks, counting from the first day of your last period, although between 38 and 42

weeks is quite normal. If you have a regular 28 day cycle, your baby will have been conceived around the 14th day after the first day of your last period. This means that by week four your baby will have actually been in existence for two weeks and will be developing from a mass of cells into an embryo consisting of three layers from which the body structures will grow.

By week six, you may be aware of the early signs of pregnancy already mentioned earlier in this chapter. The placenta which connects the baby to your womb is beginning to grow and the head is forming, the heart is beating and the legs and arms are developing in the form of limb 'buds'.

By week eight, your baby measures about one inch in length and all of his internal organs are in place, His face is recognisably human, with eyes, nose, ears, lips, tongue and the beginnings of milk teeth in the gums. He is growing at a remarkable speed, even though you probably won't notice any change around your tummy yet.

By week ten, the baby is beginning to move around quite a lot inside your womb, although you won't be aware of this until much later.

By week 12 he will be about three inches long and will weigh about an ounce. By now, you'll probably be aware of marked changes in your breasts, and it's a good idea to wear a well supporting bra to cope with the extra weight. Your body is working hard now to maintain the baby's development, so it's important to keep following all the rules of good health, including a well-balanced diet, sufficient exercise, plenty of rest and sleep and to avoid unnecessary risks.

You are entitled to take time off from work without loss of pay when you visit the antenatal clinic, so make sure you inform your employer that you're pregnant. You'll also need to decide about when you want to give up work. The rules about maternity rights are complicated, so if you aren't sure about your entitlements, contact the Maternity Alliance (see the address at the end of this book) or the equivalent organisation if you don't live in Britain.

This is also the time to make an appointment to visit your dentist for free dental treatment. You're entitled to free prescriptions, too, while you're pregnant, and women on low incomes are eligible for certain other benefits. Make sure you find out about these rights when you attend the clinic for the first time.

Common Problems Common problems during pregnancy in the early weeks for some women include a loss of desire for sex, and for others an increased desire for it. Occasionally, couples worry that the baby may be harmed in some way if they make love, but in a normal, healthy pregnancy there's no need to be concerned about this. However, if you have a history of miscarriage or bleeding, it may be advisable to abstain from sex until after the third month, when the pregnancy should be well established. If you have any worries about this, do talk to your doctor or midwife so that you can be reassured. Otherwise the ebb and flow of sexual desire during pregnancy is quite normal and most couples in a loving relationship find that they can cope with it quite successfully.

If you find it difficult to eat because of nausea or vomiting, you may find it helpful to follow these simple tips. Try to increase your intake of unrefined carbohydrate foods. These include wholemeal bread, wholegrain cereals, pulses, fresh fruit and starchy vegetables such as potatoes.

Avoid rich, fatty and fried food, including red meat, butter and full fat cheese, as these are harder to digest. Try to eat small, frequent meals, rather than two or three large meals each day.

When you feel sick, you don't want to eat anything at all, but try not to let your stomach become empty. Fruit and vegetable juices can often be tolerated and will help to provide nourishment for you and your baby.

A hot drink and some dry crackers taken before you get up in the morning can often help, so ask your partner to bring these to you while you're still in bed. Remember that if you've been eating well before you became pregnant, your body will have some reserves of nourishment to draw on, so try not to worry too much about this problem. By the end of the third month it will probably have stopped.

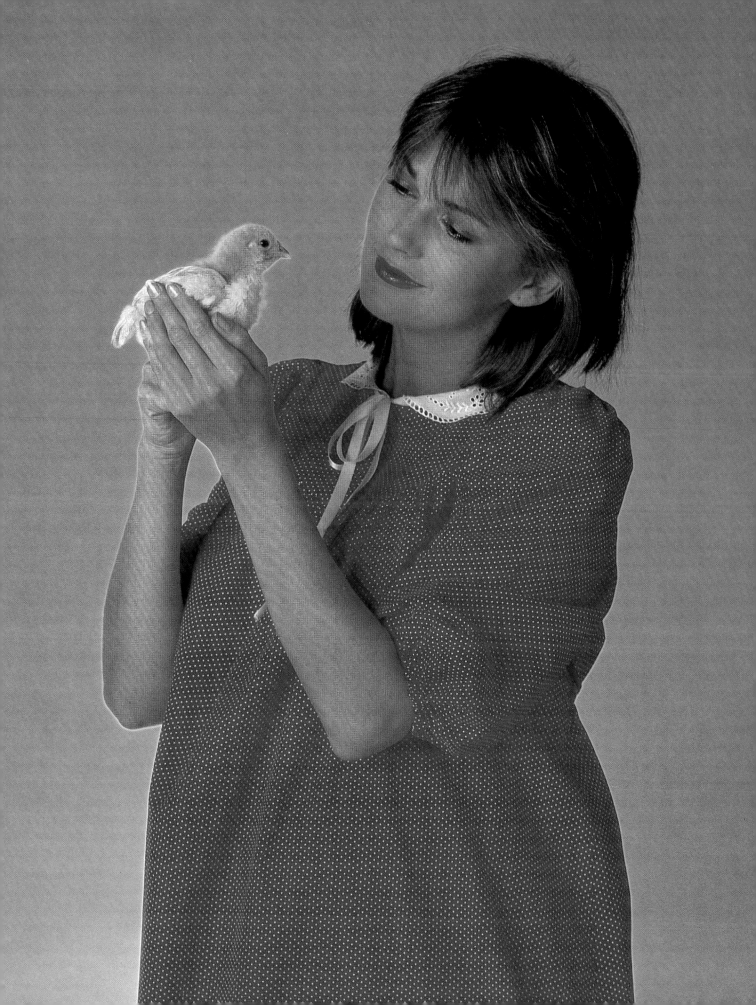

Fit for Life
Three to Nine Months

Pregnancy is divided into three stages, called *trimesters*, each of which lasts for three months. The second trimester, or middle three months, is the time when many women bloom and find they really begin to enjoy being pregnant. You may find on some days that you have lots of energy, but on others you may be tired, so do rest whenever you have the opportunity.

By the end of the fourth month (week 18), your baby is covered with a fine, downy hair called *lanugo* and his eyelashes and eyebrows are growing. His limbs are moving actively inside you and if you've already had a baby you'll probably notice these movements at around this time. You can recognise them as a light, fluttering sensation in your tummy, which first-time mothers often think is caused by wind. By the end of this month your baby is about eight inches long.

You'll notice by now that your waistline is expanding and, although your 'bump' isn't very large, you'll need to think about buying maternity clothes. Quite a lot of women start to develop stretchmarks, which are seen as pink or bluish lines around the tummy, thighs and breasts. These fade after the baby is born and become silvery white, although they never completely disappear.

By week 16, you may notice that your breasts are producing a colourless fluid known as *colostrum*, which can be expressed from the nipples. This will continue until about three days after the baby is born and is a valuable source of nutrition and protection for him until your breastmilk comes in.

During the fifth month, your baby develops a greasy, protective substance all over his body, called *vernix caseosa*. Soft hair begins to grow on his head, and his lungs develop and mature. By about week 20 his growth begins to accelerate and by week 22 he will weigh about a pound and will be about 11 inches long.

If you haven't felt your baby moving before, then you certainly will by about week 20. You'll probably have put on about a stone in weight, although women vary considerably in the amount and rate at

which they gain weight during pregnancy. On average, 20 to 30 pounds is the usual total weight gain, but some women put on less and others quite a lot more. As long as you are eating well, there's no need to worry about your weight. Your appetite is the best guide to the amount of food you should be eating. Remember that it's a myth that you need to eat for two during your pregnancy. If you have any worries about your weight, however, do talk to your doctor, midwife or dietitian for advice.

Your baby continues to grow very rapidly during the sixth month and by week 26 he weighs about 1¾ pounds and is about 13 inches long. It's not until later that he begins to develop body fat, so if you were able to see him now he would look very skinny. Babies born as early as 24 weeks have been known to survive in a few cases with skilled and dedicated care.

You'll probably find that during the sixth month you'll need a good support bra to accommodate the extra weight of your breasts. Your tummy will be quite large now, too, because your womb will have risen up from the pelvis and will reach just above your navel, or even higher if you're carrying a large baby or twins. The baby's heartbeat will be quite audible with the aid of a stethoscope and you can ask your midwife to let you listen to it, too. It's a magical sound when you hear it for the first time!

By the end of the seventh month of pregnancy, your baby's skin will look red and wrinkled and some of the downy lanugo will have begun to disappear. He will weigh about three pounds and will be about 16 inches in length. There's a much better chance of survival for babies born after the 28th week nowadays, as long as they aren't handicapped or affected by birth injury.

By 28 weeks the top of your womb will be roughly halfway between your navel and the bottom tip of your breastbone. Your tummy will be very noticeable by now and your baby's movements will be quite unmistakeable. Your partner can also feel the movements by laying his hands on your tummy, and for many men this is the first time they are really aware of their baby's existence.

The eighth month is when most babies turn from the breech position in the womb (legs first) to the vertex position (facing downwards). This is the normal position for delivery. In a few cases the baby doesn't turn until just before the birth, and some babies are born feet or buttocks first, when it is known as a *breech* delivery. By week 35 your baby will probably weigh over five pounds and has begun to develop body fat, and has almost fully grown fingernails. If he is born around this time, he has a very good chance of survival.

Your tummy will be very large now and you'll probably notice that you're beginning to slow down because of the extra weight you're carrying around, especially during the summer months. The top of your womb will be as high as it's going to reach. You may find that you become breathless at times, because there is less room for your lungs to expand and your diaphragm is compressed. Sleep may also be difficult at night, especially if you have an active baby. If you find it hard to get comfortable, try putting a small pillow under your tummy while lying on your side.

By month nine you'll probably be relieved that you only have a few more weeks to go. Your baby may increase in weight by as much as half a pound each week. He has much less room to move than before, so he may seem a bit less active, although you'll probably notice tiny limbs pushing against the wall of your tummy, which are visible from the outside.

By about week 36, feelings of breathlessness are likely to disappear. The reason for this is that the baby's head moves down into the pelvis to prepare for delivery. If you've already had one or more babies, the head may not engage until just before the birth. Most women experience 'practice' contractions towards the end of pregnancy which are felt as an alternating hardening and relaxation of the muscle of the womb. They're called Braxton-Hicks contractions and are usually painless, although the first time you feel them you may think labour has started!

Because of the long months of waiting, you may notice that you feel slightly irritable or impatient and you may be tempted to take this out on your partner, which can make life difficult for both of you. It's important to understand this and to talk about it between you, so that you can avoid any unnecessary friction just at a time when you need each other's support. Extra rest and sleep at this time are also very important – you'll need all your energy and strength for when you finally go into labour.

Looking Your Best Some women take a great pride in their changing shape during pregnancy, while others feel ungainly and clumsy and try to hide their body. Whichever group you fall into, it's a good

idea to try to make the most of yourself so that you feel you look your best, regardless of the size of your tummy.

If you can afford it, it's worth investing in a few attractive items of maternity wear. These can be whatever you feel most comfortable in and which suit your lifestyle. If you are going out to work, you can ring the changes with two or three good maternity dresses or pinafores, made up in fabrics according to the season of your pregnancy.

Baggy sweaters, overshirts, tracksuits and dungarees are ideal to wear at home or for leisure, and you may be able to borrow items from your partner's wardrobe if you don't want to spend too much money on new clothes.

It's often possible to adapt your existing clothes by inserting elastic or velcro strips in the waistbands – another simple way of saving money. Choose natural fibres wherever possible, as synthetic ones can make you feel uncomfortably hot, especially in the summer. Small prints and stripes emphasise your expanding shape less than large ones.

Fashions for pregnant women have improved enormously during the past few years and there's now a wide range of outfits to suit your budget. So it's worth shopping around before you decide what to buy, because you'll be wearing these clothes all the time for several months. If you don't have a suitable coat, choose a loose fitting A-line style or a generously cut jacket so that you can add sweaters underneath for extra warmth.

Your centre of gravity changes as the months pass and you'll notice that you develop the characteristic pregnancy 'waddle'. For this reason it's sensible to buy low or flat heeled shoes or sandals. High heels are difficult to walk in at the best of times and when you're pregnant they're likely to make you even more unstable. Low heels will help to keep your spine straight and prevent backache, which is very common in pregnancy. If your feet tend to swell, particularly in hot weather, you may find that sandals with adjustable straps, canvas shoes or trainers with laces are the most suitable footwear.

There's a wide choice of maternity tights available now, but you may find that a larger size in a non-pregnancy brand will be adequate for most of your pregnancy. Cotton or wool socks are often a better option, as long as they don't constrict the blood vessels in your legs or ankles.

As far as underwear is concerned, the most important item you'll have to buy is a well fitting support bra. It's a good idea to go to a store where you can be properly measured by a trained fitter. She will recommend that you buy two or three with wide straps which don't cut into your shoulders, a deep band under the cups and an adjustable fastening to accommodate the extra weight you'll put on around the chest.

A good bra will help to prevent the soft breast tissues from sagging, which often leads to stetchmarks. You may also want to wear a lightweight bra at night if your breasts become very heavy. Towards the end of pregnancy, you'll need to think about investing in several nursing bras if you plan to breastfeed. The best kind to choose is the type which opens in front, rather than the drop cup kind which can compress the breast tissue and milk ducts and may cause problems during the early weeks of feeding until your milk supply settles down.

It's worth paying special attention to your skin, face, nails, hair and feet, too, at this time. If you can, invest in a new, easy to manage hairstyle and an occasional visit to a beauty salon for a facial to lift your spirits when you're feeling low. Pregnancy often has a beneficial effect on a woman's skin because of the extra hormones circulating and you may find yours looks smooth and velvety. If, on the other hand, your skin feels drier than usual, soften it with a rich moisturiser and use a few drops of oil in your bathwater. Itching can be counteracted by rubbing almond oil into the skin and the gentle massage will help to ease irritation and improve the blood supply.

You may find that brown patches appear on your face and neck, especially in sunny weather. These can be disguised with a blemish cover and you can prevent them by using a sunblock cream when you're out of doors. The patches usually disappear by about the third month after your baby is born. Spider veins can also be a

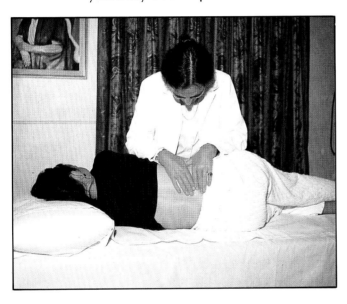

Special Tests Make sure you keep all your antenatal appointments throughout your pregnancy, because in this way any potential problems can be spotted early and dealt with. You may be asked to undergo certain special tests, of which the most common is ultrasound scanning.

This is a picture of your baby produced by bouncing very high frequency sound waves off his body and it's used to determine his age and size, your expected

minor problem – these are tiny, broken blood vessels under the surface of the skin. They also disappear in time.

Don't stop exercising in the later months of pregnancy, unless you feel it's too tiring. Walking, swimming and yoga are all good forms of exercise which help to tone the muscles and keep you in good shape right up to the birth. Some areas organise special antenatal classes in swimming and yoga and you can usually find out about these at your local public library or from your town hall. If you can't manage to get to a class, try to walk a couple of miles at a comfortable speed each day to keep yourself in trim.

date of delivery and to detect certain abnormalities. There has been some controversy about the safety of this procedure in recent years, and if you prefer not to have this test, you are entitled to refuse.

A special blood test known as *AFP screening* is carried out between 16 and 18 weeks. AFP (alpha fetoprotein) is a substance normally found in the blood in low levels, but if it is raised it may indicate that the baby has an abnormality of the brain or spine. If you have a positive result, your blood will be retested to see if it has gone back to the normal level. If it hasn't you may be recommended to undergo a

further test known as *amniocentesis* to rule out this possibility.

Amniocentesis involves taking a small sample of the fluid which surrounds your baby in the womb. This is done by inserting a special needle through your abdominal wall. The fluid can then be analysed to check for the possibility of various birth defects, including Down's syndrome and spina bifida (where the spine hasn't developed normally).

It can take up to four weeks before the results of the test are known and there is a slight risk of miscarriage associated with it, so you shouldn't have to undergo it unless the advantages outweigh the disadvantages. It's often recommended for women over 35 or so, who have a slightly higher risk of having a baby with an abnormality, but if this applies to you, you have the right to refuse the test if you wish.

Making Choices As time goes by, you'll probably find that you have a clearer idea about what to expect when your baby is born. You'll have had the chance to make your decisions about whether you want drugs or not, about how much you want

the medical staff to control the delivery, in what position you'd like to give birth and whether you want to breast or bottle feed.

Some women nowadays make a record of their choices in the form of a *birth plan*. They write their wishes down in the form of a letter after discussion with their medical advisers, and ask for this to be filed with their notes so that the staff delivering the baby know how the parents feel. If you have any strong preferences about your labour, this is a good way to make your wishes known in advance, rather than trying to communicate them at a time when you're concentrating on other things.

Your Relationship Pregnancy is a time of ups and downs in a couple's relationship, so it's important to be patient with each other. Your moods will fluctuate considerably, but if your relationship is basically sound you'll find that your pregnancy will bring you closer together. Try to talk to each other as much as possible and to share your doubts and anxieties.

The prospect of parenthood brings with it an awareness of the additional responsibilities involved and many men, in particular, can find this a bit daunting. Try to involve your partner as much as you can in what's happening to you, so that he doesn't feel left out. One very good way of doing this is for him to accompany you on some of your antenatal appointments and to attend fathers' classes, if they're available.

Pregnancy nearly always puts some kind of stress on a couple's sexual life, too. The most obvious reason is that your tummy simply gets in the way as you grow bigger. This means that you need to find different positions in which to make love, other than with the man on top. Some men are very proud of their partner's changing shape and want to make love more frequently, while others find her less desirable, with the result that they want sex less often. Some men are afraid of harming the baby in some way, but may not be aware of this fear. Your own moods and tiredness may make you feel less sexy at times, too.

If you feel that your sexual relationship is becoming a problem which you can't sort out between you, it's a good idea to talk the problem over with your doctor or a marriage guidance counsellor.

Feeding Your Baby Medical opinion is overwhelmingly in favour of breastfeeding young babies nowadays. There are many reasons for this, including the fact your own milk is perfectly designed for all the nutritional needs of your baby; it's convenient; it costs nothing, and it contains many important substances which help to protect your baby against infection during the first few months of his life. More and more mothers are breastfeeding their babies at least for the first few weeks of life and there's no reason why, with the right help and support at the beginning, you shouldn't be able to breastfeed your baby successfully for as long as you wish.

If, however, you prefer to bottle feed, then no one should make you feel that it's the wrong choice. What is important is that you feel happy with your decision and that you have your partner's support.

What You'll Need for the Baby Towards the end of your pregnancy, you'll be thinking about the clothes and equipment you'll need for the baby and, if you work out the cost, it can come to a surprising amount. The kind of clothes you'll choose will depend on the season when your baby arrives, but you'll need to make sure that you have enough underwear and outer wear for several changes. You'll probably

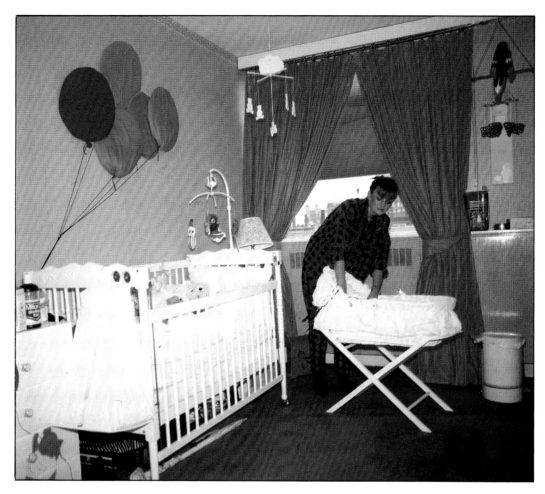

find that you'll be given quite a lot of clothing as gifts by generous friends and relations, so make sure you don't stock up on too much of the newborn size as your baby will outgrow these items very quickly.

Whether you use terry or disposable nappies depends on your domestic circumstances. There's not a great deal to choose between them when you take into account the cost of washing and drying if you use terry nappies. If you don't have a washing machine, then disposables are really your only practical option.

Your baby will need somewhere warm to sleep during the early months. Many babies sleep with their parents at the beginning, but are moved to their own room later. Make sure that the nursery has adequate heat day and night, as small babies don't retain their body heat as well as adults.

Certain essential items of equipment

have to be found before the baby arrives, including a small cot, a baby bath, a buggy or pram, bedding, toiletries and so on. You may be able to save money by buying secondhand or by borrowing from other people whose children are older. Make sure that any equipment you obtain in this way is safe, however.

If your baby is going to be born in hospital, it's a good idea to pack your case four weeks in advance, in case you go into labour early. Your midwife will probably give you a list of the things you need to take in with you. Apart from nightwear, underwear and toiletries, remember to take small change for the telephone, a needle and cotton, books or magazines, cosmetics, tissues, writing paper, your address book, stamps, towels and a shower cap. If you have all these ready, you won't be taken by surprise and have to rush around when you finally go into labour.

Fit for Life
Some Pregnancy Exercises

Many women think childbearing will spoil their figures and they'll never regain the kind of shape they had before. But the pregnancy experience could actually be turned to their advantage. If you are a little overweight, have got out of condition and into bad eating habits, then pregnancy is an ideal time to start exercising and balancing your weight through a healthier eating pattern.

Right now we are learning so much about the positive effects of physical movement and healthy eating, we may soon discover that many ailments attributed to the childbirth experience can be lessened or even avoided altogether.

Obviously the strain of carrying a baby puts a lot of pressure on the abdominal muscles, spine and pelvic floor. It makes sense to be in good shape before pregnancy, and to strengthen the abdominal muscles in particular.

If you try to get into good shape *before* you become pregnant you will find it much easier to regain your former shape – or even attain a better one afterwards.

Another sound reason for being in satisfactory physical condition before pregnancy is the fact that your legs will have to carry around so much more weight. For this reason, strong, healthy leg muscles will prove an asset. They'll improve circulation and fight against varicose veins. If you are supple around the hip and pelvic area, then this has to make the birth of the child so much easier.

After the birth, restoring your hard-worked body to good condition through sensible exercise is vital and may even help prevent problems with the pelvic floor in later life.

Here are exercises to try both during pregnancy and after the birth. Before attempting them, check with your medical supervisor that you are in good enough physical condition to embark on them.

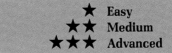

★ **Easy**
★★ **Medium**
★★★ **Advanced**

A.   B.   C.

Exercise 1. ★

A. With soles together, hands clasped behind head, pull elbows forward.
B. Now try to touch elbows together.

C. Raise right arm over head and touch left temple. Place left arm on left shoulder. Gently pull neck to right. *Repeat on other side.*

Exercise 2. ★

A. Sit upright with knees apart and soles of feet together. Grasp feet or legs.
B. Stretch neck back and to front again.
C. With hands resting on legs, raise shoulders towards ears.
D. Push shoulders down keeping ribs still.
E. With arms relaxed, stretch neck back again with mouth open.
F. Stretch neck with mouth closed.

A

B

C

D

E

F

Exercise 3. ★★

Keeping shoulders and chest open, raise one arm over head and down to meet other hand. *Repeat on other side.*

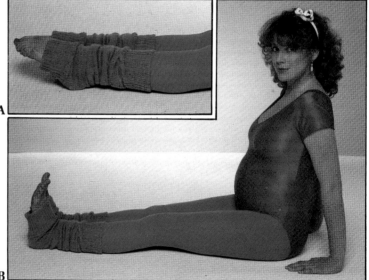

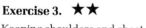

A

B

Exercise 4. ★

A. Sitting with legs in front, place arms on floor for support and point toes.
B. Now flex feet up. Repeat both exercises a few times.

Exercise 5. ★★

With legs apart, hands or arms clasped behind back, push forward from pelvis and lightly bounce downwards, flexing then pointing toes.

A

B

C

D

Exercise 6. ★★

A. Sit with legs crossed. Clasp hands behind back (or hold a handkerchief if your hands don't meet).

Repeat on other side.
B. Raising right arm above head, push right forearm down back from the elbow.

C. Take hands behind back and try to clasp hands in prayer position.
D. Now open out palms.

A

B

Exercise 7. ★

A. Sitting cross-legged, raise arms out to shoulder level with palms straight, facing down.
Flex hands upwards.

B. Flex hands downwards. Repeat a few times.

A

B

C

D

Exercise 8.   ★

A. Sit up straight with legs crossed, arms stretched forwards, hands flexed down.
B. Straighten arms above head.

C. Interlock fingers and stretch palms upwards.
D. Keeping arms raised, lean over to the right. And then lean over to the left.

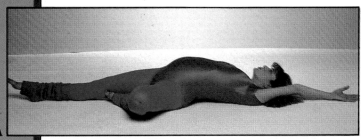

A

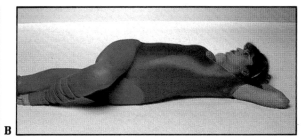

B

Exercise 9.   ★

A. Bend left knee outwards and raise left arm above head.
Repeat other side.

B. With hands behind head, shoulders on floor, bend one knee towards chest and take it over body. *Repeat other side.*

A

B

C

Exercise 10. ★★

A. Lie on floor with both knees bent. Now bend right knee to chest.

B. Now straighten leg and gently pull towards body, pointing foot.
C. Flex foot. Repeat sequence other side.

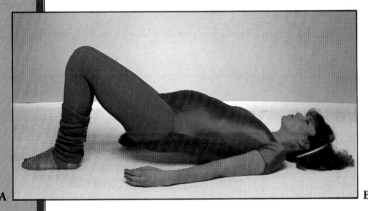

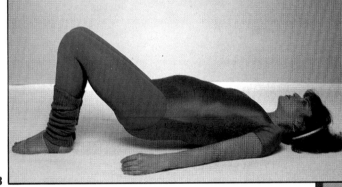

A

B

Exercise 11. ★

A. With knees bent and hands down to sides for support, gently raise buttocks upwards in small movements. Weight is on shoulders.
B. Lower slightly and repeat.

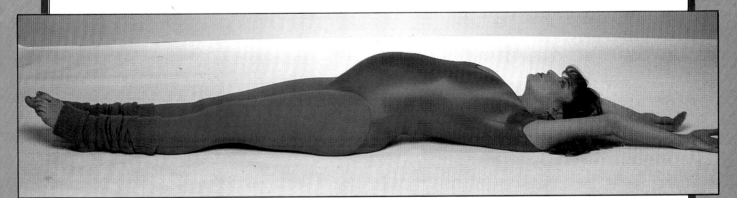

Exercise 12. ★

Lie flat on floor, feet together, arms above head and stretch out legs and arms.
Relax and repeat.

Exercise 13. ★★

A. Still with legs apart, place arms straight in front on floor and push forward from the pelvis. Point toes.

B. Turn hands to face each other, bend elbows outwards, flex feet and push forward from pelvis.

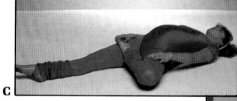

Exercise 14. ★★

A. Lie flat on floor, spine straight and comfortable with right leg extended. Place arms around left leg and gently pull towards chest.

B. Place left foot on right leg.
C. Gently push knee to floor.
Repeat sequence on other side.

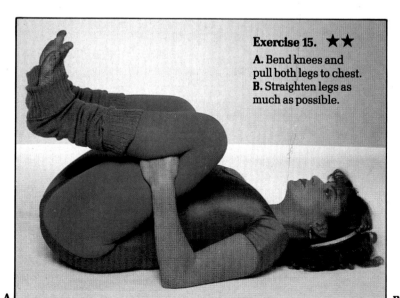

Exercise 15. ★★

A. Bend knees and pull both legs to chest.
B. Straighten legs as much as possible.

A   B   C   D

Exercise 16. ★★

A. Cross arms behind waist and step forward.
B. Bend knee slightly and lean forward.

C. Bend to knee as far as is comfortable.
D. Straighten knee and try to bend to right-angle keeping back straight.

A   B

Exercise 17. ★★

A. Sit on floor with left foot bent inwards. Take right foot over to outside of left knee. Place left hand on the floor behind. Put right hand on right foot.

B. Change position of arms and pull round to opposite side.

Repeat sequence on other side.

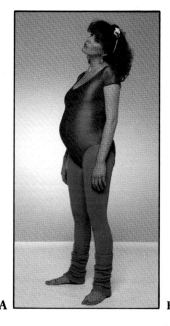

Exercise 18. ★

A. With legs apart, arms down to sides, let neck fall down to side.
Repeat other side.

Exercise 19. ★

Drop forward bending knees and slowly roll back up using the spine.

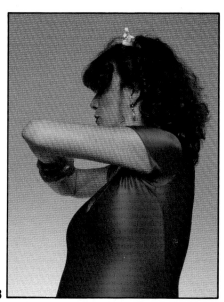

Exercise 20. ★

A. Stand with hands clasped in front, elbows out to right-angles.
B. Pull around to one side, then the other.

Exercise 21. ★★

Stand with legs apart. Take left hand as far as it will go towards left foot.
Repeat other side.

 A
 B
 C

Exercise 22. ★★★

A. Squat on floor with feet flat and hands clasped in front.
B. Straighten arms to floor and push forward onto toes, ten times.

C. With feet flat on floor, place hands behind feet.
D. Move hands forward either side of feet and pull head and body towards floor.

 A
 B
 C
 D

Exercise 23. ★★★

A. Kneel on floor supported on hands with arms straight, and bring left knee up towards chest.
B. Now take bent knee back and up.
C. Straighten bent leg out behind pushing up.

Return to **A** *and repeat sequence.*
D. Bend forward over knees and relax with head down, arms stretched out in front on floor.

 A
 B
 C
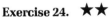

Exercise 24. ★★

A. Stand with feet apart, knees bent and stretch forward keeping back straight.
B. Swing arms to back. Repeat.

C. Extend arms in opposite directions and swing round to one side.
D. Swing round to opposite side.
E. Repeat **D** bending knees further down.

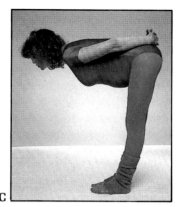

Exercise 25. ★★

A. With feet and hands apart, drop palms to floor. Walk hands back towards feet.
B. Hold position with hands near feet.
C. Straighten back to right-angle and clasp hands behind, arms straight.
D. Bend knees and bring arms to front with elbows bent and palms together.

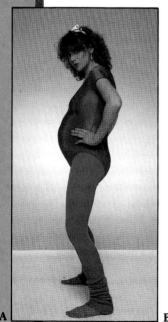

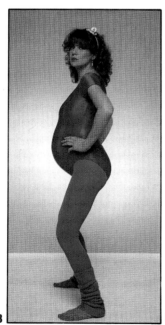

Exercise 26. ★

A. With feet apart, knees bent, hands on hips, tilt hips forwards.

B. Tilt hips backwards.
C. Bend hips to one side.

Then repeat other side.

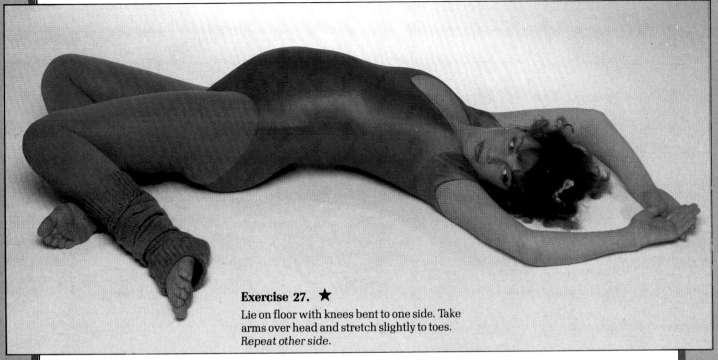

Exercise 27. ★

Lie on floor with knees bent to one side. Take arms over head and stretch slightly to toes. *Repeat other side.*

A

B

C

D

Exercise 28. ★

A. Stand up straight, feet slightly apart with elbows together in front. Point finger upwards.
B. Take arms apart.
C. Keeping elbows out at right angles, bring hands together.
D. Open arms out to sides, with palms open, level with shoulders.

Fit for Life
The Miracle of Birth

Before you go into labour, you'll probably have had the opportunity to look at the delivery rooms at the hospital. If you haven't been shown around, ask the staff to let you see where you'll have your baby so that you won't be going into a totally strange environment.

The standard delivery room in most hospitals is designed to meet emergency situations and is usually equipped with a high delivery table, bright lights, a gas and

hospitals, there may be a Borning bed in the room, which is a bed that can be adjusted to a variety of positions so that you can give birth upright if you wish.

Other hospitals may have a birthing room available, which consists of a low platform covered by a mattress on which you can sit or lie during your labour and delivery. This kind of room gives you the freedom to move about when you wish and to change your position easily, so that

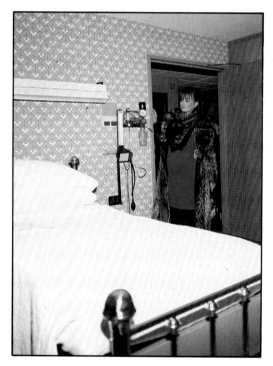

oxygen cylinder, a couple of trolleys with instruments for delivery and a cot for the baby. Other emergency equipment may be kept outside the room.

Some hospitals are providing alternative types of delivery room in response to the demand from many women for a more natural birth. In a few

you feel more comfortable, and is the sort preferred by women who want an active birth.

This term, *active birth*, is the name given to an approach to childbirth which has become widely known in recent years, largely due to the pioneering work of Dr Michel Odent. He believes, as do many

other doctors and midwives now, that pregnancy and labour are normal, healthy processes and that most women are capable of giving birth with a minimum of medical interference, as long as the emotional and physical support and the environment are right for the mother.

Active birth is a choice which more and more women are making because they feel it gives them more control over what happens to them when their baby is born. Being able to move around freely during labour helps you to cope better with the contractions and often means that your labour is shorter and easier than if you are lying on your back. You are less likely to need drugs for pain relief because the pressure of the baby is taken off your back.

Giving birth in an upright position, such as squatting or standing, helps your baby to be born more quickly because gravity is working with your body. You are also less likely to need a cut (episiotomy) to enlarge the vagina to allow the baby's head to emerge. The baby has a better supply of oxygen during the delivery, too, which means that he will be born in a better condition. In you are interested in this approach to childbirth, it's a good idea to learn about it in advance by going to special antenatal classes where it is taught.

Pain Relief Many women, however, are quite happy to accept drugs to help relieve pain during childbirth. Some plan to do without them completely in advance and then find themselves so overwhelmed by the intensity of the contractions that they are glad that the drugs are available to help them. Every woman's experience of childbirth is unique, so no matter how clear you are about what you want before your baby is born, be prepared to be flexible when the time comes and acccept whatever you need rather than suffer unnecessarily.

How much pain relief you want depends to a great extent on how you deal with pain normally in your life. You may generally prefer not to take a drug if you have a headache, for example, and try other ways of coping. On the other hand, you may be the kind of person who finds a drug the best way of dealing with a headache. Here's a summary of the most common methods of pain relief offered by hospitals during labour.

Gas and oxygen. This is a mixture of gases which you breathe in through a mask during a contraction and then stop as the contraction reaches its height. It only takes a few seconds to have its effect and if properly used it doesn't affect the baby.

Pethidine. This is an injection into a muscle or a vein in the arm. Some women find that it makes them feel sleepy or woozy, while others still feel the pain but don't care about it. One disadvantage is that it passes very quickly through to the baby and can make him drowsy or cause breathing problems after the birth. If you are worried about this possibility ask for a small dose first, and then a second one later if you need it.

Epidural. This is an anaesthetic injected into the space around your spinal cord in the lower back. It is usually very effective, but you won't be able to move around at all as the lower half of your body is numb. Disadvantages of this method include the fact that it doesn't always work completely; you are more likely to need a forceps delivery and an episiotomy; you may need a catheter to empty your bladder; you may be in labour longer and there may be an after effect, such as a headache. If you are having a Caesarean section, however, an epidural may be ideal because it allows you to remain awake while your baby is being born.

Relaxation and breathing exercises are the most popular ways of coping with pain without the help of drugs. If you want to try these methods, it's important to learn about them in advance by attending special classes during pregnancy. Your hospital may offer these classes, and most areas of the country have a branch of the National Childbirth Trust which offers regular courses of training in relaxation and breathing for expectant mothers.

When Labour Starts You'll know when you go into labour because your contractions will have started and will be strong and regular. For some women, the first sign of labour is when their waters break. This means that the bag of amniotic fluid which protects the baby during pregnancy bursts,

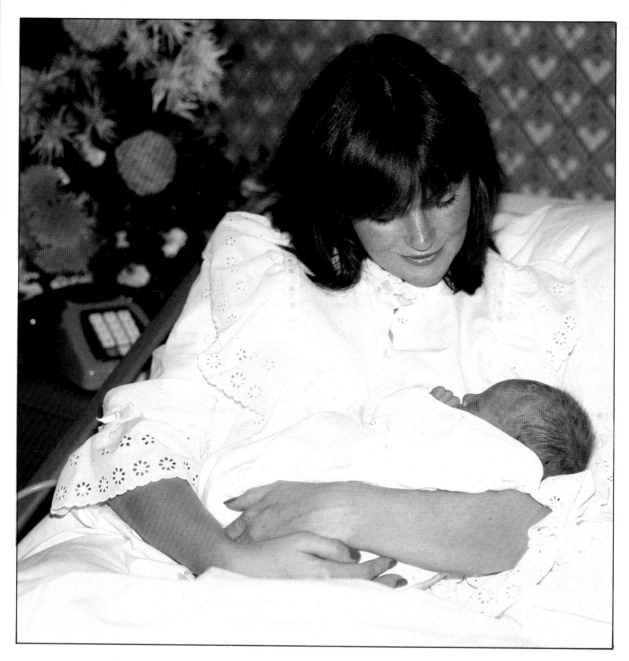

so that the water leaks or gushes out through the vagina.

Another early sign of labour is a *show*. This is when the plug of mucus which seals the cervix during pregnancy comes away. You'll recognise it as a pinkish, bloodstained blob.

Labour is divided into three stages, of which the first is the longest. During the first stage, your womb will be contracting and your cervix will be opening gradually in order to let the baby pass through the birth canal. The first stage can last many hours, although for some women it may be as little as three or four and for others as long as 36.

Some doctors and midwives prefer a mother not to be in the first stage for longer than 12 hours and offer drugs in order to speed things up. This may take the form of a pessary inserted into the vagina to stimulate the contractions, or a drip through a vein in your arm. A pessary allows you to get up and move about during labour, but this isn't possible if you're attached to a drip.

Your contractions will probably be about ten or 20 minutes apart and be very brief to begin with, but by the end of the first stage they will come every two minutes or so and last for about a minute. Let your midwife or hospital know when you think labour has started and they will tell you when to go into hospital, if that's where your baby is being born. If you're having a home birth, your midwife will call and check on your progress and probably stay with you until your baby arrives.

By the end of the first stage, your cervix will be fully dilated and will be about ten centimetres wide so that it forms a continuous passage with the vagina to allow the baby to pass through.

The Second Stage The second stage of labour begins when you feel the need to push your baby out. This may involve a lot of effort on your part, or you may find it quite easy, especially if you have given birth before. With each contraction, the baby's head comes further down the vagina, until the midwife sees it emerging. Once the head appears, she will probably tell you to stop pushing so that the baby slides gently out. If the entrance to the vagina is tight, she may make a small cut to enlarge it.

Once the head has been born, the rest of the baby's body follows quite easily. Your midwife may decide to wait until the umbilical cord has stopped pulsating in order to clamp and cut it, or she may do this immediately after the baby has been born.

The Third Stage Your baby should be given to you to hold straight away after the birth, and this is when the third stage begins. The placenta which has nourished your baby during pregnancy begins to separate from the wall of your womb and to slide down the birth canal. You'll probably notice another urge to push, and when this happens, the placenta will emerge in one large piece. The third stage can be speeded up if you put your baby to the breast straight away, as this stimulates your womb to contract.

Your Partner at the Birth For most women, their partner plays a vital role throughout labour and birth. The love, care and support that he gives you during the delivery can make all the difference to the kind of experience you have. He can help by massaging your back to ease the pain, offering sips of water when you feel thirsty and by communicating your needs to the staff.

If your partner can't be present at the birth, or if you're a single parent, you may want to have another companion to help you during labour. This could be a friend or a relative of your choice and you might want someone with you who has already had a baby of her own.

The birth of a baby is always a very emotional experience for both parents and is the beginning of a deep bonding which forms the basis of your life together as a family. Your partner should have the opportunity to hold his baby as soon as possible so that they can begin to get to know each other. Very often, however, the staff will want to examine the baby straight away to check that all is well.

Your Baby As soon as he starts breathing, the baby's colour changes from bluish to bright pink or red. He'll be covered with the remains of the vernix which protected him while he was in the womb and his head may appear slightly oddly shaped because of the pressure during delivery. This quickly goes back to normal a few days later.

The medical staff will check your baby's breathing, heart rate, muscle tone, reflexes and skin colour. His mouth and nose may be cleared of mucus to help his breathing and his body measurements will be taken. Once these checks are carried out and the baby has been cleaned, he will be given back to you to cuddle and feed. In a small number of cases, the baby may need to go into special care to be kept under observation or for treatment if there is concern about his condition.

Complications So far we've looked at what happens during a normal delivery, but it's important to be aware that things don't always go according to plan. Certain interventions may be necessary for medical reasons. For example, if your baby is thought to be overdue, you may be taken into hospital in order to be induced. This is done using a drip into a vein which contains an artificial hormone to stimulate the womb to contract.

Other common methods of induction include breaking the membranes surrounding the baby so that the fluid flows out, and inserting a pessary in the vagina.

However, it's useful to know that there are other simpler methods you can try yourself if you are overdue. Nipple stimulation by you or your partner can start

head so that he can be drawn gently out. This method usually leaves a bump on the head for several days afterwards.

Some women know in advance that they will need a Caesarean section when their baby is born. This may be because the pelvis is too narrow to allow the birth to take place in the normal way, or because the baby is in the breech position, or because the placenta is blocking the cervix so that the baby cannot pass through.

off contractions if your baby is ready to be born. The same applies to making love, as the male's semen contains the same substances that are used in the pessary for induction. So it's worth trying either or both of these before you go into hospital to be induced.

For difficult deliveries, forceps may be used to help the baby out. These look rather like large salad servers with rounded blades which are inserted into the vagina and are cradled around the baby's head. You'll need some kind of anaesthesia and also an episiotomy. An alternative to forceps is a vacuum extractor, which involves putting a suction cap on the baby's

In other cases, an emergency Caesarean may need to be carried out for urgent medical reasons, even though you had expected a normal delivery. Some women feel very disappointed when this happens and have strong feelings of failure. It's a good idea to be aware that there is a possibility you might need a Caesarean (about one in nine women do, and to learn as much about it as you can in advance so that you can cope with these feelings better afterwards. Recovering from a Caesarean takes much longer than a normal delivery and you'll need lots of help and support when you get home.

Fit for Life

Now we are Three!

Most first time mothers spend up to a week in hospital after the birth in order to give them time to rest and to get to know their baby. These early days are usually very emotional ones after the excitement and hard work of the delivery and you'll probably be very glad that the staff are there to take care of you and your baby.

If you've had an episiotomy during the birth, your stitches will have dissolved within a week. While the cut is healing you'll find it rather painful to sit comfortably and a rubber ring under your buttocks can give considerable relief. If you've had a Caesarean section, you'll probably stay in hospital for up to ten days after the delivery until the staff feel sure that everything is healing normally. Because this is a major operation, you'll find the first few days quite painful, so don't be afraid to ask for pain relief when you want it.

While you're in hospital the staff will examine you every day to make sure that your body is returning to normal. They will check to see that your womb is shrinking normally and will take your blood pressure regularly. Your breasts will be examined to ensure that your colostrum, and later your milk supply, are flowing and you'll be given internal examinations to make sure that any bruising or stitching is healing well.

There will be a bloodstained discharge (lochia) for a few weeks after the birth and this will be checked to rule out any infection. Your blood will also be tested to see if you are anaemic and you may be advised to take an iron supplement if the level is low. All these checks are routine and will be followed up by another six weeks later by your doctor, to make sure that you have completely recovered. If you are still experiencing any physical problems when you keep this appointment, do make sure you tell him or her about them so that you can get skilled help and advice.

Give yourself time to sleep while you're in hospital and, if possible, avoid having too many visitors to begin with. The ward is likely to be quite busy and noisy anyway and you'll be adjusting to a new routine with your baby. At first, he will sleep a great deal and just wake up for feeds. Many hospitals now have a rooming-in policy, which means that babies sleep in a cot beside their mothers, instead of being kept in a separate nursery. Because newborns need feeding frequently, you'll probably find that you'll be woken up several times during the night, so you'll need to catch up on your sleep at other times.

While you're in hospital, the staff will show you how to clean and bath your baby, change his nappy and help you with breast or bottle feeding. Most hospitals encourage new mothers to breastfeed their babies right from the start and will do all they can to overcome minor problems. Your milk will come in after the third day and you may notice some engorgement in your breasts until your supply settles down. Don't be afraid to ask for advice from the staff about anything that worries you.

Coming Home Coming home can be something of an anti-climax, and it's important to regard the early weeks with your baby as a time of adjustment to your new role as a mother. Your partner, too, will be adjusting to his new role and you'll both find that life is very different from before. You'll both be experiencing a mixture of emotions, ranging from excitement and passionate involvement with your baby, to feeling overwhelmed by your new responsibility and concern about his well being.

Many new mothers find they get a little depressed, too, and go through a period

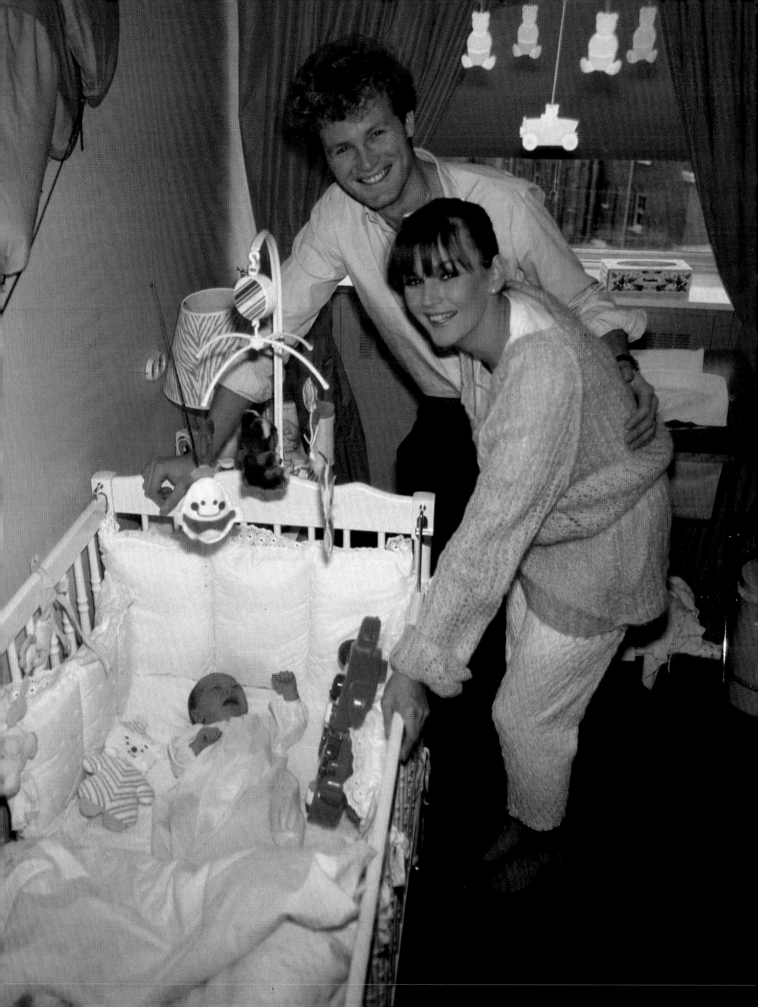

that's often called the 'baby blues'. Because of your natural preoccupation with your baby your partner may feel left out or confused, but if you can talk to each other openly during these early days and still communicate your love and care, these problems can be overcome before they become serious.

Caring for the Baby As the days and weeks pass, you'll find yourself becoming more confident in your ability to take care of the baby. He's unlikely to settle into a routine straight away and the biggest problem you'll have to cope with is tiredness. Sleepless nights can be a very real stress for both of you, so do accept all offers of help from your partner or from friends and relatives.

Cut down as much as you can on your usual household chores. Housework can be left to a minimum and what's more important is to put yourself, your baby and your partner first. Your body has gone through enormous changes and needs time to recover, and there's no point in overdoing things and wearing yourself out.

You'll probably find it easier if you have

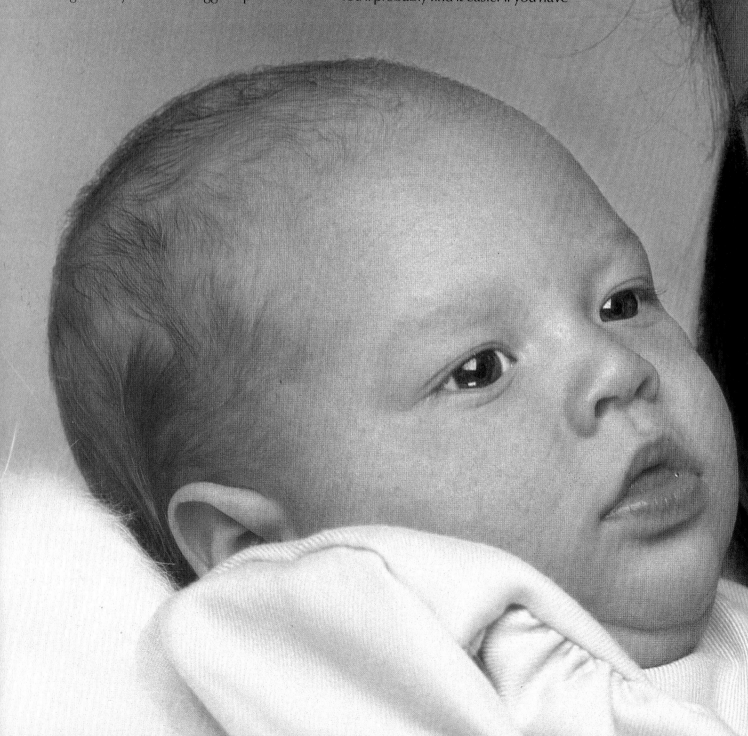

your baby sleeping next to you at night to begin with. In this way, you can respond immediately when he wakes to be fed. Many babies who are being breastfed sleep much more happily next to their mother in the same bed, where they can suckle whenever they want to, and this is often a good way to get a restful night. There's no danger to the baby as long as neither you nor your partner have had too much to drink or have taken sleeping pills, in which case you might not respond to the baby. Keep your pillow well out of the way if your baby sleeps with you, however.

If you're bottle feeding, you'll have been shown how to make up the feeds and sterilise the equipment whilst in hospital. It's essential to follow the instructions exactly and not be tempted to use an extra scoop of powder if your baby seems hungry. Your baby will thrive on breast or bottle milk exclusively for the first three or four months, as long as he is fed on demand.

Many of the problems mothers encounter over feeding stem from attempting to establish a feeding routine before the baby has settled into his own natural rhythm. So, if possible, let your baby lead you, rather than the other way round. Some babies take much longer than others to fall into a regular pattern of feeding and sleeping and it can be frustrating if yours is one of the more difficult ones. Do ask your health visitor for advice if you are having problems about this – she has lots of experience in helping new mothers and has been trained in the care of young babies.

Looking After Yourself While you were in hospital the staff will have taught you postnatal exercises to help tone up the muscles of your pelvic floor and abdomen. Try to continue these after you return home as much as you can to help you get back into shape. Don't be disappointed if you don't regain your pre-pregnancy figure straight away. You may not lose all the extra weight you've put on as soon as your baby is born because your body will have laid down additional stores of fat. Exercise, a well balanced diet and continuing to breastfeed for as long as possible will all help to shed any extra pounds you may still want to lose.

Until your figure returns to normal, you'll probably find that you won't fit into the clothes you wore before you became pregnant. If so, choose loose comfortable outfits at first to flatter your shape. Front opening dresses or blouses are the most convenient for breastfeeding, or alternatively you may prefer to wear a baggy sweater which you can lift up conveniently. A shawl thrown around your shoulders to cover the baby while you're feeding can help you cope with any feelings of modesty if there are strangers around and you'd like some privacy.

An Older Child If you have an older child, you'll need extra help when you get home because you'll have less opportunity to rest. Coping with a toddler and a new baby can make you feel that you're continually on the go, and this is where your partner's help and support are even more important. If possible, ask him to share as much of the care of your children as he can to take the burden off you. You can take it in turns to bath and change the baby and to look after the older one, who may be feeling resentful about the new arrival.

Jealousy is almost universal among youngsters when a new baby comes home, so it's important to make an older child feel extra loved and wanted at this time. You may find that a toddler becomes difficult to cope with because of his negative feelings towards the baby, so be prepared for this reaction and try to make a special fuss of him and include him in as much of the care of the baby as you can.

Many fathers try to take a week or two off work to help their partners when they come home from hospital. This is an important time for all of you, as it can help cement the relationship in your new family. Once he's returned to work, however, you may feel very alone and this is when it's important to feel that you have someone to turn to if things start to get you down. It's a good idea to stay in contact with other women you have met at your antenatal classes, so that you can share your problems with each other. Your health visitor can also put you in touch with other new mothers in your area, or there may be a postnatal support group you can contact.

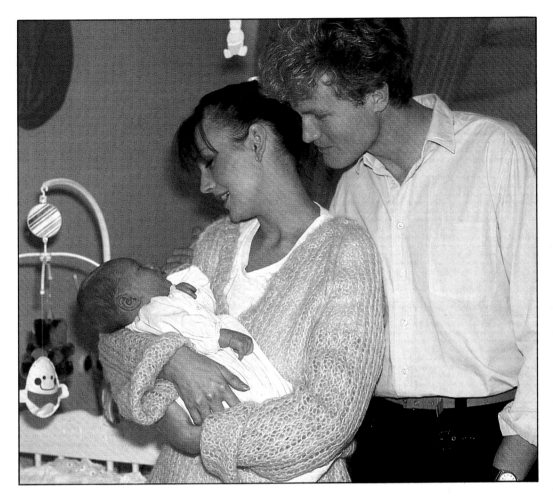

Just talking things over with other mothers can help to put a problem in perspective, and you can learn a lot from the experience of women who've had to cope with the joys and difficulties of looking after a young baby.

Making Love Many couples wonder about the right time to start making love after the birth of their baby. There's no hard and fast rule about this question and it's really a matter of when you both feel like it. Some doctors recommend waiting until after the six week check up, but if your stitches are healed and you feel physically well, there's no reason not to make love before then, if you wish.

Because of tiredness and other factors, some women feel put off sex for some time after the birth, while others who recover quickly are eager to resume it. The important thing is to be guided by your own feelings and, if your partner is patient and understanding, you should find that your sex life returns to normal in the course of time. If you find lovemaking painful or difficult, it's possible that you haven't healed properly, so do consult your doctor about this.

These early weeks will soon fly by and as you gain confidence as a mother you'll start to experience the deep happiness that comes from loving and caring for your baby. He'll be growing very fast and in a year's time will be crawling or walking around. He'll have changed a great deal from this tiny helpless creature that you've brought into the world, so do try to cherish these early days – they won't last for long!

Fit for Life
Recipes for Health...
Revitalize Your Jaded Palate

For most of us, eating is one of life's great pleasures, with delectable flavours and aromas, and bright colours and textures all stimulating our appetites. Unfortunately, these pleasurable aspects of food and eating often lead us to eat more than we need, and to crave for the wrong sorts of food. Wise decisions for healthy eating need to be made with some basic knowledge of nutrition.

What is Healthy Eating?
For optimum health we need a diet that regularly contains carbohydrates, proteins, fat, vitamins and minerals. Some foods are particularly rich in one nutrient, whereas others contain three or more. Each of the following nutrients is essential to the body.

Protein: for body growth and cell replacement.
Carbohydrate: for energy.
Fibre: aids digestion, and helps to prevent digestive-associated complaints.
Fat: concentrated source of energy; also provides vitamins A, D, E, and K.
Vitamin A: for healthy eyes and strong bones and teeth.
Vitamin B: necessary for healthy skin, as well as the digestive and nervous system and blood formation.
Vitamin C: increases resistance to infection, aids healing of wounds.
Vitamin D: helps strengthen teeth and bones.
Calcium: strengthens teeth and bones; essential to the nervous system, muscles, heart and blood.
Iron: maintains haemoglobin in the blood.

Generally speaking, we all eat a diet which is too rich in fat (especially animal fat), too high in refined sugar, too high in salt, and too low in natural fibre.

General Guidelines for a Healthy Eating Pattern.
Eat white fish, chicken, turkey and veal as the main protein meats.
Eat low fat cheeses, such as curd and cottage cheese, rather than the high fat cheeses such as Cheddar.
Use skimmed milk in place of full fat milk, both for drinks and for cooking.
Use the minimum amount of margarine or butter for spreading on bread or toast, and use olive oil for cooking wherever possible.
If dishes need sweetening, use an unrefined sugar or honey – people who are also trying to lose weight can use an artificial sweetener instead (choose a good one).
Choose breads and cereals which are rich in fibre – wholemeal bread, brown rice, wholewheat pasta etc.
Eat plenty of fresh fruits and vegetables, raw whenever possible.
Choose healthy cooking methods – poaching, baking, casseroling etc. If frying is a necessary stage in a recipe, use the minimum amount of fat.

Recipes
All the recipes have been put together in such a way that they not only offer a good balance of nutrients, but also follow the healthy eating guidelines listed above. They also taste delicious.

Fit for Life
A Flair for Fish

Smoked Haddock and Egg Quiche

PREPARATION TIME: about 25 minutes

This page: Fish, Courgette and Lemon Kebabs (top), Smoked Haddock and Egg Quiche (bottom).

Facing page: Provencale Fish Stew (top) and Baked Sea Bass with Fennel and Vegetable Julienne (bottom).

COOKING TIME: about 40 minutes

OVEN: 190°C, 375°F, Gas Mark 5

SERVES: 6 people

225g (8oz) wholemeal pastry
350g (12oz) smoked haddock fillet
Chicken stock
2 hard boiled eggs, chopped
15ml (1 tblsp) chopped chives
75g (3oz) grated cheese
300ml (½ pint) skimmed milk
3 eggs
Salt and freshly ground black pepper
   to taste

Garnish
2 hard boiled eggs
Finely chopped parsley

Roll out the pastry and use to line a 23cm (9 inch), deep fluted flan case; press up the edges well. Line with greaseproof paper and baking beans and bake 'blind' for 10 minutes. Meanwhile, poach the smoked haddock fillet gently in chicken stock for about 8 minutes, until just tender. Drain the fish and flake it, discarding any skin and bone. Put the flaked smoked haddock into the pastry case with the chopped hard boiled egg, chopped chives and grated cheese. Beat the skimmed milk with the eggs and salt and pepper to taste; pour into the pastry case. Bake for 30 minutes until the filling is just set. Meanwhile, prepare the garnish. Separate the hard boiled egg whites and yolks; chop the whites finely and sieve the yolks. The quiche can either be served hot or cold. Sprinkle the top with chopped egg white, sieved egg yolk and parsley.

Provençal Fish Stew

PREPARATION TIME: about 15 minutes

COOKING TIME: about 35 minutes

SERVES: 4 people

1 medium onion, finely chopped
2 cloves garlic, peeled and crushed
45ml (3 tblsp) olive oil
750g (1½lb) tomatoes, skinned,
   seeded and chopped
30ml (2 tblsp) tomato puree

600ml (1 pint) dry red wine
Salt and freshly ground black pepper
   to taste
1¼ litres (2 pints) mussels in their
   shells, scrubbed
8 large Mediterranean prawns
100g (4oz) peeled prawns
4 crab claws, partly shelled

To Serve
8 small slices stale French bread, or
   similar crusty bread
A little olive oil
1 large clove garlic
Bruised chopped parsley

Fry the onion gently in the olive oil for 3 minutes. Add the garlic and chopped tomatoes and fry gently for a further 3 minutes. Add the tomato puree and red wine and bring to the boil; simmer for 15 minutes. Add the mussels and simmer, covered, for 5 minutes. Add the whole Mediterranean prawns, peeled prawns and crab claws, and simmer for a further 5 minutes. Meanwhile, prepare the bread croutes. Brush the slices of French bread with a little olive oil and rub with the crushed clove of garlic. Grill until crisp and golden and then sprinkle with chopped parsley. Spoon the fish stew into a deep serving dish and top with the bread croutes. Serve immediately.

Chilled Fish Curry

PREPARATION TIME: 20 minutes, plus chilling time

COOKING TIME: about 6 minutes

SERVES: 4 people

225g (8oz) fresh salmon
350g (12oz) white fish fillet
Chicken stock
Salt and freshly ground black pepper
   to taste
150ml (¼ pint) mayonnaise
300ml (½ pint) natural yogurt
10ml (2 tsp) curry powder
Juice and grated rind of ½ lemon
100g (4oz) peeled prawns

Garnish
Sliced, peeled kiwi fruit
Sprigs fresh mint
Flaked coconut

Put the fresh salmon and white fish fillet into a shallow pan and add

sufficient chicken stock to just cover. Add salt and pepper to taste; cover and simmer gently until the fish is just tender. Remove the fish carefully from the cooking liquid and allow to cool slightly. Mix the mayonnaise with the yogurt, curry powder, lemon juice and rind, and salt and pepper to taste. Thin the curry sauce down a little with a small amount of the fish cooking liquid. Flake the cooked salmon and white fish and stir lightly into the prepared curry sauce, together with the peeled prawns. Arrange the chilled fish curry on a serving dish and garnish with slices of kiwi fruit, sprigs of fresh mint and a scattering of flaked coconut.

Plaice Tartare

PREPARATION TIME: 25 minutes, plus chilling time

COOKING TIME: 6 minutes

SERVES: 4 people

450g (1lb) plaice or sole fillets
Skimmed milk
Salt and freshly ground black pepper
   to taste
60ml (4 tblsp) olive oil
Juice of ½ lemon
2.5ml (½ tsp) soft brown sugar
4 anchovy fillets, finely chopped
1 large clove garlic, peeled and
   crushed
30ml (2 tblsp) chopped parsley
2 hard boiled eggs

Garnish
Small wedges of lemon
Green olives
Capers

Put the fish fillets into a large, shallow pan with sufficient skimmed milk to just cover; add salt and pepper to taste. Cover the pan and poach the fish gently until just tender – about 6 minutes. Meanwhile, make the dressing. Mix the olive oil with the lemon juice, sugar, anchovy fillets, garlic, and salt and pepper to taste. Stir in the chopped parsley. Separate the egg yolks from the whites; chop the whites finely, and sieve the yolks. Add the chopped egg white to the dressing. Drain the cooked fish and flake it; mix lightly with the prepared dressing. Cover and chill

Plaice Tartare (left) and Chilled
Fish Curry (below).

for 1 hour. Spoon the prepared plaice tartare onto serving plates; sprinkle each portion with sieved egg yolk. Garnish with wedges of lemon, green olives and capers.

Taramasalata

PREPARATION TIME: about 20 minutes

SERVES: 4 people

3 slices wholemeal bread, crusts removed
75ml (5 tblsp) water
100g (4oz) smoked cod's roe, skinned
1 large clove garlic, peeled and crushed
Juice of 1 lemon
90ml (6 tblsp) olive oil
Salt and freshly ground black pepper to taste

To Serve
Wholemeal pitta bread
Olives (black or green)

Note: for special occasions, serve the taramasalata in a hollowed, cooked globe artichoke. Trim and cook the globe artichoke in the usual way. Drain thoroughly, upside-down, and brush lightly all over with oil and vinegar dressing. Pull out the centre leaves and remove the hairy choke. Brush inside with a little more dressing and fill with taramasalata – the outer leaves can then be pulled off and dipped into the taramasalata. Soak the bread in the water for 10 minutes; squeeze the bread lightly between the fingers. Put the bread into the liquidiser with the cod's roe, garlic, lemon juice and 15ml (1 tblsp) of the olive oil. Blend until smooth, and then gradually blend in the remaining olive oil. Season to taste with salt and pepper. Serve with warm pitta bread and olives, or as suggested above.

Baked Sea Bass with Fennel and Vegetable Julienne

PREPARATION TIME: 30 minutes

COOKING TIME: 35-40 minutes

OVEN: 190°C, 375°F, Gas Mark 5

SERVES: 4-6 people

1 sea bass, about 1.25kg (2½lb) in weight, scaled, gutted and cleaned
Salt and freshly ground black pepper to taste
15ml (1 tblsp) chopped fresh fennel
1 large clove garlic, peeled and finely chopped
Coarsely grated rind of ½ lemon
30ml (2 tblsp) olive oil
60ml (4 tblsp) dry white wine

Vegetable Julienne
2 large carrots, peeled and cut into thin strips
3 stems celery, cut into thin strips
100g (4oz) haricots vert

Garnish
Feathery sprigs of fennel or dill

Season the sea bass inside and out; put the chopped fennel, garlic and lemon rind into the cavity of the fish. Lay the fish on a rectangle of greased foil, sitting on a baking sheet; pinch up the edges of the foil. Brush the sea bass with olive oil and spoon over the dry white wine. Pinch the foil together over the fish to completely enclose it. Bake in the oven for 35-40 minutes (the foil can be folded back for the last 10 minutes cooking time, if liked). For the vegetable julienne, steam al the vegetables over gently simmering water for about 10 minutes – they should still be slightly crunchy. Arrange the cooked sea bass on a large, oval serving platter, and surround with small 'bundles' of the steamed vegetables. Garnish with sprigs of fennel.

Sole with Anchovy, Caper and Mint Sauce

PREPARATION TIME: 10-15 minutes

COOKING TIME: 10-12 minutes

SERVES: 4 people

30ml (2 tblsp) chopped fresh mint
60ml (4 tblsp) dry white wine
60ml (4 tblsp) olive oil
1 large clove garlic, peeled and finely chopped
Juice of 1 large orange
15ml (1 tblsp) capers
3 anchovy fillets, finely chopped

Salt and freshly ground black pepper to taste
8 good size sole fillets
Seasoned flour
25g (1oz) butter

Garnish
Matchstick strips orange peel
Small sprigs fresh mint

Mix half the chopped mint with the white wine, 45ml (3 tblsp) of the olive oil, the garlic, orange juice, capers, anchovy fillets and salt and pepper to taste. Dust the sole fillets very lightly in seasoned flour. Heat the remaining oil and the butter in a large, shallow pan with the remaining mint. Fry the sole fillets for 2-3 minutes on either side (you will find this easier if you fry the fillets in two batches). Remove the cooked fillets carefully to a shallow serving dish and spoon over the prepared anchovy, caper and mint sauce. The sole fillets can either be served warm or chilled. Garnish with matchstick strips of orange peel and small sprigs of mint.

Fish, Courgette and Lemon Kebabs

PREPARATION TIME: 30 minutes, plus chilling time

COOKING TIME: about 8 minutes

SERVES: 4 people

16 small, thin sole fillets, or 8 larger ones, cut in half lengthways
60ml (4 tblsp) olive oil
1 clove garlic, peeled and crushed
Juice of ½ lemon
Finely grated rind of ½ lemon
Salt and freshly ground black pepper to taste
3 drops Tabasco
3 medium size courgettes, cut into ½cm (¼ inch) slices
1 medium green pepper, halved, seeded and cut into 2.5cm (1 inch) pieces

Facing page: Taramasalata (top) and Sole with Anchovy, Caper and Mint Sauce (bottom).

Garnish

30ml (2 tblsp) coarsely chopped parsley

Roll up each sole fillet, Swiss-roll fashion, and secure with wooden cocktail sticks. Place them in a shallow dish. Mix the olive oil with the garlic, lemon juice, lemon rind, salt and pepper to taste and the Tabasco. Spoon evenly over the fish. Cover and chill for 2 hours. Remove the wooden cocktail sticks and carefully thread the rolled fish fillets onto kebab skewers together with the courgette slices and pieces of green pepper, alternating them for colour. Brush each threaded kebab with the lemon and oil marinade. Grill for about 8 minutes, under a moderately hot grill, carefully turning the kebabs once during cooking. Brush the kebabs during cooking with any remaining marinade. Place the kebas on a serving dish and sprinkle with chopped parsley.

Fit for Life

A Shade Continental!

Noodle and Ratatouille Bake

PREPARATION TIME: 25-30 minutes	
COOKING TIME: 35-40 minutes	
OVEN: 190°C, 375°F, Gas Mark 5	
SERVES: 4 people	

1 medium onion, thinly sliced
30ml (2 tblsp) olive oil
2 cloves garlic, peeled and finely chopped
1 large green pepper, seeded and cut into cubes
1 large red pepper, seeded and cut into cubes
1 medium aubergine, cubed
6 tomatoes, skinned, seeded and chopped
15ml (1 tblsp) tomato puree
45ml (3 tblsp) red wine
Salt and freshly ground black pepper to taste
100g (4oz) green noodles, cooked
75g (3oz) grated cheese

Fry the onion gently in the olive oil for 4 minutes; add the garlic, red and green peppers, aubergine and chopped tomatoes and cook covered for 5 minutes. Add the tomato puree, wine and salt and pepper to taste; simmer gently for 10-15 minutes, until the vegetables are almost soft. Remove from the heat and stir in the cooked noodles. Spoon into a shallow flameproof dish and sprinkle with the grated cheese. Bake in the oven

This page: Wild Rice and Egg Scramble (top) and Pasta Shapes with Green Mayonnaise and Crab (bottom).

Facing page: Pasta Shells with Agliata Sauce (top) and Noodle and Ratatouille Bake (bottom).

for 15 minutes (alternatively, the dish can be flashed under a preheated grill).

Spaghetti with Sweetbread Carbonara

PREPARATION TIME: 10-15 minutes

COOKING TIME: 10 minutes

SERVES: 4 people

1 onion, chopped
45ml (3 tblsp) olive oil
350g (12oz) wholemeal spaghetti
Salt and freshly ground black pepper
   to taste
225g (8oz) calves' sweetbreads,
   blanched, skinned and chopped
90ml (6 tblsp) dry white wine
4 eggs
50g (2oz) grated Parmesan cheese
30ml (2 tblsp) chopped fresh basil
1 clove garlic, peeled and crushed

Fry the onion gently in the olive oil for 5 minutes. Meanwhile, cook the spaghetti in a large pan of boiling salted water for about 10 minutes, until just tender. Add the chopped sweetbreads to the onion and fry gently for 4 minutes. Add the white wine and cook briskly until it has almost evaporated. Beat the eggs with the Parmesan cheese, basil, garlic, and salt and pepper to taste. Drain the hot, cooked spaghetti thoroughly; immediately stir in the beaten egg mixture and the sweetbreads, so that the heat from the spaghetti cooks the egg. Garnish with basil and serve immediately.

Wild Rice and Egg Scramble

PREPARATION TIME: 10 minutes

COOKING TIME: 7-8 minutes

SERVES: 4 people

175g (6oz) wild or brown rice,
   cooked
15g (½oz) butter
1 small onion, thinly sliced
30ml (2 tblsp) olive oil
3 eggs

2.5ml (½ tsp) mixed herbs
Salt and freshly ground black pepper
   to taste

Garnish
Chopped parsley

Heat the cooked rice through gently with the butter. Fry the onion gently in the olive oil for 3-4 minutes. Beat the eggs with the herbs, salt and pepper to taste, and 15ml (1 tblsp) water. Add the beaten egg mixture to the onion and scramble lightly. Combine the hot rice and the scrambled egg and onion and serve immediately.

Pasta Shells with Agliata Sauce

PREPARATION TIME: 10 minutes

COOKING TIME: about 8 minutes

SERVES: 4 people

275g (10oz) wholemeal or plain
   pasta shells
Salt and freshly ground black pepper
   to taste

Sauce
90ml (6 tblsp) olive oil
45ml (3 tblsp) coarsely chopped
   parsley
2 cloves garlic, peeled
15ml (1 tblsp) pine kernels
15ml (1 tblsp) blanched almonds

Cook the pasta shells in a large pan of boiling salted water until just tender. Meanwhile, make the sauce. Put all the ingredients into a liquidiser and blend until smooth; add salt and pepper to taste. Drain the hot, cooked pasta shells and toss together with the prepared sauce. Serve immediately.

Chick Pea, Mint and Orange Salad

PREPARATION TIME: 15-25 minutes

SERVES: 4 people

175g (6oz) dried chick peas, soaked
   overnight and cooked

30ml (2 tblsp) chopped fresh mint
1 clove garlic, peeled and crushed
Salt and freshly ground black pepper
   to taste
Juice of 1 orange
Rind of 1 orange, cut into matchstick
   strips
45ml (3 tblsp) olive oil
Segments from 2 large oranges

Garnish
Fresh mint leaves

Mix the chick peas with half the chopped mint, garlic, and salt and pepper to taste. Mix the orange juice, strips of orange rind and olive oil together; stir into the chick peas. Lightly mix in the orange segments and garnish with the remaining chopped mint.

Spinach and Feta Cheese Lasagne

PREPARATION TIME: 20-25 minutes

COOKING TIME: about 35 minutes

OVEN: 190°, 375°F, Gas Mark 5

SERVES: 6 people

450g (1lb) cooked and drained
   spinach (or thawed frozen spinach)
Generous pinch grated nutmeg
Salt and freshly ground black pepper
   to taste
30ml (2 tblsp) natural yogurt
1 clove garlic, peeled and crushed
1 egg yolk
175g (6oz) Feta cheese, crumbled
225g (8oz) green or wholewheat
   lasagne (the non pre-cook variety)

Sauce
150ml (¼ pint) natural yogurt
1 egg, beaten
30ml (2 tblsp) grated Parmesan
   cheese
3 firm tomatoes, sliced

Mix the cooked spinach with nutmeg and salt and pepper to taste; stir in the yogurt, garlic, egg yolk and crumbled Feta cheese. Layer the lasagne and spinach mixture in a lightly greased ovenproof dish, starting with spinach and finishing with lasagne. For the sauce: mix the yogurt with

the beaten egg and half the grated Parmesan cheese; spoon over the lasagne. Top with the sliced tomato and the remaining Parmesan cheese. Bake in the oven for about 35 minutes, until golden. Serve piping hot.

Pasta Shapes with Green Mayonnaise and Crab

PREPARATION TIME: 25 minutes

COOKING TIME: 8-10 minutes

SERVES: 4 people

Green Mayonnaise
60ml (4 tblsp) mayonnaise
150ml (¼ pint) natural yogurt
45ml (3 tblsp) cooked spinach
1 clove garlic, peeled
Salt and freshly ground black pepper to taste
350g (12oz) pasta shapes – shells, wheels, twists, etc
Juice of 1 lemon
30ml (2 tblsp) olive oil

This page: Chick Pea, Mint and Orange Salad (top) and Spinach and Feta Cheese Lasagne (bottom).

175g (6oz) flaked crabmeat, or crab flavoured sticks, shredded

Garnish
Parsley sprigs

For the green mayonnaise: put all the ingredients into the liquidiser and blend until smooth. Cook the pasta shapes in boiling salted water until tender. Drain thoroughly and toss in the lemon juice and olive oil, adding salt and pepper to taste. Mix in the flaked crabmeat. Spoon into a serving dish and serve warm, garnished with parsley.

Noodles with Kidney Beans and Pesto

PREPARATION TIME:	5 minutes
COOKING TIME:	about 10 minutes
SERVES:	4 people

225g (8oz) wholemeal or plain noodles
Salt and freshly ground black pepper to taste
1 small onion, finely chopped
30ml (2 tblsp) olive oil
1 clove garlic, peeled and crushed
10ml (2 tsp) Pesto sauce (see recipe)
225g (8oz) cooked red kidney beans

Garnish
Sprigs fresh basil

Cook the noodles in a large pan of boiling salted water until just tender. Meanwhile, fry the onion gently in the olive oil for 3 minutes; mix in the garlic and Pesto sauce. Drain the cooked noodles thoroughly; add to the onion and pesto mixture, together with the red kidney beans. Stir over a gentle heat for 1-2 minutes and serve piping hot, garnished with basil.

Skillet Rice Cake

PREPARATION TIME:	25 minutes
COOKING TIME:	about 15 minutes
SERVES:	4 people

1 medium onion, thinly sliced or chopped
1 clove garlic, peeled and chopped
30ml (2 tblsp) olive oil
15ml (1 tblsp) chopped fresh thyme
1 red pepper, seeded and thinly sliced
1 green pepper, seeded and thinly sliced
4 eggs
Salt and freshly ground black pepper to taste

90ml (6 tblsp) cooked brown or wild rice
45ml (3 tblsp) natural yogurt
75g (3oz) grated cheese

Garnish
Chopped fresh thyme

Fry the chopped onion and garlic gently in the olive oil in a frying pan for 3 minutes. Add the thyme and sliced peppers and fry gently for a further 4-5 minutes. Beat the eggs with salt and pepper to taste. Add the cooked rice to the fried vegetables and then add the beaten egg; cook over a moderate heat, stirring from time to time, until the egg starts to set underneath. Spoon the yogurt over the top of the part-set egg and sprinkle with the cheese. Place under a moderately hot grill until puffed and golden. Serve immediately, straight from the pan.

Rice and Vegetable Loaf with Yogurt and Mint Sauce

PREPARATION TIME:	25-30 minutes
COOKING TIME:	53 minutes
OVEN:	190°C, 375°F, Gas Mark 5
SERVES:	6-8

1 small onion, finely chopped
30ml (2 tblsp) olive oil
1 clove garlic, peeled and crushed
225g (8oz) wild rice, cooked and drained (not rinsed)
3 courgettes, finely shredded
2 medium size carrots, finely shredded
30ml (2 tblsp) chopped parsley
Salt and freshly ground black pepper to taste
5ml (1 tsp) chopped fresh thyme
2-3 eggs, beaten
75g (3oz) grated cheese

Garnish
Fresh mint

Fry the onion gently in the olive oil for 3 minutes. Mix together with all the remaining ingredients, adding sufficient beaten egg to give a stiff yet moist consistency. Spoon the mixture into a deep, greased and lined loaf tin, smoothing the surface level. Cover with a piece of lightly greased foil. Bake in the oven for 50 minutes. Allow to cool slightly in the tin before turning out. Serve the rice and vegetable loaf cut into slices, and accompanied by the yogurt and mint sauce. Garnish with mint. For the sauce: mix 150ml (¼ pint) natural yogurt with salt and freshly ground black pepper to taste and 15ml (1 tblsp) chopped mint.

Chicken Liver Risotto with Red Beans

PREPARATION TIME:	15 minutes
COOKING TIME:	about 28 minutes
SERVES:	4 people

1 medium onion, finely chopped
30ml (2 tblsp) olive oil
1 clove garlic, peeled and crushed
175g (6oz) brown or wild rice
750ml (1¼ pints) chicken stock
Salt and freshly ground black pepper to taste
225g (8oz) chicken livers, chopped
25g (1oz) butter
175g (6oz) cooked red kidney beans
15ml (1 tblsp) chopped parsley

Fry the onion gently in the olive oil for 3 minutes. Add the garlic and the rice and stir over the heat for 1 minute, until the rice is evenly coated with oil. Gradually stir in the chicken stock. Bring to the boil and add salt and pepper to taste; cover and simmer for 20 minutes. Meanwhile, fry the chopped chicken livers in the butter for about 4 minutes, until sealed on the outside but still pink in the centre. Drain the chicken livers with a slotted spoon and stir into the cooked rice, together with the red kidney beans and chopped parsley. Heat through. Serve hot with grated Parmesan cheese, if liked.

Facing page: Chicken Liver Risotto with Red Beans (top) and Spaghetti with Sweetbread Carbonara (bottom).

Cucumber with Yogurt, Dill and Burghul

PREPARATION TIME: 25 minutes

SERVES: 4 people

90ml (6 tblsp) burghul
1 clove garlic, peeled and crushed
Juice of 1 lemon
60ml (4 tblsp) olive oil
15ml (1 tblsp) fresh dill

Salt and freshly ground black pepper
　　to taste
½ a large cucumber, halved, seeded
　　and chopped
30ml (2 tblsp) natural yogurt

Garnish
Coarsely grated lemon rind
Sprigs of fresh dill

Soak the burghul in sufficient
warm water to cover, for 10

**This page: Rice and Vegetable
Loaf with Yogurt and Mint
Sauce (top) and Skillet Rice
Cake (bottom).**

Facing page: Italian Pasta Pie.

minutes. Squeeze the drained burghul in a clean cloth to remove excess moisture. Mix the prepared burghul with the garlic, lemon juice, oil, dill and salt and pepper to taste. Stir in the cucumber and the yogurt. Spoon into a serving dish and garnish with lemon rind and dill.

Note: instead of mixing the yogurt into the burghul, make a well in the centre of the prepared burghul and spoon the yogurt into the centre.

Italian Pasta Pie

PREPARATION TIME: 35	minutes
COOKING TIME: 1 hour 5	minutes
OVEN: 190°C, 375°F, Gas Mark 5	
SERVES: 6-8 people	

600g (1¼lbs) puff pastry
450g (1lb) fresh spinach, cooked and
    drained thoroughly
175g (6oz) curd cheese
1 clove garlic, peeled and crushed
Salt and freshly ground black pepper
    to taste
Generous pinch ground nutmeg
100g (4oz) pasta shapes, cooked
    until just tender
75g (3oz) shelled mussels
15ml (1 tblsp) chopped fresh basil
1 egg, beaten
To Glaze Pastry
Beaten egg
Grated Parmesan cheese

Roll out ⅔ of the puff pastry quite thinly and use to line the sides and base of a loose-bottomed 18cm (7 inch) round cake tin; press the pastry carefully into the shape of the tin, avoiding any cracks or splits. Roll out the remaining pastry to a circle large enough to cover the top of the cake tin generously. Mix the spinach with the curd cheese, garlic, salt, pepper and nutmeg to taste, cooked pasta, mussels and the beaten egg; spoon the filling into the pastry lined tin. Brush the rim of the pastry with beaten egg; lay the rolled out portion of pastry over the filling and press the adjoining pastry edges together to seal. Trim off the excess pastry, and pinch the edges decoratively. Cut decorative shapes from the pastry trimmings and fix on top of the pie; glaze with beaten egg and sprinkle with grated Parmesan cheese. Bake in the oven for 45 minutes; cover with a piece of foil and cook for a further 20 minutes. Unmould carefully from the tin and serve the pie hot, cut into wedges.

Note: the top of the pie can be sprinkled with a few pine kernels prior to baking, if liked.

Fit for Life
Meals to Please

Chicken Moussaka

PREPARATION TIME: about 30 minutes

COOKING TIME: about 1 hour 5 minutes

OVEN: 190°C, 375°F, Gas Mark 5

SERVES: 6 people

60ml (4 tblsp) olive oil
1 medium onion, finely chopped
1 clove garlic, peeled and crushed
450g (1lb) minced raw chicken
30ml (2 tblsp) tomato puree
300ml (½ pint) chicken stock
30ml (2 tblsp) chopped parsley
Salt and freshly ground black pepper
  to taste
2 medium size aubergines, thinly
  sliced
150ml (¼ pint) natural yogurt
1 egg
50g (2oz) grated cheese
15ml (1 tblsp) grated Parmesan
  cheese

Heat half the olive oil in a pan; add the chopped onion and garlic and fry gently for 3 minutes. Add the minced chicken and fry until lightly browned. Add the tomato puree, chicken stock, parsley and salt and pepper to taste. Cover and simmer gently for 15 minutes. Lay the aubergine slices on lightly greased baking sheets and brush with the remaining olive oil; bake in the oven for 8 minutes. Arrange a layer of aubergine and then a layer of chicken in a lightly greased ovenproof dish; repeat the layers, finishing with a layer of aubergines. Beat the yogurt with the egg and grated cheese and spoon evenly over the top; sprinkle with the grated Parmesan. Bake in the oven for 35-40 minutes, until the top is bubbling and lightly golden. Serve piping hot.

Veal Paprika with Noodles

PREPARATION TIME: 10-15 minutes

COOKING TIME: about 1 hour 15 minutes

SERVES: 4 people

1 medium onion, thinly sliced
30ml (2 tblsp) olive oil
600g (1¼lb) boned leg of veal, cubed
Seasoned flour
15ml (1 tblsp) paprika
15ml (1 tblsp) tomato puree
Bayleaf
450ml (¾ pint) chicken stock
150ml (¼ pint) skimmed milk
Salt and freshly ground black pepper
  to taste
100g (4oz) button mushrooms, sliced

To Serve
Cooked green noodles

Fry the onion gently in the olive oil for 3 minutes. Dust the cubed veal lightly in seasoned flour and add to the onion; fry until the veal is evenly coloured on all sides. Add the paprika, tomato puree and bayleaf, and gradually stir in the stock and skimmed milk. Bring to the boil, stirring, and add salt and pepper to taste. Cover and simmer gently for 55 minutes. Add the sliced mushrooms and simmer for a further 10 minutes. Serve piping hot with cooked green noodles.

Veal Casserole with Apricots and Prunes

PREPARATION TIME: 30 minutes

COOKING TIME: about 1 hour 40 minutes

OVEN: 160°C, 325°F, Gas Mark 3

SERVES: 4 people

600g (1¼lb) boned leg of veal, cubed
Seasoned flour
45ml (3 tblsp) olive oil
1 large onion, thinly sliced
450g (1lb) fresh ripe apricots,
  skinned, halved and stoned
300ml (½ pint) chicken stock
300ml (½ pint) dry white wine
150ml (¼ pint) fresh orange juice
Salt and freshly ground black pepper
  to taste
75g (3oz) dried prunes, soaked
  overnight
75g (3oz) dried apricots, soaked
  overnight

Garnish
Matchstick strips of orange peel

Dust the cubed veal lightly in seasoned flour. Heat the oil in a pan; add the sliced onion and fry gently for 4 minutes. Meanwhile, put the halved and skinned fresh apricots into the liquidiser with the chicken stock and blend until smooth. Add the cubed veal to the onion and fry until evenly coloured on all sides. Gradually stir in the apricot puree, white wine and orange juice. Bring to the boil, stirring, and add salt and pepper to taste. Transfer to a casserole and add the drained prunes and apricots. Cover the casserole and cook in the oven for 1½ hours. Serve sprinkled with matchstick strips of orange peel.

Facing page: Veal Casserole with Apricots and Prunes (top) and Chicken Moussaka (bottom).

Turkey, Chestnut and Sage en Croute

PREPARATION TIME: 35 minutes, plus chilling time

COOKING TIME: about 55 minutes

OVEN: 200°C, 400°F, Gas Mark 6, and then 180°C, 350°F, Gas Mark 4

SERVES: 6-8 people

450g (1lb) minced raw turkey
1 small onion, finely chopped
45ml (3 tblsp) chestnut puree (unsweetened)
15ml (1 tblsp) chopped fresh sage
1 clove garlic, peeled and crushed
Salt and freshly ground black pepper to taste

45ml (3 tblsp) fresh brown breadcrumbs
1 egg, beaten
450g (1lb) puff pastry (preferably vegetable oil based)
Beaten egg to glaze

Mix the minced turkey with the onion, chestnut puree, sage, garlic, salt and pepper to taste, and brown breadcrumbs. Bind with the beaten egg. Form into a fat, cylindrical sausage, and chill while you prepare the pastry coating. Divide the pastry into two portions, one slightly larger than the other; roll out thinly on a floured surface into two rectangles, one slightly larger than the other. Trim neatly, reserving the trimmings. Place the smaller rectangle of pastry into a dampened baking sheet; brush the edges with beaten egg. Place the turkey 'sausage' in the centre. Lay the larger rectangle of pastry over the top, and pinch the joining pastry edges together to seal (the pastry should fit snuggly around the filling). Trim off excess pastry. Glaze the pastry all over with beaten egg and decorate with shapes cut from the pastry

This page: Turkey, Chestnut and Sage en Croute.

Facing page: Stir Fried Calves' Liver with Peppers and Carrots (top) and Veal Paprika with Noodles (bottom).

trimmings; glaze the pastry decorations. Bake in the oven at the higher temperature for 20 minutes; reduce to the lower temperature and bake for a further 35 minutes, covered with a piece of foil. Serve hot or cold, cut into slices.

Stir Fried Calves' Liver with Peppers and Carrots

PREPARATION TIME: 15-20 minutes

COOKING TIME: 10-12 minutes

SERVES: 4 people

30ml (2 tblsp) olive oil
1 onion, thinly sliced
600g (1¼lb) calves' liver cut into thin strips
Seasoned flour
60ml (4 tblsp) dry sherry
1 green pepper, seeded and cut into thin strips
3 large carrots, peeled and cut into thin strips
Salt and freshly ground black pepper to taste
1 clove garlic, peeled and cut into thin strips
100g (4oz) mung bean sprouts

Garnish
Sprigs fresh sage

Heat the olive oil in a large, shallow pan or wok; add the onion and stir fry for 3 minutes. Dust the strips of calves' liver in seasoned flour and add to the pan; stir fry until sealed on the outside but still pink in the centre. Add the sherry and bubble briskly; add 150ml (¼ pint) water or stock, green pepper, carrots, salt and pepper to taste and the garlic. Stir over a brisk heat for 3 minutes. Stir in the mung beans and heat through for 1 minute. Spoon into a serving dish and garnish with sprigs of fresh sage.

Chicken and Herb Loaf (top right), Chicken Andalusia (centre left) and Turkey, Cauliflower and Almond au Gratin (bottom).

Chicken and Herb Loaf

PREPARATION TIME: 20-25 minutes

COOKING TIME: 50 minutes

OVEN: 190°C, 375°F, Gas Mark 5

SERVES: 6 people

450g (1lb) minced raw chicken
90ml (6 tblsp) wholemeal breadcrumbs
1 small onion, grated
1 clove garlic, peeled and crushed
30ml (2 tblsp) chopped parsley
15ml (1 tblsp) chopped fresh thyme
1 medium parsnip, peeled and grated
2 eggs, beaten
Salt and freshly ground black pepper to taste

Garnish
A little olive oil
15ml (1 tblsp) chopped parsley
Sprigs fresh rosemary

Mix the minced chicken with the breadcrumbs, onion, garlic, parsley, thyme, parsnip, beaten eggs and salt and pepper to taste. Spoon the mixture into a greased and lined loaf tin. Cover with a piece of greased foil. Bake in the oven for about 50 minutes, until cooked through – test with a skewer. For a brown top, remove the foil for the last 8-10 minutes. Brush the top of the loaf with the oil, while it is still hot, and sprinkle with the chopped parsley. Carefully take the loaf out of the tin, and serve either hot or cold, garnished with rosemary.

Chicken Andalusia

PREPARATION TIME: 15 minutes

COOKING TIME: 45 minutes

OVEN: 190°, 375°F, Gas Mark 5

SERVES: 4 people

4 small poussins
Salt and freshly ground black pepper to taste
Olive oil
4 small wedges of lime or lemon
4 bayleaves

Sauce
1 small onion, thinly sliced
30ml (2 tblsp) olive oil
1 clove garlic, peeled and crushed
450g (1lb) tomatoes, skinned, seeded and chopped
150ml (¼ pint) red wine
150ml (¼ pint) chicken stock
15ml (1 tblsp) tomato puree
2 green chillies, thinly sliced
1 small red pepper, seeded and cut into thin strips
1 small green pepper, seeded and cut into thin strips
30ml (2 tblsp) chopped blanched almonds
15ml (1 tblsp) pine kernels
12 small black olives
15ml (1 tblsp) raisins

Season the poussins inside and out with salt and pepper. Rub olive oil into the skin and push a wedge of lemon or lime and a bayleaf into the centre of each one. Roast the poussins in the oven for 45 minutes, until just tender (if they start to get too brown, cover them with foil during cooking). Meanwhile, make the sauce. Fry the sliced onion gently in the oil for 3 minutes; add the remaining sauce ingredients and simmer for 10 minutes. Arrange the poussins on a serving dish and spoon over the hot sauce.

Turkey, Cauliflower and Almond Au Gratin

PREPARATION TIME: 20-25 minutes

COOKING TIME: about 16 minutes

SERVES: 4 people

1 medium size cauliflower
Juice of ½ lemon
Salt and freshly ground black pepper to taste
22g (¾oz) butter
22g (¾oz) flour
300ml (½ pint) skimmed milk
175g (6oz) cooked turkey, cut into thin strips
100g (4oz) grated cheese
30ml (2 tblsp) flaked almonds

Divide the cauliflower into good size florets; cook in boiling salted water to which you have added the lemon juice and salt to taste, until just tender. Meanwhile, make the sauce. Melt the butter in a pan; stir in the flour and cook for 1 minute. Gradually stir in the skimmed milk and bring to the boil; add salt and pepper to taste and stir until thickened. Add the strips of turkey and half the grated cheese to the sauce. Arrange the florets of cooked cauliflower in a greased heatproof dish and spoon over the prepared sauce; sprinkle with the almonds and remaining cheese and brown under a hot grill.

Turkey Meatballs with Sweet and Sour Sauce

PREPARATION TIME: 20-25 minutes, plus chilling time

COOKING TIME: about 35 minutes

SERVES: 4 people

1 small onion, finely chopped
30ml (2 tblsp) olive oil
450g (1lb) minced raw turkey
1 clove garlic, peeled and crushed
30ml (2 tblsp) chopped parsley
30ml (2 tblsp) finely chopped almonds
Salt and freshly ground black pepper to taste
1.25ml (¼ tsp) mixed spice
15ml (1 tblsp) chopped raisins
30ml (2 tblsp) wholemeal breadcrumbs
1 egg, beaten

Sauce
1 small onion, thinly sliced
300ml (½ pint) pure tomato juice
30ml (2 tblsp) tomato puree
Juice of ½ lemon
15ml (1 tblsp) honey
1 green chilli, thinly sliced
2 slices fresh pineapple, finely chopped
1 medium red pepper, seeded and cut into thin strips
2 carrots, peeled and coarsely grated

For the meatballs: fry the onion gently in the olive oil for 4 minutes. Mix with the minced turkey, garlic, parsley, almonds, salt and pepper to taste, mixed spice, raisins, breadcrumbs and beaten egg. Form into small balls, about the size of a table tennis ball. Chill for 30 minutes. For the sauce: put all the ingredients into a shallow pan;

bring to the boil and simmer gently for 10 minutes. Add the shaped meatballs and turn them in the sauce. Cover and simmer gently for a further 20 minutes, until the meatballs are tender – if the sauce evaporates too quickly, add a little stock or water. Serve piping hot with cooked brown rice or wholewheat pasta.
Note: the shaped meatballs can be lightly fried in a little oil, before being added to the sauce, if liked.

Sweetbread and Courgette Tarts

PREPARATION TIME: 40 minutes, plus chilling time

COOKING TIME: about 35 minutes

OVEN: 190°C, 375°F, Gas Mark 5

SERVES: 4 people

350g (12oz) shortcrust pastry
225g (8oz) calves' sweetbreads, soaked for 3 hours
Beaten egg
25g (1oz) butter
Finely grated rind of 1 lemon
1 clove garlic, peeled and crushed
4 courgettes, finely shredded
Salt and freshly ground black pepper to taste
Juice of ½ lemon

Divide the pastry into 4 equal portions; roll each one out to a circle and use to line an individual tartlet tin, about 10cm (4 inches) in diameter. Press up the pastry edges well. Line with greaseproof paper and baking beans, and chill for 30 minutes. Rinse the sweetbreads under cold water. Drain the sweetbreads, put them into a pan and add sufficient cold water to cover; bring to the boil slowly, covered, and simmer for 8 minutes. Drain and rinse; remove any muscly parts and skin, and chop into pieces. Bake the pastry cases for 10 minutes. Remove the paper and beans and brush the rim of each pastry case with beaten egg. Return to the oven for a further 8 minutes. Melt the butter with the lemon rind. Add the garlic and chopped sweetbreads and fry for 4 minutes. Add the shredded courgettes and salt and pepper to taste and fry together for a further 3

minutes. Spoon the hot filling into the pastry cases, squeeze over the lemon juice and serve immediately.

Tarragon Chicken Pancakes

PREPARATION TIME: about 10 minutes

COOKING TIME: 5-10 minutes

SERVES: 4 people

8 small wholemeal pancakes (using wholemeal flour and skimmed milk in the batter)
A little melted butter
22g (¾oz) butter
22g (¾oz) plain flour
300ml (½ pint) skimmed milk
Salt and freshly ground black pepper to taste
225g (½lb) cooked chicken, chopped
1 avocado pear (not over-ripe), peeled, halved, stoned and chopped
15ml (1 tblsp) chopped fresh tarragon

Brush the cooked pancakes lightly with melted butter and keep them warm in a parcel of foil in a moderately hot oven. Melt the butter and stir in the flour; cook, stirring, for 1 minute. Gradually stir in the skimmed milk; bring to the boil until the sauce has thickened. Add salt and pepper to taste and stir in the chopped chicken, avocado and tarragon. Fold each pancake in half, and then in half again, to form a triangle. Fill each folded pancake with the chicken and avocado mixture and serve piping hot. Garnish with sprigs of fresh tarragon, if liked.

Facing page: Turkey Meatballs with Sweet and Sour Sauce (top) and Sweetbreads and Courgette Tarts (bottom).

Just Desserts ...and Cakes too!

Fit for Life

Date and Pistachio Shortbreads

PREPARATION TIME: 20 minutes
COOKING TIME: 12-15 minutes
OVEN: 190°C, 375°F, Gas Mark 5
MAKES: about 12

100g (4oz) butter
50g (2oz) soft brown sugar
100g (4oz) wholemeal flour
50g (2oz) ground almonds
75g (3oz) stoned dates, chopped
30ml (2 tblsp) chopped shelled pistachios

To Decorate
Chopped shelled pistachios

Work the butter, brown sugar, wholemeal flour and ground almonds to a soft, smooth dough. Knead lightly, working in the chopped dates and pistachios. Press the mixture into small boat-shaped moulds. Press a few chopped pistachios into the top of each uncooked shortbread. Bake in the oven for 12-15 minutes.

Apricot and Walnut Teabread

PREPARATION TIME: 20 minutes
COOKING TIME: 1 hour 3 minutes
OVEN: 160°C, 325°F, Gas Mark 3
MAKES: 1 loaf

175g (6oz) softened butter
175g (6oz) light soft brown sugar
3 eggs, beaten
225g (8oz) wholemeal flour
7.5ml (1½ tsp) baking powder
30ml (2 tblsp) milk
100g (4oz) dried apricots, chopped
50g (2oz) chopped walnuts

To Decorate
30ml (2 tblsp) clear honey, warmed
Extra chopped dried apricots

Lightly grease a 1kg (2lb) loaf tin, and line the base with a piece of greased greaseproof paper. Cream the butter and sugar until light and fluffy. Gradually beat in the eggs, adding a little flour if the mixture shows signs of curdling. Mix in the flour and baking powder, together with the milk, and finally stir in the chopped apricots and nuts. Put the mixture into the prepared loaf tin, smoothing the top level. Bake in the oven for 1 hour 30 minutes. If the top of the loaf starts to darken too much, cover it with a piece of foil. As soon as the loaf comes out of the oven, brush the top with the warmed honey and sprinkle with the chopped apricots. Leave to cool in the tin for a few minutes before turning out.

Prune, Apricot and Nut Torten

PREPARATION TIME: 30 minutes. plus 'plumping' time
COOKING TIME: 25 minutes
OVEN: 190°C, 375°F, Gas Mark 5
SERVES: 6-8 people

100g (4oz) dried apricots
100g (4oz) dried prunes
300ml (½ pint) red wine, or dry cider

Nut Shortcake
100g (4oz) butter
50g (2oz) soft brown sugar
100g (4oz) wholemeal flour
50g (2oz) ground hazelnuts
45ml (3 tblsp) finely chopped walnuts

Glaze
30ml (2 tblsp) clear honey, warmed

To Decorate
15ml (1 tblsp) pine kernels
15ml (1 tblsp) hazelnuts

Put the apricots and prunes into a bowl. Warm the wine or cider and pour it over the dried fruits; leave them to 'plump' for 4 hours. For the shortcake: work the butter, brown sugar, flour and ground hazelnuts together. Knead lightly to a smooth dough, working in the chopped walnuts. Press evenly over the base of a 23cm (9 inch) fluted, loose-bottomed flan tin. Bake in the oven for 15 minutes. Drain the plumped prunes and apricots thoroughly on absorbent paper. Remove the shortcake from the oven and arrange the plumped fruits on top. Cover with a piece of foil and return to the oven for a further 10 minutes. Remove the shortcake carefully from its tin. Glaze the fruits on top with the

Facing page: Apricot and Walnut Teabread (top) and Date and Pistachio Shortbreads (bottom).

292

warmed honey and sprinkle with the nuts. This is absolutely delicious served warm from the oven, but is equally good served cold.

Honey and Apple Tart

PREPARATION TIME: about 45 minutes	
COOKING TIME: 35-40 minutes	
OVEN: 190°C, 375°F, Gas Mark 5	
SERVES: 6 people	

75g (33oz) wholemeal flour
75g (3oz) plain white flour
75g (3oz) butter
1 egg yolk
45ml (3 tblsp) cold water

Filling
300ml (½ pint) unsweetened apple puree
15ml (1 tblsp) honey
2 egg yolks
30ml (2 tblsp) ground almonds
3 large eating apples, quartered, cored and thinly sliced
A little pale soft brown sugar

Glaze
45ml (3 tblsp) clear honey, warmed

For the pastry: put the flours into a bowl; add the butter in small pieces and rub in. Beat the egg yolk with 30ml (2 tblsp) of the water and add to the dry ingredients; mix to a soft yet firm dough, adding a little extra water as necessary (wholemeal flour varies from batch to batch as to how much liquid it will absorb). Roll out the dough on a floured surface and use to line a 23cm (9 inch) loose-bottomed, fluted flan tin; pinch up the edges well. Prick the base. For the filling: mix the apple puree with the brandy, egg yolks, honey and ground almonds. Spread over the base of the pastry case. Arrange the apple slices in overlapping, concentric circles on top of the apple and almond filing. Dust lightly with soft brown sugar. Bake in the oven for 35-40 minutes (if the apples start to brown too much, cover the filling with a circle of foil). As soon as the flan comes out of the oven, brush the apple top with warmed honey. This flan can be served cold, but it is best served warm.

Mango and Orange Mousse

PREPARATION TIME: 35-40 minutes, plus chilling time	
SERVES: 4-6 people	

450ml (¾ pint) fresh mango pulp
Finely grated rind of ½ orange
Artificial sweetener to taste
15g (½oz) powdered gelatine
30ml (2 tblsp) orange juice
30ml (2 tblsp) natural yogurt
2 egg whites

To Decorate
Twisted strips orange peel

Mix the mango pulp with the orange rind and artificial sweetener to taste. Dissolve the gelatine in the orange juice. Add to the mango pulp, together with the yogurt. Leave until the mixture is on the point of setting. Whisk the egg whites until stiff but not 'dry', and fold lightly but thoroughly into the thickened mango mixture. Spoon into stemmed glasses and chill until set. Decorate with twisted strips of orange peel.

Lemon and Ginger Cheesecake

PREPARATION TIME: 45 minutes, plus chilling time	
SERVES: 6-8 people	

40g (1½oz) butter, melted
25g (1oz) soft brown sugar
75g (3oz) oatmeal biscuits, crushed

Filling
175g (6oz) curd cheese
2 eggs, separated
Finely grated rind of 1 lemon
50g (2oz) light, soft brown sugar
150ml (¼ pint) natural yogurt
15g (½oz) powdered gelatine
45ml (3 tblsp) water
Juice of ½ lemon

Facing page:
Mango and
Orange Mousse
(top) and Lemon
and Ginger
Cheesecake
(bottom). This
page: Prune,
Apricot and Nut
Torten (top) and
Honey and Apple
Tart (bottom).

3 pieces preserved stem ginger, rinsed in warm water and chopped

To Decorate
60ml (4 tblsp) thick natural yogurt
Fine matchstick strips lemon peel, or twists of lemon

Lightly grease an 18cm (7 inch) loose-bottomed cake tin. For the base: mix the melted butter, soft brown sugar and crushed biscuits together; press evenly over the base of the tin. Chill while you make the filling. For the filling: beat the curd cheese with the egg yolks, lemon rind, soft brown sugar and yogurt. Dissolve the gelatine in the water and add to the cheese mixture, together with the lemon juice; leave on one side until the mixture is on the point of setting. Whisk the egg whites until stiff but not 'dry', and fold lightly but thoroughly into the cheese mixture, together with the chopped ginger. Spoon the mixture into the prepared cake tin, smoothing the surface level. Chill for 3-4 hours, until the filling has set. Unmould the cheesecake carefully. Swirl natural yogurt over the top of the cheesecake and decorate with strips of lemon peel or lemon twists.

Golden Pistachio Meringues

PREPARATION TIME: 15-20 minutes

COOKING TIME: 1 hour

OVEN: 110°C, 225°F, Gas Mark ¼

MAKES: about 6

2 egg whites
100g (4oz) golden granulated sugar

Filling
100g (4oz) curd cheese
15ml (1 tblsp) clear honey
30ml (2 tblsp) chopped shelled pistachios

To Decorate
Chopped shelled pistachios

Whisk the egg whites until stiff but not dry and then gradually whisk in the golden granulated sugar. Pipe into 6 nest shapes on lightly

greased and floured baking sheets. Bake in the oven for 1 hour. The meringues should be fairly crisp but they should not 'colour'. Allow to cool. For the filling: cream the cheese until soft; beat in the honey and chopped pistachios. Fill the meringue nests with the cheese filling. Sprinkle each one with extra pistachios.

Strawberry and Melon Salad

PREPARATION TIME: 25 minutes

SERVES: 4 people

225g (8oz) large strawberries, hulled
1 small Charentais or Ogen melon
Juice of 1 orange
15ml (1 tblsp) brandy

To Decorate
Small sprigs fresh mint

Slice the strawberries quite thinly. Halve and de-seed the melon and then scoop it into small balls (there is a special cutter for doing this, but you can do it with a coffee spoon). Arrange the strawberry slices and melon balls on individual glass plates. Mix the orange juice with the brandy and dribble over the fruit. Decorate with mint.

Passion Fruit Ice Cream

PREPARATION TIME: 20 minutes plus freezing time

SERVES: 4 people

6 passion fruit
300ml (½ pint) thick natural yogurt
2 egg yolks
10ml (2 tsp) honey

To Decorate
1-2 passion fruit, halved and scooped

For the ice cream: halve the passion fruit and scoop all the centre pulp into a bowl. Add the yogurt, egg yolks and honey, and mix well together. Pour into a shallow container and freeze until firm. Scoop the ice cream into stemmed glasses and trickle a little passion fruit pulp over each portion. Serve immediately.

Note: this ice cream goes *very* hard and needs to be removed from the freezer several minutes before scooping.

Almond Stuffed Figs

PREPARATION TIME: 25 minutes

SERVES: 4 people

4 large ripe figs
60ml (4 tblsp) ground almonds
30ml (2 tblsp) orange juice
30ml (2 tblsp) finely chopped dried apricots

Sauce
60ml (4 tblsp) natural yogurt
Finely grated rind of ½ orange

Garnish
Wedges of ripe fig
Wedges of lime
Ground cinnamon

Make a cross cut in each fig, without cutting right down and through the base. Ease the four sections of each fig out, rather like a flower head. Mix the ground allmonds with the orange juice and chopped dried apricots; press into the centre of each fig. For the sauce: mix the yogurt with the orange rind, and thin down with *a little* water. Spoon a pool of orange flavoured yogurt onto each of 4 small plates; sit a stuffed fig in the centre of each one. Decorate with wedges of fig and lime and a sprinkling of ground cinnamon.

Cinnamon and Peanut Cookies

PREPARATION TIME: 15-20 minutes

COOKING TIME: 20 minutes

OVEN: 180°C, 350°F, Gas Mark 4

MAKES: about 20

100g (4oz) softened butter
100g (4oz) soft brown sugar
1 egg, beaten

Facing page: Passion Fruit Ice Cream (top) and Strawberry and Melon Salad (bottom).

60ml (4 tblsp) clear honey
250g (9oz) wholemeal flour
2.5ml (½ tsp) ground cinnamon
5ml (1 tsp) baking powder
Pinch salt
75g (3oz) shelled peanuts

Cream the butter and sugar until well mixed (do not over-beat). Mix in the beaten egg and honey and then mix in the flour, cinnamon, baking powder and salt. Put heaped teaspoons of the mixture onto greased baking sheets, allowing room for spreading; flatten each one slighttly with the rounded side of a dampened spoon. Stud the tops with peanuts. Bake in the oven for 20 minutes.
Note: for really golden topped biscuits bake them as above for just 15 minutes; brush each one with beaten egg and return to the oven for a further 5 minutes.

Ricotta Pancakes with Honey and Raisin Sauce

PREPARATION TIME:	10 minutes
COOKING TIME:	2-3 minutes
SERVES:	4 people

Sauce
60ml (4 tblsp) clear honey
Juice ½ lemon
15ml (1 tblsp) raisins
15ml (1 tblsp) pine kernels

Filling
225g (8oz) curd cheese, or Ricotta
Grated rind of ½ lemon
30ml (2 tblsp) raisins
15ml (1 tblsp) chopped pine kernels

8 small, hot pancakes

To Decorate
Twists of lemon

For the sauce: put all the ingredients into a small pan and warm through gently. For the filling: beat the cheese and the lemon rind until soft; mix in the raisins and pine kernels. Divide the filling amongst the hot pancakes and either roll them up, or fold them into triangles. Arrange the pancakes on warm plates, spoon

the sauce over the top and decorate with twists of lemon. Serve immediately.

Hazelnut and Apple Meringue Torten

PREPARATION TIME:	25-30 minutes
COOKING TIME:	45 minutes
OVEN:	190°C, 375°F, Gas Mark 5, then 160°C, 325°F, Gas Mark 3
SERVES:	6-8 people

100g (4oz) butter
50g (2oz) soft brown sugar
100g (4oz) wholemeal flour
50g (2oz) ground hazelnuts
30ml (2 tblsp) chopped hazelnuts
2 egg whites
75g (3oz) golden granulated sugar
300ml (½ pint) thick unsweetened apple puree

Work the butter, brown sugar, wholemeal flour and ground hazelnuts to a soft, smooth dough. Knead lightly and work in the chopped hazelnuts. Press evenly over the base of a 23cm (9 inch) fluted, loose-bottomed flan tin. Bake in the oven for 10 minutes. Meanwhile, whisk the egg whites until stiff but not 'dry'; gradually whisk in the golden granulated sugar. Remove the shortcake from the oven and pipe or swirl the meringue in a border around the edge. Return to the oven, lower the heat, and bake for a further 35 minutes, until golden. Fill immediately with the apple puree and serve while still warm.

This page: Cinnamon and Peanut Cookies (top) and Golden Pistachio Meringues (bottom). Facing page: Ricotta Pancakes with Honey and Raisin Sauce (top) and Almond Stuffed Figs (bottom).

Fit for Life

Microwave: Less Time... Less Fuss!

The microwave oven is tailor-made to today's fast pace of life. It can defrost, reheat, boil, bake – indeed perform everything that the conventional oven does, but in a fraction of the time. For the health conscious, however, this modern marvel holds a further advantage in that its use requires little or no fat to prevent foods from sticking to their containers. And if soggy, colourless vegetables put you off the meat-free regime, then the microwave has a surprise in store for you: vegetables prepared in the microwave retain much of their natural flavour as well as their crisp texture and colour.

People are usually of two minds about microwave ovens. Experienced cooks are sceptical. Inexperienced cooks are mystified. Most people who don't own one think a microwave oven is an expensive luxury. Those of us who have one, though, would find it difficult to give it up. Great advances have been made in the design and capabilities of microwave ovens since the demand for them first began in the Sixties. With so many kinds of ovens available, both beginners and advanced cooks can find one that best suits their particular needs.

How Microwave Ovens Work

Microwave ovens, whatever the make or model, do have certain things in common. The energy that makes fast cooking possible is comprised of electromagnetic waves converted from electricity. Microwaves are a type of high frequency radio wave. The waves are of short length, hence the name microwave.

Inside the oven is a magnetron, which converts ordinary electricity into microwaves. A wave guide channels the microwaves into the oven cavity, and a stirrer fan circulates them evenly. Microwaves are attracted to the particles of moisture that form part of any food. As the microwaves are absorbed, to a depth of about 4-5cm/1½-2 inches, they cause the water molecules in the food to vibrate, about 2000 million times a second. This generates the heat that cooks the food. The heat reaches the centre of the food by conduction, just as in ordinary cooking. However, this is accomplished much faster than in conventional cooking because no heat is generated until the waves are absorbed by the food. All the energy is concentrated on cooking the food and not on heating the oven itself or the baking dishes. Standing time is often necessary to allow the food to continue cooking after it is removed from the oven.

Most microwave ovens have an ON indicator light and a timer control. Some timer controls look like minute timers, while others are calibrated in seconds up to 50 seconds and minutes up to 30 minutes. This can vary slightly; some models have a 10 minute interval setting. Some ovens have a separate ON-OFF switch, while others switch on with the timer or power setting. Almost all have a bell or buzzer to signal the end of cooking time.

Microwave Oven Features

At this point, things really begin to diversify. Different terms are used for the same power setting depending on what brand of oven you buy. Some ovens have a wider range of different settings as well. Chart No. 1 on power settings reconciles most of the popular terms.

Some ovens come equipped with a temperature probe which allows you to cook food according to its internal temperature instead of by time. It is most useful for roasting large cuts of meat. The probe needle is inserted into the thickest part of the food and the correct temperature set on the attached control. When that internal temperature is reached, the oven automatically turns off, or switches to a low setting to keep the food warm. Special microwave thermometers are also available to test internal temperature and can be used inside the oven. Conventional thermometers must never be used inside a microwave oven, but can be used outside.

A cooking guide is a feature on some ovens, either integrated into the control panel or on the top or side of the oven housing. It is really a summary of the information found in the instruction and recipe booklet that accompanies every oven. However, it does act as a quick reference and so can be a time saver.

CHART 1 Power Setting Comparison Chart

	Other Terms and Wattages	Uses
Low	ONE or TWO, KEEP WARM, 25%, SIMMER, DEFROST. 75-300 watts.	Keeping food warm. Softening butter, cream cheese and chocolate. Heating liquid to dissolve yeast. Gentle cooking.
Medium	THREE or FOUR, 50%, STEW, BRAISE, ROAST, REHEAT, MEDIUM-LOW, FIVE, 40%, MEDIUM-HIGH, SIX, 60-75%.. 400-500 watts.	Roasting meat and poultry. Stewing and braising less tender cuts of meat. Baking cakes and custards. Cooking hollandaise sauces.
High	SEVEN, FULL, ROAST, BAKE, NORMAL, 100%.	Quick cooking. Meats, fish, vegetables, biscuits/cookies, pasta, rice, breads, pastry, desserts.

Turntables eliminate the need for rotating baking dishes during cooking, although when using a square or loaf dish you may need to change its position from time to time anyway. Turntables are usually glass or ceramic and can be removed for easy cleaning. Of all the special features available, turntables are one of the most useful.

Certain ovens have one or more shelves so that several dishes can be accommodated at once. Microwave energy is higher at the top of the oven than on the floor and the more you cook at once the longer it all takes. However, these ovens accommodate larger baking dishes than those with turntables.

If you do a lot of entertaining, then an oven with a keep warm setting is a good choice. These ovens have a very low power setting that can keep food warm without further cooking for up to one hour. If you want to programme your oven like a computer, choose one with a memory control that can switch settings automatically during the cooking cycle.

Browning elements are now available built into microwave ovens. They look and operate much the same as conventional electric grills. If you already have a grill, you probably don't need a browning element. Some of the most recent ovens allow the browning element to be used at the same time as the microwave setting, which is a plus.

Combination ovens seem to be the answer to the problem of browning in a microwave oven. While the power settings go by different names in different models, generally there is a setting for microwave cooking alone, a convection setting with conventional electric heat and a setting which combines the two for almost the speed of microwave cooking with the browning ability of convection heat. However, the wattage is usually lower than in standard microwave ovens, and so cooking time will be slightly longer.

On combination settings, use recipes developed for microwave ovens, but follow the instructions with your particular oven for times and settings. Some ovens have various temperature settings to choose from. Breads, poultry, meat and pastries brown beautifully in these ovens, and conventional baking dishes, even metal, can be used with a special insulating mat. Beware of certain plastics though, as they can melt in a combination oven.

You can have your microwave oven built into the same unit as your conventional oven. Microwave ovens are best situated at eye level. In fact, there are now units available with gas or electric cooktops and a microwave oven underneath where the conventional oven used to be.

Safety and Cleaning

One of the questions most commonly asked is "Are microwave ovens safe to use?" They are safe because they have safety features built into them and they go through rigorous tests by their manufacturers and by independent agencies.

If you look at a number of microwave ovens you will see that the majority of them are lined with metal, and metal will not allow microwaves to pass through. The doors have special seals to keep the microwaves inside the oven and have cut-out devices to cut off microwave energy immediately the door is opened. There are no pans to upset, no open flames or hot elements and the interior of the oven stays cool enough to touch. Although microwave ovens don't heat baking dishes, the heat generated by the cooking food does, so it is a good idea to use oven gloves or pot holders to remove dishes from the oven. It is wise periodically to check the door of your oven to make sure it has not been bent. Check latches and hinges, too, to make sure they are in good working order. Don't use baking dishes that are too large to allow the turntable to rotate freely; this can cause the motor to over-heat or cause dents in the oven sides and door, lowering efficiency and affecting safety of operation.

Microwave ovens are cleaner and more hygienic to cook with than conventional gas and electric ovens. Foods do not spatter as much and spills do not burn, so clean-up is faster. The turntables and shelves can be removed for easier cleaning. Use non-abrasive cleansers and scrubbers, and be sure to wipe up

A special microwave thermometer, which is used to test the internal temperature of the food, can be used inside the oven.

Density and Shape

The denser the food, the longer the cooking time. A large piece of meat is bound to take longer to cook than something light and porous like a cake or a loaf of bread. When cooking foods of various densities or shapes at the same time, special arrangements are necessary. For instance, place the thicker part of the food to the outside of the dish, thinner part toward the middle. Arrange pieces of food in a circle whenever possible, and in a round dish. If neither of these arrangements is possible, cover the thinner or less dense part of the food with foil for part of the cooking time. Rearrange and turn over such foods as asparagus or broccoli spears several times during cooking if they will not fit into your round dishes without considerable trimming.

Size

The smaller a piece of food the quicker it will cook. Pieces of food of the same kind and size will cook at the same rate. Add smaller or faster-cooking foods further along in the cooking time, such as mushrooms to a stew. If you have a choice of cooking heights, put food that is larger and can take more heat above food that is smaller and more delicate.

Covering

Most foods will cook, reheat or defrost better when covered. Use special covers that come with your cookware or simple cover with cling film. This covering must be pierced to release steam, otherwise it can balloon and possibly burst. Tight covering can give meat and poultry a "steamed" taste. Greaseproof paper or paper towels can also be used to keep in the heat and increase cooking efficiency.

Sugar or Fat Content

High sugar or fat content in certain foods means they will absorb microwave energy faster and reach a higher temperature. It is wise to cover food that will spatter, such as bacon, and to protect cakes that have very sugary toppings.

Standing Time

Microwave recipes usually advise leaving food to stand for 5-10 minutes after removal from the oven. Slightly undercooking the food allows the residual heat to finish it off, and microwave recipes take this into consideration. Meat and baked potatoes are usually wrapped in foil to contain the heat. Standing time also makes meat easier to carve. Cakes, breads and pastries should be left on a flat surface for their standing time as this helps to cook their bases. In general, foods benefit from being covered during standing time.

any residue so that it does not build up around the door seals. Faster cooking times and lower electricity consumption combine to make microwave ovens cheaper to run, especially for cooking small amounts of food, than conventional ovens.

Once you have chosen your oven and understand what makes it work, the fun of cooking begins. There are some basic rules to remember, however, as with conventional cooking, but most of them are common sense.

Quantity

Food quantities affect cooking times. For example, one baked potato will take about 3-4 minutes, two will take about 6-7 minutes, four will take 10-11 minutes. Generally, if you double the quantity of a recipe, you need to increase the cooking time by about half as much again.

Equipment and Cookware

The number of different baking dishes and the range of equipment for microwave cooking is vast. There are so many highly specialised dishes for specific needs that to list them all would take up almost the whole of this book!

Explore cookware departments and find your own favourites. Follow your oven instruction booklet carefully since it will give you good advice on which cookware is best for your particular oven. Some dishes, lightweight plastics and even some hard plastics can't be used on combination settings. The temperature is too high and the dishes will melt or break. Most metal cookware can be used successfully in combination ovens, following the manufacturers guidelines. I have had less than satisfactory results with certain aluminium pans in my combination oven, so experimentation is essential. Paper bags can catch fire on High settings, and I have had the same experience with silicone-coated paper, although its use is often recommended. Microwave energy penetrates round shapes particularly efficiently, so round dishes and ring moulds work very well. The turntable can also be cooked on directly for such foods as scones or meringues or used for reheating foods like bread or coffee cakes.

Above and left: the number and variety of different baking dishes and the range of equipment for the microwave is vast.

For foods that are likely to boil over, like jams and soups, use the largest, deepest bowl that will fit into the oven cavity. Whole fish can be cooked in a cooking bag and curved to fit the shape of the turntable if they are too large to lie flat.

Browning dishes do work and the results are impressive. There are different designs and some have lids so that meat can be browned and finished off as a braise or stew in the same dish. Covering foods like chops or nut cutlets also speeds up the browning process. These dishes need to be preheated for between 4 to 8 minutes, depending on manufacturers instructions, and will get extremely hot. Use oven gloves or pot holders to remove browning dishes from the oven and set them on a heatproof mat to protect work surfaces. Butter will brown very fast, and steaks and chops can be seared. Stir frying is possible in a microwave oven with the use of a browning tray, and sausages brown beautifully without the shrinkage of conventional grilling or frying. These dishes can also be useful for browning a flour and fat roux for making sauces and gravies.

Cooking Poultry, Meat and Game

Moisture evaporates less readily during microwave cooking, so meat does not dry out. The fat in poultry will turn brown during cooking, but only in whole birds. Single joints of chicken or other poultry cook too quickly for the fat to brown. A thin layer of fat left on pork or beef for roasting will also brown, although it will not crisp. Fat is important to help keep the meat moist, but if you prefer to take it off, do so after cooking, or remember to baste frequently and cover the meat. There are a number of bastes, coatings and seasonings, some especially developed for microwave cooking, that can be used to give an appetizing brownness to meat and poultry.

Choose boned and rolled joints and cuts of meat that are a uniform thickness and shape. If this isn't possible, the next best thing is covering the thinner parts with foil for part of the cooking time. This trick with foil is also useful on poultry to cover the leg ends and the meat along the length of the breast bone. For poultry joints, cover the thinner ends of the breasts and the drumsticks.

Less tender cuts of meat, such as those for stewing, need to be cooked on a medium setting after initial browning. High settings can toughen these cuts of meat. Whether or not to salt

meat before cooking depends on which book you read. I think the general rules that apply to conventional meat cooking apply to microwave cooking as well. Do not salt meat to be roasted until after cooking. Sprinkle salt inside the cavity of poultry, if desired, and lightly salt stews and braises once the liquid has been added. Charts No. 2 and 3 serve as a quick reference, for meat, poultry and game.

Cooking Fish and Shellfish

The microwave oven excels at cooking fish. You can poach fish fillets in minutes. Arrange them in a dish in a circle with the thicker part of the fillet to the outside of the dish. If preparing a sauce to go with the fish, poach in a little white wine or water and lemon juice for a little more liquid to work with. A bay leaf, slice of onion and a few peppercorns are classic additions to the poaching liquid for extra flavour.

CHART 2 Meat, Poultry and Game (per 450g/1lb.)

	Mins. on High	Mins. on Medium	Internal Temperature Before Standing	After Standing
Beef: boned and rolled				
rare	6-7	11-13	57°C/130°F	62°C/140°F
medium	7-8	13-15	65°C/150°F	70°C/160°F
well-done	8-9	15-17	70°C/160°F	78°C/170°F
Beef: bone in				
rare	5	10	57°C/130°F	62°C/140°F
medium	6	11	65°C/150°F	70°C/160°F
well-done	8	15	70°C/160°F	78°C/170°F
Leg of Lamb	8-10	11-13	78°C/170°F	82°C/180°F
Veal	8-9	11-12	70°C/160°F	78°C/170°F
Pork	9-11	13-15	82°C/180°F	85°C/185°F
Ham				
Uncooked, boned	1st 5	15-18	55°C/130°F	70°C/160°F
Bone in	1st 5	15½-18½	55°C/130°F	70°C/160°F
Pre-cooked, boned	1st 5	12-15	55°C/130°F	
Bone in	1st 5	10-15		
Chicken	6-8	9-11	85°C/185°F	94°C/190°F
Duck	6-8	9-11	85°C/185°F	94°C/190°F
Turkey	9-11	12-15	85°C/185°F	94°C/190°F
Pheasant		20 total		
Poussins	15-20 total			
Wild Duck	5	10 total		
Pigeon	10 total			
Quail	5-9 total			

CHART 3 Small Cuts of Meat, Poultry and Game

Type	Mins. on High	Mins. on Medium	Special Instructions
Steaks (3.75mm/ 1½" thick) 120g-180g/4-6oz			Use a browning dish pre-heated to manufacturer's instructions. Use timing for rare when cooking kebabs.
rare	2-3		
medium rare	3-4		
medium	5-7		
well-done	7-9		
Lamb Chops	7-9	13-15	Use a browning dish Cook in liquid
Lamb Fillet		10-12	Brown, then cook in liquid
Pork Chops	7-9	13-15	Use a browning dish Cook in liquid
Pork Fillet		15	Brown, then cook in liquid
Veal Chops	7-9	13-15	Use a browning dish Cook in liquid
Smoked Pork Chops	4-6		Pre-cooked and browned
Ham Steaks	3		Pre-cooked and browned
Minced/Ground Meat (450g/1lb)	5		Break up with a fork as it cooks
Hamburgers	2½-3		Use browning dish
Lamb Patties	2½-3		Use browning dish
Meatballs (675g/1½ lbs)	10-12		
Duck Portions			Use browning dish
1 Breast (boned)	6		
2 Legs		15	Brown each side first
Chicken			
1 Breast		2-3	Brown first if desired
1 Leg		3-4	
2 Pieces		3-6	
3 Pieces		4-7	
4 Pieces		7-9	
Turkey Escalopes/Cutlets		10-15	
Turkey Legs (450g/1lb)	1st 10	13-16	
Bacon		4 1	On rack or paper towels Per side on pre-heated browning dish
Sausages		2	Use browning dish

CHART 4 Fish and Shellfish (per 450g/1lb.)

Type	Mins. on high	Type	Mins. on high
Cod Steaks and Fillets	4-5	Salmon (Whole, 1kg/2.2lbs)	10-15
Halibut and Turbot Steaks and Fillets	4-5	Salmon Steaks and Tail pieces	2-7
Smoked Fish (poached)	1-2	Sea Bass (Whole, 1kg/2.2lbs)	10-15
Sole Fillets	2-3	Prawns/Shrimp Scampi/Langoustines	2-5
Mackerel	10-12	Scallops	2-5
Trout	8-10	Mussels	2-3
Herring Fillets	6-8	Oysters	1-2
Tuna Steaks	5	Squid	6
Monkfish Tail Portion Sliced	8-9 2-5		

Whole fish can be "fried" in a browning dish. They can also be cooked in bags, shallow covered dishes or enclosed in greaseproof paper — en papillote.

Shellfish can toughen if cooked too quickly at too high a temperature. Add them to a hot sauce and leave for 5 minutes to cook in residual heat. Alternatively, cook on their own for no more than 3 minutes.

See chart No. 4 for times and settings.

Cooking Vegetables

Microwave cooking is ideal for vegetables. Very little water is needed, so they keep their colour and nutrients. They are best cooked loosely covered, and whole vegetables like corn-on-the-cob, aubergines, artichokes and chicory can be completely wrapped in cling film and cooked without any water. Cooking bags are another alternative.

   Break broccoli into even-sized pieces and, if cooking a large quantity, be sure to put the flower ends in toward the centre of the dish. Trim down the tough ends of asparagus and peel the ends of the stalks. This will help the stalks cook quickly before the tips are overcooked. Some vegetables, like cucumbers, spring onions and button onions cook very well in butter or margarine alone, if well covered. Chart No. 5 lists suggested cooking times.

Cooking Fruit

Poach, bake and preserve fruit with ease in a microwave oven. Sterilise jars for preserving by adding a little water and heating on High for about 2-3 minutes and then draining. Metal lids and rubbers seals are best sterilised outside the microwave oven.

CHART 5 Cooking Vegetables

Type	Quantity	Water	Mins. on High	Mins. Stdg. Time
Artichokes	4	430ml/¾pt/1½ cups	10-20	5
Asparagus	450g/1lb	140ml/¼pt/½ cup	9-12	5
Aubergine/Eggplant	2 med.	30ml/2 tbsps	7-10	5
Beans Green, French	450g/1lb	140ml/¼pt/½ cup	8	3
Broad/Lima			10	3
Beetroot/Beets Whole	2	60ml/2 fl oz/¼ cup	4-5	3
Broccoli	450g/1lb	140ml/¼ pt/½ cup	4-5	3
Brussels Sprouts	450g/1lb	60ml/2 fl oz/¼ cup	8-10	3-5
Cabbage Shredded	450g/1lb	140ml/¼ pint/½ cup	7-9	3
Quartered			9-12	5
Carrots Whole	225g/8oz	140ml/¼ pint/½ cup	10	6
Sliced			7	5
Cauliflower Whole	450g/1lb	280ml/½ pint/1 cup	11	3
Florets		140ml/¼ pint/½ cup	7	3
Chicory	4	60ml/2 fl oz/¼ cup (water or stock)	5	3
Corn-on-the-Cob	2 ears	60ml/2 fl oz/¼ cup	6	3
Courgettes/Zucchini	450g/1lb	60ml/2 fl oz/¼ cup	5	3
Fennel Sliced	1 bulb	280ml/½ pint/1 cup boiling water	2-8	3
Quartered			10-12	3
Leeks, sliced	450g/1lb	140ml/¼ pint/½ cup	7-10	3
Mushrooms	225g/8oz	30ml/2 tbsps	2	3
Okra	225g/8oz	60ml/2 fl oz/¼ cup	4	3
Onions, small	225g/8oz	30ml/1 fl oz/2 tbsps	7-8	3
Sliced	2	60ml/2 fl oz/¼ cup	10	3
Parsnips	225g/8oz	140ml/¼ pint/½ cup	8-10	3
Peas, shelled	450g/1lb	140ml/¼ pint/½ cup	10-15	5
Peapods/Mangetout	225g/8oz	140ml/¼ pint/½ cup	3	3
Peppers	2 sliced	60ml/2 fl oz/¼ cup	3	3
Potatoes New	450g/1lb	140ml/¼ pint/½ cup	10-12	5
Baked	2		9-12	10
Boiled	450g/1lb	140ml/¼ pint/½ cup	6-7	5
Spinach	225g/8oz		4-5	3
Turnips	225g/8oz	60ml/2 fl oz/¼ cup	12	3

Paraffin wax for sealing jars cannot be melted in a microwave oven. The great advantages of microwave preserving are that jams and jellies can be made in small amounts and the job is much less messy and time-consuming. Whole preserved fruits and pickled vegetables can't be heated long enough to kill bacteria, so they must be kept refrigerated after bottling.

Cooking Rice, Pasta, Grains and Pulses

Rice and pasta need nearly as much cooking by microwave methods as by conventional ones. However, both pasta and rice cook without sticking together and without the chance of overcooking. This is because most of the actual cooking is accomplished during standing time. All kinds of rice and shapes of pasta benefit from being put into hot water with a pinch of salt and 5ml/1 tsp oil in a deep bowl. There is no need to cover the bowl during cooking, but, during standing time, a covering of some sort will help retain heat. Ease long spaghetti into the bowl gradually as it softens. Drain rice and pasta and rinse under hot water to remove starch. Both pasta and rice can be reheated in a microwave oven without loss of texture. Fresh pasta doesn't seem to take to the microwave oven successfully.

There is a great time saving with dried peas, beans and lentils — pulses. Cover them with water in a large bowl and heat on a High setting to bring to the boil, which takes about 10 minutes. Allow the pulses to boil for about 2 minutes and then leave to stand for one hour. This cuts out overnight soaking. The pulses will cook in about 45 minutes to one hour depending on what variety is used. This is about half the conventional cooking time. Make sure pulses are cooked completely; it can be dangerous to eat them undercooked. Refer to Chart No. 6 for cooking times.

Cooking Eggs and Cheese

When poaching eggs, always pierce the yolks with a skewer or fork to prevent them from bursting. Use individual ramekins or patty pans with a spoonful of water in each. Alternatively, bring water to the boil in a large dish and add a pinch of salt and 5ml/1 tsp vinegar to help set the egg whites. Slip the eggs in one at a time. Cook just until the whites are set. To stop the cooking and to keep the eggs from drying out, keep them in a bowl of cold water. For frying eggs, choose a browning dish, and for

scrambling use a deep bowl or glass measuring jug. Always remove scrambled eggs from the oven while they are still very soft. Stir during standing time to finish cooking. Hollandaise sause is easy to make. Choose the same kind of container as for scrambled eggs and have a bowl of iced water ready. Use a medium setting and cook the sauce at short intervals, whisking vigorously in between times. Put the sauce bowl into the iced water at the first sign of curdling or briefly when it has thickened, to stop the cooking process.

Cheese will get very stringy if it overcooks or gets too hot. When preparing a cheese sauce, stir finely grated cheese into the hot sauce base and leave to stand. The cheese will melt without further cooking. Cheese toppings will not brown except in a combination oven. A medium setting is best for cheese.

Baking

Baking is one of the most surprising things a microwave oven does. Quick breads, those leavened with baking powder or soda and sour milk, rise higher than they do in a conventional oven and bake faster. If using a square or loaf dish, cover the corners with foil for part of the cooking time to keep that part of the bread or cake from drying out before the middle is cooked. Cakes also rise much higher and a single layer will bake in about 6 minutes on a medium setting.

Microwave ovens can cut the rising time for yeast doughs nearly in half, and a loaf of bread will bake in an astonishing 8-10 minutes.

Biscuits will not usually crisp in a microwave oven except in one with a combination setting. However, they bake to a moist, chewy texture which is just as pleasing. A batch of 3 dozen will cook in about 10 minutes.

Pastry is not as much of a problem as most people believe. Prick the base and sides of the pastry well, after lining a pie or flan dish. It is essential to bake the pastry shell "blind" — without filling — in order to dry the base. Pastry will not bake to an even brown. The exception is, of course, pastry baked in a combination oven. Pastry and filling can be baked at the same time in these ovens.

CHART 6 Cooking Rice, Pasta, Grains and Pulses

Type	Quantity	Water	Mins. on High	Mins. Stdg. Time
Brown Rice	120g/4oz 1 cup	570ml/1 pint/ 2 cups	20	5
White Rice (long grain)	120g/4oz 1 cup	570ml/1 pint/ 2 cups	10-12	5
Quick Cooking Rice	120g/4oz 1 cup	430ml/¾ pint/ 1½ cups	6	5
Macaroni	225g/8oz 3 cups	1 litre/1¾ pints/ 3½ cups	6	10
Quick Cooking Macaroni	225g/8oz 3 cups	1 litre/1¾ pints/ 3½ cups	3	10
Spaghetti	225g/8oz	1 litre/1¾ pints/ 3½ cups	6-10	10
Tagliatelle/Fettucine	225g/8oz	1 litre/1¾ pints/ 3½ cups	5-9	10
Pasta Shapes	225g/8oz 3 cups	1 litre/1¾ pints/ 3½ cups	6	10
Lasagne Ravioli Cannelloni	180g-225g/ 6oz-8oz	1 litre/1¾ pints/ 3½ cups	6	10
Barley	120g/4oz/ 1 cup	570ml/1 pint/ 2 cups	20	10
Bulgur (cracked wheat)	225g/8oz/ 2 cups	570ml/1 pint/ 2 cups boiling water	4	10
Dried Beans	180g/6oz/ 1 cup	1 litre/1¾ pints/ 3½ cups	55-60	10
Dried Peas	225g/8oz/ 3 cups	1 litre/1¾ pints/ 3½ cups	45-60	10
Lentils	225g/8oz/ 3 cups	1 litre/1¾ pints/ 3½ cups	20-25	15

NOTE: Add a pinch of salt and 5ml/1 tsp oil to grains and pasta

CHART 7 Reheating

	Quantity	Setting	Time from room temp. (minutes)	Special Instructions		Quantity	Setting	Time from room temp. (minutes)	Special Instructions
Spaghetti Sauce	225g/8oz 450g/1lb	Med.	5-6 7-8	Stir several times. Keep loosely covered.	Pasta	120g/4oz 225g/8oz	Med. or High	2-3 5-6	Stir once or twice. Add 5ml/ 1 tsp oil. Use shorter time for High setting.
Beef Stew	225g/8oz 450g/1lb	Med.	5-5½ 6-7	Stir occasionally. Cover loosely.	Rice	120g/4oz 225g/8oz	Med. or High	2-3 4-5	Stir once or twice. Add 5ml/ 1 tsp oil or butter. Use shorter time for High setting.
Casseroles	225g/8oz 450g/1lb	Med.	5-7 7-8	Stir occasionally. Cover loosely. Use the shorter time for chicken, fish or vegetables.	Potatoes	120g/4oz 225g/8oz 450g/1lb	High	1-2 2-3 3-4	Use the shorter time for mashed potatoes. Do not reheat fried potatoes. Cover loosely.
Chili	225g/8oz 450g/1lb	Med.	5-5½ 6-7	Stir several times. Keep loosely covered.					
Pork Chops	2 4	Med.	5 7½	Turn over halfway through. Cover loosely.	Corn-on-the-Cob	2 ears 4 ears	High	2-3 4-6	Wrap in plastic wrap/cling film
Lamb Chops	2 4	Med.	4-5 6-10	Turn over halfway through. Cover loosely.	Carrots	225g/8oz 450g/1lb	High	1-2 2-4	Cover loosely. Stir once.
Sliced beef, pork, veal	120g/4oz 225g/8oz	Med.	3-5 6-7½	Add gravy or sauce if possible. Cover loosely.	Turnips	225g/8oz 450g/1lb	High	1-2 2-4	Cover loosely. Stir carefully.
Sliced turkey, chicken, ham	120g/4oz 225g/8oz	Med.	2½-5 4-6	Add gravy or sauce if possible. Cover loosely.	Broccoli Asparagus	120g/4oz 225g/8oz	High	2 2	Cover loosely. Rearrange once.
					Peas Beans Courgettes/ Zucchini	120g/4oz 225g/8oz	High	1-1½ 1½-2	Cover loosely. Stir occasionally.

To let air and heat circulate underneath breads, cakes and pastry shells, place them on a rack or inverted saucer. This allows the base to cook faster and more evenly. Once baked and cool, keep microwave-baked goods well covered. They seem to dry out faster than those conventionally baked.

Defrosting and Reheating

With the defrosting and reheating abilities of a microwave oven menu planning can become crisis-free. Most ovens incorporate an automatic defrosting control into their setting programs. If your oven does not have this facility, use the lowest temperature setting and employ an on/off technique. In other words, turn the oven on at 30 second-1 minute intervals and let the food stand for a minute or two before repeating the process. This procedure allows the food to defrost evenly without starting to cook at the edges. The times given in Charts No. 7 and 8 apply to ovens of 600-700 watts.

Always cover the food when defrosting or reheating. Plastic containers, plastic bags and freezer-to-table ware can be used to freeze and defrost food in. Meals can be placed on paper or plastic trays and frozen. Cover with cling film or greaseproof paper. Usually, foods are better defrosted first and cooked or reheated second. There are exceptions to this rule, so be sure to check instructions on pre-packaged foods before proceeding. Food frozen in blocks, such as spinach or casseroles, should be broken up as they defrost.

Breads, rolls and coffee cakes can be placed on paper plates or covered in paper towels to reheat or defrost. These materials will help protect the foods and absorb moisture which will come to the surface and could make these foods soggy. If you want a crisp crust on reheated bread, slip a sheet of foil under the paper towel and don't cover completely.

When reheating foods in a sauce, stir occasionally to distribute heat evenly. Spread food out in an even layer for uniform heating. Sauces and gravies can be poured over sliced meat and poultry to keep it moist while reheating. Vegetables, except for root vegetables and starchy ones like corn, lose texture when they are reheated. It is best to add them at the last

CHART 8 Defrosting

	Mins. on Low/ Defrost Setting per 450g/1lb	Mins. Stdg. Time	Instructions
Pork, Veal, Lamb, Beef for Roasting	8-10	30-40	Pierce covering. Turn frequently.
Ground/ Minced Beef or Lamb	7-8	5-6	Pierce wrapping. Break up as it defrosts.
Hamburgers	6-8	5	Use shorter time if individually wrapped. Pierce wrapper and separate when starting to defrost. Turn patties over once.
Bacon	6-8	5	Cover in paper towels. Separate as slices defrost.
Sausages	6-8	5	Cover in paper towels. Separate as defrosting.
Whole Chickens, Duck, Game Birds	5-7	30	Pierce wrapper. Remove giblets as soon as possible. Cover leg ends, wings, breast bone with foil part of the time. Turn several times.
Poultry Pieces	6-8	15-20	Pierce wrapper. Turn several times.
Casseroles, filled crêpes (for 4 people)	4-10	10	Defrost in dish, loosely covered. Stir casseroles if possible.

	Mins. on Low/ Defrost Setting per 450g/1lb	Mins. Stdg. Time	Instructions
Vegetables	1-8	3-5	Cover loosely. Break up or stir occasionally.
Fish Fillets and Steaks	6-10	5-10	Pierce wrapper. Separate during defrosting. Use greater time for steaks.
Whole Fish	6-8	10	Pierce wrapper. Turn over during defrosting. Cover tail with foil halfway through.
Shellfish	6-8	6	Pierce wrapper. Stir or break up pieces during defrosting.
Bread Loaf	2-4 (per average loaf)	5-10	Cover with paper towels. Turn over once.
1 Slice Bread	20 seconds	1	Cover in paper towels.
Rolls 6 12	1½-3 2-4	3 5	Cover in paper towels. Turn over once.
Cake	1½-2	2	Place on serving plate. Some icings not suitable.
Fruit Pie 23cm/9″	8-10	6	Use a glass dish. Place on inverted saucer or rack.

minute to other foods. To tell if reheating is completed, touch the bottom of the plate or container. If it feels hot, then the food is ready.

Foods can be arranged on plates in advance and reheated very successfully, an advantage when entertaining. With a microwave oven, you can spend more time with your guests than by yourself in the kitchen!

Recipe Conversion

Experiment with your favourite recipes and you will probably find that many of them can be converted for microwave cooking with only a few changes. Things that don't work are recipes which call for whipped egg whites, such as angel food cake and crisp meringue shells. Soft meringues for pies will work, and one of the most amazing recipe conversions is that for crisp meringues. These meringues triple in size as they cook and are made from a fondant-like mixture.

Batters for pancakes, waffles or Yorkshire pudding are impossible to cook successfully. Deep fat frying is understandably impossible. Yeast doughs and biscuit doughs must be specially formulated for microwave cooking. To convert your own recipes, the following rules will help:

✻ Look for similar microwave recipes with the same quantities of solid ingredients, dish size, techniques and times.

✻ Reduce liquid quantities by one quarter. More can always be added later in cooking.

✻ Cut down on fat and save calories as well as cooking time. Fat will attract microwave energy and slow down the cooking of the other ingredients in the recipe.

✻ Reduce the seasoning in your recipe; microwave cooking intensifies flavours.

✻ Microwave cooking takes approximately a quarter of the time of conventional cooking. Allow at least 5 minutes standing time before checking to see if the food is cooked. You can always add more time at this point if necessary.

Fit for Life
Microwave Recipes for Your Fitness and Figure

A slimmer's life is difficult enough without having to suffer the temptations of hours spent in the kitchen. A microwave oven makes dieting that little bit easier by limiting the time you spend in preparing the food, as well as keeping all those irresistible aromas, and consequently your taste buds, under control.

On its own, of course, the microwave cannot magically produce low calorie meals. Cooked in a microwave, however, low calorie recipes seem particularly appetising, as the food retains much of its texture and colours remain bright and attractive. Somehow, the lack of rich ingredients becomes less noticeable. Perhaps of even greater interest to those watching their waistline is the fact that the microwave system of cooking requires little or no use of fat, since food is unlikely to stick to the container.

The ingredients in the selected recipes have all been carefully chosen to keep the calorie count down, but this does not mean that all the more exciting foods have been cut out. With a little skilful management, a judicious mix of low-rated foods together with a minimal quantity of high-calorie ingredients can, in combination, produce mouthwatering dishes – a rosette of cream is only 15 calories.

Generally speaking, vegetables and salads are low in calories while foods containing fats and sugars are more fattening. But even the more fattening foods, eaten in moderation, have their place in your diet.

Calorie counts and the number of servings are given with each of the featured recipes, and if the recipe is stretched to serve more people, the total calories per serving will be further reduced.

Cooking times can be influenced by a variety of factors and those given should be used as a guide. Remember that you can always add extra cooking time, but overcooking cannot be rectified.

To cover the food in a microwave use either vented cling film/plastic wrap or a lid, but note that these covers should never be tight fitting unless specifically stated.

Always refer to the manufacturer's handbook for specific instructions on the use of the microwave oven.

Altering Timings The recipes given in this book can be cooked in any model of variable power microwave oven that is available today. Each of these recipes was tested in a 700W microwave oven. Convert the timings in the following way if the output of your oven is other than 700W:

If using an oven of 500W, add 40 seconds for each minute stated in the recipe.

If using an oven of 600W, add 20 seconds for each minute stated in the recipe.

If using an oven of 650W plus, you will only need to allow a slight increase in the overall time.

Fit for Life

Low Calorie Soups

Beetroot Soup

PREPARATION TIME: 10 minutes

MICROWAVE COOKING TIME:
25 minutes

MAKES: Approximately 1150ml/
2 pints/5 cups

TOTAL CALORIES: 330

450g/1lb/2 or 3 raw medium beetroots/
    beets
1 medium onion
850ml/1½ pints/3¾ cups hot stock
30ml/2 tbsps cider vinegar
1.25ml/¼ tsp bay leaf powder
140ml/¼ pint/⅔ cup skimmed milk
Salt
Freshly ground black pepper
1 small cucumber, finely diced
30ml/2 tbsps natural low fat yogurt

Peel the beetroots/beets and onion
and put into a large bowl with the
stock, vinegar and bay leaf powder.
Cover and cook for 20 minutes on
HIGH until the beetroots are tender.
Cut up the vegetables and purée in a
blender with as much of the liquid as
is needed. Pour back into the bowl
with the remaining liquid, add the
milk and season to taste with salt and
pepper. Stir in the cucumber, cover
and cook for 5 minutes on HIGH.
Remove from the microwave and stir
in the yogurt.

Chicken and Vermicelli Soup

PREPARATION TIME: 5 minutes

MICROWAVE COOKING TIME:
15 minutes

MAKES: 1150ml/2 pints/5 cups

TOTAL CALORIES: 500

285g/10oz raw chicken, skinned and
    diced
1150ml/2 pints/5 cups hot chicken stock
30ml/2 tbsps fresh lemon juice

**This page: Chicken and Vermicelli
Soup (top) and Mulligatawny Soup
(bottom). Facing page: Beetroot
Soup (top) and Mushroom Soup
(bottom).**

Salt
Freshly ground black pepper
30g/1oz/2 nests vermicelli
15ml/1 tbsp chopped chives

Put the chicken into a large bowl and pour in sufficient stock to cover. Cook uncovered for 6 minutes on HIGH. Add the remaining stock and lemon juice and season to taste with salt and pepper. Cook uncovered for 4 minutes or until boiling. Stir in the vermicelli and cook for 5 minutes, stirring once during cooking, until the chicken and vermicelli are tender. Garnish each portion with chopped chives.

Mulligatawny Soup

PREPARATION TIME: 5 minutes

MICROWAVE COOKING TIME:
8-9 minutes

MAKES: 700ml/1¼ pints/2½ cups

TOTAL CALORIES: 295

75g/3oz mixed diced vegetables
330ml/11½ fl oz can vegetable juice
425ml/15 fl oz can ready-to-serve consommé
1.25ml/¼ tsp ground coriander
1.25ml/¼ tsp ground cardamom
1.25ml/¼ tsp ground turmeric
Pinch ground cloves
15g/½ oz/2 tbsps slivered/flaked almonds, browned

Combine the vegetables, vegetable juice, consommé and spices in a large bowl. Cover and cook for 8-9 minutes on HIGH until the vegetables are tender and the soup is hot. Pour into individual bowls and garnish with the browned almonds.

Mushroom Soup

PREPARATION TIME: 10 minutes

MICROWAVE COOKING TIME:
17 minutes

MAKES: 1 litre/1¾ pints/4¼ cups

TOTAL CALORIES: 162

225g/8oz/2 cups button mushrooms
1 small onion, peeled and quartered

½ small clove garlic, peeled and crushed
1.25ml/¼ tsp dried rosemary
850ml/1½ pints/3¾ cups hot chicken stock
30ml/2 tbsp soured cream
Salt
Freshly ground black pepper

Slice and set aside two or three mushrooms. Cut up the remainder and purée in a blender with the onion, garlic, rosemary and 570ml/1 pint/2½ cups of the stock. Pour into a large bowl, cover and cook for 15 minutes on HIGH, stirring occasionally. Stir in the remaining stock and season to taste with salt and pepper. Cover and cook for 2 minutes on HIGH, stirring once during cooking. Stir in the soured cream. Garnish each portion with slices of raw mushroom.

Fish Chowder

PREPARATION TIME: 20 minutes

MICROWAVE COOKING TIME:
26-27 minutes

MAKES: 1150ml/2 pints/5 cups

TOTAL CALORIES: 685

675g/1½ lbs whole whitefish (including head and bones)
1 bay leaf
280ml/½ pint/1¼ cups water
Squeeze lemon juice
5ml/1 tsp anchovy essence
2 slices rindless bacon
1 medium potato
1 medium onion
Salt
Freshly ground black pepper
225g/8oz canned tomatoes
15ml/1 tbsp chopped parsley
75g/3oz/1 cup peeled cooked shrimp/prawns

Remove head, skin and all bones from the fish, and put them into a large bowl. Add the bay leaf, water and lemon juice. Cook uncovered for 6-7 minutes on HIGH until boiling. Reduce the setting to DEFROST/35% and cook uncovered for 10 minutes. Set aside. Meanwhile dice the bacon and peel and dice the potato and onion. Put them into a

large bowl. Cover and cook the bacon and vegetables for 5 minutes on HIGH, stirring occasionally. Strain in the fish liquor and season to taste with salt and pepper. Roughly cut up the fish and stir into the mixture. Add the tomatoes and their juice, the parsley and shrimp/prawns and cook uncovered for 5 minutes on HIGH, stirring two or three times during cooking.

Tomato and Leek Soup

PREPARATION TIME: 10 minutes

MICROWAVE COOKING TIME:
11-13 minutes

MAKES: 1½ litres/2½ pints/1½ quarts

TOTAL CALORIES: 212

2 large leeks, trimmed, washed and finely sliced
570ml/1 pint/2½ cups boiling water
570ml/1 pint/2½ cups tomato juice
Dash Worcestershire sauce
1.25ml/¼ tsp celery seeds
Shake garlic powder
Salt
Freshly ground black pepper
4 tomatoes, skinned and sliced

Put the leeks and water into a large bowl, cover and cook for 5-6 minutes on HIGH. Remove half the leeks with a slotted spoon and set aside. Purée the remaining leeks and cooking liquid in a blender. Pour back into the bowl and add the tomato juice, Worcestershire sauce, celery seeds and garlic powder. Cover and cook for 3-4 minutes on HIGH until hot, stirring once during cooking. Season to taste with salt and pepper. Stir in reserved leeks and sliced tomatoes, cover and cook for 3 minutes on HIGH, stirring once during cooking. Ladle into individual serving dishes.

Facing page: Tomato and Leek Soup.

Stir and cook for a further 2-3 minutes. Season to taste with salt and pepper. Garnish each portion with watercress leaves.

Lettuce Soup

PREPARATION TIME: 5-10 minutes	
MICROWAVE COOKING TIME: 13-14 minutes	
MAKES: 1¼ litres/2 pints/5 cups	
TOTAL CALORIES: 285	

2 medium butterhead/cabbage lettuces, rinsed and trimmed
15g/½ oz/1 tbsp low calorie margarine
½ bunch scallions/spring onions, trimmed and finely sliced
15ml/1 tbsp all-purpose/plain flour
570ml/1 pint/2½ cups hot water
1 vegetable stock/bouillon cube, crumbled
280ml/½ pint/1¼ cups skimmed milk
Salt
Freshly ground black pepper
Grated nutmeg
1 small carrot, scraped and cut into julienne strips

Coarsely shred the lettuce. Put the margarine into a large bowl with the scallions/spring onions. Cover and cook for 3 minutes on HIGH. Add lettuce, cover and cook for 5 minutes on HIGH. Blend the flour with 2 tbsps cold water and stir into the lettuce mixture, then add half of the hot water and the stock/bouillon cube. Cover and cook for 3 minutes on HIGH. Purée in a liquidiser/blender, then pour back into the bowl. Stir in the milk and remaining water. Season to taste with salt and pepper and add a dash of grated nutmeg. Reheat for 2-3 minutes on HIGH, stirring once during cooking. Garnish with the carrot strips.

Watercress Soup

PREPARATION TIME: 10 minutes	
MICROWAVE COOKING TIME: 13-21 minutes	
MAKES: 900ml/1½ pints/4 cups	
TOTAL CALORIES: 480	

2 bunches watercress
570ml/1 pint/2½ cups home-made chicken stock
30g/1oz wholemeal/whole-wheat flour
30g/1oz/¼ cup butter
280ml/½ pint/1¼ cups skimmed milk
Salt
Freshly ground black pepper

Rinse the watercress and discard any coarse stalks. Reserve a few leaves for garnish and put the remaining watercress into a large bowl with 280ml/½ pint/1½ cups of the stock. Cover and cook for 3-6 minutes on HIGH until the liquid boils, then cook for a further 8-10 minutes on HIGH until the watercress is tender. Meanwhile, blend the flour and butter together in a small bowl to form a paste. Beat the butter paste, a little at a time, into the boiling mixture. Purée in a blender with the remaining stock, pour back into the bowl and stir in the milk. Cook uncovered for 2 minutes or until bubbles appear around the edges.

This page: Fish Chowder. Facing page: Lettuce Soup (top) and Watercress Soup (bottom).

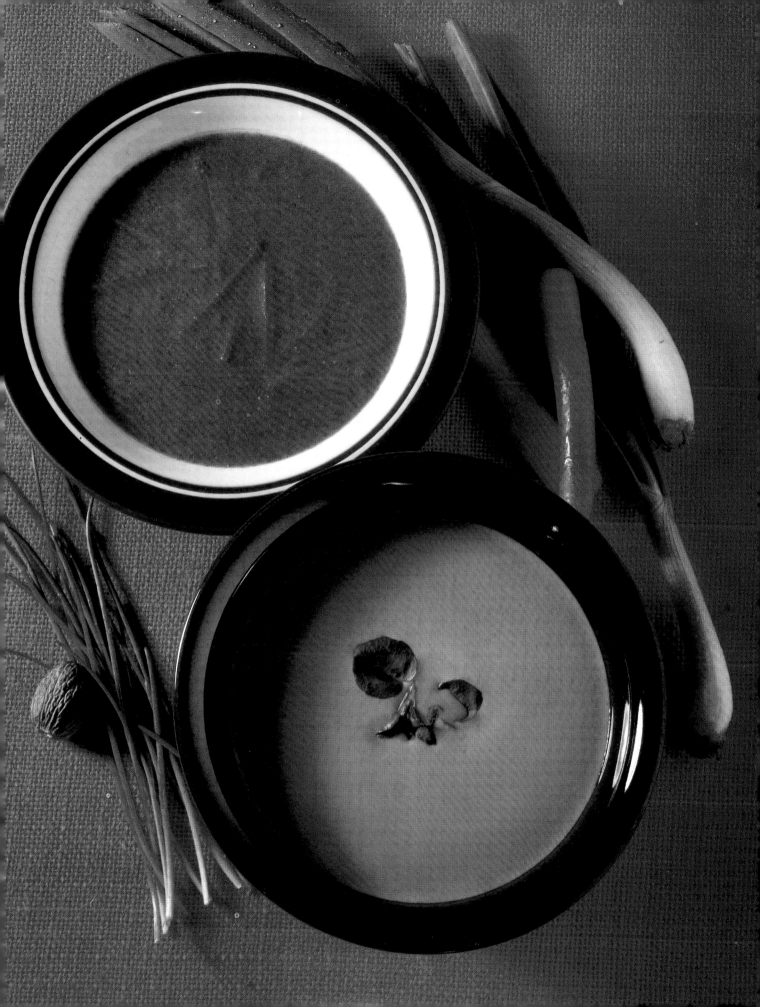

Fit for Life
Snacks Low in Calories

Tacos Mexicana

PREPARATION TIME: 10 minutes	
MICROWAVE COOKING TIME: 2 minutes	
SERVES: 4 people	
TOTAL CALORIES: 962	

120g/4oz Edam/Monterey Jack cheese, grated
2 red or green bottled chilis, seeds removed and finely sliced
60g/2oz can red kidney beans, rinsed and well drained
450g/1lb bean sprouts
8 taco shells
Green or red pepper and onion rings to garnish (optional)

Mix the cheese, chilis, beans and bean sprouts together and pile into the taco shells. Place the tacos close together and curved side down in a small, shallow dish and cook uncovered for 2 minutes on HIGH. Serve immediately.

Eggs Dolmades

PREPARATION TIME: 15 minutes	
MICROWAVE COOKING TIME: 4-5 minutes	
SERVES: 4 people	
TOTAL CALORIES: 565	

1 medium cabbage/butterhead lettuce
4 hard-boiled eggs, finely chopped/ minced
60g/2oz/¼ cup cooked long grain rice
30ml/2 tbsps low calorie mayonnaise
Salt
Freshly ground black pepper

Trim and wash the lettuce leaves. Pat dry or spin. Pile the leaves eight at a time in the microwave and cook uncovered for 30 seconds on HIGH until slightly softened. Remove with a fish slice and repeat with another batch of leaves. Mix together the eggs, rice and mayonnaise and season to taste with salt and pepper. Layer two lettuce leaves together and place a little of the egg mixture in the middle. Roll up, tucking in the sides

This page: Tacos Mexicana. Facing page: Eggs Dolmades (top) and Tuna Scramble (bottom).

to form a parcel. Repeat with the remaining leaves and filling. Arrange the lettuce parcels smooth side up in a small, shallow dish and cook uncovered for 3-4 minutes on HIGH, giving the dish a half turn halfway through cooking. Baste with the juices and serve hot or cold.

Eve's Rarebit

PREPARATION TIME: 5 minutes

MICROWAVE COOKING TIME:
2 minutes

SERVES: 4 people

TOTAL CALORIES: 842

120g/4 oz Edam/Monterey Jack cheese,
*   grated*
1 small onion, peeled and very finely
*   chopped/minced*
1 medium carrot, peeled and grated
15ml/1 tbsp bran
2 eggs
2.5ml/½ tsp mustard powder
30ml/2 tbsps skimmed milk
Salt
Freshly ground black pepper
4 thin slices bread, toasted

Thoroughly mix the cheese, onion, carrot, bran, eggs, mustard and milk together and season with the salt and pepper. Cook uncovered for 2 minutes on HIGH until thickened, beating every 30 seconds. Pile on to the toast and brown under the grill/broiler if desired.

Eggs Benedict on Wilted Watercress

PREPARATION TIME: 10 minutes

MICROWAVE COOKING TIME:
11-12 minutes

SERVES: 6 people

TOTAL CALORIES: 1004

2 bunches watercress
60g/2oz/¼ cup low calorie margarine
8 eggs
30ml/2 tbsps lemon juice
Salt
White pepper

Wash the watercress, remove and discard the thick stalks, and pat the leaves dry. Put the margarine in a small bowl and heat uncovered for

This page: Eggs Benedict on Wilted Watercress. Facing page: Almond and Pepper Timbale (top) and Eve's Rarebit (bottom).

Almond and Pepper Timbale

PREPARATION TIME: 5 minutes

MICROWAVE COOKING TIME:
15-19½ minutes

SERVES: 4 people

TOTAL CALORIES: 755

¼ green pepper, finely diced
1 medium onion, peeled and finely
*   chopped/minced*
120ml/8 tbsps skimmed milk
4 eggs, beaten
60g/2oz Edam/Monterey Jack cheese,
*   grated*
Salt

Freshly ground black pepper
25g/1oz flaked/slivered almonds,
*   browned*

Spread the pepper and onion in a 570ml/1 pint/2½ cup straight-sided soufflé dish. Cover and cook for 2½-3½ minutes on HIGH until the vegetables are cooked. Stir in the milk and, without covering, cook for 30 seconds to 1 minute until the milk is steaming but not boiling. Mix in the eggs and cheese and lightly season. Cover and cook for 12-15 minutes on LOW, giving the dish a half turn once during cooking. Garnish with the almonds and serve hot.

30 seconds on HIGH until melted. Beat two of the eggs and mix with the lemon juice, then whisk into the melted margarine and season with salt and pepper. Cook uncovered for 45 seconds to one minute on HIGH, whisking every 10 seconds until the sauce thickens sufficiently to coat the back of a spoon. Do not overcook or the sauce will curdle. Cover and set aside. Break the remaining six eggs into individual greased poachers or ramekin dishes. Cover each loosely with cling film/plastic wrap and arrange in a circle in the microwave. Cook for 8-9 minutes on LOW until the white is just set, giving each dish a half turn halfway through cooking. Arrange the watercress leaves on a micro-proof serving dish and cook, uncovered, for 1 minute on HIGH to warm and wilt. Arrange the eggs on the watercress, coating them with the sauce. Serve immediately.

Whole-Wheat Vegetable Quiche

PREPARATION TIME: 20 minutes

MICROWAVE COOKING TIME: 21-23 minutes

SERVES: 4 people

TOTAL CALORIES: 873

90g/3oz/¾ cup wholemeal/whole-wheat flour
15g/½ oz/¼ cup bran
60g/2oz/¼ cup low calorie margarine
30ml/2 tbsps cold water
1 small red pepper, cored, seeded and diced
120g/4oz courgettes/zucchini, diced
2 spring onions/scallions, trimmed and finely sliced
1 tomato, skinned and chopped
2 eggs
15ml/1 tbsp skimmed milk
Salt
Pepper

Put the flour and bran in a bowl and rub in the margarine. Add the water and mix to form a wet dough. Put into a 16cm/6½ inch shallow dish and press out to form a pie case. Cook uncovered for 4 minutes on

HIGH, turning the dish every minute. Set aside. Put the diced pepper in a bowl, cover and cook for 2 minutes on HIGH. Add the courgettes/zucchini and onions, then cover and cook for 3 minutes on HIGH. Spread the cooked vegetables and the tomato in the base of the pastry case. Beat the eggs and milk together thoroughly and season with salt and pepper, pour over the vegetables and cook uncovered for 12-14 minutes on LOW, or until set. Give the dish a turn occasionally during cooking. Serve hot or cold.

Tuna Scramble

PREPARATION TIME: 10 minutes

MICROWAVE COOKING TIME: 8-9 minutes

SERVES: 4 people

TOTAL CALORIES: 815

1 small onion, peeled and finely chopped/minced
6 eggs, beaten
6 large tomatoes, skinned and chopped
Salt
Freshly ground black pepper
1 210g/7oz can tuna in brine, drained and flaked

Put the onion in a bowl, cover and cook for 4-5 minutes on HIGH until tender, stirring occasionally. Thoroughly mix in the eggs and tomatoes and season with salt and pepper. Cook uncovered for 3 minutes on HIGH, stirring every minute until the mixture is moistly scrambled. Gently mix in the tuna and continue cooking for 1 minute, stirring gently halfway through the cooking period. Serve on thinly sliced toast if desired.

Cottage Cheese and Chervil Cocottes

PREPARATION TIME: 5 minutes

MICROWAVE COOKING TIME: 5-6 minutes plus standing time

SERVES: 4 people

TOTAL CALORIES: 370

225g/8oz cottage cheese
1 egg
2 spring onions/scallions, finely sliced
2.5ml/½ tsp dried chervil or 10ml/2 tsp fresh chervil
10ml/2 tsp freshly chopped parsley
Pinch ground mace
Salt
Pepper
30ml/2 tbsps soured cream

Mix the cottage cheese, egg, onion, chervil, parsley and mace to a smooth paste in the blender. Season to taste with salt and pepper. Divide the mixture between four individual ramekins, cover each with cling film/plastic wrap and cook for 5-6 minutes on LOW until just set. Leave to stand for 3 minutes, then uncover and pour a little cream on each. Serve hot or cold.

Soufflé Omelette

PREPARATION TIME: 10 minutes

MICROWAVE COOKING TIME: 7-11 minutes plus standing time

SERVES: 2 people

TOTAL CALORIES: 350

5ml/1 tsp vegetable oil
Non-stick vegetable parchment
190g/6¾ oz can pimentos, drained and puréed
5ml/1 tsp tomato purée/paste
15ml/1 tbsp pine kernels, finely grated
Salt
Freshly ground black pepper
3 eggs, separated
45ml/3 tbsp cold water

Brush a little of the oil round the edge and in the base of a 22cm/9 inch shallow, round dish and line the base with a disc of non-stick vegetable parchment. Mix the puréed pimentos, tomato purée/paste, nuts and seasoning in a small bowl, and cook uncovered for 1-2 minutes on HIGH, stirring occasionally. Cover and keep warm. Using grease-free

Facing page: Whole-Wheat Vegetable Quiche.

This page: Soufflé Omelette. Facing page: Cottage Cheese and Chervil Cocottes (top) and Egg, Bacon and Tomato Pots (bottom).

beaters, whisk the egg whites until stiff. In another large bowl whisk the egg yolks and water, with salt and pepper to taste. Stir in one tablespoon of the egg white, then gently fold in the remainder. Pour the egg mixture into the prepared dish and cook uncovered for 5-8 minutes on LOW until just set. Give the dish a quarter turn every minute during cooking. Leave to stand for 1 minute, then turn out onto a flame-proof dish and gently fold the omelette over. Lightly brown under the grill/broiler. Reheat the sauce for 1 minute on HIGH, then pour over the omelette. Serve immediately.

Egg, Bacon and Tomato Pots

PREPARATION TIME: 8 minutes	
MICROWAVE COOKING TIME: 20-23½ minutes	
SERVES: 4 people	
TOTAL CALORIES: 745	

4 large beef/Moroccan tomatoes
5ml/1 tsp cornstarch/cornflour
2.5ml/½ tsp bottled fruity sauce
5ml/1 tsp tomato purée/paste
Salt
Freshly ground black pepper
2 bacon rashers/slices, rind and outside fat removed
4 eggs, beaten together

Cut off a thick slice from the stalk end of the tomatoes. Scrape out all the pulp into a bowl, making sure that the tomatoes are well drained. Cover and cook for 3 minutes on HIGH, then press through a sieve into another bowl and discard the pips. Stir in the cornstarch/cornflour, sauce and tomato purée/paste and season to taste with salt and pepper. Cook uncovered for 1-2 minutes on HIGH, stirring occasionally until the mixture thickens. Dice the bacon and spread out on a saucer covered with absorbent kitchen paper. Cook for 30 seconds on HIGH. Arrange the tomato shells open side up in a shallow dish, three-quarters fill with the beaten egg and top with the bacon. Cover and cook for 10 minutes on LOW. Carefully stir the egg and bacon filling, then cook uncovered for 5-7 minutes on LOW. Remove from the microwave, then reheat the sauce, covered, for 30 seconds to 1 minute on HIGH. Pour over the tomatoes and serve hot.

Fit for Life

Slimline Fish and Seafood

Quenelles Poche au Crème de Tomates

PREPARATION TIME: 10-15 minutes

MICROWAVE COOKING TIME: 21-22 minutes

SERVES: 4 people

TOTAL CALORIES: 645

450g/1lb pike or whitefish fillet
1 bay leaf
1 spring onion/scallion, peeled and sliced
1 blade mace
140ml/¼ pint/⅔ cup water
3 thin slices white bread, crusts removed
45ml/3 tbsp skimmed milk
2 egg whites
Salt
Pepper
Pinch grated nutmeg
1 430ml/15 fl oz/2 cup can low calorie tomato soup
Freshly chopped parsley to garnish (optional)

Skin the fish and remove any bones. Cut up the skin and place with the bones, bay leaf, onion, mace and water in a bowl. Cook uncovered for 2-3 minutes on HIGH or until boiling. Reduce the setting and cook for 10 minutes on LOW. Strain the liquor and make up to 90ml/6 tbsp with water if necessary. If the liquor exceeds this quantity, continue cooking on FULL POWER until it is reduced. Cut up the fish and purée in the food processor with the bread coarsely torn, the milk, egg whites and fish liquor. Season with salt, pepper and nutmeg. Pour the soup into a large, shallow dish and cook uncovered for 2-3 minutes on HIGH until hot, stirring occasionally. Divide the fish mixture into eight oval shapes using two tablespoons and place well spaced out into the hot soup. Cover and cook for 6 minutes on HIGH, repositioning the fish quenelles halfway through cooking. Serve hot, garnished with parsley if desired.

Cutlets, Sauce Champignon

PREPARATION TIME: 10 minutes

MICROWAVE COOKING TIME: 18-20 minutes

SERVES: 4 people

TOTAL CALORIES: 794

10ml/2 tsp corn oil
1 medium onion, peeled and finely chopped/minced
1 garlic clove, skinned and crushed
10ml/2 tsp cornstarch/cornflour
140ml/¼ pint/⅔ cup dry white wine
30ml/2 tbsps tomato purée/paste
1.25ml/¼ tsp mixed dry herbs
Salt
Freshly ground black pepper
225g/8oz mushrooms, sliced
4 225g/8oz cod steaks
Low calorie sweetener

Combine the oil, onion and garlic in a bowl, cover and cook for 3 minutes on HIGH until the onion is soft. Stir in the cornstarch/cornflour, wine, tomato purée/paste and herbs and season with salt and pepper. Cook uncovered for 2 minutes on HIGH, then beat thoroughly with a whisk. Stir in the mushrooms and cook uncovered for 5-6 minutes on HIGH, stirring occasionally until the mushrooms are tender and the sauce is thick. Cover and set aside. Arrange the cod steaks in a shallow dish, the thin ends towards the centre. Cover and cook for 6-7 minutes on HIGH until the fish is cooked. Spoon the juices into the mushroom mixture, adjust seasoning to taste, adding a drop of liquid sweetener. Pour the sauce over the fish and, without covering, reheat on HIGH for 2 minutes. Serve hot.

Fish Pie

PREPARATION TIME: 10 minutes

MICROWAVE COOKING TIME: 10-12 minutes

SERVES: 4 people

TOTAL CALORIES: 1030

1 tbsp vegetable oil
30g/1oz/¼ cup flour
225ml/8 fl oz/1 cup skimmed milk
Salt
Pepper
450g/1lb whitefish fillets, skinned
4 slightly undercooked hard boiled eggs
15ml/1 tbsp capers, chopped

Stir the oil and flour together in a medium bowl and cook for 30 seconds on HIGH. Beat in the milk and cook uncovered for 1 minute on HIGH. Beat, then cook for a further 1½-2 minutes on HIGH, beating every 30 seconds. Season to taste with salt and pepper. Arrange half the fish in a round or square dish, cover with a layer of sliced eggs, then spoon over half the sauce. Repeat the

Facing page: Cutlets, Sauce Champignon.

layers, then top with a sprinkling of capers. Cook uncovered for 5-6 minutes on HIGH, turning the dish every 2 minutes until the fish is cooked. Brown under the grill/broiler if the dish is flameproof.

Fresh Salmon Steaks Royale

PREPARATION TIME: 5 minutes

MICROWAVE COOKING TIME: 11-15 minutes

SERVES: 4 people

TOTAL CALORIES: 1373

4 225g/6oz fresh salmon steaks
Salt
Freshly ground black pepper
10ml/2 tsp crushed dill weed
2 scallops, washed and sliced
60g/2oz cooked, shelled prawns/shrimp
15g/½ oz lumpfish caviar

Season the salmon with salt and pepper and sprinkle one side of the steaks with the dill weed. Arrange herb side down in a single layer, the thicker parts towards the outside in a large, shallow dish. Cover with non-stick baking parchment and cook for

This page: Fresh Salmon Steaks Royale. Facing page: Quenelles Poche au Crème de Tomates (top) and Fish Pie (bottom).

9-12 minutes on LOW. Transfer the salmon steaks to a hot serving dish. Stir the scallops and prawns/shrimp into the juices remaining in the dish. Cover tightly and cook for 2-3 minutes on LOW until the scallops are opaque. Arrange the scallops and prawns/shrimp on top of the salmon and sprinkle with caviar.

Curried Prawns/Shrimp

PREPARATION TIME: 5 minutes

MICROWAVE COOKING TIME: 8-9 minutes

SERVES: 4 people as a starter

TOTAL CALORIES: 560

5ml/1 tsp vegetable oil
1 small shallot, peeled and finely
* chopped/minced*
7.5ml/1½ tsp garam masala
⅛ tsp Cayenne pepper
Pinch salt
Pinch freshly ground black pepper
225g/8oz/1 cup shelled, cooked,
* prawns/shrimp*
¼ red pepper, cut into thin strips
15ml/1 tbsp water
180g/6oz/1 cup cooked long grain rice
15ml/1 tbsp low fat natural yogurt

Combine the oil, shallot, garam masala, Cayenne, salt and pepper in a medium bowl. Cover and cook for 2 minutes on HIGH. Drain the prawns/shrimp if freshly thawed and stir into the mixture. Cover and set aside. Put pepper strips and water in a dish, cover and cook for 2 minutes on HIGH. Drain and set aside. Arrange a border of rice on one large or four small micro-proof serving dishes. Place in the microwave and heat for 2-2½ minutes on HIGH. Heat the prawn/shrimp mixture for 2-2½ minutes on HIGH, stirring once during cooking. Stir the yogurt into the hot prawns/shrimp, then spoon into the centre of the rice. Garnish with a lattice of pepper strips and serve immediately.

Lemon Poached Trout

PREPARATION TIME: 5 minutes

MICROWAVE COOKING TIME: 16-18 minutes

SERVES: 4 people

TOTAL CALORIES: 985

1 small onion, peeled and finely chopped/
* minced*
1 celery stalk, finely chopped/minced
1 leek, trimmed, washed and thinly sliced
1 bay leaf

2.5ml/½ tsp lemon thyme
4 black peppercorns
140ml/¼ pint/⅔ cup medium white
* wine*
15ml/1 tbsp fresh lemon juice
Salt
4 225g/8oz trout, gutted and cleaned
15ml/1 tbsp cornstarch/cornflour
60ml/4 tbsps/¼ cup water
Lemon and cucumber slices to garnish

Combine the onion, celery, leek, bay leaf, lemon thyme, peppercorns, wine and lemon juice in a large bowl. Cover and cook for 5 minutes on HIGH. Add salt to taste. Leave to cool. Arrange the fish in a single layer

This page: Folded Flounder in Pernod Sauce. Facing page: Curried Prawns/Shrimp (top) and Lemon Poached Trout (bottom).

in a large, shallow dish and strain in the liquid. Cover and cook for 8 minutes on HIGH, basting occasionally with the juices. Remove the two outer fish. Cover and cook the remaining fish for 2 minutes on HIGH, then remove from the dish. Peel off the skin and remove the heads from the fish if desired. Blend the cornstarch/cornflour with the water, stir into the liquid remaining

in the dish and cook uncovered for 1-2 minutes on HIGH, stirring halfway through cooking. When the sauce thickens pour over the fish and garnish with lemon and cucumber slices cut into triangles.

Folded Flounder in Pernod Sauce

PREPARATION TIME: 5 minutes

MICROWAVE COOKING TIME: 25-29 minutes

SERVES: 4 people

TOTAL CALORIES: 604

225g/8oz bulb fennel, trimmed and shredded
140ml/¼ pint/⅔ cup skimmed milk
15ml/1 tbsp Pernod
Salt
Freshly ground black pepper
4 120g/4oz plaice/flounder fillets, skinned if preferred
1 egg yolk
15ml/1 tbsp cold water
Green fennel sprigs to garnish

Put the fennel in a bowl, cover and cook for 4-5 minutes on HIGH until soft, stirring once during cooking. Without uncovering, set aside. Put the milk and Pernod in a suitable shallow dish and cook uncovered for 2½-3 minutes on HIGH or until boiling. Reduce the setting and cook for 5 minutes on LOW. Season the fish with salt and pepper and fold each fillet in half. Arrange slightly overlapping in the liquid in the dish. Cover and cook for 10-12 minutes on LOW until the fish is just cooked. Arrange the shredded fennel on a suitable micro-proof serving dish. Using two fish slices place the fish on top of the fennel. Pour the remaining liquor into a bowl. Blend the egg yolk and water together, mix into the liquid and cook uncovered for 2½-3 minutes on HIGH, beating every 15-20 seconds until the sauce thickens to the consistency of thin cream. Do not overcook or the sauce will curdle. Lightly cover the fish and fennel and reheat for 1 minute on HIGH, then pour the sauce over the fish and garnish with fennel sprigs.

Luxury Seafood Shells

PREPARATION TIME: 10 minutes

MICROWAVE COOKING TIME: 4½-5½ minutes

SERVES: 4 people

TOTAL CALORIES: 765

4 90g/3oz plaice/flounder fillets, skinned
10ml/2 tsp lemon juice
120g/4oz/½ cup cooked shelled prawns/shrimp
4 scallops, washed and cut into quarters
90g/3oz crabmeat
15g/½ oz/1 tbsp butter
Salt
Freshly ground black pepper
Pinch grated nutmeg
Cayenne pepper

Cut the fish lengthwise into 2.5 cm/1 inch wide strips, sprinkle with lemon juice and roll up. Arrange the fish rolls, prawns/shrimp and scallops in four individual shells and top with the crabmeat. Put the butter, salt, pepper and nutmeg in a small jug and heat uncovered for 30 seconds on HIGH until melted. Pour over the fish and sprinkle with Cayenne. Arrange the shells in a circle in the microwave and cover each with a disc of non-stick vegetable parchment. Cook for 2-3 minutes on HIGH, give the dishes a half turn then continue cooking for 2-3 minutes on HIGH until the fish and scallops are cooked. Do not overcook.

Smoked Trout Mousse

PREPARATION TIME: 10 minutes

MICROWAVE COOKING TIME: 1 minute

MAKES: Approximately 570ml/1 pint/2½ cups

SERVES: 4-8 people)

TOTAL CALORIES: 450

225g/8oz smoked trout (weight after skinning and boning)
1 small shallot, peeled and quartered
140ml/¼ pint/⅔ cup low fat natural yogurt
1.25ml/¼ tsp grated mace
Salt
Freshly ground black pepper
60ml/4 tbsps/¼ cup water
15g/½ oz envelope gelatine
2 egg whites
Orange or lemon slices to garnish

Make sure that all the bones have been removed, then liquidise/blend the fish with the shallot, yogurt and mace, seasoning sparingly with salt and pepper. Put the water in a jug and heat uncovered for 30 seconds on HIGH. Sprinkle the gelatine over the surface, then stir and cook for 20 seconds on HIGH. Stir until the gelatine has dissolved. Leave to cool for 5 minutes, then pour gradually into the puréed fish, beating continuously. Whisk the egg whites until stiff and fold into the fish mixture. Pour into a mould and chill until set. Garnish with orange or lemon slices.

Mackerel in Gooseberry Sauce

PREPARATION TIME: 15 minutes

MICROWAVE COOKING TIME: 14-15 minutes

SERVES: 4 people

TOTAL CALORIES: 1570

225g/8oz/1¼ cups gooseberries, fresh or frozen
120ml/4 fl oz water
5ml/1 tsp grated lemon zest
5ml/1 tsp caster sugar
Low calorie sweetener to taste
Freshly ground black pepper
4 285g/10oz mackerel, cleaned and heads removed

Top and tail the gooseberries if necessary and put them into a bowl with the water, lemon zest and sugar. Cook for 5-6 minutes, stirring once during cooking until the gooseberries are soft. Purée in the blender, then rub through a sieve/strainer. Add

Facing page: Luxury Seafood Shells (top) and Smoked Trout Mousse (bottom).

sweetener to taste. Season the mackerel and arrange in a single layer in a large, shallow dish. Cover with non-stick vegetable parchment or a lid and cook for 4 minutes on HIGH. Reposition, putting the two fish on the outside in the middle. Cover and cook for a further 3 minutes on HIGH. Pour the gooseberry sauce over and cook uncovered for 2 minutes on HIGH, or until the fish is cooked.

Smoky Fish Kebabs

PREPARATION TIME: 10 minutes

MICROWAVE COOKING TIME: 4-7 minutes

SERVES: 8 people

TOTAL CALORIES: 550 excluding rice

450g/1lb thick smoked cod fillet, skinned
180g/6oz cucumber
16 pearl baby onions
4 tomatoes
8 wooden skewers
120g/4oz long grain rice cooked in saffron (optional)

Cut the fish into sixteen cubes. Cut the cucumber into eight 1cm/½ inch slices, then cut each slice in half again. Halve the tomatoes. Thread each skewer in the following order – cucumber, fish, onion, tomato, onion, fish, cucumber. Arrange the skewers on a shallow dish or plate and cook for 4-7 minutes on HIGH, repositioning halfway through the cooking time.

Fillets Stälhammer

PREPARATION TIME: 15 minutes

MICROWAVE COOKING TIME: 10-11 minutes

SERVES: 4-6 people

TOTAL CALORIES: 972

1 large leek, trimmed, rinsed and finely sliced
12 spring onions/scallions, trimmed, rinsed and finely sliced
105ml/6 tbsps white wine

1 210g/7oz can shrimp
Pinch saffron
10ml/2 tsp arrowroot
60ml/4 tbsps cold water
Salt
Freshly ground black pepper
1 125g/4oz can mussels
450g/1lb whitefish fillet
2 tomatoes, skinned and sliced
Chopped parsley to garnish

Put the leek and spring onions/scallions in a medium bowl with the wine, the drained liquor from the shrimp and the saffron. Stir

This page: Smoky Fish Kebabs (top) and Fillets Stälhammer (bottom). Facing page: Middle European Gratinee.

thoroughly, then cover and cook for 5 minutes on HIGH, stirring once during cooking, until the vegetables are tender. Mix the arrowroot and water together and season with salt and pepper. Stir into the vegetables, cover and cook for 1-2 minutes on HIGH, stirring frequently until the

sauce thickens. Drain the mussels, discarding their liquor, rinse and drain. Add the mussels and shrimps to the vegetable mixture. Arrange the fish fillets in a single layer in a shallow dish and season with salt and pepper. Top with the tomato slices. Pour the sauce over, then cover the dish and cook for 4 minutes on HIGH, giving the dish a half turn halfway through cooking. Sprinkle with the parsley and serve hot.

Middle European Gratinee

PREPARATION TIME: 15 minutes	
MICROWAVE COOKING TIME: 14-16 minutes	
SERVES: 4 people	
TOTAL CALORIES: 842	

1 medium onion, peeled and finely chopped/minced
6 medium tomatoes, skinned and chopped
5ml/1 tsp dry basil
Salt
Freshly ground black pepper
450g/1lb whitefish fillet, skinned
450g/1lb courgettes/zucchini rinsed, topped and tailed and thinly sliced
60g/2oz Edam/Monterey Jack cheese
30ml/2 tbsps fresh breadcrumbs

Put the onion into a bowl, cover and cook for 1 minute on HIGH. Stir in the tomatoes and basil and season with salt and pepper. Arrange layers of fish, onion mixture and courgettes/zucchini in a shallow dish, finishing with a layer of courgettes/ zucchini. Cover and cook for 10 minutes on HIGH, turning the dish three times during cooking. Mix the cheese and breadcrumbs together and sprinkle over the courgette/ zucchini. Without covering, cook for 3-5 minutes on HIGH or until the fish and courgettes/zucchini are cooked. If the dish is flameproof brown under the grill/broiler.

This page: Mackerel Gooseberry Sauce. Facing page: Welsh Ham Rolls.

Fit for Life

Main Meals that won't put on Inches!

Welsh Ham Rolls

PREPARATION TIME: 12 minutes

MICROWAVE COOKING TIME:
12-14 minutes

SERVES: 4-6 people

TOTAL CALORIES: 688

450g/1lb leeks, washed, trimmed and
  finely sliced
140ml/¼ pint/⅔ cup salted water
Freshly ground black pepper
180g/6oz/¾ cup cottage cheese
2 sping onions/scallions, trimmed and
  finely sliced
1 egg
6 30g/1oz even shaped, lean, cooked ham
  slices

Put the leeks and water into a
casserole. Cover and cook for
6 minutes on HIGH. Without
draining, purée in the liquidiser or
food processor. Season with pepper
and add salt if necessary. Spread the
purée in a shallow oval dish, and
cook for 2-3 minutes on HIGH.
Thoroughly mix the cottage cheese,
spring onions/scallions with the egg
and pile a border of the mixture
along one edge of each ham slice.
Roll up and arrange on top of the
purée. Cover and cook for 4-6
minutes on HIGH. Serve hot.

Chicken Indienne

PREPARATION TIME: 2 minutes
plus marinating time

MICROWAVE COOKING TIME:
9-11 minutes

SERVES: 4 people

TOTAL CALORIES: 614

60ml/4 tbsps/¼ cup low fat natural
  yogurt
15ml/1 tbsp curry paste
1.25ml/¼ tsp salt
4 120g/4oz boneless chicken breasts
Fresh coriander leaves to garnish

In a shallow micro-proof dish
combine the yogurt, curry paste and
salt. Add the chicken breasts, turning
the pieces until all are well coated.
Cover and refrigerate for 12 hours,
turning the chicken pieces over

30ml/2 tbsp dry sherry
30ml/2 tbsp tomato purée/paste
30ml/2 tbsp Tamari sauce
10ml/2 tsp clear honey

Separate the ribs and trim away excess fat. Rub with salt and pepper. In a large dish combine the vinegar, sherry, tomato purée/paste, Tamari sauce and honey. Add the ribs and turn them until they are well coated. Cover the dish and leave to marinate in a cool place for 3-4 hours, turning the ribs occasionally. Pile the ribs on a rack in a shallow dish. Cover with non-stick paper and cook for 5 minutes on HIGH. Reposition and brush with marinade. Cover and cook for 5 minutes on HIGH, brushing with any remaining marinade. Cover and cook for 20 minutes on LOW until the meat is cooked. Serve hot.

Bombay Chicken Salad

PREPARATION TIME: 8 minutes plus marinating time	
MICROWAVE COOKING TIME: 5-6 minutes	
SERVES: 4-8 people	
TOTAL CALORIES: 1070	

450g/1lb boneless raw chicken
Grated zest and juice of one lemon and
*   grated zest and juice of one lime*
30ml/2 tbsps garam masala
4 dessert apples
½ head/bunch celery, finely sliced
10 spring onions/scallions, finely sliced
4 fresh dates, stoned and finely sliced
280ml/½ pint/1¼ cups low fat natural
*   yogurt*
Salt
Freshly ground black pepper

Dice the chicken and put into a bowl with the citrus zest and juices. Mix in the garam masala thoroughly. Cover and leave to stand for 20 minutes, stirring once. Cover and cook for

occasionally. Cover with non-stick baking parchment and cook for 4 minutes on HIGH. Reposition and turn the chicken pieces over and cook for 3 minutes or until the chicken is cooked. Transfer the chicken breasts to a serving plate and keep warm. Stirring frequently, cook the remaining sauce uncovered for 2-4 minutes on HIGH until slightly reduced. Spoon the sauce over the chicken. Garnish with fresh coriander leaves and serve with a tomato and onion salad.

Barbecued Spare Ribs

PREPARATION TIME: 10 minutes	
MICROWAVE COOKING TIME: 30 minutes	
SERVES: 4 people	
TOTAL CALORIES: 360	

8 pork spare ribs, total weight
*   approximately 900g/2lb*
Salt
·Freshly ground black pepper
30ml/2 tbsp vinegar

This page: Barbecued Spare Ribs. Facing page: Bombay Chicken Salad (top) and Chicken Indienne (bottom).

5-6 minutes on HIGH, stirring once during cooking until the chicken is cooked. Cool rapidly. Drain away surplus juices. Core and dice the apples and mix into the chicken with the remaining ingredients. Season to taste. Chill for one hour before serving. Not suitable for freezing.

Turkey Fillet en Papillote

PREPARATION TIME: 15 minutes

MICROWAVE COOKING TIME:
6 minutes plus standing time

SERVES: 4 people

TOTAL CALORIES: 575

450g/1lb raw turkey breast fillet, about
  1cm/½ inch thick
120g/4oz button mushrooms, sliced
Salt
Freshly ground black pepper
1 large red pepper, cored, seeded and cut
  into rings
Paprika

Cut the fillet into four even pieces. Slash each piece vertically in three places part way through, and insert mushroom slices into these slits. Season with salt and pepper. Put each piece onto a sheet of non-stick baking parchment. Top each turkey piece with two pepper rings and sprinkle with paprika. Wrap each parcel separately, making sure that the turkey portion is completely enclosed. Secure with wooden pick/cocktail stick if necessary. Arrange the parcels in a circle in the microwave and cook for 6 minutes on HIGH, repositioning halfway through cooking time. Leave wrapped for 5 minutes. Open the parcels and baste the turkey with the juices. Re-wrap and add extra cooking time if necessary. Serve hot.

Chinese Meatballs

PREPARATION TIME: 10 minutes

MICROWAVE COOKING TIME:
6 minutes

SERVES: 4 people

TOTAL CALORIES: 1050

450g/1lb/2 cups lean raw minced/
  ground beef
30ml/2 tbsps bran
1 egg
Grated zest and juice of 1 lemon
15ml/1 tbsp tomato purée/paste
15ml/1 tbsp French/Dijon mustard
Salt
Freshly ground black pepper
450g/1lb/8 cups bean sprouts, rinsed
  and drained
1 small red pepper, seeded, cored and
  diced
1 large carrot, peeled and cut into thin
  strips
15ml/1 tbsp dark soy sauce

Mix together the meat, bran, egg, lemon juice and zest, tomato purée/paste and mustard. Season with salt and pepper. Form into sixteen balls and arrange in a shallow dish. Cover and cook for 5-6 minutes on HIGH, repositioning the meatballs once during cooking. Meanwhile, pat the bean sprouts dry in a clean cloth, then combine with the diced pepper and carrot strips. Arrange in nests in individual dishes. Put three or four meatballs in the centre of each nest. Sprinkle with soy sauce and serve immediately.

Chicken and Ham Stuffed Mushrooms

PREPARATION TIME: 10 minutes

MICROWAVE COOKING TIME:
6½ minutes

SERVES: 4 as a main course or
6 as a starter

TOTAL CALORIES: 395

8 7.5cm/3 inch open flat mushrooms
90g/3oz cooked minced/ground chicken
30g/1oz lean cooked ham, finely chopped
1 egg, separated
2 spring onions/scallions, finely sliced
Salt
Freshly ground black pepper
1.25ml/¼ tsp cornstarch/cornflour
30ml/2 tbsps soured cream
Paprika
Spring onions/scallions to garnish

Remove and finely chop the mushroom stalks, then mix with the chicken, ham, egg yolk and onions and season with salt and pepper. Beat egg white until stiff and fold in. Arrange the mushroom caps dark side up in a shallow dish. Pile the filling on the mushrooms and cook uncovered for 6 minutes on HIGH until the mushrooms are tender. Remove to a hot serving dish. Mix together the cornstarch/cornflour and cream and stir into the juices remaining in the dish. Cook uncovered for 30 seconds on HIGH. (Do not overcook or the cream will curdle.) Pour a little sauce on each mushroom, sprinkle with paprika and garnish with spring onions/scallions. Serve immediately.

Saucy Meatloaf

PREPARATION TIME: 5 minutes

MICROWAVE COOKING TIME:
11 minutes plus standing time

SERVES: 4 people

TOTAL CALORIES: 960

225g/8oz/2 cups lean raw minced/
  ground beef
225g/8oz/2 cups lean raw minced/
  ground pork
120g/4oz carrots, peeled and grated
1 egg
60g/2oz chives, chopped or 30ml/2 tbsps
  dried chives
15ml/1 tbsp finely chopped celery
30ml/2 tbsp bottled fruity sauce
Salt
Freshly ground black pepper
Parsley sprigs, chives and carrot flowers to
  garnish

Mix together the beef, pork, carrot, egg, chives, celery and 1 tbsp of the fruity sauce. Season with salt and pepper. Press the mixture into a 19 x 9 x 5cm/7 x 3½ x 2 inch/1½ pint glass, loaf-shaped dish. Cook uncovered for 10 minutes on HIGH,

Facing page: Chicken and Ham Stuffed Mushrooms.

turning occasionally. Drain away fat. Cover and leave to stand for 10 minutes. Turn out onto a dish or non-stick paper and quickly reverse onto a suitable flameproof serving dish. Spread the remaining sauce over the top and down the sides of the meatloaf using a round-bladed knife. Cook uncovered for 1 minute on HIGH or brown under the grill/broiler. Garnish with parsley sprigs, chives and carrot flowers.

This page: Turkey Fillet en Papillote. Facing page: Chinese Meatballs (top) and Saucy Meatloaf (bottom).

Lamb Chops with Currant Sauce

PREPARATION TIME: 5 minutes	
MICROWAVE COOKING TIME: 6 minutes	
SERVES: 4 people	
TOTAL CALORIES: 760	

4 120g/4oz loin lamb chops, well
*   trimmed*
45g/1½ oz/¼ cup currants
90ml/6 tbsps water
30g/1oz/½ cup fresh brown breadcrumbs
Pinch ground cloves
40ml/2½ tbsp red wine
1.25ml/¼ tsp butter
Cooked French/green beans to garnish

Arrange the chops in a shallow dish or preheated, oiled browning dish, the bones towards the centre. Cover with wax/greaseproof paper and cook for 2½ minutes on HIGH. Place the currants in a bowl with the water, cover and cook for 2 minutes on HIGH. Add all the remaining ingredients, cover and cook for 1½ minutes on HIGH. Transfer the chops to a micro-proof serving dish and top each with the sauce. Cook uncovered for 5 minutes on LOW. Garnish with the French/green beans.

Liver and Tomato Slaw

PREPARATION TIME: 15 minutes	
MICROWAVE COOKING TIME: 14 minutes plus heating browning dish	
SERVES: 4 people	
TOTAL CALORIES: 1230	

285g/10oz white cabbage, finely
*   shredded*
1 small onion, peeled and finely chopped
1 carrot, peeled and grated
60ml/4 tbsps/¼ cup natural low fat
*   yogurt*
15ml/1 tbsp horseradish sauce
15ml/1 tbsp low calorie mayonnaise/
*   salad dressing*
15ml/1 tbsp finely chopped parsley
15ml/1 tbsp vegetable oil

450g/1lb lambs liver, trimmed and sliced
Salt
Freshly ground black pepper
8 tomatoes, sliced
5ml/1 tsp gravy powder

Mix the cabbage, onion and carrot in a large bowl. Combine the yogurt, sauces and parsley in a smaller bowl. Season the liver with salt and pepper. Preheat a large browning dish to maximum, add the oil and quickly brown half of the liver slices on both sides. Remove them from the browning dish and set aside. Reheat the browning dish for 2 minutes on HIGH, then brown the remaining liver slices. Layer the liver slices and tomatoes in the browning dish or a suitable casserole, finishing with a layer of tomato. Sprinkle with the gravy powder. Cover and cook for 8-10 minutes on HIGH until the liver is just cooked. Cover and leave to stand for 5 minutes. Meanwhile cook the vegetables uncovered for 4 minutes on HIGH, stirring once. Stir the sauce into the warm vegetables and serve with the liver.

Chicken Escalopes in Paprika Sauce

PREPARATION TIME: 20 minutes	
MICROWAVE COOKING TIME: 16-18 minutes plus standing time	
SERVES: 4 people	
TOTAL CALORIES: 876	

15g/½ oz/1 tbsp butter
1 small green pepper, cored, seeded and
*   diced*
1 small onion, peeled and finely chopped/
*   minced*
1 garlic clove, peeled and crushed
7.5ml/1½ tsp mild paprika
15g/1 tbsp all-purpose/plain flour
140ml/¼ pint/⅔ cup dry white wine
140ml/¼ pint/⅔ cup hot chicken stock
2 tomatoes, skinned and chopped
Salt
Freshly ground black pepper
4 120g/4oz boneless chicken breasts,
*   skinned*

Put the butter in a medium bowl and

add the pepper, onion and garlic. Cover and cook for 4-5 minutes on HIGH, stirring occasionally, until the vegetables are tender. Stir in the paprika and flour, and cook uncovered for 1 minute on HIGH. Stir in the wine, stock and tomatoes and season to taste with salt and pepper. Cook uncovered for 4 minutes on HIGH until the mixture thickens, stirring occasionally during cooking. Cover tightly and set aside. Arrange the chicken in a shallow dish, cover and cook for 3 minutes on HIGH. Reposition and turn the pieces over, then cover and cook for 2-3 minutes on HIGH until the chicken is cooked. Leave for 1 minute, then uncover and transfer the chicken to a hot serving dish. Pour the sauce over, cover and cook for 2 minutes on HIGH until the sauce is hot.

Tropical Lamb Kebabs

PREPARATION TIME: 20 minutes plus standing time	
MICROWAVE COOKING TIME: 18-20 minutes	
SERVES: 4 people	
TOTAL CALORIES: 920	

450g/1lb lean leg of lamb, cut into
*   2½ cm/1 inch cubes*
2.5ml/½ tsp meat tenderising powder
3 thick slices fresh pineapple, each cut
*   into 8 wedges*
Salt
1.25ml/¼ tsp ground cumin
1.25ml/¼ tsp turmeric
15ml/1 tbsp black treacle/molasses
1 small onion, peeled and sliced into thick
*   rings*
¼ head Chinese leaves, shredded
Alfalfa to garnish

Sprinkle the lamb with meat tenderising powder and set aside in a cool place for 1 hour. Thread the

Facing page: Lamb Chops with Currant Sauce (top left) and Liver and Tomato Slaw (top right and bottom).

meat cubes and pineapple wedges alternately onto twelve cocktail sticks. Season with salt and sprinkle with cumin and turmeric. Put the treacle/molasses into a shallow dish and heat uncovered for 20 seconds on HIGH. Carefully place kebabs in the dish, turning them in the molasses mixture until they are well coated. Cook uncovered for 15-20 minutes on LOW until the lamb is just cooked. Serve on a bed of onion and Chinese leaves. Garnish with alfalfa.

Kidneys in Creamy Wine Sauce

PREPARATION TIME: 15 minutes	
MICROWAVE COOKING TIME: 12 minutes	
SERVES: 4 people	
TOTAL CALORIES: 540	

450g/1lb/8 lambs kidneys, skinned
1 medium onion, peeled and very finely chopped
1 small garlic clove, peeled and crushed with 2.5ml/½ tsp salt
30ml/2 tbsp medium red wine
10ml/2 tsp French/Dijon mustard
Shake Tabasco (optional)
Freshly ground black pepper
60ml/4 tbsp/¼ cup low fat skimmed milk soft cheese (Quark)

Quarter the kidneys, removing the core with scissors. Set aside. Mix the onion, garlic and wine together in a casserole dish, cover and cook for 3 minutes on HIGH. Stir in the mustard, Tabasco and pepper to taste, then stir in the kidneys. Cover and cook for 3 minutes on HIGH. Stir and cook for a further 2 minutes on HIGH until the kidneys are just pink inside. Stir in the cheese (Quark) and cook uncovered for 4 minutes on LOW, stirring once during cooking.

This page: Chicken Escalopes in Paprika Sauce. Facing page: Tropical Lamb Kebabs (top) and Kidneys in Creamy Wine Sauce (bottom).

Fillet Steak au Poivre

PREPARATION TIME: 5 minutes

MICROWAVE COOKING TIME:
4-6 minutes plus heating browning dish

SERVES: 4 people

TOTAL CALORIES: 1150

4 120g/4oz fillet steaks
15ml/1 tbsp brandy
15ml/1 tbsp vegetable oil
30ml/2 tbsp green peppercorns
60ml/4 tbsp/¼ cup soured cream

Salt
4 small tomatoes, halved and cooked

First brush the steaks with brandy and then with the oil. Crush the peppercorns with a rolling pin and press onto one side only of each steak. Preheat a large browning dish to maximum, then immediately press in the steaks, peppercorn side uppermost. Cook uncovered for 1 minute on HIGH. Turn steaks over and for medium rare, cook uncovered for a further 3 minutes on HIGH. (Shorten or lengthen the

This page: Fillet Steak au Poivre. Facing page: Aubergine/Eggplant Loaf (top) and Okra Alabama (bottom).

cooking time according to preference.) Remove the steaks to a hot serving platter. Stir the cream into the juices remaining in the dish and add salt to taste. Spoon the cream over the steaks and serve immediately, accompanied by a green salad and tomato halves.

Fit for Life Vegetable Fare

Okra Alabama

PREPARATION TIME: 10 minutes

MICROWAVE COOKING TIME: 16 minutes

SERVES: 4 people

TOTAL CALORIES: 120

450g/1lb okra
225g/8oz can chopped tomatoes
4 spring onions/scallions, peeled, trimmed
   and finely sliced
Dash Worcestershire sauce
Dash Tabasco
Salt
Freshly ground black pepper
5ml/1 tsp cornstarch/cornflour
15ml/1 tbsp cold water

Wash, top and tail the okra, place in a casserole and add the tomatoes and their juice, the onions, sauces and seasoning to taste. Mix well, then cover and cook for 10 minutes on HIGH, stirring occasionally. Remove the lid and cook uncovered for a further 5 minutes on HIGH, stirring twice during cooking. Transfer the okra with a slotted spoon to a warm serving dish. Blend the cornstarch/cornflour and cold water together and stir into the cooking liquor. Cook uncovered for 1 minute on HIGH, stirring once during cooking until thickened. Pour the sauce over the okra and serve immediately.

Aubergine/Eggplant Loaf

PREPARATION TIME: 15 minutes

MICROWAVE COOKING TIME: 14-18 minutes

SERVES: 4 people

TOTAL CALORIES: 442

450g/1lb aubergine/eggplant
1 small onion, finely chopped/minced
Pinch salt
5ml/1 tsp oregano

1 egg
30ml/2 tbsp skimmed milk powder
75ml/5 tbsp/⅓ cup fresh breadcrumbs
2.5ml/½ tsp ground coriander
Freshly ground black pepper
15ml/1 tbsp grated Parmesan cheese

1 large onion, peeled and finely chopped/
   minced
1 garlic clove, peeled and crushed
1 small courgette/zucchini, topped, tailed
   and diced
3 tomatoes, skinned and chopped
5ml/1 tsp chopped basil leaves
30ml/2 tbsp tomato purée/paste
30g/1oz/¼ cup grated Edam cheese
Salt
Freshly ground black pepper
Parsley sprigs to garnish

Use the oil to grease a 7 inch non-stick pan, then make up the batter and cook four pancakes in the usual way. Put the peppers, onion and garlic in a bowl, cover and cook for 5-6 minutes on HIGH. Add the courgette/zucchini, cover and cook for 5-6 minutes on HIGH until all the vegetables are soft. Stir in the tomatoes, basil, tomato purée/paste and cheese, cover and cook for 2 minutes on HIGH. Season to taste with salt and pepper. Divide the mixture between the pancakes, roll up, place on a suitable serving dish and reheat, uncovered, on HIGH for 1 minute. Serve at once.

Cauliflower Parma

PREPARATION TIME: 10 minutes

MICROWAVE COOKING TIME:
12-13 minutes

SERVES: 4 people

TOTAL CALORIES: 344

15ml/1 tbsp flour
Salt
Freshly ground black pepper
1 small onion, peeled and cut into rings
15g/½ oz low calorie margarine
450g/1lb cauliflower florets
2 thin slices Parma ham, diced
2.5ml/½ tsp dried marjoram, soaked in
   5ml/1 tsp cold water for 15 minutes
   before draining

Season the flour with salt and pepper, toss in the onion rings, then

Rinse, dry, then peel and thinly slice the aubergine/eggplant. Place in a bowl with the onion, salt and oregano. Cover and cook for 6-8 minutes on HIGH until the aubergine/egg plant is soft. Stir the mixture occasionally during cooking. Transfer the mixture to the blender and add the egg, milk powder, 60ml/4 tbsp/¼ cup of the breadcrumbs, the coriander and pepper to taste. Process to mix coarsely, then put the mixture into a suitable loaf-shaped microwave dish. Cook uncovered for 8-10 minutes on LOW, then turn out on to a flameproof serving dish. Mix the Parmesan cheese with the remaining breadcrumbs, sprinkle over the top of the loaf, then brown under the grill/broiler.

Pancakes Provençale

PREPARATION TIME: 15 minutes plus cooking the pancakes

MICROWAVE COOKING TIME:
12-14 minutes

SERVES: 4 people

TOTAL CALORIES: 585

PANCAKE BATTER
2.5ml/½ tsp vegetable oil
50g/2oz/½ cup all-purpose/plain flour
Pinch salt
1 small egg
140ml/¼ pint/⅔ cup skimmed milk

2 medium green peppers, cored, seeded
   and diced
1 large red pepper, cored, seeded and diced

This page: Cauliflower Parma.
Facing page: Pancakes Provençale.

shake off the surplus flour. Put the margarine in a casserole and cook for 20 seconds on HIGH until melted, then add the onion rings and cook uncovered for 4-5 minutes on HIGH, turning them over once until golden. Fill a 570-850ml/1-1½ pint/2½-3 cup basin with cauliflower florets, arranging them so that the cauliflower shape is reconstructed in the base. Cover and cook for 6 minutes on HIGH or until only just tender. Leave to stand covered. Stir the ham and drained marjoram into the onions, cover and cook for 1 minute on HIGH. Turn the cauliflower out on to a hot serving dish, reshaping the vegetables if necessary, and garnish with the ham and onion mixture.

Tomato Supper Ring

PREPARATION TIME: 10 minutes plus setting time

MICROWAVE COOKING TIME: 1 minute

SERVES: 6 people

TOTAL CALORIES: 340

430ml/¾ pint/2 cups tomato juice
15g/½ oz powdered gelatine
5ml/1 tsp fresh lemon juice
15ml/1 tbsp tomato purée/paste
Salt
Freshly ground black pepper
120g/4oz cooked mixed diced vegetables
120g/4oz cooked chicken, diced
Lettuce leaves and onion rings to garnish

Rinse a 570ml/1 pint/2½ cup ring mould with cold water and shake out the surplus. Put 75ml/5 tbsp/⅓ cup of tomato juice into a bowl and cook uncovered for 40 seconds on HIGH until hot but not boiling. Sprinkle gelatine over the surface and stir thoroughly. Cook uncovered for a further 20-30 seconds on HIGH, then stir briskly until dissolved. Whisk in the remaining tomato juice, the lemon juice and tomato purée. Season to taste with salt and pepper. Set aside in a cool place until just on the point of setting. Mix in the vegetables and chicken, then pour into the mould and leave in a cool

place until set. When ready to serve, arrange a salad of lettuce and onion rings on a suitable dish, dip the base of the mould in hot water, then turn out onto the salad.

Poached Fennel

PREPARATION TIME: 5 minutes

MICROWAVE COOKING TIME: 12 minutes plus standing time

SERVES: 4 people

TOTAL CALORIES: 124

2 large fennel bulbs
15ml/1 tbsp fresh lemon juice
60ml/4 tbsp water
5ml/1 tsp fennel seeds
5ml/1 tsp vegetable oil
Salt
Freshly ground black pepper

Wash the fennel, remove a slice from the bottom and discard the outside leaves if necessary. Cut each bulb into six or eight wedges. Combine the lemon juice, water, fennel seeds and oil in a casserole and season to taste with salt and pepper. Put in the fennel, cover with a lid and cook for 12 minutes on HIGH, repositioning the wedges once during cooking. Leave to stand for 3-4 minutes, then serve hot.

Hot Cucumber in Ginger Mint Sauce

PREPARATION TIME: 10 minutes

MICROWAVE COOKING TIME: 13-15 minutes

SERVES: 4 people

TOTAL CALORIES: 239

1 large cucumber
½ small onion, peeled and finely chopped/minced
15ml/1 tbsp vegetable oil
15g/½ oz/1 tbsp all-purpose/plain flour
140ml/¼ pint/⅔ cup home-made chicken or vegetable stock
Salt
Freshly ground black pepper
Few sprigs fresh ginger mint

Peel the cucumber, roughly chop and reserve the peel. Cut the cucumber into half lengthwise, then into 1cm/½ inch chunks and set aside. Combine the onion and oil in a bowl, cover and cook for 2 minutes on HIGH. Stir in the flour and stock, then cook for 2 minutes on HIGH, whisking once during and once after cooking. Season to taste with salt and pepper, stir in most of the mint, reserving some for garnish if desired and add the chopped cucumber peel. Cover and cook for 6-8 minutes on LOW, stirring once during cooking. Liquidise in the blender and adjust the seasoning if necessary. Put the cucumber chunks into a dish, cover and cook for 2 minutes on HIGH until only just tender. Mix in the sauce and cook uncovered for 1 minute on HIGH. Garnish with the reserved mint leaves if desired.

Artichokes Sauce Maigre

PREPARATION TIME: 10 minutes

MICROWAVE COOKING TIME: 30-31 minutes

SERVES: 4 people

TOTAL CALORIES: 95

4 well-rounded globe artichokes
140ml/¼ pint/⅔ cup hot water
5ml/1 tsp lemon juice

SAUCE
200g/7oz can tomatoes
2 spring onions/scallions, trimmed and finely sliced
1.25ml/¼ tsp bay leaf powder
Salt
Freshly ground black pepper
5ml/1 tsp cornstarch/cornflour

Remove tips from leaves and long stem from base of artichokes. Wash artichokes thoroughly. Combine water and lemon juice in a large, deep casserole and arrange the artichokes bottom ends towards the outside. Cover tightly and cook for

Facing page: Hot Cucumber in Ginger Mint Sauce (top) and Tomato Supper Ring (bottom).

Remove the tough ends from the asparagus, then pare or scrape the stalks. Arrange the asparagus in two layers in a rectangular casserole so that half the stalks point in one direction and the other half in another. Smaller spears should be placed in the centre. Pour in the stock, cover and cook for 9-14 minutes on HIGH until the tips are just tender (cooking time depends upon the size of the asparagus). While the asparagus is cooking mix the cream and lemon juice together, and season to taste with salt and pepper. Serve the asparagus well drained with a light dressing of the cream.

Yogurty Sweetcorn

PREPARATION TIME: 5 minutes	
MICROWAVE COOKING TIME: 8 minutes	
SERVES: 4 people	
TOTAL CALORIES: 380	

1 small onion, peeled and finely chopped/ minced
15ml/1 tbsp vegetable oil
225g/8oz/1½ cups frozen corn/ sweetcorn kernels
Salt
Freshly ground black pepper
60ml/2 fl oz/¼ cup natural low fat yogurt
5ml/1 tsp cornstarch/cornflour
Chopped chives to garnish

Mix the onion and oil together in a medium casserole, cover and cook for 3 minutes on HIGH. Stir in the sweetcorn and season to taste with salt and pepper. Cover and cook for 4 minutes on HIGH, stirring once during cooking. Blend together the yogurt and cornstarch/cornflour and stir into the sweetcorn. Cover and cook for 1 minute on HIGH. Stir and serve garnished with the chopped chives.

10 minutes on HIGH. Reposition artichokes, replace cover and cook for 10 minutes on HIGH or until a leaf pulls away easily. Leave to stand covered while preparing the sauce. Drain tomatoes, reserving the juice. Put the tomatoes and onions in a bowl, and cook uncovered for 8 minutes on HIGH, stirring occasionally. Add the bay leaf powder and salt and pepper to taste. Blend cornstarch/cornflour with the reserved juice, stir into the mixture and cook uncovered for 2-3 minutes on HIGH, stirring occasionally until the sauce thickens. Drain the artichokes and serve the sauce as a hot dip.

Fresh Asparagus with Soured Cream

PREPARATION TIME: 5-10 minutes	
MICROWAVE COOKING TIME: 9-14 minutes	
SERVES: 4 people	
TOTAL CALORIES: 220	

450g/1lb asparagus
140ml/¼ pint/⅔ cup well-flavoured chicken stock
60ml/4 tbsps/¼ cup soured cream
1.25ml/¼ tsp fresh lemon juice
Salt
Freshly ground black pepper

This page: Poached Fennel (top) and Persian Courgettes/Zucchini (bottom). Facing page: Fresh Asparagus with Soured Cream.

Persian Courgettes/Zucchini

PREPARATION TIME: 5 minutes

MICROWAVE COOKING TIME:
4 minutes plus standing time

SERVES: 4 people

TOTAL CALORIES: 295

450g/1lb firm courgettes/zucchini
1.25ml/¼ tsp coriander
1.25ml/¼ tsp ground cardamom
1.25ml/¼ tsp salt
1.25ml/¼ tsp freshly ground black pepper
30g/1oz/⅙ cup seedless raisins
30g/1oz/¼ cup chopped cashew nuts

Rinse, top and tail the courgettes/
zucchini and cut them into 5cm/
2 inch sticks. Mix the spices and
seasoning together. Arrange layers of
courgettes/zucchini in a small dish,
sprinkling each layer with the spice
mixture, the raisins and the nuts.
Cover and cook for 4 minutes on
HIGH, then leave to stand for 2
minutes. Stir just before serving.

Spinach and Pepper Casserole

PREPARATION TIME: 15 minutes

MICROWAVE COOKING TIME:
24-25 minutes

SERVES: 4 people

TOTAL CALORIES: 491

450g/1lb spinach, tough stalks removed
1 medium red pepper, cored, seeded and
*   cut into thin strips*
1 medium green pepper, cored, seeded and
*   cut into thin strips*
4 celery stalks, thinly sliced
2 medium onions, peeled and finely
*   chopped/minced*
30g/1oz/⅙ cup sultanas/golden raisins,
*   chopped*
1.25ml/¼ tsp sweet paprika
Generous pinch sugar
Pinch ground cinnamon
5ml/1 tsp salt
30ml/2 tbsp tomato purée/paste
10ml/2 tsp cornstarch/cornflour
30g/1oz/¼ cup grated Cheddar cheese
30ml/2 tbsp fresh breadcrumbs

Wash the spinach in plenty of cold
water and shake off the excess water.
Put the spinach in a roasting bag and
seal loosely with an elastic band,
leaving a gap for steam to escape. Put
the bag upright in the microwave and
cook for 5-6 minutes on HIGH.
Drain, reserving the liquid. Put the
peppers, celery and onion into a
shallow casserole, cover tightly and
cook for 15 minutes on HIGH,
stirring several times during cooking.
Stir in the spinach, cover and set
aside. Mix together the sultanas/
raisins, paprika, sugar, cinnamon, salt,
tomato purée, cornstarch/cornflour
and reserved spinach liquor
(approximately 10 tbsps) and cook
for 2-3 minutes on HIGH, stirring
occasionally until thickened. Stir into
the vegetables, then cover and cook
for 2 minutes on HIGH. Spoon into
individual flame-proof dishes. Mix
the cheese and breadcrumbs together,
sprinkle over the vegetables and
brown under the grill/broiler.

Austrian Red Cabbage

PREPARATION TIME: 10 minutes

MICROWAVE COOKING TIME:
15 minutes

SERVES: 4-6 people

TOTAL CALORIES: 276

450g/1lb red cabbage, thick stem
*   removed*
2 red dessert apples, cored
30g/1oz/⅙ cup raisins
140ml/¼ pint/⅔ cup salted water
15ml/1 tbsp fresh lemon juice
Freshly ground black pepper
Sweetener
15ml/1 tbsp soured cream

Finely shred the cabbage and put
into a large casserole. Grate in the
apple and add the raisins, salted
water, lemon juice and a dash of
pepper. Cover and cook for 15
minutes on HIGH or until the
cabbage is just tender, stirring three
times during cooking. Leave to stand
covered for 5 minutes, then sweeten
to taste. Swirl the soured cream on
top just before serving.

Brussels Sprouts in Orange Juice

PREPARATION TIME: 5 minutes

MICROWAVE COOKING TIME:
8 minutes plus standing time

SERVES: 4 people

TOTAL CALORIES: 147

1 large orange
2.5ml/½ tsp salt
450g/1lb Brussels sprouts, fresh or frozen

Grate the orange zest and set aside.
Squeeze the juice into a casserole and
stir in the salt. Trim and rinse the
fresh sprouts, then stir the vegetables
into the orange juice. Cover and
cook for 8 minutes on HIGH, until
the sprouts are tender, stirring once
during cooking. Leave covered for
5 minutes, then drain and serve
sprinkled with the grated zest.

Carrot Ramekins

PREPARATION TIME: 10 minutes

MICROWAVE COOKING TIME:
17-20 minutes

SERVES: 4 people

TOTAL CALORIES: 459

120ml/8 tbsp water
Salt
285g/10oz carrots, peeled and finely
*   sliced*
280ml/½ pint/1¼ cups skimmed milk
3 eggs, at room temperature, beaten
1.25ml/¼ tsp mustard powder
Freshly ground black pepper

Put the water into a dish and add salt
to taste. Stir in the carrots, then
cover and cook for about 6 minutes
on HIGH until soft. Drain and set
aside. Meanwhile grease four
individual ramekin dishes. Put the
milk in a bowl and heat uncovered
for 1-2 minutes on HIGH until warm.
Beat in the eggs, mustard powder and

Facing page: Austrian Red Cabbage
(top), Spinach and Pepper
Casserole (centre) and Yogurty
Sweetcorn (bottom).

season to taste with salt and pepper. Divide the carrots between the dishes, then pour in the milk mixture. Cover each ramekin with cling film/plastic wrap and arrange in a circle in the microwave. Cook for 10-12 minutes on LOW or until just set. Turn out if desired. Serve warm or cold.

Mushrooms in Tarragon Sauce

PREPARATION TIME: 5 minutes

MICROWAVE COOKING TIME: 7-8 minutes

SERVES: 4 people

TOTAL CALORIES: 324

450g/1lb button mushrooms, quartered
15ml/1 tbsp vegetable oil
15g/½ oz skimmed milk powder
30ml/2 tbsp all-purpose/plain flour
Salt
Freshly ground black pepper
1.25ml/¼ tsp dried tarragon
60ml/4 tbsp/¼ cup medium white wine
Fresh tarragon leaves to garnish

Put the mushrooms into a large bowl, add the oil and stir to coat them. Cover and cook for 5 minutes on HIGH, stirring occasionally. Remove the mushrooms with a slotted spoon and set aside. Whisk the milk powder and flour into the juices remaining in the bowl and season to taste with salt and pepper. Add the dried tarragon. Cook uncovered for 30 seconds on HIGH, then whisk in the wine and cook for a further 1-1½ minutes on HIGH, whisking frequently until thickened. Stir in the mushrooms and cook uncovered for 1 minute on HIGH, stirring once during cooking. Stir again before serving. Garnish with fresh tarragon leaves.

Chicken Stuffed Peppers

PREPARATION TIME: 20 minutes

MICROWAVE COOKING TIME: 19 minutes

SERVES: 4 people

TOTAL CALORIES: 532

4 180g/6oz green peppers
2 225g/8oz cans tomatoes
3 stalks celery, finely chopped/minced
1 small onion, peeled and finely chopped/minced
5ml/1 tsp chopped basil
Small clove garlic, peeled and crushed
225g/8oz cooked chicken, chopped
15ml/1 tbsp cornstarch/cornflour

Remove a slice from the top of each pepper. Discard the core and seeds. Chop and reserve the flesh from the pepper lids. Drain the tomatoes, reserving the juice. Mix the chopped peppers, celery, onion, basil,

This page: Carrot Ramekins (top) and Chicken Stuffed Peppers (bottom). Facing page: Stuffed Crispy Potatoes (top) and Mushrooms in Tarragon Sauce (bottom).

tomatoes and garlic together in a bowl, cover and cook for 7 minutes on HIGH, stirring occasionally until the vegetables are tender. Season to taste with salt and pepper, then mix in the chicken. Stuff the mixture into the peppers, then stand them in a shallow dish, cover and cook for 10 minutes on HIGH. Give each pepper a half turn halfway through

cooking. Transfer the peppers to a serving plate and keep warm. Blend the cornstarch/cornflour with the reserved tomato juice and stir into the juices remaining in the dish. Cook uncovered for 2 minutes on HIGH, stirring occasionally until thickened. Serve the sauce with the peppers.

Savoury Celery

PREPARATION TIME: 15 minutes

MICROWAVE COOKING TIME: 14-15 minutes

SERVES: 4 people

TOTAL CALORIES: 250 plus approximately 100 for corn chips

1 head/bunch celery, rinsed, trimmed and cut into 2.5cm/1 inch lengths
60ml/4 tbsps chicken stock
120g/4oz chicken livers, rinsed and trimmed
Salt
Freshly ground black pepper
15ml/1 tbsp all-purpose/plain flour
15g/½ oz corn chips, lightly crushed

Put the celery into a casserole with the chicken stock. Cover and cook for 12 minutes on HIGH or until the celery is tender, stirring twice during cooking. Meanwhile coarsely chop the livers and season to taste with salt and pepper. Mix in the flour, then add the livers to the celery, stirring thoroughly. Cover and cook for 2-3 minutes on HIGH or until the liver is cooked. Garnish with crushed corn chips.

Stuffed Crispy Potatoes

PREPARATION TIME: 10 minutes

MICROWAVE COOKING TIME: 20-25 minutes

SERVES: 4 people

TOTAL CALORIES: 635

2 285g/10oz baking potatoes
15ml/1 tbsp vegetable oil
1 small green pepper, cored, seeded and diced
1 small onion, peeled and chopped

1 clove garlic, peeled and crushed
Pinch ground ginger
Pinch saffron powder
Salt
Freshly ground black pepper

Wash and dry the potatoes and prick deeply with a fork. Place on paper towels and cook uncovered for 5 minutes on HIGH. Reposition and turn the potatoes over and continue cooking for 5-6 minutes until soft.

This page: Leeks Mimosa. Facing page: Brussels Sprouts in Orange Juice (top) and Savoury Celery (bottom).

Cut in half lengthwise and scoop out the pulp. Mash lightly with a fork. Arrange the potato skins in a shallow dish and pour a little of the oil around the insides. Brush the remaining oil over the outside of the

skins. Cook uncovered for 4-6 minutes on HIGH until the skins are crispy, removing each skin as it is ready. Put the green pepper, onion, garlic, ginger and saffron in a small bowl and season to taste with salt and pepper. Cover tightly and cook for 3-4 minutes on HIGH until soft. Mix into the mashed potatoes, then pile the mixture into the potato skins. Reheat uncovered for 2-3 minutes until hot.

Leeks Mimosa

| **PREPARATION TIME:** 10 minutes |
| **MICROWAVE COOKING TIME:** 13-14 minutes |
| **SERVES:** 4-6 people |
| **TOTAL CALORIES:** 325 |

280ml/½ pint/1¼ cups hot water
Salt
6 medium leeks (each weighing
*   approximately 120g/4oz), washed and*
*   trimmed*
10ml/2 tsp cornstarch/cornflour
15ml/1 tbsp cold water
60ml/4 tbsp skimmed milk soft cheese
*   (Quark)*
Freshly ground black pepper
1 hard boiled/hard cooked egg
5ml/1 tsp freshly chopped parsley

Pour the hot water into a shallow dish and add salt to taste. Cut the leeks so that there is an equal amount of white and green and put in the dish. Cover and cook for 12 minutes on HIGH until tender, repositioning the leeks once during cooking. Meanwhile blend the cornstarch/cornflour and cold water together in a jug, then separate the yolk and the egg white. Sieve the yolk and chop the white separately. When the leeks are tender, transfer them to a warm serving dish using a slotted spoon. Stir 140ml/¼ pint/⅔ cup of the liquid into the blended cornflour. Cook uncovered for 1-2 minutes on HIGH, stirring occasionally until thickened. Season the cheese with pepper and stir into the thickened juices. Spoon over the leeks and garnish with the egg white, yolk and parsley.

Fit for Life
Lightweight Desserts

Apple Snow

PREPARATION TIME: 15 minutes

MICROWAVE COOKING TIME:
5½-7 minutes

SERVES: 4 people

TOTAL CALORIES: 385

*450g/1lb dessert apples, peeled, cored and
 sliced*
5ml/1 tsp finely grated lemon zest
2 egg whites
30g/1oz/2 tbsp sugar
2 drops almond essence/extract
15g/½ oz flaked/slivered almonds

Put the apple and lemon zest in a
medium bowl, cover tightly and cook
for 4-5 minutes on HIGH until
pulpy. Purée in the blender. Beat the
egg whites until stiff and fold half the
mixture into the apple purée. Beat
the sugar and almond essence/extract
into the remaining beaten whites.
Half-fill four sundae dishes with the
purée and pile the mallow on top.
Arrange the dishes in a circle in the
microwave and cook uncovered for
1½-2 minutes on HIGH until the
mallow puffs up. Sprinkle with flaked
almonds and quickly brown at a
15cm/6 inch distance from a hot
grill/broiler.

Rhubarb, Orange and Strawberry Comfort

PREPARATION TIME: 5 minutes

MICROWAVE COOKING TIME:
10-12 minutes

SERVES: 4-6 people

TOTAL CALORIES: 202

*450g/1lb canned rhubarb, cut into
 2.5cm/1 inch lengths*
1.25ml/¼ tsp ground ginger
*1 298g/10½ oz can mandarin orange
 segments in natural juice*
Liquid sweetener
30ml/2 tbsp low fat natural yogurt
180g/6oz strawberries, halved and rinsed
30ml/2 tbsp crunchy muesli

**This page: Rhubarb, Orange and
Strawberry Comfort (top) and
Apple Snow (bottom). Facing page:
Hot Fruit Salad Cups.**

Put the rhubarb in a large bowl, add
the ground ginger and strain in the
juice from the mandarin oranges.
Cover and cook for 10-12 minutes on
HIGH, stirring twice during cooking

until the rhubarb is mushy. Mix in sweetener to taste. Stir in the yogurt and fold in the orange segments, cover and leave to cool. Reserve four strawberries for decoration and thinly slice the remainder. Mix the sliced strawberries into the rhubarb, then spoon the mixture into individual goblets. Just before serving, sprinkle with the muesli and top with a half or whole strawberry.

Tipsy Berries

PREPARATION TIME: 5 minutes

MICROWAVE COOKING TIME:
7 minutes plus chilling

SERVES: 4-6 people

TOTAL CALORIES: 408

30ml/2 tbsps sugar
225ml/8 fl oz/1 cup sweet red wine
30ml/2 tbsps tequila
Low calorie sweetener
450g/1lb raspberries
120g/4oz blackcurrants } *or use all*
120g/4oz redcurrants } *blackcurrants*

Mix the sugar and the wine in a medium bowl and cook uncovered for 2 minutes on HIGH. Stir until the sugar is dissolved. Cook uncovered for 5 minutes, then stir in the tequila and add liquid sweetener to taste. Trim and rinse the fruit and place in a serving bowl, then pour the syrup over. Chill thoroughly in the refrigerator, stirring occasionally.

Hot Fruit Salad Cups

PREPARATION TIME: 10 minutes

MICROWAVE COOKING TIME:
6½ minutes

SERVES: 4 people

TOTAL CALORIES: 457

2 large oranges
30g/1oz/2 tbsps sugar
5ml/1 tsp rum
1 small dessert apple
1 slice fresh or canned pineapple
1 banana
8g/¼ oz shelled pistachios, skinned and chopped

Halve the oranges and put in a shallow dish, cut side down. Cook uncovered for 2 minutes on HIGH until the juice can be easily squeezed. Gently squeeze the juice and scrape out most of the flesh. Set the shells aside. Stir the sugar into the juice and cook uncovered for 1-1½ minutes on HIGH until boiling. Stir, then cook uncovered for 2 minutes on HIGH. Add the rum. Core and cube the apple, cut the pineapple into wedges and peel and slice the banana, and mix all the fruit into the juice. Cook uncovered for 30 seconds on HIGH, then stir and cook for a further 30 seconds on HIGH. Spoon the fruit into the orange shells and pour the syrup over. Decorate with pistachio nuts.

Blackberry and Raspberry Jellies

PREPARATION TIME: 5 minutes

MICROWAVE COOKING TIME:
7 minutes plus setting time

SERVES: 4 people

TOTAL CALORIES: 290

225g/8oz fresh or frozen blackberries
225g/8oz fresh or frozen raspberries
Approximately 225ml/8 fl oz/1 cup fresh orange juice
30ml/2 tbsps cold water
10ml/2 tsp gelatine
Liquid sweetener
4 rosettes whipping cream

Put the blackberries in one bowl and the raspberries in another and cook each separately, uncovered, for 3 minutes on HIGH or until the juice runs freely. Strain the juices into a wide-necked jug and make up to 280ml/½ pint/1¼ cups with the orange juice. Put the water into a small dish or glass and cook for 30 seconds on HIGH until hot but not boiling. Sprinkle the gelatine over the surface and stir thoroughly. Cook for 20 seconds on HIGH, then stir until the gelatine is completely dissolved. Leave to cool for a few moments before pouring into the fruit juices. Stir in liquid sweetener to taste. Chill until just beginning to set. Divide the blackberries between four tall glasses and cover with the jelly. Refrigerate until set, then top up with the raspberries. Decorate each with a rosette of cream.

Home Made Yogurt

PREPARATION TIME: 5 minutes

MICROWAVE COOKING TIME:
12-13 minutes plus setting time

MAKES:
approximately 570ml/1 pint/2½ cups

TOTAL CALORIES: 262

430ml/¾ pint/2 cups skimmed milk
60ml/4 tbsps skimmed milk powder
60ml/4 tbsps low fat yogurt

Put the milk in a large bowl and cook uncovered for 2 minutes on HIGH. Stir and cook for a further 2-3 minutes on HIGH until the milk boils. Reduce the setting and cook uncovered for 8 minutes on DEFROST (35%), stirring occasionally until the milk is slightly reduced. Whisk in the milk powder and leave to cool until comfortable to the touch. Whisk in the yogurt, then pour into a wide-necked flask or divide between the glasses in a yogurt maker. Cover and leave for 8 hours until the yogurt is just set, then refrigerate covered for a further 3-4 hours.

Chocolate Creams

PREPARATION TIME: 5 minutes

MICROWAVE COOKING TIME:
5 minutes plus chilling time

SERVES: 4 people

TOTAL CALORIES: 568

30g/1oz/¼ cup cocoa powder, sifted
45g/1½ oz/⅓ cup custard powder
570ml/1 pint/2½ cups skimmed milk

Facing page: Home Made Yogurt (top) and Tipsy Berries (bottom).

Low calorie sweetener
1 milk coated chocolate digestive/
Graham cracker, grated

Mix the cocoa and custard with a
little of the cold milk in a medium
bowl. Whisk in the remaining milk
and cook uncovered for 5 minutes
on HIGH, whisking frequently until
thickened. Add sweetener to taste.
Divide the cream between four
individual moulds and leave to cool
for 30 minutes, then cover with cling
film/plastic wrap and refrigerate until
cold. Remove the cling film/plastic
wrap and decorate the tops of the
creams with grated biscuit/cracker.

Coffee Soufflés

PREPARATION TIME: 20 minutes	
MICROWAVE COOKING TIME: 40 seconds	
SERVES: 4 people	
TOTAL CALORIES: 795	

140ml/¼ pint/½ cup double strength hot
  black coffee
15ml/1 tbsp powdered gelatine
2 eggs, separated
30ml/2 tbsp sugar
170ml/6 fl oz/¾ cup canned evaporated
  milk, well chilled
2.5ml/½ tsp vanilla essence/extract
1 small bar dairy flake chocolate, finely
  crushed
4 rosettes whipping cream

Cut four strips wax/greaseproof
paper and attach to four individual
ramekins with an elastic band,
making sure that the collars protrude
2.5cm/1 inch above the rims. Put half
the coffee in a medium jug and heat
uncovered for 30 seconds on HIGH.
Sprinkle on the gelatine and stir to
dissolve. If necessary return to the
microwave for a further 10 seconds.
Beat the egg yolks and sugar until
thick and mousse-like. Beat in the
remaining coffee, then mix in the
dissolved gelatine. In another bowl
whisk the milk and vanilla essence/
extract until very thick, then fold
into the coffee mixture. Leave in a
cool place until on the point of
setting, then beat the egg whites until
stiff and fold into the mixture. Pour
evenly into the prepared dishes and
chill until set. With the aid of a
round-bladed knife dipped into hot
water, remove the paper collars.
Decorate the soufflés with crushed
flake and a cream rosette.

**This page: Blackberry and
Raspberry Jellies. Facing page:
Chocolate Creams (top) and Apple
and Cherry Sponge Cakes (bottom).**

Beat the eggs, cream of tartar, sugar and vanilla essence/extract together until thick. Fold in the flour and the chopped apple. Divide the mixture between approximately fifteen double thickness paper cases and sprinkle the cherries over each. Arrange five at a time in a circle in the microwave and cook for 45 seconds to 1 minute on HIGH until the cakes are just dry on top. Do not overcook.

Baked Bananas Sauce au Poire

PREPARATION TIME: 15 minutes	
MICROWAVE COOKING TIME: 6 minutes	
SERVES: 4 people	
TOTAL CALORIES: 375	

1 large orange
2 ripe pears
Low calorie sweetener
4 small bananas

Pare thin strips of orange and shred finely. Put into a jug, cover with cold water and cook on FULL POWER for 2 minutes or until tender. Drain and set aside. Halve the orange and squeeze the juice of one half into a blender. Remove and chop the segments from the remaining half of orange and set aside. Peel, core and cut up the pears, and blend with the orange juice to a smooth purée, adding sweetener to taste. Peel the bananas and put into a small dish. Cook uncovered for 2 minutes on HIGH, then reposition the fruit, placing the two outside bananas into the middle. Pour the pear purée over the bananas and cook uncovered for 2 minutes on HIGH. Top with the chopped orange and decorate with the reserved shreds. Serve immediately.

Apple and Cherry Sponge Cakes

PREPARATION TIME: 15 minutes	
MICROWAVE COOKING TIME: 2-3 minutes	
MAKES: approximately 15	
TOTAL CALORIES: 590	

2 large eggs
Pinch cream of tartar
25g/1oz/2 tbsps sugar
2.5ml/½ tsp vanilla essence/extract
60g/2oz/½ cup all-purpose/plain flour, sifted
1 dessert apple, peeled, cored and finely chopped
30g/1oz/⅛ cup glacé/candied cherries, finely chopped

This page: Coffee Soufflés. Facing page: Baked Bananas Sauce au Poire.

Fit for Life

What... No Meat?
Vegetarian Recipes for You!

The microwave oven has a brilliant way with vegetables. Fast cooking times mean vegetables keep their fresh colour and crisp texture. Low evaporation means vegetables need very little water to cook, so they keep their nutrients. Fresh vegetables cook as quickly as frozen vegetables do by conventional methods, and frozen vegetables are cooked beautifully in almost the blink of an eye.

Vegetarian diets are losing their "cranky" image as more people turn to that way of eating because of weight and nutrition consciousness. The humble dried bean or lentil has an abundant supply of protein to add to our diets, with the added plus of more fibre than many other protein foods.

The microwave method of rehydrating pulses – dried peas, beans and lentils – eliminates overnight soaking. Just cover the dried pulses with water and bring them to the boil, which usually takes about 10 minutes on the highest setting. After that, allow the pulses to boil for 2 minutes. Leave them standing, covered, in the hot water for 1 hour and they will be ready to cook according to your recipe. Dried pulses usually take about an hour to cook. If that doesn't seem like convenience cooking, remember that conventional methods would take twice as long. It is essential, though, that dried peas, beans and lentils are thoroughly cooked. Eating insufficiently cooked pulses can be dangerous.

Vegetarian menus have suffered from the image that they are composed solely of nut cutlets. I have always found that unfair, since well seasoned cutlets are a delicious alternative to meat and a good addition to a healthy diet. Nut cutlets, escalopes and croquettes are very easy to cook in a microwave oven with the use of a browning dish. Be creative with shapes, too, because nut mixtures hold up better in a microwave oven than they do when fried or baked conventionally.

When organising the recipes into chapters, I was amazed to find just how many recipes could fit easily in several different categories. Pulses can be used in salads, appetizers or entrées. Main courses can be cut down and used as appetizers and appetizers can be expanded to main-meal-sized portions. Even desserts and puddings can be based on vegetables. Which all goes to prove that, vegetarian or not, we can all enjoy more creative meals thanks to the versatility of vegetables.

Fit for Life

Kick off in Style

Tomato and Tarragon Creams with Sweetcorn Salad

PREPARATION TIME: 25 minutes

MICROWAVE COOKING TIME: 9-10 minutes

SERVES: 4 people

400g/14oz plum tomatoes, canned
30ml/2 tbsps tomato purée/paste
1 onion, finely chopped
5ml/1 tsp chopped tarragon
1 bay leaf
Salt and pepper
225g/8oz low fat or cream cheese
2 eggs
280ml/½ pint/1 cup whipped cream
15g/½ oz/1 tbsp gelatine or agar-agar
45ml/3 tbsps water and lemon juice
    mixed
Salt and pepper

SALAD
225g/8oz/baby corn-on-the-cob
1 green pepper, cut in thin strips
4-6 tomatoes, peeled, seeded and cut in
    strips
4-6 spring/green onions, shredded
45ml/3 tbsps salad oil
15ml/1 tbsp white wine vinegar
5ml/1 tsp white wine vinegar
5ml/1 tsp Dijon mustard
5ml/1 tsp chopped fresh tarragon
Lettuce leaves

GARNISH
Whole tarragon leaves

Sprinkle the gelatine on top of the water and lemon juice in a small ramekin/custard cup. If using agar-agar in leaf form, dissolve with the water or lemon juice in a small cup. Combine the tomatoes, onion, tarragon, bay leaf, tomato purée/paste, salt and pepper in a deep bowl. Cook, uncovered, 5 minutes on HIGH. Sieve the pulp and set it aside to cool. Beat the eggs and cheese together until smooth. Add the

This page: Tomato and Tarragon Creams with Sweetcorn Salad. Facing Page: Danish Egg Salad (top) and Pasta and Asparagus Salad (bottom).

cooled tomato pulp. Melt the gelatine or agar-agar for 30 seconds on HIGH. Pour into the tomato mixture and stir well. Set briefly over ice and stir constantly until beginning to thicken. Fold in the cream and adjust the seasoning. Brush 4 ramekin dishes/custard cups lightly with oil and spoon in the tomato mixture. Chill until firm. Put the corn into a large bowl with enough hot water to cover. Cover loosely and cook for 3-4 minutes on HIGH until tender. After 2-3 minutes add the pepper strips. Remove the vegetables with a slotted spoon and rinse under cold water. Set aside to drain. Put the tomatoes into the same water and cook 30 seconds on HIGH. Put into cold water immediately. Remove the skins, cut in half and scoop out the seeds. Slice the flesh into thin strips. Mix the oil, vinegar, tarragon, salt and pepper and combine with the vegetables. Add the spring/green onions just before serving. Arrange lettuce leaves on serving plates and carefully turn out the tomato creams. It may be necessary to dip the moulds briefly into hot water to loosen. Decorate the creams with whole tarragon leaves and serve surrounded with the corn salad.

Danish Egg Salad

PREPARATION TIME: 20 minutes

MICROWAVE COOKING TIME:
7 minutes

SERVES: 4 people

4 eggs
30ml/2 tbsps cream
30g/1oz/2 tbsps butter or margarine
225g/8oz/1 cup frozen peas, thawed
1 cucumber, cut into 1.25cm/½ inch dice
6 sticks of celery, diced
3 spring onions, chopped
30ml/2 tbsps chopped dill
120g/4oz/1 cup diced cheese
280ml/½ pint/1 cup sour cream
60ml/2 fl oz/¼ cup mayonnaise
Paprika
Salt and pepper
1 head Chinese cabbage/leaves, shredded

Beat the eggs and cream together with salt and pepper. Heat a browning dish 5 minutes on HIGH, melt the butter or margarine for 1 minute on HIGH. Pour in half the egg mixture and cook the omelette on one side for 1 minute on HIGH. Turn over and cook a further 1 minute. Cook the egg in two batches. Cook the peas for 1 minute on HIGH with 2 tbsps water. Rinse under cold water and drain to dry. Mix the sour cream, mayonnaise, dill, salt and pepper together. Reserve 30ml/ 2 tbsps dressing and mix the remaining dressing with the peas, celery, cheese and cucumber. Arrange the Chinese cabbage/leaves on serving plates. Pile on the salad. Cut the omelettes into strips and arrange on top. Drizzle the remaining dressing over the omelette strips and sprinkle with paprika.

Warm Salad with Avocado, Grapes, Blue Cheese and Walnuts

PREPARATION TIME: 20 minutes

MICROWAVE COOKING TIME:
1-2 minutes

SERVES: 4 people

1 head curly endive
1 head Belgian endive (chicory)
1 head radicchio
1 small bunch lambs lettuce or watercress
1 head Chinese leaves/cabbage
1 head leaf or iceberg lettuce
4 tbsps chopped fresh herbs
120g/4oz/1 cup walnuts
120g/4oz/1 cup blue cheese crumbled
1 large or 2 small avocados
1 small bunch purple/black grapes

DRESSING
90ml/6 tbsps walnut oil and grapeseed oil mixed
30ml/2 tbsps lemon vinegar or white wine vinegar and lemon juice mixed
Pinch sugar

Tear the curly endive, Belgian endive, radicchio and lettuce into small pieces. If using lambs lettuce separate the leaves. If using watercress remove any thick stalks. Shred the Chinese

leaves/cabbage and peel and slice the avocado. Cut the grapes in half and remove any seeds/pips. Combine all the salad ingredients in a large bowl. Mix the salad dressing ingredients and toss with the salad. Arrange on individual salad plates and heat each plate for 1-2 minutes on HIGH before serving.

Pasta and Asparagus Salad

PREPARATION TIME: 15 minutes

MICROWAVE COOKING TIME:
11 minutes plus 8 minutes standing time

SERVES: 4 people

120g/4oz tagliatelle/fettuccine
450g/1lb asparagus, trimmed and cut into 5cm/2 inch pieces
2 courgettes/zucchini, cut into 5cm/ 2 inch sticks
1 lemon, peeled and segmented
30g/2 tbsps chopped parsley
30g/2 tbsps chopped marjoram
Grated rind and juice of 1 lemon
90ml/3 fl oz/⅓ cup salad oil
Pinch sugar (optional)
Salt and pepper
1 head lettuce
1 head Belgian endive (chicory)

Put the pasta into a large bowl with 570ml/1 pint/2 cups hot water, a pinch of salt and 5ml/1 tsp oil. Cook 6 minutes on HIGH and leave to stand in the water for 8 minutes. Drain and leave to cool completely. Cook the asparagus in 140ml/ ¼ pint/½ cup water for 5 minutes on HIGH or until tender. Add the courgettes/zucchini after 3 minutes cooking time. Rinse under cold water and drain. Combine the pasta, asparagus, courgettes/zucchini, parsley, marjoram and lemon segments in a large bowl. Mix the lemon rind, juice, oil, salt and pepper together to blend well. Pour over the

Facing page: Warm Salad with Avocado, Grapes, Blue Cheese and Walnuts.

combined ingredients and toss to coat. Arrange lettuce and endive on serving plates and pile on the salad to serve.

Eggs Primavera

PREPARATION TIME: 20 minutes

MICROWAVE COOKING TIME: 12-14 minutes

SERVES: 4 people

4 eggs
120g/4oz peapods/mangetout
2 large carrots
225g/8oz asparagus
1 small cauliflower
4 spring onions/green onions
1 small head Chinese leaves/cabbage, shredded

DRESSING
280ml/½ pint/1 cup yogurt
1 ripe avocado
140ml/¼ pint/½ cup cream

Put 570ml/1 pint/2½ cups water in a shallow dish with 15ml/1tbsp vinegar and 5ml/1 tsp salt. Heat the water on HIGH for 3-4 minutes or until boiling. Break the eggs one at a time into a cup and slide them into the water. Pierce the yolks once with a small knife or skewer. Cover the dish loosely and cook for 2-3 minutes on MEDIUM. When the whites are set lift the eggs out of the dish and put them immediately into a bowl of cold water. Trim the asparagus spears and cut them into 5cm/2 inch pieces. Separate the head of cauliflower into individual flowerets. Put the asparagus into a casserole with 30ml/ 2 tbsps water. Cook for 5 minutes on HIGH. After 1 minute add flowerets of cauliflower. Three minutes before the end of cooking time add the mangetout/peapods and the carrots, cut into ribbons with a vegetable peeler. Leave the vegetables to stand, covered, for 1 minute and then rinse under cold water and dry well. Slice the spring/green onions and add to the rest of the vegetables. Pile the Chinese leaves/cabbage onto 4 individual plates. Put the mixed vegetables on top. Drain the poached eggs well and put 1 egg on top of each

salad. Peel the avocado and combine with the yogurt in a food processor and purée until smooth. Stir in the cream and season with salt and pepper. Coat some of the dressing over each egg and serve the rest separately.

Red Pepper Pâté in Lemon Shells

PREPARATION TIME: 20 minutes

MICROWAVE COOKING TIME: 8-9 minutes

SERVES: 4 people

4 lemons, cut in half
6 red peppers, cored, seeded and cut in pieces
60ml/2 fl oz/4 tbsps white wine
1 bay leaf
450g/1lb cream cheese
½ chili pepper, finely chopped
Pinch ground oregano
Salt
Pinch sugar (optional)

This page: Red Pepper Pâté in Lemon Shells. Facing page: Oeufs à la Russe (top) and Eggs Primavera (bottom).

GARNISH
8 thin slices of red pepper
8 small fresh bay leaves
Chinese cabbage/leaves, shredded

ACCOMPANIMENT
Melba or hot buttered toast

Scoop out the pulp from the lemon. Squeeze the juice and set it aside. Trim a slice from the bottom of each lemon half so that they stand upright. Combine peppers, wine and bay leaf in a medium size casserole. Cover and cook 8-10 minutes on HIGH until very soft. Remove the bay leaf and purée the peppers and wine in a food processor. Add the cream cheese, chili pepper, oregano, salt, lemon juice and sugar (if using). Process until smooth. Adjust the seasoning and pipe or spoon the pâté into the lemon shells. Chill briefly

aside. Chop the mushroom stalks and combine with the walnuts, pimento, chives, mustard, salt, pepper and breadcrumbs. Add any cooking liquid from the mushrooms and the beaten egg. Mound the filling onto the mushroom caps. Cook on MEDIUM for 6-8 minutes until the filling is set. Mix the topping ingredients and spoon onto the mushroom filling. Cook a further 2 minutes on MEDIUM or 3 minutes on a combination setting of a microwave convection oven. Serve immediately. The cheese topping may be sprinkled lightly with paprika before the final cooking if desired.

Spinach-Stuffed Artichoke Hearts

PREPARATION TIME: 25 minutes

MICROWAVE COOKING TIME: 19-20 minutes

SERVES: 4 people

4 globe artichokes
450g/1lb fresh spinach, stalks removed and well washed
1 shallot finely chopped
1 egg, beaten
140ml/¼ pint/½ cup heavy/double cream
2 slices bread, made into crumbs
15g/½ oz/1 tbsp butter or margarine
Nutmeg
Cayenne pepper
Salt

TOPPING
60g/2oz/½ cup grated Cheddar cheese
60ml/4 tbsps heavy/double cream

Cut all of the top leaves off the artichokes. Trim the remaining leaves down to the thickest part. Cut out as much of the choke as possible. Cover the artichokes with water and cook in a covered casserole for 7-8 minutes on HIGH. Drain well and remove any remaining choke. Trim the remaining leaves down further until

This page: Spinach-Stuffed Artichoke Hearts (top) and Stuffed Mushrooms (bottom). Facing page: Aubergine/Eggplant Caviar (top) and Avocado, Tomato and Mozzarella on Garlic Toast (bottom).

before serving. Garnish each with a slice of red pepper and one bay leaf. Arrange on a bed of Chinese cabbage/leaves. Serve with hot buttered toast or melba toast.

Stuffed Mushrooms

PREPARATION TIME: 15 minutes

MICROWAVE COOKING TIME: 8-11 minutes

SERVES: 4 people

4 very large or 8 medium-size mushrooms
30g/2 tbsps butter
3 slices white bread, made into crumbs
120g/4oz/1 cup chopped walnuts
3 pimento caps, chopped
1 egg, beaten
1 small bunch chives, snipped
15ml/1 tbsp Dijon mustard
Salt and pepper

TOPPING
30g/1oz/2 tbsps cream cheese
15g/½ oz/1 tbsp grated Gruyère or Cheddar cheese
90ml/3 fl oz/⅓ cup heavy/double cream
Pinch cayenne pepper

Melt the butter in a large, shallow dish. Remove the stalks from the mushrooms and set them aside. Cook the whole mushroom caps for 2 minutes on HIGH, remove and set

only the thick, edible part remains. Cook the spinach in the water that clings to the leaves on HIGH for 5 minutes. Melt the butter 30 seconds on HIGH in a small bowl. Cook the shallot for 1 minute until softenend. Combine with the spinach, breadcrumbs, egg, cream, nutmeg, cayenne pepper and salt. Mound the filling onto the artichoke bottoms. Arrange in a circle and cook 5 minutes on MEDIUM or until set. Mix the topping ingredients together and spoon onto the spinach filling. Cook a further 2 minutes on MEDIUM to melt the cheese, or for 3 minutes on a combination setting in a microwave convection oven. Sprinkle lightly with more grated nutmeg before serving.

Courgette/Zucchini and Carrot Terrine

PREPARATION TIME: 20 minutes

MICROWAVE COOKING TIME: 17 minutes plus 10 minutes standing time

SERVES: 4-6 people

6-8 large, green cabbage leaves
340g/12oz low fat cheese
4 slices bread, made into crumbs
2 eggs
140ml/¼ pint/½ cup cream, lightly whipped
1 bunch chives, snipped
Salt and pepper
1-2 carrots, cut in strips
1-2 courgettes/zucchini, cut in strips

SAUCE
280ml/½ pint/1 cup sour cream or plain yogurt
140ml/¼ pint/½ cup mayonnaise
2 tomatoes, peeled, seeded and cut in small dice
30ml/2 tbsps chopped parsley
15ml/1 tbsp lemon juice or white wine
Pinch sugar (optional)
Salt and pepper

Trim the spines of the cabbage leaves to make them thinner. Place the leaves in a shallow dish with 30ml/ 2 tbsps water and a pinch of salt. Cover the dish loosely and cook for

1 minute on HIGH. Line a 450g/1lb loaf dish with the cabbage leaves. Mix together the cheese, breadcrumbs, eggs, cream, chives and salt and pepper. Cook the carrots in 30ml/2 tbsps water for 5 minutes on HIGH. Add the courgettes after 3 minutes cooking time. Drain and dry both vegetables very well. Put a quarter of the mixture into the bottom of the loaf dish on top of the cabbage leaves. Place on 1 layer of carrots and cover with another quarter of the cheese mixture. Place on a layer of courgettes and repeat the process until all the mixture and the vegetables are used. Wrap over the overlapping cabbage leaves. Cover the dish with the cling film/ plastic wrap, pierce several times to release the steam. Put into the microwave oven with a small dish of hot water and cook for 10 minutes on MEDIUM. Allow to cool in the dish. Combine the sauce ingredients. Slice the terrine and arrange on lettuce leaves or watercress. Spoon over some of the sauce and serve the rest separately.

Aubergine/Eggplant Caviar

PREPARATION TIME: 20 minutes

MICROWAVE COOKING TIME: 7-9 minutes

SERVES: 4 people

1 large or 2 small aubergines/eggplants
60ml/4 tbsps oil
Juice of ½ lemon
1 clove garlic, minced
Pinch cayenne pepper
Salt

GARNISH
2 hard boiled eggs
1 small onion, finely chopped
30g/2 tbsps chopped parsley
4-8 slices French bread, toasted

Remove the stem from the eggplant/ aubergine, cut it in half and lightly score the flesh. Sprinkle with salt and leave to stand for 30 minutes to draw out any bitterness. Rinse and pat dry. Put into a covered casserole and

cook on HIGH for 7-9 minutes. Allow to cool and cut into small pieces. Combine in a food processor with the garlic, lemon juice, salt and pepper. Blend until smooth. Pour the oil gradually through the feedtube with the machine running. Adjust the seasoning and chill. Sieve the egg yolk and finely chop the white. To serve, pile the aubergine/eggplant caviar on top of the French bread toast and sprinkle on the onion, egg and parsley.

Oeufs à la Russe

PREPARATION TIME: 20 minutes

MICROWAVE COOKING TIME: 35-40 minutes plus 10 minutes standing time

SERVES: 4 people

4 eggs
3 beetroot/beets
120g/4oz mushrooms
4 sticks celery
2-3 potatoes, depending on size
15ml/1 tbsp butter or margarine
180g/6oz fresh spinach

DRESSING
430ml/¾ pint/1½ cups sour cream
5ml/1 tsp white wine vinegar
2.5ml/½ tsp sugar
1 bunch chives, chopped
Salt and pepper

Poach the eggs as for Eggs Primavera. Leave in cold water until ready to use. Put the beetroot/beets into a deep bowl with 140ml/¼ pint/½ cup water and a pinch of salt. Cover the bowl loosely with cling film/plastic wrap and cook on HIGH for 12-16 minutes, stirring once or twice. Remove the beetroot/beets from the bowl and set aside to stand 10 minutes before peeling. Rinse out the bowl and add the potatoes cut in 1.25cm/½ inch dice. Add 140ml/ ¼ pint/½ cup water and a pinch of

Facing page: Broccoli and Hazelnut Terrine (top) and Courgette/ Zucchini and Carrot Terrine (bottom).

salt and cover the bowl loosely with cling film/plastic wrap. Cook the potatoes on HIGH for 8-10 minutes, stirring once. Leave to stand while preparing the rest of the salad. Heat the butter in a small bowl for 30 seconds on HIGH and add the mushrooms, quartered, and the celery, cut in small dice. Cook for 1 minute on HIGH, stirring occasionally. Drain the potatoes and add them to the celery and mushrooms. Leave to cool. Combine the dressing ingredients and set them aside. Wash the spinach leaves well and dry and shred them finely. Add 60ml/2 fl oz/¼ cup of the dressing to the potatoes, celery and mushrooms and stir to coat. Add the beetroot/beets and stir very carefully. Pile the salad onto the spinach and top each salad with 1 drained poached egg. Coat the remaining dressing over each egg before serving.

Avocado, Tomato and Mozzarella on Garlic Toast

PREPARATION TIME: 15 minutes

MICROWAVE COOKING TIME: 9 minutes

SERVES: 4 people

4 slices French or Vienna bread, sliced 1.25cm/½ inch thick, on the diagonal
60g/2oz/4 tbsps butter or margarine
15ml/1 tbsp oil
1 clove garlic, crushed
2-4 beefsteak tomatoes
1-2 ripe avocados
120g/4oz mozzarella cheese, sliced
30ml/2 tbsps capers
30ml/2 tbsps salad oil
10ml/2 tsps lemon juice
2.5ml/½ tsp oregano
Salt and pepper

Heat a browning dish for 5 minutes on HIGH. Add the oil, butter and garlic. Put in the bread slices, two at a time if necessary. Brown for 1 minute on HIGH and turn over. Cook another 1 minute on HIGH and set on paper towels to drain. Peel the avocados, remove the stones and slice. Slice the tomatoes and the

cheese and arrange on top of the bread slices, alternating with the avocado slices. Scatter over the capers. Mix the oil, lemon juice, oregano, salt and pepper and spoon on top. Heat 2 minutes on MEDIUM to melt the cheese. Serve immediately.

Salad of Wild Mushrooms and Artichokes

PREPARATION TIME: 20 minutes

MICROWAVE COOKING TIME: 9-11 minutes

SERVES: 4 people

2-3 globe artichokes, depending on size
1 slice lemon
1 bay leaf
6 black peppercorns
225g/8oz oyster mushrooms (other varieties of wild mushrooms may be substituted)
30ml/2 tbsps oil
1 head radicchio (red or Italian lettuce)
1 head iceberg or leaf lettuce
1 bunch watercress
1 small bunch fresh chives, snipped

DRESSING
90ml/6 tbsps oil
30ml/2 tbsps white wine vinegar
15ml/1 tbsp Dijon mustard
Salt and pepper

GARNISH
Fresh chervil or dill

Trim the tips of the artichoke leaves. Put the artichokes into a large bowl with the lemon, bay leaf, peppercorns and enough water to cover. Cook 7-8 minutes or until the bottom leaf pulls away easily. Drain upside-down. Remove the stalks and slice the mushrooms thickly. Cook for 1-2 minutes in 30ml/2 tbsps oil and set aside. Tear the radicchio and lettuce into small pieces. Add the watercress leaves and toss together with the chives. Mix the salad dressing ingredients together until very well blended. Remove the leaves of the artichokes and arrange them on 4 plates. Top with the radicchio and watercress. Remove the chokes from

the artichoke hearts and discard. Cut the artichoke hearts into thin slices and combine with the mushrooms. Toss with half of the dressing, spoon equal amounts over the salads. Reheat each for 1 minute on HIGH. Garnish with the chervil and serve the remaining dressing separately.

Broccoli and Hazelnut Terrine

PREPARATION TIME: 20 minutes

MICROWAVE COOKING TIME: 10 minutes plus 10 minutes standing time

SERVES: 4-6 people

6-8 large or 12-14 small whole spinach leaves
450g/1lb broccoli
1 shallot, finely chopped
180g/6oz/¾ cup low fat cheese
4 slices bread, made into fine crumbs
2 eggs
280ml/½ pint/1 cup cream, lightly whipped
120g/4oz/1 cup coarsely chopped, roasted hazelnuts
Pinch nutmeg
Pinch thyme
Salt and pepper

SAUCE
280ml/½ pint/1 cup mayonnaise
140ml/¼ pint/½ cup plain yogurt
Grated rind and juice of 1 lemon
Pinch cayenne pepper
Salt

Trim away any coarse stalks from the spinach but leave the leaves whole. Wash them well and put them into a shallow dish with a pinch of salt. Loosely cover the dish and cook for 1 minute on HIGH with only the water that clings to the leaves. Remove from the dish and press on paper towels to drain. Line a 450g/1lb loaf dish with the spinach leaves and set aside. Chop the broccoli finely. Mix the eggs, cheese, cream, breadcrumbs, shallot, thyme, nutmeg and salt and pepper together. Stir in the broccoli and the hazelnuts. Spoon the mixture into the loaf dish on top of the spinach leaves and pack down well.

Fold the spinach leaves over on top of the mixture. Cover the dish with 2 layers of cling film/plastic wrap, pierced several times to let out steam. Put a ramekin/custard cup of water into the microwave oven with the terrine and cook on MEDIUM for 10 minutes or until just barely set. Allow to cool in the dish. Mix the sauce ingredients together. Turn the terrine out of the dish and slice. Arrange on lettuce leaves or

This page: Salad of Wild Mushrooms and Artichokes.

radicchio (red or Italian lettuce) and spoon over some of the sauce. Serve the remaining sauce separately.

Fit for Life

Vegetable Soups

Cream of Watercress Soup

PREPARATION TIME: 20 minutes

MICROWAVE COOKING TIME:
12-13 minutes plus 5 minutes
standing time

SERVES: 4 people

2 medium potatoes, cut in even-size
   pieces
3 bunches watercress, well-washed and
   root ends removed
1 litre/1¾ pints/3½ cups vegetable stock
Juice of ½ lemon
1.25ml/¼ tsp ground nutmeg
280ml-430ml/½-¾ pint/1-1½ cups
   single/light cream
Salt and pepper

GARNISH
120ml/4 tbsps heavy/double cream
Reserved watercress leaves

Put the stock and the potatoes into a
large bowl with a pinch of salt.
Partially cover and cook for 10
minutes on HIGH or until the
potatoes are tender. Allow to stand
for 5 minutes. Add the lemon juice,
salt, pepper, watercress and nutmeg
and purée in a food processor until
smooth. Stir in the cream and
process once more. Heat 2-3 minutes
on HIGH before serving. Garnish
with a swirl of cream and the
reserved watercress leaves.

Tomato and Dill Bisque

PREPARATION TIME: 20 minutes

MICROWAVE COOKING TIME:
7½ minutes

SERVES: 4 people

900g/2lbs tomatoes
850ml/1½ pints/3 cups vegetable stock
30ml/2 tbsps tomato purée/paste
1 onion, peeled and chopped
2 sprigs fresh dill
Salt and pepper
10ml/2 tsps chopped fresh dill
140ml/¼ pint/½ cup double/heavy
   cream

**This page: Beetroot and Sour
Cream Soup with Horseradish.
Facing page: Tomato and Dill
Bisque (top) and Cream of
Watercress Soup (bottom).**

GARNISH
1 slice tomato
4 small sprigs fresh dill
60ml/2 fl oz/¼ cup plain yogurt

Cut half of 1 cucumber into small dice and set aside. Peel the other half and the remaining 2 cucumbers and chop them roughly. Place the cucumbers in a large bowl with the stock and salt and pepper. Remove the mint leaves from the stalks and add the stalks to the cucumbers. Cover the bowl loosely and cook 6 minutes on HIGH or until the cucumbers are tender. Remove the mint stalks and purée the soup in a food processor. Strain if desired and add the cream and cucumber dice. Re-heat for 2 minutes on HIGH. Chop the mint leaves just before serving and add to the soup. Garnish with yogurt.

Sweetcorn and Red Pepper Soup

PREPARATION TIME: 20 minutes

MICROWAVE COOKING TIME: 14 minutes plus 5 minutes standing time

SERVES: 4 people

4 medium potatoes, cut in even-size
* pieces*
570ml/1 pint/2 cups vegetable stock
225g/8oz/1½ cups corn/sweetcorn
1 bay leaf
15ml/1 tbsp butter or margarine
1 red chili pepper
1 large, sweet red pepper
1 onion, chopped
Salt and pepper
570ml/1 pint/2 cups milk

GARNISH
Chopped parsley

Pour the stock into a large bowl and add the potatoes, bay leaf and a pinch of salt. Partially cover and cook 10 minutes on HIGH or until the potatoes are tender. Leave to stand for 5 minutes and remove the bay leaf. Purée until smooth. Melt the butter 30 seconds on HIGH and

Cut the tomatoes in half, remove the seeds and strain the juice into a large bowl. Add the onion, sprigs of dill, tomato purée/paste, halved tomatoes, salt, pepper and stock. Partially cover and cook on HIGH for 7 minutes or until the tomatoes have broken down and the onions are soft. Remove the sprigs of dill and pour the soup into a food processor. Purée the soup until smooth, and strain to remove any tomato skins. Adjust the seasoning and add a pinch of sugar if necessary to bring out the tomato flavour. Stir in the cream and chopped dill and re-heat for 30 seconds on HIGH. Garnish each serving with a spoonful of yogurt, a tomato strip and a sprig of fresh dill.

Cream of Cucumber Soup with Mint

PREPARATION TIME: 20 minutes

MICROWAVE COOKING TIME: 7-8 minutes plus 5 minutes standing time

SERVES: 4 people

3 large cucumbers (seedless variety)
1 litre/1¾ pints/3½ cups vegetable stock
2-3 sprigs mint
280ml/½ pint/1 cup single/light cream
Salt and pepper

GARNISH
Cucumber dice
60ml/2 fl oz/¼ cup plain yogurt

This page: Sweetcorn and Red Pepper Soup. Facing page: Cream of Cucumber Soup with Mint (top) and Fresh Pea Soup with Thyme (bottom).

cook the onion, pepper, and chili pepper for 2 minutes on HIGH. Add to the puréed potato along with the corn/sweetcorn and milk. Cook 2 minutes on HIGH and adjust the seasoning. Garnish with chopped parsley.

Purée of Asparagus Soup

PREPARATION TIME: 15 minutes

MICROWAVE COOKING TIME:
11 minutes plus 5 minutes standing time

SERVES: 4 people

1340g/3lbs asparagus
1 litre/1¾ pints/3½ cups vegetable stock
1.25ml/¼ tsp ground mace
280ml/½ pint/1 cup single/light cream
Salt and pepper

GARNISH
140ml/¼ pint/½ cup whipped cream, unsweetened
Ground mace

Trim the thick ends of the asparagus and chop the spears to even-sized pieces. Place in a large bowl with the stock, mace, salt and pepper. Partially cover and cook 10 minutes on HIGH or until the asparagus is soft. Leave to stand for 5 minutes. Purée in a food processor and strain if desired. Add the cream and heat 1 minute on HIGH. Garnish each serving with a spoonful of whipped cream and sprinkle with mace.

Fresh Pea Soup with Thyme

PREPARATION TIME: 20 minutes

MICROWAVE COOKING TIME:
7-13 minutes

SERVES: 4 people

1.8kg/4lbs fresh peas, shelled (1.3kg/3lbs frozen peas may be substituted)
1 litre/1¾ pints/3½ cups vegetable stock
2 sprigs fresh thyme
280ml/½ pint/1 cup single/light cream
Salt and pepper

GARNISH
140ml/¼ pint/½ cup heavy/double cream
Reserved peas

Place the peas in a large bowl with the stock, thyme, salt and pepper. Partially cover and cook for 10 minutes on HIGH or until the peas are soft. If using frozen peas, cook for 5 minutes on HIGH. Leave to stand for 5 minutes. Remove the thyme and discard. Remove about 60g/4 tbsps peas to reserve for garnish. Purée the remaining peas and stock in a food processor until smooth. Strain the soup if desired. Stir in the cream and adjust the seasoning. Add the reserved peas and re-heat 2-3 minutes on HIGH. Before serving, swirl a spoonful of cream through each bowl.

Beetroot and Sour Cream Soup with Horseradish

PREPARATION TIME: 20 minutes

MICROWAVE COOKING TIME:
22-23 minutes plus 10 minutes standing time

SERVES: 4 people

225g/8oz turnips, peeled and cut in even-size pieces
450g/1lb beetroot/beets
1 litre/1¾ pints/3½ cups vegetable stock
1 bay leaf
Salt and pepper
280ml/½ pint/1 cup sour cream
15ml/1 tbsp grated fresh or bottled horseradish

GARNISH
Chopped chives
Reserved sour cream

Cook unpeeled beetroot/beets in a large bowl, covered, with 60ml/2 fl oz/¼ cup stock for 10 minutes on HIGH. Leave to stand for 10 minutes before peeling. Pre-cooked or canned beetroot may be substituted. Cut into small pieces and return to the bowl with the turnips, remaining stock, bay leaf, salt and pepper. Partially cover the bowl and cook for a further 10 minutes on HIGH. Remove the bay leaf and purée the soup in a food processor until smooth. Reserve 60ml/4 tbsps sour cream and add the rest to the soup along with the horseradish. Heat 2-3 minutes on MEDIUM. Do not allow the soup to boil. Serve topped with sour cream and chopped chives.

Lettuce Cream Soup with Coriander

PREPARATION TIME: 20 minutes

MICROWAVE COOKING TIME:
15-16 minutes plus 5 minutes standing time

SERVES: 4 people

2 medium-sized potatoes, cut into even-size pieces
1 litre/1¾ pints/3½ cups vegetable stock
2 small heads lettuce, washed and shredded
2.5ml/½ tsp ground coriander
280ml-430ml/½-¾ pint/1-1½ cups single/light cream
Salt and pepper

GARNISH
Reserved shredded lettuce
Chopped parsley

Place the potatoes, stock and a pinch of salt in a large bowl. Partially cover the bowl and cook 10 minutes on HIGH or until the potatoes are tender. Add the lettuce, reserving about a quarter for garnish. Add the coriander and pepper and cook a further 3 minutes on HIGH. Leave to stand 5 minutes before blending in a food processor until smooth. Add 280ml/½ pint/1 cup cream (add more cream if the soup is too thick). The soup should be the consistency of lightly-whipped cream. Add the reserved shredded lettuce and parsley and re-heat for 2-3 minutes on HIGH.

Facing page: Lettuce Cream Soup with Coriander (top) and Purée of Asparagus Soup (bottom).

Mushroom and Sherry Cream Soup

PREPARATION TIME: 20 minutes

MICROWAVE COOKING TIME:
9-11 minutes plus 5 minutes standing time

SERVES: 4 people

900g/2lbs mushrooms, chopped
5-6 slices bread, crust removed
700ml/1¼ pints/2½ cups vegetable stock
1 sprig fresh thyme
1 bay leaf
½ clove garlic, crushed (optional)
430ml/¾ pint/1½ cups light/single
  cream
60ml/2 fl oz/¼ cup sherry
Salt and pepper

GARNISH
140ml/¼ pint/½ cup whipped cream
Grated nutmeg

Combine the mushrooms, bread, stock, thyme, bay leaf, salt, pepper and garlic (if using) in a large bowl. Partially cover and cook on HIGH for 7-8 minutes. Leave to stand for 5 minutes. Remove the thyme and the bay leaf and purée in a food processor until smooth. If the soup is not thick enough, add 1-2 slices more bread with the crusts removed. Add the sherry and process once more. Re-heat 2-3 minutes on HIGH. Garnish each bowl with a spoonful of whipped cream and a sprinkling of nutmeg.

Purée of Leek and Potato Soup

PREPARATION TIME: 20 minutes

MICROWAVE COOKING TIME:
12 minutes plus 5 minutes standing time

SERVES: 4 people

3 medium-size potatoes, cut in even-size
  pieces
4 leeks, depending on size
1 litre/1¾ pints/3½ cups vegetable stock
1 bay leaf
2 sprigs thyme
1.25ml/¼ tsp ground nutmeg

Salt and pepper
280-430ml/½-¾ pint/1-1½ cups single/
  light cream

Wash leeks well and shred the light green portion of 1 of the leeks and reserve. Slice the remaining leeks and combine with the potatoes in a large bowl. Pour on the stock and add the bay leaf, thyme and a pinch of salt. Partially cover the bowl and cook on HIGH for 10 minutes or until the potatoes and leeks are tender. Leave to stand for 5 minutes. Remove the bay leaf and thyme and purée the soup in a food processor until smooth. Add the nutmeg, pepper

This page: Purée of Leek and Potato Soup (top) and Mushroom and Sherry Cream Soup (bottom). Facing page: Spring Vegetable Soup.

and 280ml/½ pint/1 cup cream. Process again and add more cream if the soup is too thick. It should be the consistency of lightly whipped cream. Put the reserved leek into a small dish with 30ml/2 tbsps water and cook for 2 minutes on HIGH. Drain and garnish the soup with a spoonful of sour cream and the reserved leek strips.

Purée of Carrot Soup

PREPARATION TIME: 20 minutes

MICROWAVE COOKING TIME:
16-17 minutes

SERVES: 4 people

1340g/3lbs carrots, scraped and grated
1 litre/1¾ pints/3½ cups vegetable stock
2-3 sprigs rosemary
280ml/½ pint/1 cup milk or light/single
   cream
Salt and pepper

GARNISH
140ml/¼ pint/½ cup unsweetened
   whipped cream
Chopped parsley

Combine the carrots, rosemary, salt,
pepper and stock in a large bowl.
Partially cover and cook 15 minutes
on HIGH or until the carrots are
very tender. Remove the rosemary
and purée the soup in a food
processor. Add the milk or cream and
process until smooth. Adjust the
seasoning and re-heat 1-2 minutes on
HIGH before serving. Top with
spoonfuls of whipped cream and
chopped parsley.

Spring Vegetable Soup

PREPARATION TIME: 25 minutes

MICROWAVE COOKING TIME:
30 minutes plus 15-20 minutes
standing time

SERVES: 4-6 people

VEGETABLE STOCK
225g/8oz carrots, roughly chopped
6 sticks celery, roughly chopped
1 turnip, roughly chopped (optional)
3 onions, chopped and the peel of 1
   reserved for colour
1 tomato, quartered and seeded
3 parsley stalks
1 whole clove
1 bay leaf
1 blade mace
2 sprigs thyme or other fresh herbs
6 black peppercorns
Pinch salt
1150ml/2 pints/4 cups water

SOUP
1 litre/1¾ pint/3½ cups vegetable stock
1 head green cabbage, shredded
120g/4oz asparagus cut in 2.5cm/1 inch
   pieces
120g/4oz French/green beans cut in
   2.5cm/1 inch pieces
3 carrots, cut in 5cm/2 inch strips
120g/4oz fresh or frozen peas
1 large red pepper, thinly sliced
3 spring/green onions, sliced
60ml/2 fl oz/¼ cup white wine, optional
Salt and pepper

Combine all the ingredients for the
stock in a large bowl. Half cover the
bowl with cling film/plastic wrap and
cook 15 minutes on HIGH. The
stock will boil, so the bowl must be
deep enough to contain it. Allow to
stand for 15-20 minutes before
straining. The stock will keep up to
3 days in the refrigerator or frozen in

**This page: Purée of Carrot Soup.
Facing page: French/Green Beans
with Lemon Herb Sauce (top) and
Asparagus Tied with Fresh Herbs
(bottom).**

ice cube trays for convenience. To
prepare the soup, pour the measured
stock into a large bowl. If using fresh
peas add them to the stock and
partially cover the bowl. Cook the
peas for 5 minutes on HIGH. Add
the carrots and cook a further 5
minutes on HIGH. Add the beans,
asparagus and cabbage and cook for
5 minutes further on HIGH. Add the
onions, peppers and wine after
2 minutes cooking time. If using
frozen peas, add them with the
onions and peppers. Season with salt
and pepper to taste before serving. If
preparing the soup in advance, re-
heat it for 5-6 minutes on HIGH
before serving.

Fit for Life

Never Just a Salad!

French/Green Beans with Lemon Herb Sauce

PREPARATION TIME: 10 minutes

MICROWAVE COOKING TIME:
7 minutes

SERVES: 4 people

450g/1lb French /green beans
60ml/4 fl oz/¼ cup water
Salt

SAUCE
280ml/½ pint/1 cup low fat soft cheese
   or fromage blanc
60-140ml/2 fl oz-¼ pint milk
30g/1oz/1 cup watercress leaves, and
   thin stalks
30ml/2 tbsps chopped fresh herbs
Juice and grated rind of ½ lemon
Salt and pepper

Combine the beans, water and salt in a casserole dish and cover loosely. Cook on HIGH for 4 minutes, stirring once or twice. Leave to stand while preparing the sauce. Heat the milk for 3 minutes on HIGH. If using low fat soft cheese, use the greater quantity of milk. Combine with the remaining ingredients, except the lemon rind, in a food processor and work until well blended. Drain the beans and pour over the sauce. Sprinkle on the lemon rind, and toss just before serving.

Asparagus Tied with Fresh Herbs

PREPARATION TIME: 15 minutes

MICROWAVE COOKING TIME:
14 minutes

SERVES: 4 people

900g/2lb asparagus spears
8 sprigs of fresh thyme or marjoram or
   8 chives

SAUCE
3 egg yolks
180g/6oz/¾ cup butter
30ml/2 tbsps white wine
Squeeze of lemon juice

5ml/1 tsp chopped thyme, marjoram or
  chives
Salt and pepper

Trim the thick ends of the asparagus
and place the spears in a shallow
dish. Add 140ml/¼ pint/½ cup water
and cover the dish loosely. Cook on
HIGH for 10 minutes. Drain and
keep warm. In a small, deep bowl,
heat the wine and butter for 2
minutes on HIGH. Remove from the
oven and gradually beat in the egg
yolks. Cook on HIGH 10 seconds
and then stir. Repeat the process
until the sauce thickens, which takes
about 2 minutes. Add the lemon
juice, chopped herbs, salt and pepper.
Tie up 4 bundles of asparagus with
the chosen herbs. Serve the
asparagus with the sauce.

Broccoli with Toasted Sunflower Seeds

PREPARATION TIME: 10 minutes

MICROWAVE COOKING TIME:
4½-5½ minutes

SERVES: 4 people

450g/1lb broccoli
30g/2 tbsps butter or margarine
120g/4oz/1 cup toasted, salted sunflower
  seeds
Pepper
5ml/1 tsp lemon juice (if desired)

Trim the ends of the broccoli stalks
and separate into even-sized pieces.
Place in a large casserole or shallow
dish with 60ml/2 fl oz/¼ cup water.
Cover loosely and cook 4-5 minutes
on HIGH. Melt the butter for
30 seconds on HIGH, stir in the
sunflower seeds and add pepper and
lemon juice. Drain the broccoli and
sprinkle over the sunflower seeds to
serve.

Broccoli and Cauliflower Mold with Salsa

PREPARATION TIME: 25 minutes

MICROWAVE COOKING TIME:
7½ minutes

SERVES: 4-6 people

1 small head cauliflower
225g/8oz broccoli

DRESSING
45ml/3 tbsps oil
15ml/1 tbsp wine vinegar
5ml/1 tsp ground mustard
½ clove garlic, minced
Salt and pepper

SALSA
4-5 tomatoes, depending on size
1 green pepper, chopped
15ml/1 tbsp oil
1 green chili pepper, finely chopped
5ml/1 tsp cumin seed or ground cumin
4 spring onions, finely chopped
Salt and pepper

This page: Broccoli and
Cauliflower Mold with Salsa.
Facing page: Broccoli with Toasted
Sunflower Seeds (top) and Brussels
Sprouts and Hazelnuts (bottom).

Divide the cauliflower into flowerets
and trim down any long, thick stalks.
Trim the broccoli stalks to within
5cm/2 inches of the flowerets and
combine with the cauliflower in a
deep bowl. Add 30ml/2 tbsps water
and a pinch of salt. Cover loosely
and cook 3 minutes on HIGH. Mix
the dressing ingredients together
thoroughly. Drain the vegetables well
and pour the dressing over the
vegetables while still warm. Arrange
the vegetables in a deep 570ml/
1 pint/2 cup bowl, alternating the

2 vegetables. Press lightly to push the vegetables together. Leave the vegetables to cool in the bowl and then refrigerate. Put the tomatoes in a bowl of very hot water. Microwave 30 seconds on HIGH. Put the tomatoes into cold water and then peel and chop roughly. Heat the oil in a large bowl for 30 seconds on HIGH. Add the green pepper, chili pepper and cumin. Cook for 2 minutes on HIGH. Stir in the tomatoes, onions, salt and pepper and leave to cool. Turn out the vegetables carefully onto a serving plate and spoon the salsa around the base. Serve cold. Both the mold and the salsa may be prepared several hours in advance. If left overnight, the broccoli may discolour the cauliflower.

Vegetable Stir Fry with Tofu

PREPARATION TIME: 20 minutes

MICROWAVE COOKING TIME: 7½ minutes

SERVES: 4 people

60ml/2 fl oz/¼ cup oil
Blanched whole almonds
225g/8oz tofu
4 spears broccoli
120g/4oz peapods/mangetout
120g/4oz bean sprouts
120g/4oz baby corn-on-the-cob
1 red pepper, sliced
60g/2oz/½ cup water chestnuts, sliced
1 clove garlic, minced
140ml/¼ pint/½ cup vegetable stock
10ml/2 tsps cornstarch/cornflour
60ml/2 fl oz/4 tbsps soy sauce
Dash sherry
Dash sesame oil
Salt and pepper
4 spring onions/green onions, sliced

Heat a browning dish for 5 minutes on HIGH. Add the oil and fry the almonds for 5 minutes, stirring often to brown evenly. Remove the almonds from the dish and set them aside. Cut out the broccoli flowerets and reserve. Slice the stalks diagonally. If the corn cobs are large cut in half lengthwise. Cook the broccoli and the corn together for 1 minute on HIGH. Add the garlic, red pepper, peapods/mangetout, water chestnuts and the broccoli flowerets. Mix the soy sauce, sesame oil, sherry, stock, and cornstarch/cornflour together. Pour over the vegetables and cook 1 minute on HIGH. Add the bean sprouts, almonds, spring/green onions and the tofu, cut in small cubes. Cook 30 seconds on HIGH. Serve immediately.

Vegetables Mornay

PREPARATION TIME: 25 minutes

MICROWAVE COOKING TIME: 24-28 minutes

SERVES: 4-6 people

225g/8oz new potatoes, scrubbed but not peeled
125g/8oz button or pickling onions, peeled
15g/1 tbsp butter
Pinch sugar
2-3 carrots, cut in strips
2 parsnips, cut in strips
120g/4oz mangetout/peapods
120g/4oz button mushrooms
30g/2 tbsps butter
Salt

SAUCE
45g/3 tbsps butter
45g/3 tbsps flour
5ml/1 tsp dry mustard
Pinch cayenne pepper
570ml/1 pint/2 cups milk
120g/4oz/1 cup Cheddar cheese, shredded
Salt and pepper
Nutmeg

Cook the new potatoes in 60ml/ 2 fl oz/¼ cup water with a pinch of salt for 8-10 minutes on HIGH in a deep, covered dish. Leave to stand 5 minutes. Cook the carrots and parsnips together in 60ml/2 fl oz/ ¼ cup water in a covered dish for 6 minutes on HIGH. Combine the onions with the sugar and 15g/1 tbsp butter in a deep bowl. Cook, covered, for 7 minutes on HIGH. Stir twice while cooking. Melt the remaining butter for the vegetables and add the mangetout/peapods and mushrooms. Cook for 2 minutes on HIGH. Leave all the vegetables covered while preparing the sauce. Melt the butter for 1 minute on HIGH in a glass measure. Stir in the flour, mustard and cayenne pepper. Gradually whisk in the milk and add the salt and pepper. Cook for 3-4 minutes on HIGH, whisking after 1 minute, until the sauce has thickened and is bubbling. Stir in the cheese to melt. Arrange the vegetables on a serving dish, keeping each different vegetable in a separate pile. Coat with some of the sauce and sprinkle on nutmeg. Serve remaining sauce separately.

Brussels Sprouts and Hazelnuts

PREPARATION TIME: 20 minutes

MICROWAVE COOKING TIME: 20-21 minutes

SERVES: 4 people

60g/2oz/½ cup hazelnuts
450g/1lb Brussels sprouts
30g/2 tbsps butter or margarine
Salt and pepper

Put the nuts into a small, deep bowl. Cover with hot water and heat 3 minutes on HIGH. Leave to soak for 10 minutes. Drain and rub off the skins. Leave the nuts to dry. Heat a browning dish 5 minutes on HIGH and drop in the butter. Add the nuts and cook 5 minutes on HIGH, stirring every 30 seconds to brown the nuts evenly. Cook the Brussels sprouts with 30ml/2 tbsps water and a pinch of salt in a lightly covered bowl or a cooking bag. Cook for 7-8 minutes on HIGH or until tender. Drain and combine with the nuts and butter.

Facing page: Vegetable Stir Fry with Tofu.

Ginger Sesame Carrots

PREPARATION TIME: 10 minutes

MICROWAVE COOKING TIME:
7½-10½ minutes

SERVES: 4-6 people

900g/2lb carrots, sliced diagonally
30g/1oz/2 tbsps butter or margarine
30g/1oz/2 tbsps brown sugar
7.5ml/1½ tsps ground ginger or 1 small
    piece fresh ginger, grated
30g/1oz/¼ cup sesame seeds
Dash soy sauce
Dash sesame oil
Salt and pepper

Place the carrots in a casserole dish
with 60ml/2 fl oz/¼ cup water. Add
a pinch of salt, cover and cook on
HIGH for 7-10 minutes. Leave to
stand while melting the butter for
30 seconds on HIGH. Stir in the
brown sugar, ginger, sesame seeds,
sesame oil, soy sauce, salt and pepper.
Add 15-30ml/1-2 tbsps of the
cooking liquid from the carrots to
the sesame-ginger mixture. Stir in the
carrots to coat with the sauce.

Pommes Noisettes

PREPARATION TIME: 15 minutes
plus overnight refrigeration

MICROWAVE COOKING TIME:
14-15 minutes

SERVES: 4-6 people

450g/1lb potatoes, scrubbed but not
    peeled
30ml/2 tbsps water
30g/1oz/2 tbsps butter
Salt and pepper
60g/2oz/½ cup grated Gruyère cheese
60g/2oz/½ cup ground browned
    hazelnuts
Chopped parsley

Prick the potato skins with a fork.
Put the potatoes and water into a
covered dish and cook 12 minutes on
HIGH until tender. Drain the
potatoes and cut in half. Scoop out
the pulp and mash with a fork or
potato masher. Beat in the butter,
salt, pepper and cheese. Allow to
cool and then refrigerate until cold.

Shape into 2.5cm/1 inch balls. Roll
the potatoes in the nuts. Place in a
circle on a baking sheet or serving
dish and heat 2-3 minutes on HIGH.
Sprinkle with chopped parsley before
serving.

Dilled White Cabbage

PREPARATION TIME: 10 minutes

MICROWAVE COOKING TIME:
8 minutes plus 5 minutes
standing time

SERVES: 4-6 people

**This page: Vegetable Mornay.
Facing page: Ginger Sesame Carrots
(top) and Pommes Noisettes
(bottom).**

1 medium head white cabbage or Dutch
    cabbage, shredded
30g/2 tbsps butter or margarine
Pinch sugar
30ml/2 tbsps dill seed
30ml/2 tbsps white wine vinegar
30ml/2 tbsps chopped fresh dill
Salt and pepper

Place the cabbage in a large casserole or bowl with 30ml/2 tbsps water and the remaining ingredients except the chopped fresh dill. Cover loosely and cook 8 minutes on HIGH, stirring twice. Leave to stand, covered, 5 minutes before serving. Sprinkle with the fresh dill.

Beets with Sour Cream and Dill

PREPARATION TIME: 20 minutes

MICROWAVE COOKING TIME: 13-17 minutes plus 10 minutes standing time

SERVES: 4 people

4-8 beetroot/beets, depending on size
280ml/½ pint/1 cup sour cream
2.5ml/1 tsp grated fresh horseradish
1 small bunch dill
Salt and pepper

Place raw beets, unpeeled, in 140-280ml/¼-½ pint/½-1 cup water depending on the number of beets. Use a casserole or a bowl covered with pierced cling film/plastic wrap. Cook 12-16 minutes. Leave to stand 10 minutes before peeling. If using pre-cooked beets, just peel them and heat through 1 minute on HIGH. Slice into 6mm/¼ inch slices. Arrange in a serving dish. Mix the sour cream, horseradish, dill, salt and pepper together. Spoon over the beets and heat through 30 seconds to 1 minute on HIGH. Do not allow the sour cream to boil. Garnish with a few sprigs of fresh dill and serve immediately.

Sweet and Sour Red Cabbage with Apple

PREPARATION TIME: 15 minutes

MICROWAVE COOKING TIME: 9-10 minutes plus 5 minutes standing time

SERVES: 4-6 people

30g/2 tbsps butter or margarine
1 medium head red cabbage, shredded
1 small onion, finely chopped

1 apple, cored and chopped
30g/2 tbsps brown sugar
30ml/2 tbsps red wine vinegar
140ml/¼ pint/½ cup water
Pinch cinnamon
Salt and pepper

GARNISH
15g/1 tbsp butter or margarine
1 apple, cored and chopped
Chopped parsley

Melt the butter or margarine in a deep casserole dish for 30 seconds on HIGH. Add all the remaining ingredients except the garnish and cover with pierced cling film/plastic wrap. Cook on HIGH for 8 minutes. Leave to stand, covered, 5 minutes while preparing the garnish. Melt the butter or margarine 30 seconds on HIGH in a small bowl. Add the apple and cook 1 minute on HIGH, uncovered, to partially soften. Toss with the parsley and sprinkle on top of the cabbage.

This page: Beets with Sour Cream and Dill. Facing page: Sweet and Sour Red Cabbage with Apple (top) and Dilled White Cabbage (bottom).

Creamed Spring/Green Onions

PREPARATION TIME: 10 minutes

MICROWAVE COOKING TIME: 5 minutes

SERVES: 4 people

2 bunches spring/green onions
15g/½ oz/1 tbsp butter or margarine
Salt and pepper
280ml/½ pint/1 cup low fat soft cheese or fromage blanc
5ml/1 tsp chopped basil
5ml/1 tsp chopped parsley
140ml/¼ pint/½ cup milk

60g/2oz/½ cup chopped pine-nuts or
   walnuts
1.25ml/¼ tsp ground nutmeg
Squeeze lemon juice
Salt and pepper

GARNISH
Whole pine-nuts

ACCOMPANIMENTS
Lettuce
Buttered toast or rolls

Cook the spinach for 4 minutes on
HIGH in a loosely covered bowl.
Cook in the moisture that clings to
the leaves. Rinse under cold water,
drain very well and chop finely. Mix
with the cheese and milk and add the
garlic, nuts, nutmeg, lemon juice, salt
and pepper. Cut about 5cm/2 inches
off the tops of the peppers. Remove
the stems and chop the flesh finely.
Remove the cores and seeds from the
peppers. Place the whole and
chopped peppers into a large bowl or
casserole and cover with hot water.
Cook for 2-3 minutes on HIGH, and
rinse immediately under cold water.
Drain the whole peppers upside-
down on paper towels. Drain the
chopped peppers well and add to the
spinach pâté. Fill the drained pepper
cups with the spinach mixture.
Arrange on serving plates with the
lettuce leaves and top with whole
pine-nuts. Serve with hot buttered
toast or rolls.

Ratatouille

PREPARATION TIME: 35 minutes
MICROWAVE COOKING TIME: 14 minutes
SERVES: 4-6 people

30ml/2 tbsps oil
1 onion, sliced
1 aubergine/eggplant
2 courgettes/zucchini
1 green pepper
1 red pepper

**This page: Creamed Spring/Green
Onions (top) and Spinach with
Blue Cheese and Walnuts (bottom).
Facing page: Ratatouille.**

Wash the onions, barely remove the
root ends and trim off about 5cm/
2 inches off the green tops. Melt
butter in a casserole for 30 seconds
on HIGH. Add the onions, salt,
pepper and cover loosely with cling
film/plastic wrap. Cook 3 minutes
on HIGH. Remove the onions and
keep covered in a serving dish. Add
the cheese, herbs, milk, salt and
pepper to the casserole and stir
together well. Cook 1 minute on
HIGH. Add the onions and heat
through 30 seconds on HIGH. Serve
immediately.

Spinach and Ricotta Pâté in Red Pepper Cups

PREPARATION TIME: 20 minutes
MICROWAVE COOKING TIME: 6-8 minutes
SERVES: 4 people

4 medium-size sweet red peppers
900g/2lb fresh spinach, washed with
   stalks removed
450g/1lb ricotta, cottage or cream cheese
45ml/3 tbsps milk
1 small clove garlic, crushed

120g/4oz mushrooms, sliced
1 clove garlic, crushed
10ml/2 tsps chopped fresh basil
5ml/1 tsp chopped parsley
15ml/1 tbsp tomato purée/paste
1 bay leaf
30ml/2 tbsps white wine
Salt and pepper

Cut the aubergine/eggplant in half, score the flesh lightly and sprinkle with salt. Leave on paper towels for ½ hour to draw out any bitterness. Heat the oil in a casserole for 30 seconds on HIGH. Add the onion and garlic and cook 2 minutes on HIGH. Wash the aubergine/eggplant and dry it well. Slice it thinly and slice the courgettes/zucchini and peppers and add to the onions. Cook 5 minutes on HIGH, loosely covered. Add the herbs, bay leaf, tomato purée/paste, wine, salt and pepper and cook a further 5 minutes on HIGH. Add the mushrooms and tomatoes and cook 2 minutes on HIGH. Remove the bay leaf before serving.

Spinach with Blue Cheese and Walnuts

PREPARATION TIME: 15 minutes

MICROWAVE COOKING TIME:
4½ minutes

SERVES: 4-6 people

900g/2lb fresh spinach, washed with stalks removed
30g/1oz/2 tbsps butter or margarine
Nutmeg
Salt and pepper

This page: Spinach and Ricotta Pâté in Red Pepper Cups. Facing page: Red Lentil and Mushroom Loaf.

120g/4oz/1 cup coarsely chopped walnuts
120g/4oz/1 cup crumbled blue cheese

Place spinach in a large bowl with a pinch of salt. Cover the bowl loosely and cook in the water that clings to the leaves. Microwave on HIGH for 4 minutes. Press between 2 plates to drain thoroughly. Melt the butter in a serving dish for 30 seconds on HIGH. Add the spinach, pepper, nutmeg, walnuts and cheese and toss together to serve.

Fit for Life
Recipes with Pulses

Red Lentil and Mushroom Loaf

PREPARATION TIME: 20 minutes

MICROWAVE COOKING TIME: 25-28 minutes plus the indicated standing times

SERVES: 4-6 people

180g/6oz/1 cup red lentils, picked over and washed
340ml/12oz/1½ cups vegetable stock or water
1 clove garlic, finely chopped
15ml/1 tbsp chopped parsley
15ml/1 tbsp chopped tarragon
90g/3oz mushrooms, coarsely chopped
120g/4oz/½ cup cream cheese
1 egg plus 30ml/2 tbsps heavy/double cream
Salt and pepper

QUICK TOMATO SAUCE
1 400g/14oz can tomatoes
15ml/1 tbsp tomato purée/paste
5ml/1 tsp dry tarragon
Pinch sugar
Salt and pepper
15ml/1 tbsp chopped fresh tarragon

Cover the lentils with water and leave to stand overnight or microwave 10 minutes to boil the water. Allow the lentils to boil 2 minutes further on HIGH. Allow to stand 1 hour. Combine the lentils with stock or fresh water in a large bowl. Partially cover the bowl and cook 10-12 minutes on HIGH or until the lentils are very soft. Check the amount of liquid and add more if necessary as the lentils cook. Allow to stand for 5 minutes. Mash to a thick purée. Beat the eggs and cream together and add to the purée. Stir in the remaining ingredients and press into a lightly greased loaf dish. Cover with cling film/plastic wrap pierced several times. Cook on MEDIUM for 7-8 minutes until firm around the edges but soft in the middle. Leave to stand 5-10 minutes to firm. May be served hot with the sauce or cold. To prepare the sauce combine all the ingredients except the fresh tarragon. Cook, uncovered, 8 minutes or until thickened. Purée in a food processor and strain to remove the seeds if desired. Add the chopped fresh tarragon and serve with the red lentil and mushroom loaf.

Beans Bourguignonne

PREPARATION TIME: 20 minutes

MICROWAVE COOKING TIME:
1 hour 43 minutes plus indicated
standing times

SERVES: 4 people

*225g/8oz/2 cups field beans (other dark
    coloured beans may be substituted)*
45ml/3 tbsps oil
4 carrots
*225g/8oz small onions, peeled and left
    whole*
225g/8oz mushrooms, quartered
140ml/¼ pint/½ cup vegetable stock
280ml/½ pint/1 cup red wine
1 bay leaf
5ml/1 tsp chopped thyme
10ml/2 tsps chopped parsley
45g/3 tbsps butter or margarine
*4 slices wholemeal/whole-wheat bread,
    crusts removed*

Cover the beans with water and
leave to stand overnight or
microwave for 10 minutes on HIGH
to bring to the boil. Allow the beans
to boil for 2 minutes. Leave to stand
for 1 hour before using. Cover with
fresh water and add the bay leaf and
a pinch of salt. Loosely cover the
dish and cook on MEDIUM for
45 minutes. Leave to stand for
10 minutes before draining. Heat a
browning dish for 5 minutes on
HIGH. Pour in the oil and add the
carrots, onions and mushrooms.
Cook on HIGH for 2 minutes,
stirring frequently to brown slightly.
Remove the vegetables from the
browning dish and add 45g/3 tbsps
butter or margarine. Heat the butter
for 1 minute on HIGH and put in the
bread, cut into triangles. Brown the
croutes 1 minute on HIGH and turn
over. Brown the other side for
1 minute on HIGH and drain on
paper towels. Put the beans into a
casserole with the vegetable stock
and the red wine. Cover the
casserole and cook an additional
15 minutes on HIGH or until the
beans are almost tender. Add the
carrots, onions, mushrooms, thyme,
parsley and additional salt and
pepper. Re-cover the casserole and
cook a further 15-20 minutes on
HIGH or until the vegetables and the

beans are completely tender. Leave to
stand for 15 minutes before serving.
Re-heat the bread for 1 minute on
MEDIUM. Remove the bay leaf and
the beans and transfer them to a
serving dish and surround with the
croutes to serve.

Red Beans Creole

PREPARATION TIME: 20 minutes

MICROWAVE COOKING TIME:
1 hour 23 minutes plus standing
times indicated in the recipe

SERVES: 4 people

180g/6oz/1 cup red kidney beans
180g/6oz/1½ cups long-grain rice
30g/2 tbsps butter or margarine
1 green pepper, cut in strips
*3-4 tomatoes, peeled, seeded and cut in
    strips*

**This page: Red Beans Creole.
Facing page: Chickpea and Pepper
Casserole (top) and Beans
Bourguignonne (bottom).**

120g/4oz mushrooms, sliced
4 spring/green onions, chopped
30ml/2 tbsps chopped parsley
Cayenne pepper
Ground nutmeg
1 bay leaf
Salt and pepper

Cover the beans with water and
leave overnight, or microwave 10
minutes to boil the water. Allow the
beans to boil for 2 minutes. Leave to
stand 1 hour. Cover with fresh water
and add a pinch of salt and the bay
leaf. Cook on MEDIUM for 55
minutes to 1 hour. Allow to stand
10 minutes before draining. The
beans must be completely cooked.

Save the cooking liquid to use as stock in other recipes if desired. Place rice in a large bowl or casserole dish, add 570ml/1 pint/2 cups water and a pinch of salt. Cook about 10 minutes on HIGH. Leave to stand for 5 minutes before draining. Heat the butter or margarine 30 seconds on HIGH in a casserole dish, and add the pepper strips and mushrooms. Cook for 2 minutes, stirring once. Stir in the cayenne pepper, nutmeg, salt, pepper, rice and beans. Cook 1 minute on HIGH. Add the spring/green onions, parsley and tomatoes and cook a further 30 seconds on HIGH.

Chickpea and Pepper Casserole

PREPARATION TIME: 20 minutes

MICROWAVE COOKING TIME:
51 minutes to 1 hour 6 minutes

SERVES: 4 people

225g/8oz/1⅓ cups chickpeas (garbanzo beans)
30ml/2 tbsps oil
1 large onion, sliced
1 green pepper, sliced
1 red pepper, sliced
1 clove garlic, minced
10ml/2 tsps chopped parsley
5ml/1 tsp chopped mint
2.5ml/½ tsp ground cumin
Salt and pepper
4 tomatoes, seeded and cut in strips

ACCOMPANIMENT
1 cucumber, thinly sliced
280ml/½ pint/1 cup yogurt
Salt and pepper

Leave the chickpeas to soak in water overnight or use the microwave rehydrating method. Cover with fresh water and add a pinch of salt. Cover the bowl and cook 45 minutes to 1 hour until tender. Drain and reserve the liquid. Heat the oil 30 seconds on HIGH. Add the onion, peppers, garlic and cumin. Cook 1 minute on HIGH. Add the chickpeas and half the cooking liquid. Cook a further 5 minutes on HIGH. Add parsley, mint, tomatoes, and

season with salt and pepper. Cook 30 seconds on HIGH. Combine the accompaniment ingredients and serve with the casserole.

Vegetable Cassoulet

PREPARATION TIME: 20 minutes

MICROWAVE COOKING TIME:
1 hour 40 minutes plus indicated standing times

SERVES: 4 people

225g/8oz/2 cups haricot/navy beans
60ml/2 fl oz/¼ cup oil
2 cloves garlic, minced
2 small leeks, cut in 2.5cm/1 inch pieces
3 carrots, cut in 2.5cm/1 inch chunks
4 sticks celery, cut in 2.5cm/1 inch pieces
2 parsnips, halved, cored and cut in 2.5cm/1 inch pieces
2 turnips, peeled and cut in 2.5cm/1 inch pieces
120g/4oz mushrooms, quartered
15ml/1 tbsp Worcestershire sauce
1 bay leaf
15ml/1 tbsp marjoram, chopped
430ml/¾ pint/1½ cups vegetable stock
Salt and pepper

TOPPING
30g/2 tbsps butter or margarine
60g/2oz/½ cup dry breadcrumbs

Heat a browning dish for 5 minutes on HIGH. Melt the butter for the topping and add the crumbs. Stirring frequently, cook on HIGH for 2-3 minutes until the crumbs are golden brown and crisp. Set them aside. Add the oil to the browning dish and heat for 1 minute on HIGH. Add all of the vegetables and cook 2 minutes on HIGH to brown. Stir frequently. Remove the vegetables from the browning dish and de-glaze the dish with the vegetable stock. Stir to remove any sediment from browning the vegetables. Cover the beans with water and leave to soak overnight or microwave for 10 minutes to bring the water to the boil. Allow the beans to boil for 2 minutes. Leave them to stand for 1 hour. Drain the beans and put them into the casserole dish with the garlic, bay leaf, Worcestershire sauce, marjoram,

season with salt and pepper. Add half the stock, cover and cook for 1 hour on HIGH. Add more stock as necessary during cooking. The mixture should be fairly thick at the end of the cooking time. Add the vegetables and re-cover the dish. Cook an additional 15-20 minutes on HIGH, adding more stock if necessary. When the beans are tender and most of the liquid has been absorbed, sprinkle on the brown crumbs and cook for 5 minutes on HIGH. Leave the cassoulet to stand for 15 minutes before serving. The cassoulet may be prepared in advance and refrigerated. Re-heat 2-3 minutes on HIGH. Add the crumbs and cook a further 5 minutes on HIGH before serving.

Chinese Black Bean Casserole

PREPARATION TIME: 20 minutes

MICROWAVE COOKING TIME:
1 hour 33 minutes plus indicated standing time

SERVES: 4 people

450g/1lb black beans
1 small piece fresh ginger root, grated
1 clove garlic, minced
10ml/2 tsps 5-spice powder
1 piece star anise
6-8 sticks celery
1 small can water chestnuts, drained and sliced
90ml/3 fl oz/⅓ cup sherry
15ml/1 tbsp soy sauce
5ml/1 tsp sesame seed oil

GARNISH
120g/4oz bean sprouts
4 spring/green onions shredded

Cover the beans with water and leave to stand overnight, or microwave on HIGH for 10 minutes to boil the water. Allow the beans to boil for 2 minutes and leave to stand for 1 hour before using. If using salted

Facing page: Chinese Black Bean Casserole (top) and Vegetable Cassoulet (bottom).

Chinese black beans, soak in cold water for ½ hour and drain. Cut the cooking time in half. Cover the beans with water and add the grated ginger, star anise, 5-spice powder and garlic. Add a pinch of salt and pepper and loosely cover the bowl. Cook for 1 hour on HIGH, stirring occasionally. Add the celery and cook a further 15 minutes on HIGH. Add the sherry, soy sauce and sesame oil and cook a further 5 minutes on HIGH. If a lot of liquid remains, continue to cook until the liquid is absorbed. Add the water chestnuts just before serving and cook 1 minute on HIGH to heat through. Garnish with the bean sprouts and shredded spring/green onion to serve.

Butter Bean, Lemon and Fennel Salad

PREPARATION TIME: 15 minutes

MICROWAVE COOKING TIME:
1 hour 12 minutes plus standing times indicated in the recipe

SERVES: 4 people

225g/8oz/2 cups butter beans
1 large bulb Florentine fennel, thinly sliced
Juice and rind of 1 lemon
60ml/4 tbsps oil
Pinch sugar
Salt and pepper

Cover the beans with water and leave overnight, or microwave 10 minutes to boil the water and allow the beans to boil for 2 minutes. Leave to stand for 1 hour. Cover with fresh water and add a pinch of salt. Cook on MEDIUM for 55 minutes to 1 hour. The beans must be cooked all the way through. Allow to stand for 10 minutes before draining. Boil 570ml/1 pint/2 cups water for 10 minutes on HIGH. Reserve the green tops of the fennel and blanch the sliced bulb in the water for 2 minutes on HIGH. Drain thoroughly. Pare the rind from the lemon and scrape off any white pith. Cut the rind into very thin strips and squeeze the juice from the lemon. Mix with the oil, pinch sugar, salt and

pepper. Chop the fennel tops and add to the dressing. Pour over the drained beans and fennel slices. Toss to coat thoroughly. Serve on a bed of lettuce or radicchio.

Black-Eyed Bean/Pea and Orange Salad

PREPARATION TIME: 20 minutes

MICROWAVE COOKING TIME:
1 hour plus 10 minutes standing time

SERVES: 4 people

225g/8oz/1½ cups black-eyed beans/
  peas
1 bay leaf
1 slice onion
Salt

SALAD
4 oranges
Small handful fresh basil leaves
30ml/2 tbsps chopped parsley
6 black olives, pitted
1 large bunch watercress

DRESSING
Juice and rind of 1 orange
75ml/5 tbsps oil
4 spring/green onions, chopped
Salt and pepper

Cover the beans with water and leave overnight, or microwave for 10 minutes to boil the water. Allow the beans to boil for 2 minutes. Leave to stand for 1 hour. Cover with fresh water and add a pinch of salt, the bay leaf and the slice of onion. Cook on MEDIUM for 55 minutes to 1 hour. Allow to stand 10 minutes before draining. Mix the oil and the juice and grated rind of 1 orange with the basil leaves, chopped, chopped parsley, chopped spring/green onions and salt and pepper. Pour the dressing over the beans and add the black olives, sliced, and toss. Peel and segment the remaining four oranges. Chop the segments of two of the oranges and add those to the bean salad. Arrange the watercress on 4 individual plates and pile on the bean salad. Arrange the remaining orange segments on the plates and serve immediately.

Curried Lentils

PREPARATION TIME: 25 minutes

MICROWAVE COOKING TIME: 36 minutes plus 5-10 minutes standing time

SERVES: 4 people

225g/8oz lentils, brown or green
60g/2oz/¼ cup butter or margarine
1 large onion, chopped
1 clove garlic, chopped
1 red or green chili pepper, finely chopped
5ml/1 tsp cumin
5ml/1 tsp coriander
5ml/1 tsp turmeric
2.5ml/½ tsp cinnamon
2.5ml/½ tsp nutmeg
60g/2oz/½ cup whole blanched almonds
570ml/1 pint/2 cups vegetable stock
Salt and pepper
Desiccated coconut
Coriander leaves

APPLE AND CUCUMBER RELISH
2 apples, cored and chopped
60g/2oz/½ cup raisins
120g/4oz/1 cup chopped cucumber
60ml/2 fl oz/¼ cup mango chutney

SPICED BANANAS
2 bananas, sliced
30g/2 tbsps butter or margarine
Pinch nutmeg
Pinch cinnamon
15ml/1 tbsp brown sugar
15ml/1 tbsp lemon juice
Garam masala

TOMATO AND ONION RELISH
2 tomatoes, chopped
1 green pepper, chopped
1 small onion, chopped
Juice of ½ lemon
10ml/2 tsps oil
Pinch cayenne pepper
Salt

Cover the lentils with water and leave to soak overnight. Alternatively microwave 10 minutes to boil the water and allow the lentils to boil 2 minutes. Leave to stand for 1 hour. Melt the butter for 1 minute on HIGH in a large casserole dish. Add the onion, garlic, chili pepper and spices. Cook 4 minutes on MEDIUM. Drain the lentils and add to the casserole with the vegetable stock. Cover and cook on HIGH for 30 minutes until the lentils are tender. Allow to stand 5-10 minutes before serving. Heat a browning dish for 5 minutes on HIGH. Melt the

Facing page: Butter Bean, Lemon and Fennel Salad (top) and Black-Eyed Bean/Pea and Orange Salad (bottom). This page: Curried Lentils.

butter and add the sliced bananas. Cook 30 seconds on HIGH on one side and turn over. Cook a further 30 seconds and sprinkle with the spices and the lemon juice. Sprinkle with garam masala just before serving. Combine the ingredients for the apple and cucumber relish and those for the tomato and onion relish and serve the accompaniments with the curried lentils. Sprinkle the lentils with desiccated coconut and garnish with coriander leaves before serving.

Fit for Life
Vegetarian...with Panache

Curried Vegetables

PREPARATION TIME: 20 minutes

MICROWAVE COOKING TIME:
17 minutes

SERVES: 4 people

2 medium-size potatoes, peeled and cut
　　into 2.5cm/1 inch chunks
3 carrots, cut into 2.5cm/1 inch chunks
3 courgettes/zucchini, sliced
120g/4oz okra, stems trimmed
60g/2oz mushrooms, quartered
2 tomatoes, quartered
1 large onion, sliced
45ml/3 tbsps oil
1 clove garlic, minced
1 red or green chili pepper, minced after
　　removing the seeds
30ml/2 tbsps flour
5ml/1 tsp ground cumin
5ml/1 tsp ground coriander
5ml/1 tsp turmeric
10ml/2 tsps mustard seed
2.5ml/½ tsp paprika
Pinch ground cloves
Bay leaf
570ml/1 pint/2 cups vegetable stock or
　　vegetable cooking liquid and water
140ml/¼ pint/½ cup natural yogurt
Salt and pepper

GARNISH
Chopped coriander leaves

Cook the potatoes and carrots
together in a large, covered casserole.
Add just enough salted water to
cover the vegetables. Cook on HIGH
for 8 minutes. Add the courgettes/
zucchini and okra after 6 minutes
cooking. Leave the vegetables to
stand, covered, for 5 minutes.
Reserve the quartered tomatoes and
mushrooms. Heat the oil for 1 minute
on HIGH and add the onion, garlic,
chili pepper and mushrooms. Cook

for 1 minute on HIGH. Stir in the
flour and spices and cook a further
1 minute on HIGH. Add the liquid
gradually, stirring until smooth. Add
the bay leaf, salt and pepper and
cook 5 minutes on HIGH, stirring
frequently after 1 minute. When
thickened, remove the bay leaf and
add the cooked vegetables and the
quartered tomatoes. Heat through
1 minute on HIGH. Serve with rice
and chutney. The accompaniments
from the Curried Lentil recipe may
also be served.

**This page: Pasta, Peas and Peppers.
Facing page: Gratin of Vegetable
Oliver (top) and Curried Vegetables
(bottom).**

Pasta, Peas and Peppers

PREPARATION TIME: 20 minutes

MICROWAVE COOKING TIME:
10 minutes plus 10 minutes
standing time

SERVES: 4 people

225g/8oz/3 cups plain and whole-wheat
 pasta shells, mixed
225g/8oz/1 cup frozen peas
1 green pepper, shredded
1 yellow pepper, shredded
1 red pepper, shredded
4 spring/green onions, shredded
120g/4oz grated Parmesan cheese

DRESSING
140ml/¼ pint/½ cup oil
60ml/2 fl oz/¼ cup white wine vinegar
15ml/1 tbsp Dijon mustard
10ml/2 tsps poppy seeds
10ml/2 tsps chopped parsley
5ml/1 tsp chopped thyme
Salt and pepper

Cook the pasta 6 minutes in a large
bowl with 570ml/1 pint/2 cups
salted water. Leave to stand, covered,
10 minutes before draining. Cook the
peas and peppers in 30ml/2 tbsps
water for 2 minutes. Drain and allow
to cool, uncovered. Mix the dressing
ingredients together until well
blended. Pour over the pasta, add the
cheese and toss to coat the pasta
well. Add the peas, peppers and
spring/green onions and toss again to
mix all the ingredients before serving.

Pasta-Stuffed Cabbage Leaves

PREPARATION TIME: 20 minutes

MICROWAVE COOKING TIME:
29 minutes plus 10 minutes
standing time

SERVES: 4 people

1 head cabbage, white or green

FILLING
120g/4oz/¾ cup soup pasta
1 hard boiled egg, finely chopped
60g/2oz/½ cup walnuts, roughly
 chopped
15ml/1 tbsp chopped chives
30ml/2 tbsps chopped parsley
5ml/1 tsp chopped marjoram
Salt and pepper

SAUCE
1 450g/1lb can tomatoes
15ml/1 tbsp oil
120g/4oz mushrooms, sliced

1 small onion, diced
1 green pepper, diced
30ml/2 tbsps tomato purée/paste
1 bay leaf
Pinch sugar
Salt and pepper

Place the pasta in a large bowl with
570ml/1 pint/2 cups salted water
and cook for 5 minutes on HIGH.
Leave to stand, covered, 10 minutes
before draining. Put the cabbage
leaves in a large bowl or roasting bag
with 30ml/1 fl oz/2 tbsps water with
a pinch of salt. Cook 3-4 minutes on
HIGH. Lay flat on paper towels to
drain. Heat the oil for 30 seconds on
HIGH. Add the onions and peppers
for the sauce and cook 1 minute on
HIGH. Add the remaining sauce
ingredients and cook 8 minutes on
HIGH. Combine the drained pasta
with the remaining filling ingredients
and spoon on to the cabbage leaves.
Roll up the leaves, tucking in the
ends, and lay them in a serving dish.
Pour over the sauce and cook on
MEDIUM for 8 minutes. Serve
immediately.

Gratin of Vegetables Oliver

PREPARATION TIME: 20 minutes

MICROWAVE COOKING TIME:
12-13 minutes

SERVES: 4 people

TOPPING
120g/4oz/½ cup butter or margarine
 melted
225g/8oz/1 cup chopped, pitted black
 olives
120g/4oz/1 cup dry breadcrumbs
180g/6oz/1½ cups shredded Cheddar
 cheese
120g/4oz/1 cup chopped walnuts
10ml/2 tsps chopped fresh basil
Pinch cayenne pepper

VEGETABLES
4 courgettes/zucchini, sliced
1 bunch broccoli
4 carrots, sliced
225g/8oz French/green beans
2 red peppers, sliced
8 spring/green onions, sliced
Salt and pepper

Melt the butter for the topping for
30 seconds on HIGH. Stir in the
remaining ingredients and set aside.
Cook the carrots in 60ml/4 tbsps
water with a pinch of salt for 8
minutes. After 5 minutes add the
courgettes/zucchini, broccoli and
beans. Add the peppers and spring/
green onions 1 minute before the end
of cooking time. Drain the vegetables
and arrange in a serving dish.
Sprinkle lightly with salt and pepper
and sprinkle over the topping
ingredients. Bake 4 minutes on
MEDIUM or 5 minutes on a
combination setting in a microwave
convection oven. Serve immediately.

Watercress-Stuffed Potatoes

PREPARATION TIME: 25 minutes

MICROWAVE COOKING TIME:
27-29 minutes plus 5 minutes
standing time

SERVES: 4 people

4 large baking potatoes
140ml/¼ pint/½ cup milk
120g/4oz mushrooms, sliced
1 shallot, chopped
15g/1 tbsp butter or margarine
4 eggs
1 bunch watercress

SAUCE
45g/1½ oz/3 tbsps butter or margarine
30g/1oz/2 tbsps flour
Pinch dry mustard
Pinch cayenne pepper
280ml/½ pint/1 cup milk
60g/2oz/½ cup grated cheese
Salt and pepper

GARNISH
30g/1oz/¼ cup grated cheese
Reserved watercress

Wash and prick the potato skins
several times with a fork. Bake the
potatoes 10-12 minutes on HIGH.
Wrap them in foil and leave to stand
5 minutes. Pour 1150ml/2 pints/
4 cups hot water into a large, shallow
dish. Add 15ml/1 tbsp vinegar and
5ml/1 tsp salt. Heat the water 5
minutes on HIGH or until boiling.

reserving 4 sprigs for garnish. Add the chopped watercress to the potatoes and beat in the hot milk. Add salt and pepper to taste and pipe or spoon the potatoes on top of the cheese sauce in the potato shells. Sprinkle on cheese and cook for 3 minutes on HIGH to heat through and melt the cheese. Alternatively, heat 5 minutes on a combination setting in a microwave convection oven. Garnish with the watercress and serve immediately.

Mushroom Croquettes with Green Peppercorn Sauce

PREPARATION TIME: 25 minutes

MICROWAVE COOKING TIME: 16-17 minutes

SERVES: 4 people

120g/4oz/1 cup finely chopped mushrooms
90g/3oz/1¾ cups fresh breadcrumbs
30g/1oz/2 tbsps butter or margarine
1 shallot, finely chopped
30g/1oz/2 tbsps flour
140ml/¼ pint/½ cup milk
5ml/1 tsp chopped parsley
5ml/1 tsp chopped thyme
1 beaten egg
Salt and pepper

COATING
Remaining beaten egg
Dry breadcrumbs
30-60ml/2-4 tbsps oil for frying

SAUCE
15g/1 tbsp butter or margarine
1 shallot, finely chopped
15g/1 tbsp flour
30ml/2 tbsps vermouth or white wine
280ml/½ pint/1 cup heavy/double cream
30ml/2 tbsps green peppercorns, drained and rinsed
1 small cap pimento, diced
Salt and pepper

Melt the butter for the croquettes for 1 minute on HIGH. Add the shallot and the mushrooms and cook 30

Break the eggs into a cup and slide them, one at a time into the water. Prick the yolks once with a sharp knife or skewer. Cook on MEDIUM for 3 minutes. Remove from the dish and place in enough cold water to cover them. Melt the 15g/1 tbsp butter in a small bowl for 30 seconds on HIGH. Add the mushrooms and shallot. Cook for 1 minute on HIGH and set aside. Melt the butter for the sauce for 30 seconds on HIGH in a glass measure. Add the flour, mustard, and cayenne pepper. Stir in the milk gradually and cook 3

This page: Pasta-Stuffed Cabbage Leaves (top) and Watercress-Stuffed Potatoes (bottom).

minutes on HIGH. Stir after 1 minute. Add the cheese and stir to melt. Cut a slice off the top of each potato and scoop out the pulp, leaving a border inside the skin. Fill with the mushrooms and top with one of the drained eggs. Spoon over the cheese sauce. Mash the potato and heat the milk for 2 minutes on HIGH. Chop the watercress leaves and thin stalks in a food processor,

1 shallot, finely chopped
30g/1oz/2 tbsps flour
140ml/¼ pint/½ cup milk
5ml/1 tsp chopped parsley
5ml/1 tsp chopped thyme
1 beaten egg
Salt and pepper

COATING
Beaten egg
Dry breadcrumbs
30-60ml/2-4 tbsps oil for frying

SAUCE
280ml/½ pint/1 cup heavy/double
    cream
15ml/1 tbsp pear brandy
60g/2oz/½ cup grated Parmesan cheese
Coarsely ground black pepper
Salt

GARNISH
4 small, ripe, unpeeled pears, halved and
    cored
Lemon juice
8 fresh sage leaves

Melt the butter for the escalopes for 1 minute on HIGH. Add the shallot and cook 30 seconds on HIGH. Stir in the flour and add the milk gradually. Cook for 2 minutes on HIGH until thickened. Add the remaining escalope ingredients and half the beaten egg. Spread the mixture into a square pan and chill until firm. Cut the mixture into 8 equal pieces and flatten into thin patties. Coat with the remaining egg and dry breadcrumbs, shaking off the excess. If the patties become difficult to handle, chill for 10 minutes in the refrigerator before coating with egg and crumbs. Heat a browning dish for 5 minutes on HIGH and pour in the oil. Heat for 30 seconds on HIGH; put in the escalopes and cover the dish. Cook for 2-3 minutes on HIGH, turning over halfway through the cooking time. Drain the escalopes on paper towels. Boil the cream and brandy for 6 minutes on HIGH in a glass measure. Stir in the

This page: **Walnut Cutlets with Three Pepper Salpicon. Facing page: Mushroom Croquettes with Green Peppercorn Sauce (top) and Hazelnut Escalopes with Pear Brandy Cream Sauce (bottom).**

seconds on HIGH. Stir in the flour and add the milk gradually. Cook for 2 minutes on HIGH until thickened. Add the remaining croquette ingredients and half the beaten egg. Spread the mixture into a square pan and chill until firm. Cut the mixture into 16 equal pieces and shape into small ovals. Coat with the remaining egg and press on the dry crumbs, shaking off the excess. Heat a browning dish for 5 minutes on HIGH and pour in the oil. Heat for 30 seconds on HIGH and put in the croquettes. Cover and cook 3-4 minutes on HIGH, turning over after 2 minutes. Drain on paper towels. Heat the butter for the sauce for 30 seconds on HIGH in a small, deep bowl. Add the shallot, finely chopped and cook for 30 seconds on HIGH. Stir in the flour, vermouth or white wine and the cream. Season

lightly with salt and pepper and cook for 3-4 minutes on HIGH, stirring frequently. Add the green peppercorns and the pimento 1 minute before the end of cooking time. Arrange the croquettes in a serving dish and pour over the sauce to serve.

Hazelnut Escalopes with Pear Brandy Cream Sauce

PREPARATION TIME: 25 minutes
MICROWAVE COOKING TIME: 17-18 minutes
SERVES: 4 people

120g/4oz/1 cup ground hazelnuts
60g/2oz/1⅓ cups fresh breadcrumbs
30g/1oz/2 tbsps butter or margarine

cheese and pepper. Taste and add salt if desired. Heat for 30 seconds on HIGH to melt the cheese. Place a spoonful of the sauce on each of 4 serving plates. Brush the cut sides of the pears with lemon juice and arrange on the plates with the sage leaves. Place on the cutlets and spoon over some of the sauce to serve. Hand the rest of the sauce separately.

Walnut Cutlets with Three Pepper Salpicon

PREPARATION TIME: 25 minutes

MICROWAVE COOKING TIME: 17-18 minutes

SERVES: 4 people

CUTLETS
120g/4oz/1 cup walnuts, ground
60g/2oz/1⅓ cups fresh breadcrumbs
5ml/1 tsp chopped parsley
5ml/1 tsp chopped thyme
30g/1oz/2 tbsps butter or margarine
1 shallot, finely chopped
30g/1oz/2 tbsps flour
140ml/¼ pint/½ cup milk
1 beaten egg
Salt and pepper

COATING
Remaining beaten egg
Dry breadcrumbs
30-60ml/2-4 tbsps oil for frying

SALPICON
30g/1oz/2 tbsps butter or margarine
1 small onion, thinly sliced
15g/1 tbsp flour
Juice of 1 lemon
90ml/3oz/⅓ cup vegetable stock
1-2 green peppers, sliced
1-2 red peppers, sliced
1-2 yellow peppers, sliced
Pinch cayenne pepper
10ml/2 tsps capers
Salt and pepper

Melt the butter for the cutlets for 1 minute on HIGH. Add the shallot and cook 30 seconds on HIGH. Stir in the flour and add the milk gradually. Cook for 2 minutes on HIGH until thickened. Add the remaining cutlet ingredients and half the beaten egg. Spread the mixture

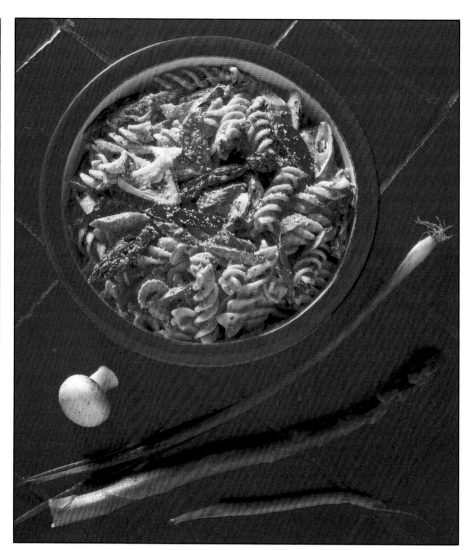

into a square pan and chill until firm. Cut the mixture into 8 equal portions and shape into cutlets or patties. Coat with the remaining egg and the dry breadcrumbs, shaking off the excess. Heat a browning dish for 5 minutes on HIGH. Pour in the oil and heat 30 seconds on HIGH. Put in the cutlets, cover the dish and cook 3-4 minutes on HIGH, turning over after 2 minutes. Drain on paper towels. Heat the butter for the salpicon 30 seconds on HIGH in a casserole. Add the onion and cook for 1 minute on HIGH. Stir in the flour and add the lemon juice and stock and cook for 1 minute on HIGH until very thick. Add the peppers and capers and cook a further 3 minutes on HIGH. Add the cayenne pepper, salt and pepper and serve with the cutlets.

Pasta Primavera

PREPARATION TIME: 20 minutes

MICROWAVE COOKING TIME: 14 minutes plus 10 minutes standing time

SERVES: 4 people

450g/1lb/6 cups pasta shapes, or noodles
225g/8oz asparagus
120g/4oz French/green beans
60g/2oz mushrooms, sliced
2 carrots
3 tomatoes peeled, seeded and cut in strips
6 spring/green onions
30ml/2 tbsps chopped parsley
10ml/2 tsps chopped tarragon
140ml/¼ pint/½ cup heavy/double cream
Salt and pepper

Cook the pasta 6 minutes on HIGH in 1150ml/2 pints/4 cups hot water with a pinch of salt and 15ml/1 tbsp oil. Cover and leave to stand 10 minutes before draining. Leave to drain completely. Slice the asparagus diagonally, leaving the tips whole. Cut the beans and carrots diagonally into thin slices. Cook the carrots and asparagus in 30ml/2 tbsps water for 4 minutes on HIGH, loosely covered. Add the beans and mushrooms and cook an additional 2 minutes on HIGH. Add to the drained pasta and stir in the cream, salt and pepper. Cook 1 minute on HIGH to heat the pasta. Add the tomatoes, onions, herbs and toss gently. Cook an additional 1 minute on HIGH. Serve immediately with grated cheese if desired.

Aubergine/Eggplant Rolls

PREPARATION TIME: 25 minutes

MICROWAVE COOKING TIME: 20-23 minutes

SERVES: 4 people

2-3 aubergines/eggplants, depending on size, sliced 1.25cm/½ inch thick
45ml/3 tbsps oil, or more as needed, for frying
120g/4oz/1 cup grated mozzarella cheese

SAUCE
1 450g/1lb can plum tomatoes
30ml/2 tbsps tomato purée/paste
1 onion, finely chopped
Pinch sugar
Pinch oregano
1 bay leaf
2 parsley stalks
Salt and pepper

FILLING
225g/8oz ricotta cheese
120g/4oz pitted black olives, chopped
60g/2oz/¼ cup grated Parmesan cheese
60g/2oz/¼ cup pine-nuts
15ml/1 tbsp white wine
1 clove garlic, finely minced
5ml/1 tsp each chopped parsley and basil
Pinch nutmeg
Salt and pepper

Facing page: Pasta Primavera. This page: Aubergine/Eggplant Rolls.

Lightly score the slices of aubergine/eggplant on both sides and sprinkle with salt. Leave on paper towels to stand for 30 minutes to draw out any bitterness. Combine all the sauce ingredients in a small, deep bowl. Cook, uncovered, for 8 minutes on HIGH. Remove the bay leaf and parsley stalks and purée in a food processor. Strain to remove the seeds if desired. Rinse the aubergine/ eggplant and pat dry. Heat a browning dish for 5 minutes on HIGH. Pour in the oil and heat for 1 minute on HIGH. Add the aubergine/eggplant slices and brown for 1 minute per side. Cook in 2 or 3 batches if necessary and add more oil if needed. Drain on paper towels. Mix the filling ingredients and fill half of each aubergine/eggplant slice. Fill the bottom of a large, shallow baking dish with half the sauce. Fold the aubergine/eggplant slices in half and place on top of the sauce. Spoon over the remaining sauce, cover the dish loosely with cling film/plastic wrap and cook 3 minutes on HIGH. Sprinkle on the cheese and cook, uncovered, a further 2-3 minutes on MEDIUM. Alternatively, coat with sauce and sprinkle on the cheese and cook for 8 minutes on a combination setting of a microwave convection oven.

Vegetable Moussaka

PREPARATION TIME: 55 minutes

MICROWAVE COOKING TIME: 29 minutes

SERVES: 4 people

2 potatoes, peeled and sliced
1 aubergine/eggplant
120g/4oz mushrooms sliced
2 courgettes/zucchini
4 tomatoes, peeled and sliced
1 green pepper, sliced

TOMATO SAUCE
15ml/1 tbsp oil
1 onion, finely chopped
1 clove garlic, minced
1 400g/14oz can tomatoes
15ml/1 tbsp tomato purée/paste
1.25ml/¼ tsp ground cinnamon
1.25ml/¼ tsp ground cumin
Salt and pepper
Pinch of sugar

EGG SAUCE
30g/2 tbsps butter or margarine
30g/2 tbsps flour
280ml/½ pint/1 cup milk
1 egg, beaten
60g/2oz/½ cup feta cheese
Nutmeg
Salt and pepper

Cut the aubergine/eggplant in half and lightly score the cut surface. Sprinkle with salt and leave to stand for ½ hour. Put the potatoes into a roasting bag, seal and cook 10 minutes on HIGH. Heat the oil for the tomato sauce 30 seconds on HIGH. Add the onions and garlic and cook 1 minute on HIGH. Add the remaining ingredients and cook a further 6 minutes on HIGH. Wash the aubergine/eggplant well and dry. Slice it thinly and cook in 30ml/2 tbsps oil for 2 minutes on HIGH in a covered dish. Remove the slices and drain. Add the mushrooms to the dish and cook for 2 minutes on HIGH. Remove and set aside. Add the green pepper and the courgettes/zucchini and cook for 1 minute on HIGH. Layer the vegetables, starting with the aubergine/eggplant and ending with the potatoes. Spoon the tomato sauce over each layer except the potatoes. Cook the butter for the egg sauce for 30 seconds on HIGH. Stir in the flour, nutmeg, salt and pepper. Add the milk gradually and cook for 3 minutes on HIGH, stirring after 1 minute. Add the cheese and egg and stir well to blend. Pour over the potatoes and cook 4 minutes on HIGH or 5 minutes on a combination setting in a microwave convection oven, or until set.

This page: Sweet and Sour Nuggets. Facing page: Vegetable Moussaka (top) and Mushrooms Florentine (bottom).

Sweet and Sour Nuggets

PREPARATION TIME: 25 minutes

MICROWAVE COOKING TIME: 15½-16½ minutes

SERVES: 4 people

60g/2oz/½ cup ground almonds
60g/2oz/½ cup finely chopped water chestnuts
30g/1oz/2 tbsps butter or margarine
1 shallot, finely chopped
30g/1oz/2 tbsps flour

5ml/1 tsp chopped parsley
5ml/1 tsp ground ginger
140ml/¼ pint/½ cup milk
1 beaten egg
Salt and pepper

COATING
Remaining beaten egg
Dry breadcrumbs
Sesame seeds
30-60ml/2-4 tbsps oil for frying

SWEET AND SOUR SAUCE
60g/2oz/¼ cup brown sugar
60ml/2 fl oz/¼ cup vinegar
30ml/2 tbsps tomato ketchup
30ml/2 tbsps soy sauce
1 225g/8oz can pineapple chunks/pieces
30g/2 tbsps cornstarch/cornflour
1 green pepper
2 green/spring onions, sliced
1 small can bamboo shoots

ACCOMPANIMENT
225g/8oz bean sprouts

Melt the butter for the nuggets for 1 minute on HIGH. Add the shallot and cook 30 seconds on HIGH. Stir in the flour and add the milk gradually. Cook for 2 minutes on HIGH until thickened. Add the remaining nugget ingredients and half the beaten egg. Spread the mixture into a square pan and chill until firm. Shape the mixture into an even number of 2.5cm/1 inch balls. Coat with the remaining egg and the dry breadcrumbs and sesame seeds, shaking off the excess. Heat a browning dish for 5 minutes on HIGH and pour in the oil. Put in the nuggets and cover the dish. Cook for 3-4 minutes on HIGH, turning frequently. Drain on paper towels. Combine the sugar, vinegar, ketchup, soy sauce, pineapple juice and cornstarch/cornflour in a small, deep bowl. Cook for 2-3 minutes on HIGH until thickened, stirring frequently. Add the peppers and onions and cook 1 minute on HIGH. Add the pineapple pieces and the bamboo shoots and cook a further 30 seconds on HIGH. Place the bean sprouts in a serving dish and heat 1 minute on HIGH. Put the nuggets in the middle. Coat over with the sweet and sour sauce to serve.

Japanese Steamer

PREPARATION TIME: 20 minutes

MICROWAVE COOKING TIME: 13 minutes

SERVES: 4 people

3 packages tofu, drained
16 dried black mushrooms, soaked and stems removed
120g/4oz small mushrooms
8 baby corn-on-the-cob
1 small diakon (mooli) radish, sliced
1 bunch fresh chives, left whole
120g/4oz buckwheat noodles or other variety Japanese noodles
1 package dried sea spinach
1 lemon, sliced

SAUCE
1 small piece fresh ginger root, grated
140ml/¼ pint/½ cup soy sauce
60ml/4 tbsps vegetable stock
15ml/1 tbsp sherry or white wine
5ml/1 tsp cornstarch/cornflour

Cover the noodles with 570ml/1 pint/2 cups water and a pinch of salt. Cook on HIGH for 6 minutes and leave to stand, covered, for 10 minutes before using. Put the mushrooms and spinach into 2 separate bowls, fill both bowls with water and leave the spinach to soak. Put the mushrooms into the microwave oven and heat for 5 minutes on HIGH and set aside. Put the small mushrooms and the baby corn-on-the-cob into a small bowl with 15ml/1 tbsp water. Cover the bowl with pierced cling film/plastic wrap and cook for 2 minutes on HIGH and set aside. Combine all the ingredients for the sauce in a glass measure. Cook on HIGH for 3 minutes or until thickened. Stir after 1 minute. Slice the tofu into 1.25cm/½ inch slices. Drain the black mushrooms and remove the stalks. Drain the noodles and arrange in 4 separate serving dishes. Add the spinach, tofu, whole black mushrooms and small mushrooms, baby ears of corn, radish slices, and lemon slices. Pour some of the sauce over each serving and garnish with the fresh chives. Heat the dishes through for 1 minute on HIGH and serve the remaining sauce separately.

Mushrooms Florentine

PREPARATION TIME: 20 minutes

MICROWAVE COOKING TIME: 17 minutes

SERVES: 4 people

60g/2oz/¼ cup butter or margarine
450g/1lb large mushrooms
900g/2lb fresh spinach, stalks removed and leaves washed
2 shallots, finely chopped
4 tomatoes, peeled, seeded and diced
Salt and pepper
Nutmeg

SAUCE
45g/3 tbsps butter or margarine
45g/3 tbsps flour
570ml/1 pint/2 cups milk
180g/6oz/1½ cups grated Cheddar cheese
2.5ml/½ tsp dry mustard
Pinch cayenne pepper
Salt and pepper
60g/2oz/¼ cup Parmesan cheese, grated
Paprika

Place the washed spinach in a large bowl or a roasting bag with a pinch of salt. Cover or seal and cook 4 minutes in the water that clings to the leaves. Set aside. Melt the butter in a large casserole for 30 seconds on HIGH. Cook the mushrooms for 3 minutes on HIGH, turning often. Remove the mushrooms and set them aside. Add the shallots to the butter in the bowl, cover, and cook 2 minutes on HIGH. Chop the spinach roughly and add to the shallots with the tomato, salt, pepper and nutmeg. Place in the bottom of the casserole dish and arrange the mushrooms on top. Melt the butter for the sauce 1 minute on HIGH. Stir in the flour, mustard, salt, pepper and a pinch of cayenne pepper. Add the milk gradually, beating until smooth. Cook, uncovered, 4 minutes on HIGH, stirring twice after 1 minute's cooking. Add Cheddar cheese and stir to melt. Coat over the mushrooms and spinach and sprinkle the Parmesan and paprika on top. Cook 3 minutes until bubbling.

Facing page: Japanese Steamer.

Escalopes d'Aubergines au Fromage

PREPARATION TIME: 25 minutes

MICROWAVE COOKING TIME:
14-15 minutes

SERVES: 4 people

1 large or 2 small aubergines/eggplants
Seasoned flour for coating
45ml/3 tbsps oil for frying

TOPPING
15g/1 tbsp butter
2 shallots, finely chopped
10ml/2 tsps chopped tarragon
10ml/2 tsps chopped chervil
225g/8oz cream cheese
120g/4oz/1 cup grated Gruyère or Swiss
  cheese
180ml/6 fl oz/¾ cup heavy/double
  cream
Dry breadcrumbs

VEGETABLES
12 small new potatoes
8 baby carrots
4 small turnips
4 small fresh beets
8 spring/green onions
4 very small courgettes/zucchini
120g/4oz French/green beans, trimmed
120g/4oz mangetout/peapods, trimmed
120g/4oz/½ cup butter, melted
Chopped parsley

Slice the aubergines/eggplants into
8 2.5cm/1 inch thick slices. Score the
slices lightly on both sides and
sprinkle with salt. Leave to stand for
30 minutes to draw out any
bitterness. Melt the butter for the
topping for 30 seconds on HIGH.
Add the shallot and cook for 2
minutes. Cool and mix with the
other topping ingredients, except the
dry breadcrumbs, and set aside.
Cook the vegetables in 60ml/2 fl oz/
¼ cup salted water as follows:–
new potatoes for 10 minutes
baby carrots for 10 minutes
fresh beets for 8-9 minutes
turnips for 8 minutes
spring/green onion for 2-3 minutes
French/green beans for 2-3 minutes
courgettes/zucchini for 2-3 minutes
mangetout/peapods for 2-3 minutes.
Cook the vegetables in a loosely
covered casserole and keep the
beetroot separate. Melt the butter for
1 minute on HIGH and pour over
the vegetables. Sprinkle the carrots
and the new potatoes with chopped
parsley. Leave the vegetables covered
while preparing the aubergines/
eggplants. Rinse the aubergines/
eggplants well and pat dry. Mix the
flour with salt and pepper and lightly
coat the aubergine/eggplant slices.
Heat a browning dish for 5 minutes
on HIGH. Pour in the oil and put in
the aubergine/eggplant slices. Cover
the dish and cook for 2-3 minutes,
turning halfway through the cooking
time. Remove the aubergines/
eggplants from the browning dish
and drain them on paper towels.
Place them in a clean casserole or on
a plate and top each slice with a
spoonful of the cheese mixture.
Sprinkle on the dry breadcrumbs and

This page: **Escalopes d'Aubergines
au Fromage.** Facing page: **Pasta
Spirals with Walnuts and
Gorgonzola (top) and Forester's
Pasta (bottom).**

cook on MEDIUM for 2 minutes.
Arrange on serving plates with the
vegetables.

Macaroni, Cheese and Tomato Squares

PREPARATION TIME: 15 minutes

MICROWAVE COOKING TIME:
14 minutes plus 10 minutes
standing time

SERVES: 4 people

225g/8oz/3 cups macaroni
60g/2oz/¼ cup butter or margarine

60g/2oz/4 tbsps flour
Pinch dry mustard
Pinch cayenne pepper
850ml/1½ pints/3 cups milk
120g/4oz/1 cup grated Cheddar cheese
Salt and pepper
2 tomatoes

Put the macaroni into a large bowl with 1150ml/2 pints/4 cups salted water. Cook on HIGH for 6 minutes and leave to stand, covered, for 10 minutes before draining. Melt the butter for 1 minute on HIGH and stir in the flour, mustard, cayenne pepper, salt and pepper. Add the milk gradually and cook for 3-4 minutes on HIGH, stirring after 1 minute. Add the cheese to the sauce and stir to melt. Drain the macaroni well and mix it with half of the sauce. Press the macaroni mixture into a 20cm/ 8 inch square pan and chill until firm. Dilute the remaining sauce with 280ml/½ pint/1 cup milk. When the macaroni mixture is firm, cut it into 8 squares and remove from the tin. Place on a serving dish and slice the tomatoes, putting 1 slice on top of each square. Reheat the sauce for 1 minute on HIGH and pour over the macaroni squares. Reheat the squares on a serving dish for 2 minutes on HIGH. Serve immediately.

Forester's Pasta

PREPARATION TIME: 15 minutes

MICROWAVE COOKING TIME:
18 minutes plus 10 minutes standing time

SERVES: 4 people

450g/1lb spinach and plain tagliatelle/
   fettucine
2 carrots, shredded
90ml/3oz oyster or wild mushrooms
30g/2 tbsps butter or margarine
1 clove garlic
30ml/2 tbsps chopped herbs such as
   thyme, parsley and sage
180ml/½ pint/1 cup heavy/double cream
Salt and pepper
60g/2oz fresh Parmesan cheese, ungrated

Place the pasta in a large bowl with 1150ml/2 pints/4 cups hot water, a

pinch of salt and 15ml/1 tbsp oil. Cook for 6 minutes on HIGH. Cover and leave to stand 10 minutes before draining. Rinse in hot water and leave to dry. Heat a browning dish 5 minutes on HIGH. Melt the butter 1 minute and add the garlic and carrots. Cook 1 minute on HIGH. The garlic should brown slightly. Add the mushrooms and cook 1 minute further on HIGH. Add the herbs, cream, salt and pepper and cook 2 minutes on HIGH. Toss with the pasta. Use a cheese slicer or a knife to shave off thin slices of Parmesan cheese to serve on top.

Stuffed Vine Leaves

PREPARATION TIME: 25 minutes

MICROWAVE COOKING TIME:
26-34 minutes

SERVES: 4 people

1 package vine leaves

FILLING
180g/6oz/1½ cups rice
1 onion, finely chopped
60g/2 tbsps butter or margarine
120g/8oz/1 cup black olives, stoned and
   chopped
1 green pepper, chopped
120g/4oz/1 cup pine-nuts
120g/4oz/1 cup feta cheese, crumbled
30g/2 tbsps chopped parsley
5ml/1 tsp ground coriander

TOMATO SAUCE
1 400g/14oz can tomatoes
15ml/1 tbsp tomato purée/paste
1 onion, finely chopped
15ml/1 tbsp oil
1 clove garlic
1.25ml/¼ tsp cinnamon
1.25ml/¼ tsp ground cumin
Salt and pepper

If the vine leaves are packed in brine, soak them in cold water for 30 minutes before using. Cook the rice 8-10 minutes in 570ml/1 pint/2 cups water with a pinch of salt. Leave the rice to stand, covered, for 5 minutes. Melt the butter for 30 seconds on HIGH and add the onion, pepper and coriander. Cook for 2 minutes on HIGH. Stir in the drained rice,

cheese, parsley, salt and pepper. Fill the leaves and roll them up, tucking in the ends. Arrange the leaves in a baking dish and set aside while preparing the sauce. Heat the oil for the sauce 30 seconds on HIGH and add the onion and garlic and cook for 1 minute on HIGH. Add the remaining ingredients and cook 6 minutes on HIGH. Leave to stand for 5 minutes before pouring over the vine leaves. Cook the vine leaves for 16 minutes on HIGH. Garnish with more chopped parsley if desired.

Pasta Spirals with Walnuts and Gorgonzola

PREPARATION TIME: 15 minutes

MICROWAVE COOKING TIME:
12 minutes plus 10 minutes standing time

SERVES: 4 people

450g/1lb pasta spirals
450g/1lb Gorgonzola cheese
120g/4oz/1 cup walnut halves
280ml/½ pint/1 cup heavy/double
   cream
Coarsely ground pepper

GARNISH
2 ripe figs
4 sprigs fresh thyme

Place the pasta in a large bowl with 1150ml/2 pints/4 cups hot water, a pinch of salt and 15ml/1 tbsp oil. Cook for 6 minutes on HIGH. Cover and leave to stand for 10 minutes before draining. Rinse in hot water and leave to dry. Combine the cream and crumbled cheese in a deep bowl. Cook on MEDIUM for 4 minutes until the cheese melts. Do not stir too often. Add the walnut halves and the coarsely ground pepper. Taste, and add salt if desired. Pour over the pasta in a serving dish and toss to coat. Cut the figs in half and then in half again. Put one half fig on each plate with a sprig of thyme to garnish.

Facing page: Stuffed Vine Leaves (top) and Macaroni, Cheese and Tomato Squares (bottom).

Fit for Life

Index to the Recipes for Health